MOTORCYCLE REPAIR MANUAL

INTRODUCTION

Because of the number, nearness and convenience of the commercial repair shop, we become lazy and ultimately cowardly toward the prospect of doing our own work until we are driven to it by rising labor costs, shop waiting lines, sloppy professional work or a frightening in-field catastrophe that warns of one's vulnerability.

To overcome these obstacles is the challenge of this book, for most of the included tasks are not all that bewildering or difficult for the enthusist of even modest experience and tools when the procedure is properly presented. The prime mover is desire, wanting to be able to do one's own work. Once that is established, panic straightens out into fun, and where the novice once doubted his own ability, he boldly questions the workmanship or thoroughness of the pro. When that frame of mind is achieved, he has arrived. Watch for it, for it is a measure of progress as you approach the criterion.

Start with the smallest, most inconsequential repair possible if timidity or fear of making a goof stands in the way. But no matter how small the task, there is only one requirement: do a super-sanitary job of it, as neat and tight as you know how. Move on to progressively more critical work as confidence builds. Don't underestimate the importance of the most menial solution to a problem, and don't forget it, for somewhere along the line it will inevitably pop up again. For double trouble is not all that rare, since one malfunction often occasions that of another if repair is not made in short order, especially in the field of electrics. These "Why me?" specials offer the ultimate incentive for doing one's own work for they can break your wallet rather than your temper when they *are* farmed out on an hourly basis.

As you go through the *Motorcycle Repair Manual* you'll notice that it may not include your exact brand or model. It can't handle them all. No book can. You couldn't lift it if we made one. Although some specific examples are given, we must deal mostly in generalities or theory, or take a specific component, work it over, then point out peculiarities of similar types and let you feed them in to what we have done. For this reason, it is advisable to supplement the *Repair Manual* with a shop manual on your particular model. Actually I've got the cart before the horse; the shop manual is the bible, but in some instances it's a tad stiff. But by playing the two against one another, you'll find that they will not only generally agree, but complement one another to the extent that your understanding is measurably reinforced. Sometimes, especially in foreign-oriented technical translations, the text absolutely defies comprehension, or it may have you holding your sides with laughter, but as a general rule the factory manuals are worth every penny of the sometimes high cost involved.

If I could leave you with a single thought, it would be this: don't be afraid to tackle the job. You can always throw it in a box and take it to the store if you fail.

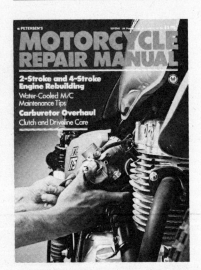

COVER: Whether your bike is a four-stroke, fire-breathing street machine or a two-cycle trail mount, there's valuable information on the following pages for you. You may not be able to perform carburetor surgery from start to finish as depicted on our cover, but you can learn a great deal about the components of your bike and how they work—to the extent of fixing many problems yourself and handling routine maintenance. Photograph by Pat Brollier, PPC Photographic. Cover design by Dick Fischer.

PETERSEN'S MOTORCYCLE REPAIR MANUAL

Edited by the Specialty Publications Division staff of Petersen Publishing Company. Copyright © 1976 by Petersen Publishing Co., 8490 Sunset Blvd., Los Angeles, Calif. 90069. Phone (213) 657-5100. All rights reserved. No part of this book may be reproduced without written permission. Printed in U.S.A.

Al Hall/Editor
Dick Fischer/Art Director
Eric Rickman/Technical Editor
Bob Greene/Contributing Editor
Angie Ullrich/Associate Editor

ISBN 0-8227-0651-2

Library of Congress Catalog Card Number 76-18641

SPECIALTY PUBLICATIONS DIVISION

Erwin M. Rosen/Executive Editor
Spencer Murray/Editor
Al Hall/Managing Editor
Jay Storer/Feature Editor
Jim Norris/Associate Editor
Richard L. Busenkell/Associate Editor
Eric Rickman/Special Assignments
Dick Fischer/Art Director
George Fukuda/Artist, Design
Glenn Hamaguchi/Artist, Design
Angie Ullrich/Editorial Assistant

PETERSEN PUBLISHING COMPANY

R.E. Petersen/Chairman of the Board

F.R. Waingrow/President
Philip E. Trimbach/V.P., Finance
Herb Metcalf/V.P., Circulation Marketing
William Porter/Director, Circulation
Jack Thompson/Assistant Director, Circulation
Spencer Nilson/Director, Administrative Services
Alan C. Hahn/Director, Market Development
James J. Krenek/Director, Manufacturing Services
Al Isaacs/Director, Graphics
Bob D'Olivo/Director, Photography
Maria Cox/Manager, Data Processing Services

CONTENTS

TOOL UP

Before you can even think of working on your bike, there are a few things you'll need. But remember, there's no such thing as a "good" cheap tool

BY DALE BOLLER

There's an old quotation by that famous scribe, "Anonymous" which says, "A good workman is known by his tools." How many times have you lost faith in a mechanic upon discovering his workshop was some cluttered corner in a dark garage with bent and battered tools strewn about in greasy disarray? His work is probably just as makeshift and inferior as his workshop. Indeed, miracle machines often come out of the most unsuspecting locations, but in general, a clean and well-equipped shop produces the best motorcycle repair. A professional mechanic will accumulate tools worth as much as two or three brand new 750's and the home mechanic will require about

$300.00 in tools to do a complete tune-up, minor repairs and routine maintenance. Therefore it's important to know how to purchase, use and maintain tools and which ones to buy in the first place. This article will discuss these subjects in terms of the home mechanic.

Another famous scribe, Carlyle, said, "The tools to him that can handle them." The most important tool in a rider's possession is his mechanical ability. Anyone without some measure of proven technical skill, or a budding potential eager to be developed with proper guidance, should leave repairs to the pros. There's too much at stake for a natural bungler to start aligning wheels or just touch-

ing a nut with a wrench. A person is only as safe as his own riding, and the bike, and an amateur wrench unknowledgeable or incompetent to the point of endangering the safety of a bike must steer clear of mechanics. Save your money in some other area if you don't know what you're doing.

There are about as many ways to go with tools and a home workshop as there are tools in the Snap-On catalog, and that's a bunch. Most mechanics agree that a complete shop grows slowly over the years. A beginner will have and need only a few tools commensurate with his mechanical ability and complexity of his motorcycle. His shop will grow in pro-

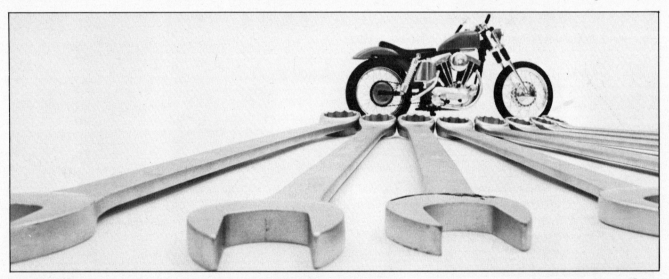

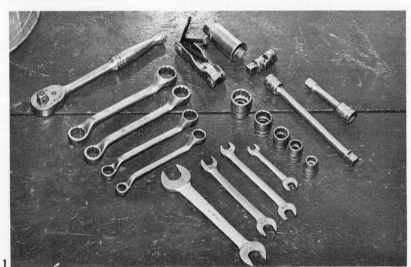

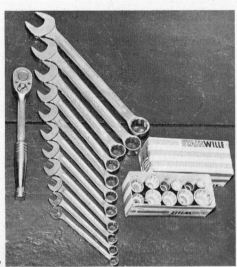

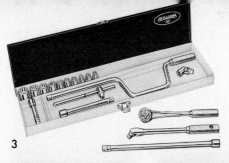

3

4

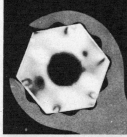

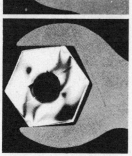

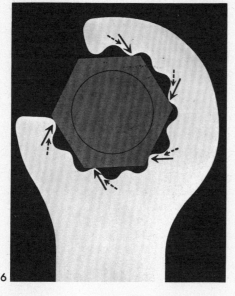

5

6

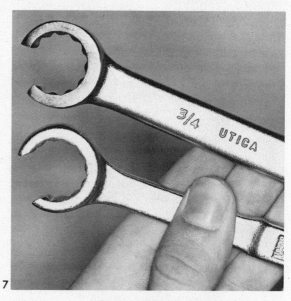

7

1. Most home workshops already have a small collection of American inch tools. Some interchange with metric.

2. Most all imported motorcycles today use metric-sized hardware. An investment in good metric open/box combo wrenches and sockets saves working time and damage to hardware.

3. Top quality socket sets aren't cheap, but will last for many years. Start off with basic set, then expand.

4. Handy LocRite wrench fits over metal gas line, then onto soft fuel nut for damage-free tightening.

5. Infra-red X-ray shows minimal stress with LocRite tool while conventional open end wrench exerts center directed force which distorts nut head.

6. Lobes exert a true twisting force tangent to the bolt's center as opposed to center-directed crushing force exerted by conventional wrench.

7. Lobular surfaces of LocRite wrench on right differ only subtly from flat surfaces of standard design, left.

8. Convincing demonstration measures torque at which various wrenches round off the corners of hex head bolt or nut at 22 foot pounds.

9. Standard open end wrench slipped over hex corners at 22. ft, lbs. The damage incurred is enough to render the nut or bolt useless to torque down to proper specs again.

10. LocRite wrench torqued down the same damaged hex to 60 foot pounds torque without slipping or causing further damage to the corners.

portion to his interest in motorcycle repair and his budget.

Inexpensive tools versus quality tools: Starting with cheap tools will build a large working set more quickly, but once you've tried a slick-fitting Williams socket or drooled over a Proto catalog, you'll end up replacing many of your original purchases. Personal pride in owning what you know are quality tools is also another factor in buying the best. Pick up a quality wrench and it's like examining a fine piece of sculpture, perfect in every detail, almost too good to use and certainly conducive to proper care and handling. If the aesthetics of quality tools don't convince you of their worth, the short life of cheap ones and damage they do to nuts and bolts certainly will. Good tools are something you buy once, for with care, they will last a lifetime. Do it in the beginning and you will save money in the end. Just as the motorcyclist starts with a 90cc trail bike and is soon shopping for a Triumph, the mechanic will eventually want the correct tool for every job, and preferably the best tool.

Admittedly, it takes experience to know what you're doing, so how can you gain experience? Here are five ways: First, have confidence in yourself—you can do it. Second, read up on motorcycle and engine theory to build a strong foundation. There are

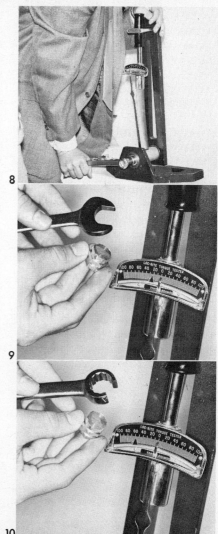

8

9

10

TOOL UP

about half a dozen good books on the subject available through Bagnall Publishing Company and Clymer Publications. Your closest dealer may be able to suggest a few titles also. Read the technical pieces which appear in the monthly magazines since they are more current than books and may often deal with a specific problem on a bike you are intending to repair. Third, consider one of the many courses presently offered in motorcycle mechanics by trade schools. They are usually a minimum of one semester in length, but difficult to enroll in because of a waiting list and sometimes costly in tuition. But other than full-time apprenticeship next to a factory-trained mechanic, the schools are the best way to go. Fourth, buy the factory service manual ($5.00 to $10.00 from your dealer) for the bike you will repair and watch for the distributor's service bulletins which should be posted in your dealer's shop; if not, ask him to see them and transfer any specifications or procedure changes in the bulletins to your service manual. Fifth, talk to people. Discuss your bike and its idiosyncracies with other owners of the same model at every chance you have. Someone who recounts cam chain trouble on his bike at 6000 miles has just tipped you off to adjust yours carefully at 4500 miles, well in advance of any possible trouble. Talk to mechanics at the dealership. Talk to race tuners who build competition bikes out of your model. But if these sources can't tell you *why* your problem occurred, beware of *how* they said to fix it. A good mechanic knows both; otherwise he's just a grease monkey.

Confidence, theoretical back-ground, service manuals and other people are all part of your tools. But now down to the basic hardware—wrenches, pliers, sockets and the like.

When you're faced with a choice between similar, but different tools—such as six-point box wrenches versus 12-point box wrenches or a "soft" rating on a plastic hammer tip versus a "medium hard" rating—ask a seasoned mechanic the differences and which is best for motorcycle work. He'll tell you to buy the 12-point wrench because it requires less throw to take a new bite and thus can be used to more advantage in the many limited access areas on a bike. Then he'll explain that hammers are available with removable tips and you need one soft enough to push in with your thumb nail and one irresistable completely to thumb-nail pressure. He'll tell you which screw extractors work and that pre-set torque wrenches with an audible signal are easier to use than the deflecting-beam type.

Common sense, your professional friend and the accompanying "Basic Workshop Tools" chart will help you decide what tools to buy. Common sense, professional advice and the following suggestions will help you to buy them for the least amount of money. Top-rate tools are extremely expensive and are rarely discounted to individuals. However, industries buying in volume, wholesalers, distributors and retailers obtain their supplies considerably below list price and their employees are often allowed to purchase tools at company cost. Make friends with someone who has such a privilege and buy your tools through him. Another way to save up to 25 percent is to find a wholesaler willing to sell to you direct; it's not illegal if you can justify professional

BASIC WORKSHOP TOOLS	
(Prices may vary depending on whether tools are purchased new or used.)	
Allen wrench set	$ 1.00
C-clamp, 6-inch	5.00
Calipers, dial-type	30.00
Center punch	1.00
Chain breaker	4.00
Circuit tracer	5.00
Drill, electric (3/8-inch)	25.00
Drill bits, set of 10	12.00
Feeler gauge	5.00
Files, triangular, flat, rattail	10.00
Hacksaw, adjustable	4.00
Hammers:	
Ball-peen	5.00
Soft tip	4.00
Knife	4.00
Paint brush (for cleaning)	1.00
Pans (for oil draining)	3.00
Pencil magnet	1.00
Pliers:	
Needle nose	4.00
Wire cutter	4.50
Regular	2.75
Channellock	4.00
Vise, grip-type	4.00
Circlip remover	3.00
Propane torch	10.00
Puller, universal-type	10.00
Rule, metal	1.00
Screwdrivers:	
4-piece blade set	8.00
4-piece Phillips set	8.00
Sockets (3/8), 20-piece set	30.00
Soldering iron or gun	10.00
Strap wrench	3.50
Tin snips, right- and left-hand	5.00
Wrenches	
Adjustable:	
6-inch	2.75
10-inch	3.75
12-inch	6.00
Combination, 8-piece set	20.00
Impact	12.00
Torque	25.00
Extras: Loctite, grease, oil can, etc.	10.00
TOTAL, approx.	**$300.00**

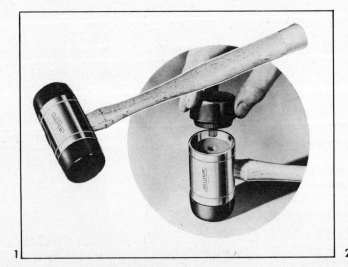

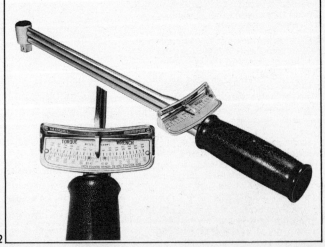

3

4

use of your tools in almost any remote way, such as working on a race bike which competes for money or working as a mechanic for pay. You can save about 10 percent by buying tools finished in industrial black; they are no different from the satin-chromed version in metal, machining or broaching. Then there are the occasional

1. Soft tips of plastic, leather or lead are a real necessity around the garage. Some hammers have replacement tips as shown. This permits a soft metal on one side, plastic on other.

2. An absolute necessity is a torque wrench. This Sturtevant wrench is calibrated in meter-grams and inch-pounds. Others are available that give both foot and inch pounds.

3. You won't get to first base working on an engine without an impact driver for slotted and Phillips screws. Keep this in your tool box.

4. Feeler gauges are the only way some measurements can be taken. They are flat steel or wire. Be sure the ones you get are stainless steel.

5. Trying to get engines and wheels apart is virtually impossible without snap ring pliers. They come in two types, open-out and close-in, with tips.

6. There's just no replacement for a ring compresser when needed.

sales on name brands. Wait for them. In some brands you save money by purchasing a set instead of individual tools. But beware of enormous sets that include many specialized items you'll never use. Sets also preclude mixing brands which often occurs when you prefer one maker's sockets but not his pliers, or go to a third manufacturer for screwdrivers simply because you like their feel. Brand loyalty toward tools among mechanics is often quite strong, but regardless of brand, most everyone succumbs to a bargain price on a top-line item.

Choosing the right tool is like choosing the right wife. Both have to give you good results for the rest of your life. Selecting the tool is a lot easier than finding the chick. Simply round up a few catalogs from some of the following major manufacturers: Blackhawk, Bonney, Craftsman, Crescent, Indestro, Mac, OTC, Proto, S-K Wayne, Snap-On, Utica and Williams.

There are others but these manufacturers are the biggies and their wares are superior. Thumb through the catalogs to determine what is available and at what cost. You'll have

to request a separate price list since cost rarely accompanies catalog descriptions. An evening with a catalog is fascinating and informative and gives you an idea of how much there is to learn about the subject. Did you know there are special pliers which automatically twist lock wire in seconds? That hacksaw blades come in 18, 24 or 32 teeth per inch? That Utica makes a tangental-drive Loc-Rite wrench which will unscrew bolts hopelessly buggered or rounded-off by conventional wrenches? Or that Williams offers a torque multiplier capable of displacing 2000 foot-pounds which weighs 102 pounds and sells for $1532.50? Becoming aware of both the basics and exotica is the first (and interesting) step.

Next, go directly to the retail outlets so you can see and handle the merchandise. Wander through your local Sears tool department for a variety of mechanics tools. Look for the word "Forged" or "Drop Forged" stamped on the tool; every maker who uses this superior process will so indicate. Check on the guarantee. It should be cut and dried: If a tool breaks in normal use, it's replaced

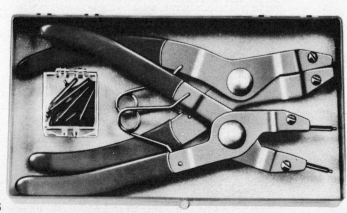

5

6

TOOL UP

free of charge. Ask if the tool has a "military description" or "military order number." If so that means the Army buys it and it's up to rigid government specs. Bring a bolt along on your browsing session and check the fit of various wrenches; if your selection has noticeably more play than a Williams, Snap-On or Proto wrench, don't buy it. Examine the mesh of pliers, the thickness and uniformity of screwdriver blades and the amount of slop in the moving jaw of adjustable wrenches. You'll soon know how much of what certain deficiency is intolerable.

SPECIAL TOOLS

Although the special factory tools available through dealers for specific jobs on your bike such as removing fork seal covers or pulling cam gears are of main concern to professionals, the shade-tree mechanic should be aware of their existence. The service manual generally pictures all the special tools available for that particular model. Sometimes a couple of pullers, a flywheel holder and an odd-shaped wrench comprise the whole assortment and cost is around $20.00, but often carb synchro gauges and electronic timing equipment can raise the price of a factory tool set up to $100.00 as is the case with Honda Fours. It's usually wise to buy only the

items you need for home workshop jobs—why pay for a main bearing removal tool when you'll never use it?

One piece of equipment which all mechanics must have is a torque wrench and its importance bears special mention here. There is an engineering phrase that says, "An over-torqued bolt is already half broken." If torque was no big thing, there wouldn't be long lists of twisting limits in service manuals or 50 different kinds of torque wrenches on the market. For most all motorcycle work, a torque wrench that reads in "inch pounds" is best. All bolts stretch slightly when tightened. Torque is the force required on the bolt to produce the desired degree of stretch to mate surfaces evenly with just the right amount of tension to withstand heat expansion, protect the gasket and prevent warping from overtightening.

Riders plagued with engine oil leaks (most of us) can reduce seeping by 70 to 80 percent by fitting new gaskets with weather stripping and torquing bolts to factory specifications. A wrench capable of this job will cost about $25.00. Torque is measured on the basis of a fundamental law of physics regarding leverage: Force times distance equals torque (twisting force) around a pivot point (bolt head). If one pound of force is exerted around the bolt center at one foot from that center, the torque is one foot-pound. If the distance is meas-

ured in inches, then the torque is read as 12 inch-pounds.

The easiest place to shop for tools is at an automotive parts jobber or major hardware store. Some brands, including one of the best available, Snap-On, are not sold in retail stores, but only by factory-franchised agents who sell out of trucks. You can locate these agents in the phone book and they will come directly to your house whether you want one pair of pliers or a complete set. Don't ignore the mail order houses either. Note well that the catalog price is usually a bit less than the over-the-counter cost.

Many people weigh the price of a repair job by the dealer with the cost of the tool necessary to do it them-

1. In time you can accrue a supply of sundry tools for the special tasks of your particular machine. Don't lend these to your friends.

2. Plan on having a gear puller of some type in your supply. They come in two or three prong varieties. Keep away from cheap imported pullers.

3. Many of the magneto and alternator rotors are very difficult to remove, particularly if they've been LocTited. A shock puller (shown) can be ordered from your dealer or special made.

4. Speciality tools include a mixed set of small files, deburring tool and jewelers magnifying glass. These are often found during special sales.

5. Bolt head markings indicate SAE tensile strength ratings. Always use grade five or better on your bike.

6. If you progress up to having compressed air a high speed impact driver will save hours of wrench turning. There are also electric models.

7. One of the musts is a set of good grade high speed drill bits. A practiced mechanic will learn how to sharpen drills on a bench grinder.

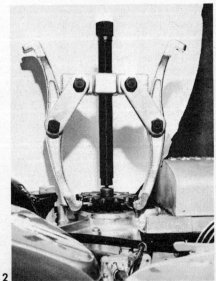

selves. If the costs are at all close, you are better off doing it yourself and ending up with the tool. In a few years you'll have a self-contained shop which prevents the frustration of being halfway through an engine teardown only to be stopped for lack of a certain tool. Once your shop is self contained, new tools will be luxury additions to make things faster or easier. Most mechanics never stop buying tools. Tools are in the same category as vehicles for hauling bikes—expenditures for them can exceed the value of the motorcycle.

TOOL SAFETY

Be careful when using your tools. Tool safety is almost an insulting subject until you are hurt or become aware of the following statistics: There is an industrial accident every 15 seconds in America today; someone is killed on the job every 39 minutes. Disabling injuries totaled just under 2,000,000 in 1968 with unsafe use of hand tools contributing to more than six percent of all industrial injuries. The Pennsylvania Department of Labor and Industry reports that using defective tools or equipment and using them in an improper manner are the principal unsafe acts contributing to 54.7 percent of injury cases analyzed. The assumption that common sense will dictate proper use of hand tools is not borne out by the accident records. Here are some rules: Don't use a pipe for extending a wrench handle, use a bigger wrench. Always pull a wrench instead of pushing it so your hand won't be smashed by ramming into the work if the wrench slips. Don't use screwdrivers on objects held in your hand. Carve and file in strokes away from your body. Don't substitute tools, such as using a pliers for a wrench job. Before doing any extensive work around the shop area, remove rings and wristwatches; they catch on things and if bumped on a battery terminal, can burn. Beware of battery acid which eats clothing. Fumes from a battery are explosive so keep anything capable of sparking away from the battery, including a hot light bulb. While charging, a battery

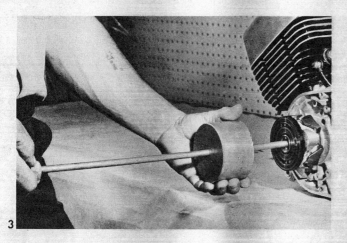

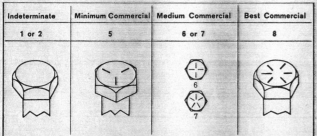

Indeterminate	Minimum Commercial	Medium Commercial	Best Commercial
1 or 2	5	6 or 7	8

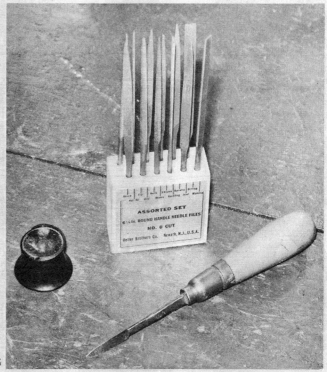

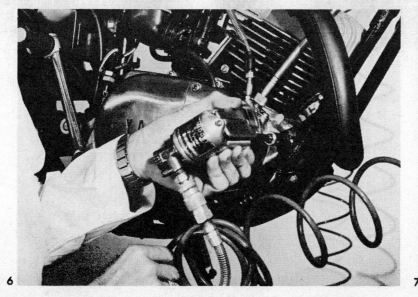

TOOL UP

expels hydrogen, another explosive gas which must be isolated or vented away from spark or flame. If you must store oily rags between washings, keep them in a closed metal container to prevent spread of flames if fire starts by spontaneous combustion. Just in case, keep your fire extinguisher easily accessible. Be sure the plastic insulation on pliers handles is intact before tackling the ignition system. If your power tools come with a ground wire, use it. Always wear safety glasses when there is any chance of eye damage, especially around grinders. It's pretty hard to ride and point a white cane at the same time. Finally, realize that every worn or mutilated hand tool is a potential accident, and so is every distraction while you're working, so keep the dog, the kids and your girl friend at a safe distance. Using tools safely is quite simple really. Employ logic, set them down carefully—don't drop them with a clang—don't loan them out, identify them with your initials and keep your hands clean and dry when using them.

CLOSE AT HAND

Storing tools is not as easy as it sounds. They are among the most commonly stolen items in existence, along with motorcycles, Corvettes and car stereos, so a chest with adequate theft prevention is important. Furthermore, tools exposed to the air will suffer from corrosion and rust speckling in just a few months, so a relatively airtight storage method is important. Tools will maintain their lustre inside a good chest. Elaborate wall mounting inside a dealer's shop is fine, but garage air will take its toll soon unless tools are sprayed with a light oil—but this coating often inhibits their use by staying slippery. A chest can be just as convenient if it has built-in casters or you mount it on a home-made rolling platform to enable easy placement close to the work. Here are some toolbox tips: Choose a chest large enough to contain your working set but not too heavy for two people to lift into your truck. Make sure the drawers will pull all the way out; some only have ⅔ travel which impedes access to the rear area. Make sure the vertical reinforcing sections in the middle of the drawer don't divide it in such a way that precludes storage of longer wrenches, drill motors or other large and bulky

items. Oil the runners carefully with 90 weight gearbox oil—it won't push out or thin enough in summer heat to drip. Finally, hit up the seller for free lining material—either vinyl, plastic, rubber or cork.

What if you live in an apartment and have no place to work on your bike? Here's where a good set of tools comes in handy to negotiate with a homeowner for space in return for use of your tools. Loaning tools is usually strictly taboo, but it will be easy to locate a working and storage area with a good set of tools to bargain with. Some groups combine forces and finances to really go whole hog on a workshop. Several wallets can afford a roller chest, welding equipment and even an air compressor in addition to hand tools. Groups can be club members, owners of the same brand motorcycle, friends, relatives, even car people. An important rule in group buying is to establish beforehand what happens to a drop-out's share. Usually his portion stays with the group, members buying him out. 🏍

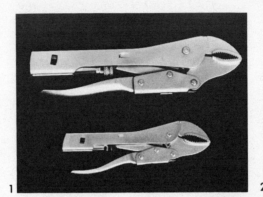

1. Vise-grip pliers can be a lifesaver when removing stuck muffler baffles. Note curved jaws, some have the less versatile straight jaws.

2. A high-speed polisher/grinder such as this flexible shaft unit, saves much hand labor. Look for a unit with lots of torque and rpm.

3. An ideal home motorcycle workshop should look like this. Plenty of elbow room to work around bike and bench with vise and grinder.

4. Two-stroke or four, an accurate degree wheel is a necessity for the home mechanic. Dialing in a cam is rough without an indicator wheel.

5. Gear ratio calculator solves the math problem when changing gearbox or rear wheel sprockets. Just locate ratio desired and buy cogs indicated.

6. Measuring flat plate, crankshaft supporting V-blocks and dial indicator are used to check the crank end bearing for excessive play.

7. Instant and inexpensive motorcycle lift is what this tube-like thing is. The lift is made from joined pipe tubing and 90° bracket.

8. Super deluxe cycle lift is for those who want the very best. Craftsmanship is first class. It tilts for easy bike loading and off-loading.

SOFT TOOLS

"Plastic" used to be a dirty word, now, no thinking cyclist can afford to be without it

BY STEVE GREENE

Dad had just put the finishing touch on the big black thumper and stepped back to run through the check-off sheet a final time . . . "Rear chain, gearbox, air cleaner, plug, points, spares, primary oil; yep, we're all . . ." His voice broke off, the sentence unfinished. I could tell by the set look on his face that something was wrong, we were in trouble.

The 500-mile National was only hours away now, the stage was set, preliminary markings were up, mileage taken, checkpoints established and the machinery already in motion. There was nothing we could do to stop it, or even slow it, for any emergency. The countdown had already begun and we—Dad's giant 600cc Matchless single and my 650 Trumpet—were dedicated, committed to marking 137 miles of desert wasteland in the next three days.

"There's a crack in my primary case. The oil's running out. I'm dead, Steve!" Sure enough, our last scouting mission over agonizing, boulder-laced Devil's Staircase had center-punched the thin aluminum, and the primary oil supply obviously wouldn't last half a day at the rate it was oozing from the hairline crack down the front of the case. And anybody'd be a fool to venture forth in the no-man's-land that lies ahead with a bike in anything short of perfect mechanical condition. "Oh man," he said, "no welding shops open this time of day and worse yet, no time to pull the case, even if there were a shop open—no way!" Panic reared its ugly head.

Then, through some blessed instinctive reaction to a distasteful situation, my attention shifted from the ailing Matchless to the ready Triumph. There it was . . . the answer, in plain sight, smeared all over the exposed rocker-shaft end in the rocker box. Only the day before I had dried-up a persistent oil seepage with a new RTV (room temperature vulcanizing) plastic by General Electric. If it worked on a hot engine head, why not on a lousy primary case? Sure as shootin' we were back in business!

As fast as it takes to tell, the single had been laid on its side, front end

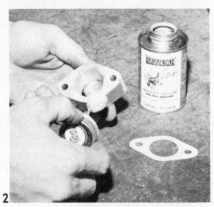

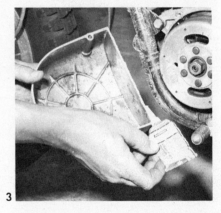

high to allow the oil to drain away from the fractured nose of the primary case, while the raw edges were generously swabbed clean with lacquer thinner preparatory to applying the magic patch. Squeezing it on like toothpaste, the GE Silicone Seal took only seconds to apply, spread to cover with the fingers. The job was done—it couldn't have taken over 5 minutes.

A lot of earth-shaking things had transpired in that brief interval. We had saved the day; the answer to a traumatic situation which would have seriously jeopardized months of planning and layout work came squirting out of a tube. Several hours' labor and chasing around town had been saved and, perhaps best of all, we had cheated the welder out of a ten-spot

at least. No, really more important were the in-the-field possibilities that loomed from this simple back-yard find. For suddenly it became clear that the motorcyclist need no longer be vulnerable to a whole class of minor-yet-crippling failures which regularly bring down even the fleetest, best-prepared set of wheels, in the darndest God-forsaken places. It's so good we'll call it Cycle Lib. Stick it in your pocket. Take it with you. Be free.

No more need the cyclist fear a holed engine or primary case, a torn fork boot or a serious engine oil loss anywhere from tank to oil pump. Here at last was a versatile "jelly band aid" that was almost tantamount to having a portable, pocket-size welding torch at your disposal wherever you go.

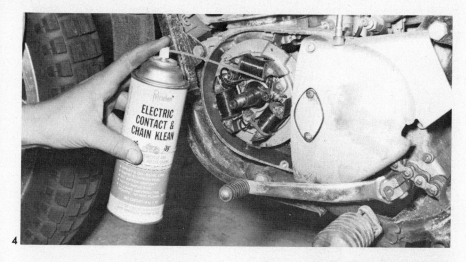

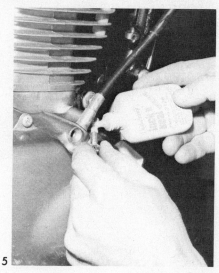

1. No shop is really complete unless it includes a set of soft tools. They are available in tubes, cans and spray cans and may just save the day.

2. Products like Gasgacinch can be used when installing new gaskets or in place of gaskets. Applied in liquid form, it dries to form air and oil tight seal.

3. Waterproofing ignition systems is a job for silicone sealant. Many types are available from bike and auto stores and can be used all over bike.

4. Spray can ignition point cleaners like this one from Petrochem remove oil and dirt without need for disassembly. Also good for cleaning spark plugs.

5. LocTite manufactures a number of products that are a must around the home workshop. A little applied to a screw before assembly assures that it will never come out till you want it to. They make various grades for various uses.

About the size of a regular tube of Ipana, it can be stuffed in a toolbox or slung on the frame or even carried in a shirt pocket. And with it and half-a-dozen inner-tube rubber bands, there's darned little you can't mend on the spot outside of a broken frame or wheel hub.

Are we over-playing it? After all, plastic patch-kits-in-a-tube have been around since Hector was a pup and at best are only temporary get-by gimmicks that seldom live up to their maker's wild boasts. Wrong, wrong, wrong—on all three counts. The good space-age stuff is only now beginning to filter back to earth; several of the plastics we will talk about weren't available to the public two years ago. And although some of them must be considered temporary, depending upon how critical the application, most of the instances to be cited are not only permanent but provide the best practical solution possible. More important is the fact that, as with First Aid, they can be applied at the time of need, like the best brain surgeon in the world, your favorite welder is

of no help if he is not at your side when you're hurtin'. And no longer is the word plastic to be associated with a trinket from Hong Kong; no more must metal be something that can only be formed in a factory. Now the motorcyclist can shape and improvise both of these materials with his bare hands.

Yesterday a punctured case, fractured gas or oil tank in the wilderness meant abandonment or, hopefully, hours, maybe even days at the end of a tow rope, at best an extremely dangerous situation in itself. Today the odds have turned in our favor, and there is every likelihood that the cyclist in distress can ride out under his own power, with a minimum of time lost or danger to his being. It's that great. Inexpensive, easy to use and durable, the new miracle plastics and metals have the added attraction of being readily available at almost any neighborhood hardware store or auto parts house. They're tailor-made for the motorcyclist.

Having been "saved" on this particular occasion, I was moved to ex-

plore further into several similar products and their uses. Although they are only a few of the many brands offered, and the applications shown here barely scratch the surface, it is hoped that they will set you to thinking and improvising, in which case the editors of MSQ will be interested, I am sure, to bank your findings with ours for future reference in this field of repair. Plastics are extremely simple to apply, the only bit of advice we could give is to clean the working area as scrupulously as possible, using lacquer thinner if available, to remove surface film or oils. In the field this should be done with gasoline, but if this is impractical a dry cloth and some elbow grease will probably do the trick. Remember that most of the included products are best suited as a patch, filler or adhesive, and that sheer-strength is not normally their forte. So experiment, determine their limitations for yourself—you'll be amazed in most instances. Now let's take a closer look at some of the practical applications that first served as the inspiration for this article, and a few others that followed as a result of our continuing curiosity and amazement.

Probably the most versatile of the lot is the GE Silicone Seal that starred in our introduction. A soft, pliable solid, it comes in shades of either white or clear. It seems to have an affinity for almost anything, sticking to and sealing aluminum, steel, rubber, glass, leather . . . you name it. It also sets up rather quickly, becoming dry enough to hold back lightly-pressurized oil (such as in our primary case application) within seconds, and completely curing in 24 hours. One of GE Silicone Seal's features is its tenacity and refusal to run when applied, simplifying vertical applications. It remains semi-resilient and can be peeled off by hand at any time, but resists normal wear and tear. We used Silicone Seal in several different circumstances, all with total success.

Silicone Seal has the ability to withstand some fairly high temperatures; not only did it easily handle the primary case caper, but it proved itself in the cylinder-head rocker box as well, pretty warm country. It stopped dead the aforementioned rocker shaft seepage, a cylinder-base nut leak and a right-side gear case oil mist between crankcase and cover that refused to respond to tightening of the cover screws. None of these applications have fallen off or given up in several

SOFT TOOLS

months of extremely hot off-road work during the summer months. Nor has any one of them permitted the slightest sign of oil seepage. The alternative to any one of these solutions would have been the removal of case, cover or cylinder at the expense of much time and no guarantee of equal results. Up until this point, I had been unable to seal off long, obstinate oil seepages, such as are common between crankcase and primary cover, without removing the cover and fitting a new gasket. Silicone Seal has the muscle to do it from the outside, without taking anything apart.

In fact, so unreal was GE's Silicone in its sealing performance that it was decided to give it the super-acid test, that of sealing a gasoline leak. Not wishing to puncture a gas tank, a coffee can was substituted; a hole was first punched in the bottom with an ice pick, then the hole was sealed with Silicone Seal and the can filled with gas. The next morning, the gas was still in the can, the bottom dry. Was there nothing this stuff wouldn't do? This clear plastic rubber was defiant, but I'd break it yet! This time the punctured can was filled with gas first, then while the gas was actually running out the bottom of the can, a wad of Silicone Seal was jammed into the hole. I couldn't believe my eyes! It stopped the leak cold and started to set up instantly! The next morning the patch was still holding, the bottom of the can dry. That did it. There was absolutely nothing we could do for an encore. And the guy who doesn't take a tube of this stuff along on his next excursion just doesn't have it all together—like going off without your sparkplug wrench. Imagine, repairing a split gas tank seam in the middle of nowhere and being back on the road in a matter of minutes!

Have you ever noticed how a headlight often grows dim with age? Dust and moisture gain easy access to the reflector around headlight rim and bulb base, eventually eroding the mirror finish on the reflector. The same can happen to a speedometer; dust blows into the inner workings and speeds wear. To seal the headlight, merely smear Silicone Seal around the base of the bulb while in place in the reflector, then, with the lens and rim mounted back in the shell, force the clear plastic in around the rim, between rim and housing and

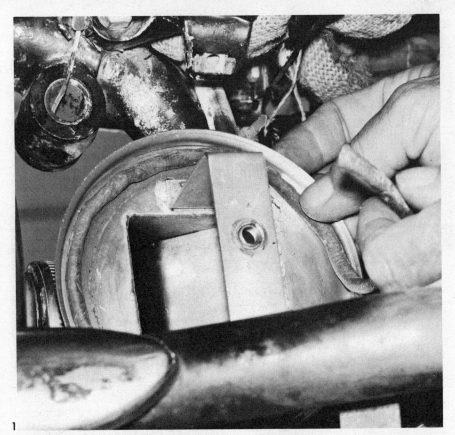

1

2

rim and glass, then wipe away the excess. Being clear, it will not be noticeable on glass or chrome, and the lens should be bright as new forever. On the speedometer, the clear plastic can be rubbed around the light socket and also the glass bezel while all is intact.

And with our increasingly worse atmospheric conditions, rubber goods are not long for this world. If the smog or fork springs take a bite out of your fork boots, don't sweat it. You don't have to replace the boot if you don't want to. Why spend an hour and a half removing the wheel and fender, pulling the old boot down off the leg, greasing a new one and

slipping it back in place before refitting wheel and fender again? Cycle Lib to the rescue! Just clean the surface, whip out Silicone Seal and cover the hole. A similar tear from a greasewood bush, patched in this matter, survived two months of desert riding and is still going strong, standing the torment of a constantly flexing accordion fork boot and looking for all the world as if it is going to go the route. Fork covers aren't cheap; this stuff is, and quick to boot.

The possibilities are seemingly endless. A torn saddle cover, an electrical connection, or a surface tear in a tire casing; all can be made to lie down tight with this stuff. Often a snag from a rock will peel back the thin outer skin of rubber that covers the first layer of cord in a tire sidewall. Although the tire is not physically weakened (unless the cord is torn too), subsequent exposure to smog, water and dirt will prematurely rot the cord. But a cover of Silicone Seal will permanently protect it from the elements and preserve the tire as though it had never been violated.

Another company which has made the motorcyclist's life a little easier is the Devcon Corporation. They manufacture several products which will heal many of your motorcycle's ailments. Their claim to fame is a product called Plastic Steel. It comes in a small tube along with a companion tube of hardener and boasts of being "the strongest, toughest repair material available today." It is an epoxy resin that contains plastic and steel and bonds with a multitude of metals including iron, steel, brass, bronze and aluminum. It is not recommended for temperatures above 250°, so let your hot little barrel be your guide. Hardening takes two hours, but can be accelerated with low heat.

Besides Plastic Steel, Devon comes up with Liquid Aluminum, Rubber, ST-50 (Steel), and 2-Ton. The 2-Ton product is an "epoxy super glue" and Devcon states that two drops of this potent mixture will hold two tons! Got anything on your scooter that's about to fall off, like a hand grip, taillight lens, foot peg rubber, exhaust guard, etc.? A few drops of this brew ought to do it ten times over—just be sure not to get a patch of it between tire and ground or you might need a crane to pull it loose! The Liquid Aluminum and ST-50, when hard, can be drilled, sanded and painted. Both set up in two hours. The ST-50 can also be threaded! It could come in handy should you strip a bolt hole in an engine case; just wash it out, squirt in some ST-50, let it harden for two hours and tap the hole with a fresh set of threads.

The Liquid Aluminum can also be used as a backup to GE's Silicone Seal regarding a cracked aluminum outer case or punctured steel case. The Silicone can be used to seal the opening until such time as routine maintenance requires that the cover be removed, upon which occasion the inside of the cover an be treated with the more permanent Liquid Aluminum. After removing the cover, clean it, then rough it up and apply the

1. Scotch-Calk is like plastic taffy, can be used around the air cleaner backing plate when hard paper element is used, to seal leaks behind filter.

2. Worn fiber washer on fork drain plug can be replaced or Silicone Seal can be substituted. Drys to become plastic rubber that defies even gasoline leaks.

3. Even tires can be repaired with the magic Silicone Seal. This sidewall was returned to like new conditioning with just a small dab after cleaning.

4. Devcon Rubber, one of their many tough products, was used to repair a V-shaped tear in this well-used seat. After drying, the seat is tough as new.

5. Minnesota Mining & Manufacturing have been the motorcyclist's friend for many years. Their "3M," or yellow peril, is found in the toolbox of every racer in the country. Primarily intended for weatherstripping, it does everything.

plastic alloy and it's fixed for good. Just for good measure, depending upon the severity of the fracture, both outer and inner surfaces can be filled, and since it is a non-stressed area, the plastic patch should serve the purpose as well as a weld. Common sense must be used, however, for it is doubtful that one of the plastic metals would hold on a cracked fender, for example, because of the vibration factor and lack of grip area between the broken edges.

Devcon's Rubber is also a versatile product that remains flexible and resists oil but is not up to gasoline. It does an excellent job of mending rips in a saddle or fork boots. Or if that plastic tank badge on your gas

tank persists in cracking and loosening or falling off, the Rubber will help secure it even if the screws should wind out due to vibration. The Rubber also is a natural in reference to electrical connections. Since we all encounter dust or water, it is a good idea to seal electrical terminals with this product, as well as beefing-up wiring insulation at potential friction points around forks and tank to preclude shorting-out from inevitable wear—a natural for waterproofing magnetos, etc. Since it is oil resistant, the Rubber could also be employed to secure a rubber oil-line-to-pipe connection by smearing a little on the pipe prior to slipping on the hose, further ensuring against the loss of oil by building up

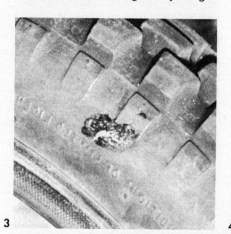
3

4

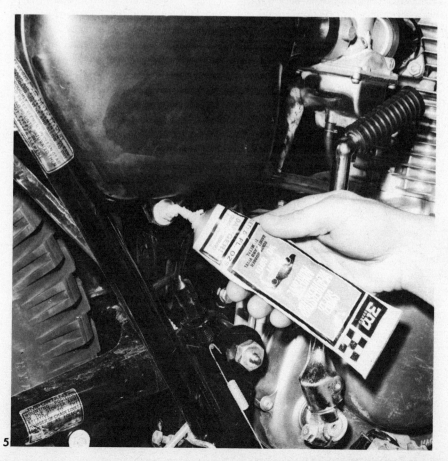
5

SOFT TOOLS

around the end of the hose from the outside once installed. Footpeg, kickstarter rubbers and handlebar grips can also be kept in place, held from sliding off or even turning by the super adhesive. Smear it generously on the shaft, then on the inside of the rubber, and jam it home—a little messy to work with but it gets the job done.

The Minnesota Mining and Manufacturing Company has pioneered its share of versatile products that can be applied to motorcycles. Their one product which really excels, and I have used for years, is Super Weatherstrip Adhesive. It is so tough that I have nicknamed it Yellow Peril because of its tenacity. This gooey yellow substance sticks to everything it comes in contact with, including your fingers. By the same token, it's one of the motorcyclist's best friends, for it will hold any nut or bolt in place against the most extreme vibration—especially good for the off-road enthusiast. Spread it on the threads, prior to installing the nut, and forget about it coming off . . . until you put the wrench to it. For despite its ability to hang in there, Super Weatherstrip gives away to a wrench and has no damaging effect to threads. And like GE's Super Silicone, it is very good about stopping an oil leak around a cylinder-base nut or oil-line flare-nut fitting, although it seems to be less versatile when it comes to sealing a crack in a case or the long parting line between a case and a cover usually served by a gasket.

Another little helper from 3M is their Scotch Calk, a tacky gray plastic that is packaged in long strips. It never changes its putty-like consistency, neither softening nor hardening, and is ideal for forming around such places as carburetor tops and the like—a good dust-proofer. Scotch Calk is waterproof and fuel resistant and can be reshaped and reused indefinitely. A favorite application is between air filter element and outer cover, to preclude the entry of dust that might otherwise sneak around the filter element rather than through it.

Leaving the subject of preventative maintenance, let's check out the sheetmetal department and see how the wonderful world of plastics can again come to our rescue. Nobody's perfect, and one of our family—I'd rather not mention any names—recently had occasion to lament a fist-sized depression in an up-to-now-cherry oil tank. That was bad enough, but trotting it around from one auto body metal shop to another, in search of a repair estimate, turned up another disappointing fact: because of the small job, and even considering the ridiculously high price of $25 to refill the depression, sand and repaint it, none of the shops really wanted to bother with it. One finally did, and after a week and a half it still sat in a corner covered with overspray from the more lucrative car jobs. In desperation, the oil tank was retrieved, with the sworn oath: "I'd rather do it myself than suffer this hassle." Sure enough, it wasn't all that difficult, and the backyard result turned out as good as any professional shop could have attained. Although there are many fine body filler products on the market, we picked up a tube of 3M's Acryl-Blue Spot Putty (part No. 5960) and a borrowed body rasp and went to work. After sanding to bare metal on the tank, the putty was applied in layers of about 3/16-inch per application, letting it dry overnight between build-ups until the area had come out to slightly past the original contour, to allow for filing. When the surface was restored, it was contoured with the body rasp, then sanded down with coarse paper, finally ending up with No. 600 paper and wet-sanded to a smooth finish. Several coats of excellent Krylon spray paint, available in most hard-

1. Silicone Seal can also be used to prevent dirt or water from entering the delicate items like headlights and taillights. Once dry, there's no way that the bad stuff can get into the works.

2. Petrochem's Anti Rust comes in a spray can and will prevent corrosion build up. Any spare parts laying around the shop can be sprayed for protection.

3. On some machines there are certain areas that will seep some oil after hard use. This Triumph rocker arm shaft was sealed with Silicone Seal in a minute.

4. Devcon Liquid Aluminum was used to repair this broken primary case, saving the cost of a welding job. Once the crack was clean and roughed up with sand paper, the sealant was applied and allowed to dry. That's all it takes.

5. Spark plug caps can be made to stay on forever with a dab of Loctite Lock N' Seal. It only takes a minute and will stay intact indefinitely.

6. ESP is yet another product from the people at Petrochem. It cleans away any corrosion and lubricates at same time.

ware stores, provides the glossy black finish to this strictly amateur effort that couldn't be told from new.

What's next? Let's say it's Saturday night before the club road run, and close inspection shows the old heap is in need of a fresh gasket. Can't buy one. Shops are closed. Never fear, Loctite's here. One of the Loctite Corporation's anaerobic adhesives can make a custom gasket of any configuration as fast as you can lay it on. The product is called Fit-all Gasket, which replaces soft gaskets. Fit-all Gasket cures overnight if you use Loctite's Klean N' Prime, which speeds the cure of all Loctite products and assures part-use in half an hour. Some of Loctite's products can be cured in 15 minutes at 200°. Still an-

other product similar to Fit-all Gasket is Plastic Gasket, which replaces paper gaskets; it is completely water- and air-tight. Two more materials vital to motorcyclists are Lock N' Seal and Nutlock. Both secure nuts, bolts and screws firmly in place so that they won't vibrate out, while Lock N' Seal has the added advantage of being able to seal leaks at oil, air and gasoline fittings.

Loctite anaerobic adhesives are kept wet by the presence of air, but when the liquid is placed between close-fitting metal parts, it then hardens into a solid resin because it is out of contact with the air. Put it on a nut and bolt and, as a liquid, it conforms to the microscopic surface roughness. Later, after it has hardened, the solid is actually keyed to the two opposing surfaces, with the result that the two parts can be separated with the use of ordinary tools but defy accidental loosening.

Going back to our previous situation calling for the need of a new gasket, let's assume that you have the critter but need some way of sealing it because previous experience has proven that, due to surface irregularities or whatever, a positive oil seal is difficult to achieve. The Porter Manufacturing and Supply Company has solved the problem with a product they call Gasgacinch. Again make

sure all surfaces are sanitary, then swab-on Gasgacinch to both sides of the gasket and both mating surfaces of the metal, let it all become a little tacky, then assemble. Properly done, your oil leak worries are over.

Still another neat little product is the Hercules Chemical Company's All purpose Tape Dope, made from Dupont Teflon. Actually it is a pipe-joint compound incorporated in tape form that lubricates and rust-proofs large threaded joints or even fuel line fittings. Tape Dope withstands temperatures from −450 to +500°F. It is ideal for such applications as motorcycle fork-bearing seal-cups, helping not only to seal against leaks but also to lubricate the threads as well. It never hardens, and prevents corrosion.

And there are more. The plastics mentioned and shown here are only those which I have "discovered" for personal use. Most of them have counterparts by other companies, possibly equally as versatile and durable, and at least worth trying since all are relatively inexpensive. You'll want to make your own discoveries, no doubt, for the trick lies in the imaginative application to the task at hand. Let's just hope that yours will be under more leisurely circumstances. The age of miracles has arrived. But who ever thought it would come in a tube!

3

4

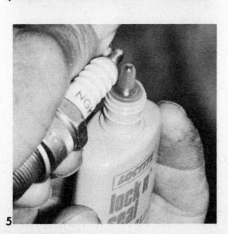

5

6

MY BIKE'S GONE LAME!

You can cure it if you use a logical approach to troubleshooting

BY BOB GREENE

Be thankful for the day your scooter refuses you in the bright morning sunshine of your driveway; it sure beats the bejabbers out of a dead motor in the middle of the night, fifty miles out of East Overshoes on a lonely stretch of swamp-bordered highway. But assuming the worst, let's picture you there, bathed in darkness, with a fistful of stamped factory wrenches or their superior, one 6-in. Vise Grip, in a heap o'trouble. All you need remember is that our little two-wheeled buddy needs gas, spark, air, compression and timing, in about that order of incidence, if it's going to get up and roar again.

FUEL

After turning off both petcocks, pull a fuel line at the carb, crack the petcock open and determine if gas is getting to the carb. If not, you're either out of gas, the gas cap breather is clogged and creating an air lock or the petcock filter has a stoppage. Let the gas run a bit, for if it is a vacuum lock it may start and then stop when the vacuum becomes sufficient.

Suzuki road bikes and some Kawasakis feature vacuum-operated fuel lines. A positive way to check their operation is to pull the vacuum hose off at the carburetor and suck on it; if fuel flows, it is working. Should it fail, merely turn the valve to Prime position, which is not vacuum controlled and is always open.

Or the opposite might prevail— flooding. If the carburetor float is stuck, tap the float body repeatedly with pocket knife or wrench; this usually frees it. Or perhaps you've picked up a load of water at that last gas stop, leaning out the mixture to where it won't fire. If so, drop the float bowl, crack the petcock and purge the line of impurities for a second or so. Rarely, a carburetor float will rupture, fill with gas and sink, causing flooding. Hold the float up tight against your ear and shake your head slowly from side to side as if saying, "Oh

no, oh no." If it gurgles, it's filled with gas. Prick a tiny hole in the top side, blow the gas out and patch both holes with the first thing that comes to hand, like soap or Silicone Seal (always carry a tube).

Perhaps the main jet has unscrewed and fallen out. Or the retaining clip has bounced off the top of the metering needle in the slide, allowing the needle to drop and wedge in the main jet. I've also had the nipple on the carburetor end of the throttle cable pull off and be blown harmlessly through the engine, but leaving the throttle slide incapacitated. Or the idle system could be at fault. If you think so, turn the idle needle jet on the outside of the carburetor body all the way in until it stops, counting the turns so you'll know where to reset it, then take it completely out, pucker up and blow into the orifice as hard as you can without bringing on a case of piles. The smallest particle of dirt or lint can bugger the idle system. If air pressure doesn't clear it, try a fine wire.

SPARK

Confident the fuel system is blameless, pull a spark plug, re-

place the lead on the plug and lay the plug on the cylinder head while cranking the engine over; you should be able to see a spark jump the electrodes. No? Fit a new plug or, failing that, use your pocket knife to clean the old sparkler, check the gap and test it again. No? Is the plug porcelain cracked? No? Has the plug wire withdrawn or otherwise separated from the cap? No? Is there a fuse in the ignition system? If there is, and it's blown, follow the wires leading from it for a short to ground. Is the coil lead tight in the coil? Yup!

The bike is probably a battery ignition job. Let's check the coil. With the spark plug out and the ignition turned off, remove the ignition points cover and kick the engine over to make sure that the points are opening and closing. Now turn the engine over until the points close, reattach the lead wire to the plug and lay the plug on the cylinder head. Turn the ignition key on and, with your fingernail hooked under the movable breaker point, work the points open and closed while observing the spark plug. If the coil is kosher, there should be a spark at the plug as you manually diddle the points.

If the bike's a multi, and one coil lead or coil has gone south, the engine will probably at least run erratically and the offending cylinder can be isolated by feeling for the lone cool cylinder head or exhaust pipe—Ouch! One of the most common bits of trouble stems from rider neglect to maintain point gap; the rubbing block wears down, the gap goes away and the engine "mysteriously" quits. If you're guilty and curb bound, file the points and make sure the gap is set at about .015 and you shouldn't be over 20 minutes late for dinner.

If you've got a pure mag job, it's a pretty bullet-proof lashup, and if one of these fails to fire it's just about got to be either the plug or the mag. After checking the gap and physical condition of the plug, file the mag points with that flexible 80-grit Rimac Flex-Stone file you carry in your wallet. Obtainable at any auto parts store, this tiny lifesaver is made of plastic and can be cut with ordinary household scissors to fit any wallet. Clean the points by drawing a business card through them, check the clearance and it had better run—always has.

Alternators are generally very dependable, unless a wire has come loose or tangled with the primary chain. If it's an off-road scooter, take a look at the outside of the primary cover to see if it has been dented to the extent that the case

has bumped the stationary winding in against the rotor and closed the gap to less than .008. If so, or if the winding is rubbing the rotor, the electrics are dead until the proper clearance has been restored.

Some motors use the zener diode system of charging control. A zener diode is an electrical voltage-amperage control bolted into a small finned heat sink, or radiator, about the size of your brain (you know best) that turns surplus electrical energy to heat which is released to the air through its radiator

fins. In really hot weather the zener diode can get so hot that it developes an internal short and fails, blows the fuse, brings the bike to a halt and turns out the lights. 'Taint necessarily so; my son Steve has piloted his 40-in. Triumph through day after day of relentless 100° Mojave hell in deep sand on innumerable occasions without a hint of trouble. But we still know that it *can* happen.

Point is, if it should, don't go through a box of fuses before realizing that this won't git it. Here's the quick and easy fix: Turn off all lights, ignition and accessories to take the load off the battery. Then, with the fuse out of the system, touch the two bare wire ends on either side of the fuse holder together. If they spark, it indicates a short in the system, which must be fixed before installing a new fuse. To determine if the zener diode is at fault, unhook the wire leading to the zener diode and let it hang. Return to the battery and repeat the sparking test between the wires on either side of the fuse holder. If no spark occurs, the zener diode was the problem. Otherwise there is likely a short in the wire that runs be-

2

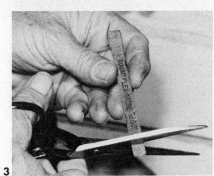

3

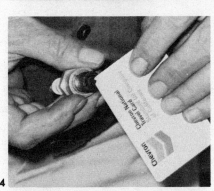

4

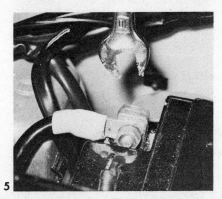

5

6

7

1. Pretty drastic measures to use on a faithful old friend when the chances are good you can find the problem by following our handy guide.

2. You get a free feeler gauge with this article. Pick up a match book at the breakfast stop; it'll be about .012-in. Right on for gapping a mag.

3. Plastic Rimac Flex-Stone is flexible, can be cut with scissors to fit any wallet, is better than steel file for dressing ignition points.

4. Got a gas company credit card? If so, you're carrying a .030-in. feeler gauge and don't know it. Between it and match book, you're all set.

5. The electrical fungus on this wrench came off battery terminal bolt. Is enough to cause flame-out. Baking soda in hot water neutralizes it.

6. Check to make sure ignition point rubbing block hasn't worn down and caused point gap to close. Book spec aside, .012 will get it running fine.

7. Checking the coil: With points in closed position, live plug on head and ignition on, work points open and closed with finger. Plug should spark.

LAME BIKE

tween the ignition switch and the coil—shorted to ground. If the zener diode was the culprit, leave the wire leading into it unattached but run with your lights on to burn off surplus juice until the new zener diode is fitted. Working this logic backward, you can lessen the load on the zener diode and minimize failure by running lights-on in very hot weather. Come to think of it, Steve always ran with his lights when working on Greenhorn layout, explaining his trouble-free rides.

Quite common is an ignition switch failure due to one of its electrical connections shaking loose or breaking just before entering the switch. Many machines seem to have about three hundred thousand wires inside the headlight, some of them in the ignition circuit. Pop the lens out and check them for security, also the fuses, but remember that a blown fuse is usually the sign of an overload, or short, and merely replacing the fuse without first remedying the cause reminds me of the Far East Indian custom of covering your face with one hand while picking your nose with the other—only covering up what's really going on. So make sure that you've got a tight electrical connection in back of the ignition switch and that the wire, although it looks to be intact, hasn't broken inside its sheath where it is offered up to the switch. Spring-loaded kill buttons, although still the most practical, can also short out on occasion. If necessary, pull the button off and inspect it to make sure it is not shorting out.

And corroded battery posts frequently knock engines out of the running. If they look the least bit grubby, or you've tried everything else, pull them and scrape the terminal posts and cable ends with a pocket knife, wipe them dry and pull them up tight with a wrench. Bared wires, too, can short to ground, so follow the wiring harness around to ascertain that they are not pinched by saddle or gas tank, or caught up in a fork bind.

Perhaps the battery's gone flat. Turn on the lights and honk the horn. If either one seems noticeably weak or completely out to lunch, an improperly set regulator, wasted alternator, dry battery plates, cracked battery case or wiring short has

probably caused the battery to discharge. Some motorcycles will start with a low battery nevertheless, so often a push will generate enough electricity to set it popping. It applies to dirt bikes as well; even if the engine fails to fire by kicking, many times a push from another bike or even a run-and-jump will bring it to life. Here's how: With the gearbox in low (street bike) or second (dirt bike), back it up until the piston backs up on compression, then pull in the clutch and run with it, hopping aboard and popping the clutch when your legs get up to speed. Immediately upon firing, clutch it and wing the engine to keep the revs on the boil. Bye! *Es por nada.*

AIR

It is unlikely that an engine's air supply would suddenly be cut off, but there is a remote possibility, so let's jaw about it. Usually this would be a gradual build-up due to air filter neglect, but one should always consider the possibility of a rag or tool pouch suffocating the filter mouth under the saddle. Or the airflow may be upset by such as a carburetor manifold gasket leak or

a ruptured filter-to-carburetor connector tube. Manifold or exhaust leaks usually announce their presence with an exhaust backfire. Especially if filter ducting is bent around corners, be sure that it is not collapsing at higher engine speeds. I've had this condition strangle my engine, and just the other day it was noticed that the corrugated carburetor ducting on a showroom Ducati was half collapsed at rest. A new bike! Unbelievable! If you suspect a vacuum leak around the manifold, douse it with soap suds, spit, whatever, and watch for action around the joint.

COMPRESSION

To properly fire the inducted charge, it must be compressed. Lack of compression can result from a blown head gasket or broken piston rings, or crankcase seals in a two-stroke. The head gasket will manifest itself by a hissing sound, and you may be able to limp in by tightening down the head bolts or nuts. If broken rings are the cause, or possibly a sticking valve guide that is holding a valve open, you can get a clue by removing the spark plug and kicking the engine through the spark plug hole. Compression while holding your thumb tightly over the spark plug hole. Compression should be at least strong enough to bounce your thumb off the hole. The check

two-stroke engine due to worn intracase seals (twin-cylinder model) or outer crank end seals (single or twin) is made by removing the air cleaner and holding your hand tightly over the carburetor mouth to determine if suction is less than normal. Of course, you won't know what normal is unless you go out now and test your engine while it's still healthy. The guy who blew the crankcase seal can start walking now, ditto for the ring casualty.

TIMING

It is extremely unlikely that spark or valve timing will slip suddenly; it's usually a gradual thing that will surface in the previously mentioned ignition points closure. So this is the last item on the trouble shooter's menu. Considering its remoteness and variables from brand to brand, we'll leave this one between you and your rider's handbook. Know where the timing marks are on your engine's flywheel or circuit breaker, and how to read them. Then should it happen, or should it

become suspect, a ballpark check can be made by laying the live plug on the cylinder head and seeing that its firing coordinates with the timing mark when the engine is slowly revolved by hand.

PARTING WORD

It should be obvious by now that trouble shooting is best done at home rather than at roadside. Then it becomes preventive maintenance, and that's the best kind. The mechanics of trouble shooting are relatively simple, a blend of horsepower and horse sense. And attitude and frame of mind have equal powers of persuasion at an engine revival. I've known some uncanny veteran shooters; to the man they exude a certain naive fascination and interest, as though each encounter were a brand new experience, an

exciting challenge. For they have learned that one never knows it all, and that the engine's cunning bag of tricks is bottomless. In so knowing, their mind never falls into the hard and fast rut that closes the door to the "impossible." They remain open to anything, constantly and rapidly exploring every avenue of *possibility* as they proceed along the more obvious and likely paths of *probability*. And they always have a long fuse, usually jovial and calm even under duress, having learned that panic leads only down the road to confusion and poor results, if not danger. It's a game with them, one that they relish, one that pays off not only in the reputation it earns but in pride and strength of knowing that they can handle it, no matter where or when. It's certainly a great feeling. 🜨

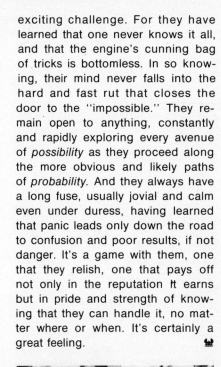

1. Find out where top dead center and firing marks are on your machine. They may be on flywheel or, as on this Benelli Four, behind breaker plate.

2. This ignition switch, behind headlight, broke twice, stopped engine. Now wire is reinforced with tapered tape wrapped a couple inches down.

3. Okie credit card, surgical rubber tube the length of handlebar, is always ready to transfer gas from one bike to another in the boonies.

4. Some Japanese bikes have vacuum-operated fuel valve pointed out here. If line cracks and leaks, vacuum drops and fuel flow stops. Switch to Prime position on the valve.

5. Drain float bowl for water and impurity detection and eyeball jets for clogged passage. Drop bowl and inspect float, and needle for shutoff.

6. With float bowl removed, fuel should stop when fuel valve is turned on and float raised fully. If not, jet's worn and carb will flood.

7. Sometimes fuel starvation is just due to float hanging up or needle sticking. Tapping against side of bowl usually frees needle or float.

8. Clogged idle jet needle causes erratic idle. Before removing and blowing into orifice, mark needle and count turns required for removal.

9. Before all else, check tank for fuel! Next, remove fuel inlet hose from carb and check selector valve for fuel flow. Valve could be faulty.

10. With thumb held tightly over spark plug hole, kick engine over; compression should blow thumb away.

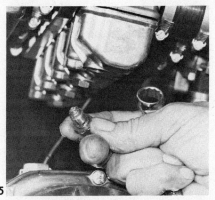

5

6

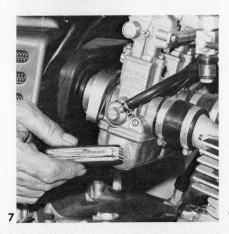

7

8

9

10

MAJOR ENGINE TUNING

Don't give up on that old bike—give it a new life
BY BILL OCHELTREE

Feelin' down in the dumps 'cause Old Faithful is letting you down lately? Maybe it would be nice to get a new bike, but the bread is a little short these days? How about the thing down the street? It's been in the guy's garage for two years and he only wants $250 for it. Looks alright but sounds like it's going to fall apart? Well take heart, things aren't as bad as they may seem. A trip around the world is no reason to go to the junk heap, it's only 25000 miles. Somebody else's miseries could be your pleasure. Here's the ticket: as long as it runs, has all the gears, and looks like everything is there, chances are that a major tune-up will make it just like new. Give it a try!

Major tune-up is type of work falling somewhere in the realm between minor tune-up and complete overhaul. This chapter will deal in more than just the engine, though. Actually, what is involved could be called a major "inspect/repair as necessary." That's old Air Force jargon more commonly referred to as IRAN. It means going over everything on the vehicle to see that it's in good working order. This is something that should be done about once a year whether or not you think it needs it; you'd be surprised at how many things wear or get out of adjustment, but that you're unaware of because they've happened gradually. Of course all these things have their limit, and when they finally do give out it seems that it's always at a bad time, and at the maximum distance from any help. The best way to be prepared for trouble is to go out of your way to avoid it, so instead of worrying about what might go wrong get busy and find out!

As we say throughout this book, you have to have the minimum equipment by way of tools and facilities for any job, and neatness and cleanliness are important too. The tools you'll need for a major tune-up aren't very elaborate and a lot of make-shift goodies can be put together from bits and pieces that have been laying around. A basic hand tool set is, of course, essential, along with a few feeler gages and some 'heavy' type automotive tune up gages (available at Western Auto or the like for a paltry sum). If the bike is caked with mud, grease or a few years of neglect, gunk it, de-grease it, steam it, wash it and perfume it: we won't touch it

1. About one evening a month is all the time needed to keep your bike in top condition. A clean, well-equipped shop is a definite asset.

2. Parts cleaning is an art that can be practiced with much make-shift equipment. Here is a gallon can with a side cut out. Be real careful with flammables! Don't use gasoline or other fuels, and NO SMOKING!

3. Special tools can be improvised in many ways. Often a standard tool can be modified to do the job. This wrench for a crank nut was milled from a large socket.

til it's clean! You're going to need a few road maps too, so hustle down to the dealer and get the service manual, owner's handbook, parts books, and any other publications that have plenty of pictures of the particular model you have. You can never have too much information. Now that everything's ready, let's go to work.

Most of the subjects covered in this chapter are treated in great detail in other chapters of this book. Also, there just isn't enough room here to tell you eveything about your bike so you'll have to do some digging in the service manual. What we'll do here is outline the things to be done and refer you to other chapters or your service manual, and we'll elaborate on some things that aren't covered elsewhere and show you some 'hot set-ups'.

A real thorough going-over of your bike can get pretty involved. Let's break it down to get a clear picture of what we're going to talk about. We'll break this up two ways: types of work to be done, and major components and systems of the bike itself. Let's break it down further so you can see the line of thought here:

TYPES OF WORK

a. Cleaning
b. Teardown/assembly
c. Inspection
d. Repair/replacement
e. Paint/finishing/lubrication
f. Adjustment/tightening/securing

MAJOR COMPONENTS & SYSTEMS

a. Engine/fuel/oil
b. Intake/exhaust
c. Drive train
d. Wheels/brakes
e. Suspension
f. Frame
g. Controls
h. Electrical/instruments

CLEANING

Cleaning methods and techniques are many and varied; each having its best application and some being very special. The alchemists of yore called water the "universal solvent" and that it is; it's a great cleansing agent and also a good corroder. Dont' get that wrong, a good bath is the best thing

you can do for a bike at regular intervals, provided the water is kept out of critical areas and the drying out process is hastened. A do-it-yourself car wash of the hand-held nozzle variety is the easiest way to clean your bike. The engine exterior and wheels are a snap and its about the only way to get into all those nooks and crannies in the frame and underneath. Be careful around the carburetor air intake, ignition parts, instruments, exhaust pipe, chain and brakes. Water in these areas can mean trouble. This is a good method for cleaning a caked-up chain but it must be run immediately to throw off the water and then well oiled. A brief ride to warm up the engine and dry out the brakes is recommended after any wash job. Don't confuse the car wash type gun with a commercial steam cleaner; the soap used in the steam cleaner will take the hide off an elephant, whereas car wash will only take off mud, oil and road film and leave the paint intact. If you don't have access to a car wash, the old bucket of suds and a large toilet bowl brush will have to do, followed by a rinse with a garden hose.

A really tough engine de-greasing job will require one of the water soluble degreasing solvents sold at most auto supply stores. These require extra care because they contain strong alkalis which convert greases into soaps that can be rinsed with water but which will eat away at just about anything including paint, aluminum and your body. Be real careful with these, follow the instructions on the can and rinse well with hot water.

A good all around solvent is a petroleum by-product called 'Stoddard Solvent.' This is similar to kerosene but does not leave an oily residue and is easily rinsed with water. The next best substitute for Stoddard solvent

MAJOR TUNING

is ordinary paint thinner, not turpentine or synthetic enamel thinner; they can really gum things up. *Warning: fuels such as gasoline, kerosene, naptha and benzene are very dangerous and should not be used.* The reason for this is that these have low flash points. The flash point of a flammable liquid is the temperature at which the quantity of the fumes given off by the liquid forms an explosive mixture with the surrounding air. For these fuel-type liquids the flash point is near ordinary room temperature and the least amount of spark or flame can set them off. For this reason use only high flash point solvents or thinners and then exercise caution. If you have a water heater or furnace in the garage, move out into the driveway to do any cleaning. Those fumes are heavier than air and can get pretty deep along the floor, and a pilot light is just the thing to raise the temperature enough to start a fire. Stoddard solvent is available at most gas stations under that name or as 'cleaning solvent.'

Pans and brushes for cleaning are available at most auto supply stores or as a make-shift, a large roasting pan or refrigerator pan will do. Always store cleaning solvents in closed metal containers for safety. Covered coffee cans are handy for storage and are convenient for small cleaning jobs.

One other handy cleaning agent that must be used very sparingly is lacquer thinner. This is best for preparing surfaces for the application of cements or 'stick-ons.' Apply only with a cloth and then wipe immediately with a clean, dry cloth. Be very careful on painted surfaces and plastics; try a test spot first.

TEARDOWN & ASSEMBLY

This is a subject that nobody gives much lip service to, but everybody has given some thought to at one time or another. Thoughts like "What did I do that for?" or "I guess I should have done that first before I tried to do this," or "I could have sworn that thing took five screws, where does this one go?". Moments like this are the result of just plain poor planning, and the frustrations and wasted time could easily be saved by giving a little forethought to the job. Things like special tools, work stands, bench & vise, something like an anvil to hammer on, cans, boxes and shelves to store loose parts and all of the things that go to make up the "compleat shop" are easy to come by if you just keep your eyes open. Getting the most done with the least amount of work is a matter of studying the job and staying awake while you're at it.

First of all don't skimp on the removal of things that get in the way. When diving into a big job on a motorcycle, the tank and seat should be the first things to come off. Be careful where you set the tank, if there are any exposed threads on the fuel line fitting, protect them from being dinged up. Things like carburetor, oil tank and battery should come off if they can possibly get in the way, and they should be protected from the entry of any dirt or foreign particles with suitable plugs, covers or tape. If you are going to do any electrical work, at least disconnect the battery, it could save the charge along with avoiding

1

2 ▶

burning up wiring. As you take apart complicated assemblies, store the parts in their own container to avoid mixing them with something totaly unrelated. This will greatly speed things when putting them back together. One last word on this subject: don't ignore the shop manual. If they have a recommended procedure for doing something, it's probably the best way.

INSPECTION

This is another field where staying awake, along with a lot of horse sense and some experience, will pay dividends in having to do the job only once. Careful examination of everything on the bike is sort of a detective game. Just the appearance of something can give you clues to impending trouble, or where some unseen trouble lurks. A lot can be told about a bike prior to taking anything apart. Oil leaks; loose, & sloppy or rough and jerky operation of controls; noisy gears, chains or bearings; these are sometimes thought of as normal for many motorcycles but they are only indications of careless assembly, or shoddy maintenance, or just plain old age. Things *are* supposed to work smooth, quiet and clean; don't believe any excuses to the contrary.

When tearing things down an eagle eye should be kept out for any evidence of wear or the presence of unwanted dirt or particles. Measurements of course should be made to determine whether or not some parts have gone beyond reasonable limits of wear. Here again the right tools make the job easier, but a lot can be done with the simplest of devices. In any case, the lack of something like a micrometer is no excuse for not somehow doing the job. Feeler gages are very inexpensive and can be used for many precision measuring jobs with a little ingenuity.

REPAIR/REPLACEMENT

Here is where sound judgement based on knowledge and experience comes into play in making decisions concerning the wisdom and economics of either making do with something of doubtful quality, applying practical techniques for the restoration of worn or damaged parts, or completely replacing it with a new one. We'll try to cover this in more detail when discussing the different types of bike parts and hardware, and when in doubt there's no substitute

1. The top plug on the front forks can be ground like this to clean up bad threads. It can still be used as a plug, too. Apply heavy grease when using it, to catch chips.

2. Touching-up worn and sand-blasted areas on the frame will prevent rusting and keep your bike looking 'sanitary.' Wash it first, and wipe it down with thinner before painting.

3. This is an age-old trick for keeping cables smooth as silk. Disconnect the lower end and put a can under it. A light engine oil will run through overnight.

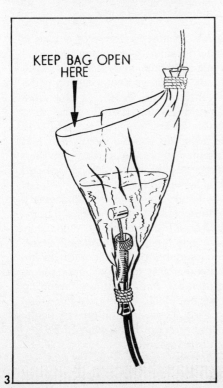

KEEP BAG OPEN HERE

3

for the experience of someone who's done the same thing before. Don't be afraid to ask and keep in mind that the cheap and easy way out now could cost you more later.

PAINT/FINISH/LUBE

Virtually all materials used in the manufacture of familiar things require a protective coating of some sort. Most people consider that these coatings are primarily for the purpose of enhancing the appearance of things, but in actuality, they are necessary for the preservation of the materials from the destructive effects of nature. There are a few exceptions to this in plastics and some aluminum alloys, but generally speaking 'what you see is *not* what you get.'' The paint, plating and brightwork on the bike make it look nice of course, and you probably want to keep it looking good, if not out of personal pride, certainly from the standpoint of resale value.

Don't consider finish from the standpoint of appearance only, the unseen areas are the ones that can cause trouble from the standpoint of safety and reliability. Climates with high humidity and rainfall can generate a lot of rust on unprotected steel, and salt air will raise havoc with aluminum and magnesium. Water will often easily find its way into closed areas and then become trapped and begin to perform its insidious habit of helping the air to eat away at everything it comes in contact with.

A good example of this is in the rear wheel swing arm pivot. If you ever have to replace the bushings in that area, you will probably find that a large drift pin and a very heavy hammer are required to remove the pivot bolt or shaft. The parts will seem to have been welded together with rust and the inside of the swing arm crossmember will look like the inside of an old water pipe. Aside from nickel plating the whole thing to prevent a repeat, a good scrubbing with a wire brush, a coat of zinc chromate or lead oxide primer and then assembling everything with a second coat of primer while it is still wet, is the best way to slow down the rusting process. A hole drilled in the bottom of the crossmember will admit water when the bike is running through deep stuff but it will also provide a drain for all the water that might get in there from any point.

Nuts and bolts are also a good ex-

ample for the requirements for a protective finish if you have ever had to remove an old rusty, unplated one. The cadmium and zinc plating used on modern fastenings has cut into the sales of penetrating oils and if you don't want to do the "soak and wait" routine, then make sure to replace those that are on the verge of rigor-mortis.

Parts that slide or turn within each other won't hold a finish very long so the next best thing to preserve them and to make their operation a little smoother is lubrication of some sort. It's amazing what a little bit of oil or grease can do to something that seems to be on the verge of seizure. Every moving part on the bike requires lubrication of some sort and even the latest trick Nylon and Teflon bushings can go to pot pretty quick in the presence of dirt and grit.

Here's a brief list of the minimum supplies you should have on hand to accomplish basic touch-up and lube:

—Primer: A small spray can of zinc chromate or lead primer. "Rustoleum" makes a good variety of these.

—Touch-up paint. Black lacquer in

ENGINE TOP-END CHECK LIST

HEAD

De-carbonize
Check for warp, look for gasket leaks
Check valve guides and springs
Lap valves

VALVE TRAIN

Check cam lobes and lifters for scoring, galling
Check push rods for straightness, ends for wear
Check rocker arms & shafts for wear, lubrication

CYLINDER

Top ridge
Taper
Scoring
Base leaks
Two-stroke port clean up

PISTON

De-carbonize
Ring grooves
Sand scuff marks
Measure skirt wear
Ring end gap
Wrist pin fit

ROD

Pin fit/bushing
Crank side clearance
Big end up-down play

MAJOR TUNING

a spray can is ideal for keeping the frame looking new. If yours is another color a close match can usually be found.

—Chain oil: The foam spray motorcycle chain lubes are good for all around use, and in a lot of water the industrial chain and cable oil that looks like asphalt is a mess to put on, but it won't wash off!

—Grease: No shop should be without a can of sticky old grease to hold things in place and maybe even be used on something like a bearing once in a while. The best general-use type for these purposes is a marine or boat trailer wheel bearing grease.

—Oil: Don't forget the trusty oil can. Drippings from motor oil cans are an endless free source to keep an inexpensive squirt can full.

—Special lubricants: Small amounts of these will last a lifetime and are indispensible for certain jobs. Molybdenum disulfide is superior to graphite for a dry lube and is available in powder form or as a paint-on. A high-temp grease such as 'Lubriplate' is a must. A lightweight penetrating/lubricating oil such as 3-IN-1 or WD-40 comes in real handy for those real sticky ones.

ADJUSTMENT/TIGHTENING/SECURING

These are either the most ignored, neglected or forgotten things that contribute the greatest amount of anxiety to the average motorcyclist. Just about everything in any sort of mechanical assemblage requires some periodic attention to its condition and appropriate action to either restore or maintain it in its proper state. When ignored, neglected or forgotten the gremlins arise to bring about faulty operation, no operation at all, or possibly failure or complete loss of the parts involved.

Adjustment is involved in many functions of the motorcycle. Here is a handy check list of adjustments that should be made periodically. Your owner's manual specifies different periods for most of these and may not mention some of them, but in any case the heading implies that about once a month you should at least consider the list and make appropriate adjustments according to your own personal needs and experience.

30-DAY CHECK LIST

Points
Timing
Valves
Carburetor—air, idle, float, needle, synchronization
Oil injector/pump
Cam chain
Primary chain
Clutch
Rear chain
Front brake cable
Clutch cable
Throttle cable
Choke cable
Compression release cable
Gear shift
Rear brake pedal
Rear brake rod/cable
Stop light switch
Brake actuating arms
Steering head bearings
Headlight aim
    Other points, not strictly adjustments, demanding equal attention:
Tire pressure
Air cleaner
Exhaust mufflers
Battery water
Oil—engine, gear box, primary

The subject of tightening applies to every nut, bolt, screw and threaded device or fastener on a motorcycle. Anything that you can put a wrench or screwdriver on should be checked at least twice a year. The vibration that

1. The ignition system is the heart of the engine and should be kept in sharp tune. An occasional drop of oil on the wick will slow down wear. Too much will foul the contacts.

2. Carburetor adjustments on the big multi's can get pretty involved, but the effort can be worth it for super-smooth operation. See 'Minor Engine Tuning' for a way around this set-up.

3. A neglected centrifugal advance mechanism has caused many puzzling tuning hang-ups. See that yours is working free and give it a little 'Lubriplate' to keep it that way.

exists in the operation of a bike is much greater than normally found in most vehicles, and this can cause many problems that only constant attention can avoid. A new bike should be completely gone over within its first week of use, and then followed up about a month later with another tightening, and then another a month after that! Anything loose on that last exercise must be considered for either safetying or replacement with something that will hold. Important points to take note of immediately are: axle nuts, swing arm bolt, steering head, handle bars, control levers, engine mount, foot pegs, drain plugs, and most important and needing continuous monitoring are the wheel spokes. These are the primary safety items and worthy of more than just a casual glance.

Tightening brings up the question of: how tight? Our chapter titled

securing device for nuts and bolts and is found in nearly all installations. When the lockwasher doesn't do the job then more drastic steps must be taken in the form of locking tabs, self locking nuts, cotter pins, bonding resins such as Loctite, external seals like 3M 8001 Weatherstrip Cement, or safety wire. We'll note the application of these various methods as we get into the details of the bike.

justing screws and pull off the air cleaner, but nobody likes to dig into the innards of the carburetor for fear of losing some of the parts. Ridiculous! You may have been snowed at some time by the fearsome looking guts of a four-barrel Rochester but a motorcycle carburetor is about as complicated as changing the overhead lights in the bathroom so get with it.

The first thing to look for is dirt. Pull the float bowl off the carburetor and the sediment bowl off the tank and be careful to not spill anything; you're looking for clues. Pour the contents into a light colored, shallow container and keep an eye out for blobs of water and rust scale. Water may be the result of a careless wash job or a night in the rain, but it may also be in the gas you've been buying, so check into the tank to see if there's any accumulation. Rust scale or other solid particles can give all sorts of intermittent running problems so anything more than a couple of specks would indicate that the entire fuel system needs cleaning.

Carefully drain the tank into a proper gas can and then remove it from the bike. Pull all plugs, petcocks and caps and turn a high pressure stream of water into the tank and try to dislodge as much loose matter as possible. Drain and shake the water out and if compressed air is available this will help to dry it out. A rinse with alcohol will also soak up moisture, and the best thing is a day in the sun to thoroughly dehydrate it. If you want to use the gas that was drained from the tank, strain it through a chamois when pouring it back.

A good cleaning of the fuel supply system may cure a lot of problems, and a great accumulation in the tank and lines will also mean something is probably making a home in the carburetor itself. A carburetor rebuild isn't very difficult if you follow the instructions and keep things clean and orderly. Be sure to check the jet, slide and needle sizes against the service manual specs if someone has had the bike before you. Some guys seem to have a talent for tuning things into a complete botch by changing jets and adjustments without really knowing what they are doing. Don't forget the float setting when re-assembling the carb. It's easy to forget but can make a big difference.

Of course you have set up the ignition system to perfection, but have you checked out these items? If the

ENGINE/FUEL/OIL

Now that we've covered all the preliminaries, let's get down to the nitty-gritty of the bike itself. The biggest single thing and the source of most problems is the engine. In doing a tune-up as such, the only things to be covered here are those which can be done without removing the engine from the frame. Check into the appropriate chapters on engine rebuilding, carburetion and tune-up for the details of the things that we'll point you to.

Let's assume that you have an engine that's running but doesn't seem to perform like it should. A minor tune-up is what you should have done first to make sure that all the usual fine points had been covered. If the engine is still misbehaving, then you will have to look further. The two most likely places to find trouble are the ignition and fuel systems.

Everybody likes to diddle the ad-

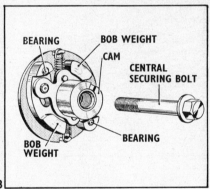

"Specs and Formulas" has a listing of recommended torque values for various structural-grade bolts. The grading symbols are not always on the bolts so the values given must be considered only as a guide, and the manufacturer's recommendations for special fastenings, especially in the engine and gearbox, should be closely followed. Impact and torque wrenches are valuable items for obtaining proper tightness, so have a look at the chapter on tools; it will give you a good idea of what is needed. When it comes to small bolts and screws the only torque measuring device available is your wrist, so be very careful if you don't want to suffer skinned knuckles and exasperation.

Securing and safetying methods vary depending on the type of fastener, its application and the degree of safety required. The lowly lockwasher is the most common form of

MAJOR TUNING

ignition has an automatic advance, the point cam should be able to rotate freely on the shaft within its limits and the springs should return it solidly to the retard position. A little high temperature grease like 'Lubriplate' is just the ticket here. If you're using flywheel marks to set the timing but something tells you it's not quite right, better check it against the piston position with a dial indicator. Sometimes those marks can be off enough to really louse things up. If the bike starts and runs alright when cold but then gives up and quits after it's warmed up only to be alright again after cooling down, you may have a bad ignition coil. Get it tested or borrow another one and try it. Badly burned points are a symptom of a bum condenser, but sometimes the points themselves can be defective. If no immediate improvement is seen after dressing the points with a tungsten file then chances are that's where the trouble lies.

Let's back up now to the basics of the minor tune-up. A compression check should be the first order of business and if you have obtained low readings (100 to 125 psi is borderline depending on compression ratio; anything below 75 psi is zilch) it will take more than a clean carburetor and hot ignition to make that engine put out. Rings and valves are the things that hold the air in, so if it's not pumpin', you'll have to start humpin' on a top end job. With a two-stroke you've got it made. Just pull the barrel and give it a bore and/or ring job. The chapter on two-stroke engine rebuilding will show you how to check the piston and cylinder bore with feeler gages and clean up the piston just like new. With a four-stroke the valves may have to be re-seated by lapping them in, just as you would after a re-grind. If an engine is in a condition where cylinder boring and valve grinding or replacement are required, then consideration should be given to a complete rebuild, which will put you beyond the realm of major tune-up.

Whether or not an engine needs a complete rebuild depends on its age, mileage, type of service and care. If you know the engine or its previous owner, you can probably make pretty good judgement as to its condition. If you aren't familiar with the engine history, you'll have to do some detective work once you've pulled the top end off. Even if you know the bottom

end is OK it wouldn't hurt to spend a little time to make sure. We've included a check list of things to do or look for when doing a top end job.

ENGINE OILING

The engine lubrication system is probably the most taken for granted yet vital part of the bike. Without oil the engine not only doesn't run very well, but it can cost some big bucks to fix the damage incurred. Changing the oil just isn't enough if you use the bike anywhere outside of a dust and moisture free environment. That eliminates just about everywhere and the amount of crud that builds up in the oil system is just a matter of time depending on how much off-road riding you do. Two stroke lubrication is a fairly straightforward way of doing things; the oil is burned almost immediately after it is used. The only hooker here is that nothing can be taken for granted. YOU better remember to put oil in the gas on your

primitive pre-mix scooter and keep the tank full on the 'mix-it-as-you-ride' model or you'll be in the same fix as the guy with a broken oil line on his Triumph.

The two-stroke oil injection systems are simple enough to check out, and most owner's manuals have instructions for checkout and adjustment. Passage of the oil through the system is strictly a one-way affair, so there shouldn't be any dirt accumulation if you have been somewhat careful when filling the tank. Just the same, it wouldn't hurt to take it off now and then and wash it out with solvent. Although pressures in the system are low enough to preclude leaky fittings, the hoses can deteriorate with age, so make sure they are in good shape. Four-stroke engine oil systems are the ones that are taken for granted as long as there is a reading on the dip stick. This is alright for a while but the nature of the system is such that metal chips, dirt and sludge are recir-

1

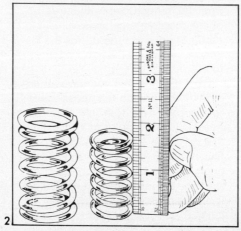

2

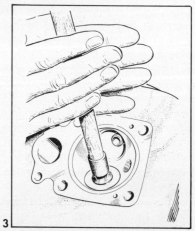

3

culated through the system and eventually find places to accumulate and block the intended flow path for the oil.

Four-stroke oil systems fall into two general categories: wet-sump and dry-sump. Wet sump systems are found on all but the rarest of automobile engines. The oil is carried in a large reservoir at the bottom of the crankcase where it can provide a continuous bath of cooling and lubrication in addition to the pressure feed directed at crank and cam bearings and up to the valve rocker shaft. Most motorcycles use the wet-sump system with the notable drawback of combing engine lubrication with gear box and clutch. The main disadvantage of this is that metallic particle accumulation takes place at a greater rate than separate engine lubrication and the manufacturer's recommendations for oil change interval should be closely adhered to if reasonable engine life is to be expected.

1. A degree wheel is a must for checking timing marks or valve timing. Make sure it's firmly tied to the crank, and a pointer can be easily improvised.

2. Check valve spring lengths against factory specs or compare them with new ones when doing a top overhaul. Weak springs will cause poor sealing and allow valve 'float' at high speed.

3. Re-seating the valves will assure a perfect seal for maximum combustion efficiency. Lapping compound and suction cup tool are available at auto parts stores.

4. Clean up the head and lightly polish it with emery paper. Smooth off sharp edges of plug threads to prevent pre-ignition-causing 'hot spots.'

In addition to regular oil changes, the things to be watched with these systems are the screens, filters and traps that are built in to intentionally trap unwanted bits and pieces. These should be cleaned out at the first couple of oil changes on a new engine or fresh rebuild and about every third oil change thereafter. Some engines (just about all Hondas) have a centrifugal filter which spins the oil as it passes through and forces heavy particles to its outer periphery where they pack in and stay until cleaned out. This should be cleaned out annually and instructions can be found in the shop manual. Some of the new models come equipped with automotive-type paper filters which should be replaced at the recommended interval. The shop manual will usually give instructions for checking oil pump operation and this should also be done at your annual check-up session.

Dry-sump systems are patterned after the aircraft philosophy of keeping the crankcase as small and light as possible and then finding a convenient place to stow the oil in a light-weight tank. This is a universal practice on all British bikes and is the exception to Honda's wet-sump policy in their 750-Four. In these set-ups, the clutch and gearbox have their own oil supplies so that eliminates one source of contamination. A necessary requirement for the dry-sump system is a dual pump lash-up. Half of the pump supplies high pressure oil for bearing and valve lubrication and the other half scavenges the expended oil from the crankcase and returns it to the oil tank. The oil tank is generally a

two to three quart container located under the seat area, and the latest wrinkle from England is to incorporate the oil reservoir as an integral part of the frame structure as in the latest series of BSA and Triumph bikes. The separate tank and pump arrangement require suitable connecting plumbing and check valves to prevent the oil from seeping into the crankcase when the engine is idle. This complicates the system and brings on another source of contamination. As long as the engine is operated to maintain uniform temperatures (long trips or warm climate) the oil stands a pretty good chance of doing its job for a reasonable length of time. The external oil system has pretty good cooling capacity and short trips in a cool climate make for pretty high moisture accumulation and a consequent formation of sludge in the tank and lines. You may think you're running your engine in the best of conditions but unless that oil gets heated up enough to dry out, you're no better off than a desert racer.

Whether it's a wet or dry sump engine, taken for granted it shouldn't be, wet sump systems should be flushed regularly, depending on conditions, with a 50-50 mixture of light oil and cleaning solvent. There are usually screens installed in the tank and scavenging pick-up and the cleaning schedule described above for wet-sumpers should be adhered to. The external feed and return lines should also be checked regularly for fitting security and flex hose condition. If your engine has been running strong and has good compression, but suddenly there is a rash of oil consumption accompanied by a smoky exhaust and wet breather spray, you're 'wet-sumping.' If this happens only when you first start the engine and then clears up, it's probably the return line check valve letting oil drain from the tank to the crankcase overnight. If wet-sumping conditions persist while the engine is running, you've got a bum scavenger pump. The shop manuals describe all the necessary maintenance and test procedures for the dry sumpers, so take heed and they won't give you any unwanted surprises.

INTAKE & EXHAUST SYSTEMS

Here are two more items that can bring no end of grief to the unwary. The symptoms of a sick intake or exhaust are similar to the symptoms of

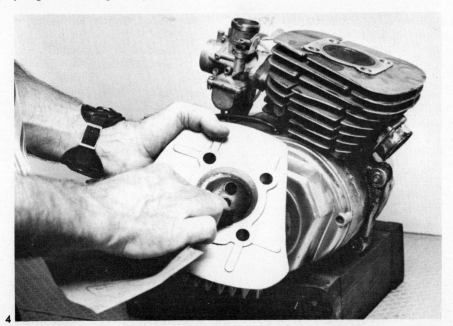

MAJOR TUNING

other illnesses, and after all kinds of tuning and troubleshooting you can be tearing your hair out 'til some wise guy comes along and tells you it's a plugged air cleaner or exhaust. As in everything else, care and maintenance are the only things that will prevent trouble in this area so don't overlook them.

Air filter cleaning or replacement requirements vary widely with the type of filter and operating conditions. Paper filters are the type that general purpose and touring bikes are most often equipped with. These are actually the finest grade of filter and will provide a very long service life under normal road conditions. Being capable of stopping very fine particles makes these filters subject to very rapid clogging under extreme dust conditions and will require frequent replacement. The blotter-type nature of the paper used in these filters also makes them vulnerable to moisture of any type.

The basic symptom of a plugged air cleaner is the inability of the engine to operate at full throttle; it's as though the choke were partially closed and when the throttle is opened to match the choke opening, no more air can flow but the fuel will continue, making for an extremely rich mixture. A paper filter will show this phenomenon immediately after having run through water deep enough to wet it or after being inadvertently hit with the hose during a washing. About all that can be done under these circumstances is to nurse it along at part throttle until the filter dries out. After about a hundred miles in extreme dust conditions, a paper filter will begin to behave like it is wet. The symptoms come on gradually at first and as the surface becomes completely caked the engine will barely run at all.

Paper filters may be re-conditioned by gently rapping them to dislodge heavy surface dust and carefully blowing from the inside with compressed air. Don't use a real strong blast of air or you'll tear the paper, and never use compressed air on a wet paper filter, it'll blast it to shreds. Reconditioning of this sort may be done several times before the surface of the paper becomes so impregnated with fine particles that it loads up after a very short time. Another application of the dry paper filter that has proved to be very unsatisfactory is on pis-

ton-ported two-stroke engines where the filter is in close proximity to the mouth of the carburetor. In this case the spit-back spray from the carburetor leaves an oily wetness on the inside of the filter which will bring about complete saturation in a fairly short time and render the filter completely useless.

This brings us to the wet-type foam or felt filtering element. These are not only ideal for piston-port two-strokes but find wide use in all types of off-road and competition bikes because they will last much longer in heavy dust conditions and may be washed and re-used indefinitely. Rather than rely on 'screening' action to keep out particles as the dry-type filter does, the wet filter performs an 'entrapping and retaining' action to hold the fine particles. The porous foam filters are of the 'depth loading' type wherein the particles actually penetrate the foam to a depth of around .10 to .20 inch. As the inner compartments become filled with dust particles the entrapment proceeds outward to the surface until the filter begins acting as a 'face loading' type. Contrary to some belief, the foam filters do not require cleaning after every ride, but are capable of operating at full capacity for several hundred miles. As long as the filter element has a damp appearance on the surface it is

1. A simple piece of string can do much to prevent problems. You can always be sure parts will go back in the way they came out if you use string on them instead of your finger.

2. When checking piston wear, measure the skirt diameter in several locations. Vernier calipers like this cost about $25 and are about the best investment you can make.

3. When checking the cylinder, measure both top and bottom to determine taper. A heavy ridge at the top will also indicate the need for a re-bore.

operating as a depth loader. When large, dry powder areas begin to show, then the filter is going into the face loading phase of operation and will require servicing within a short period.

The wet felt filter is a compromise between the face loading dry type and the depth loading wet type. It will operate for a short time as a depth loader but because of the finer texture of the fabric it will become a face loader much sooner. Its greatest advantage over the other types is that it is virtually unaffected by water. The dry paper filters are badly affected by water and the foam types will show some affect for a short time if drenched, but the felt type are the best compromise under combined conditions of both dust and water.

The proof of the operation of any

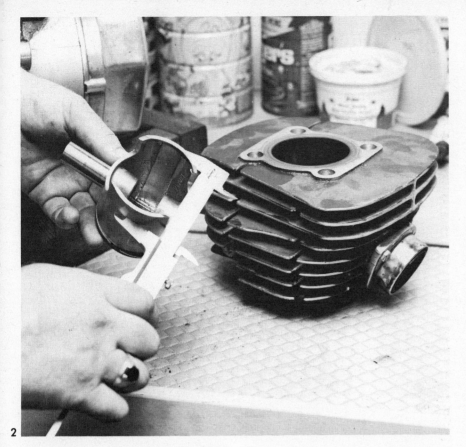

2

3

filter is what it looks like on the inside after a long period of use. When doing a major or minor tune-up or during routine maintenance on a strictly dirt bike, the filter should be carefully removed so as not to disturb the evidence, and examined on its inside surface and at the points where it makes contact with its housing. The inner surface of the filter element should look like the outside of a brand new element no matter what conditions it has been run in. Areas of dark brown blotches are evidence of where water has hit the filter and been drawn through. If the entire inside looks like this, you need better shielding around the filter. The surfaces where the filter contacts the housing may show a little dust around the outer edges, but the inner side should be clean with no evidence of dust having gone

through. A look at the inside of the filter housing and down into the intake pipe should reveal no dust whatsoever. Shine a flashlight in there and look for leakage at any hose joints also.

Cleaning of the wet-type filters is accomplished by thoroughly rinsing in cleaning solvent, drying by shaking or blowing the felt type and squeezing the foam type and then oiling with the heaviest engine oil available. Squirt the oil on the felt filters and dip or squirt the foam ones and squeeze the excess. When possible allow the elements to stand overnight in a pan to let excess oil drain, otherwise immediate use may result in a smokey exhaust and possible plug fouling, almost like wet or plugged filter operation. The reason for using heavy oil is merely to prevent 'migration' of the oil to the housing and on to the garage floor; light oil will help trap dust as well as heavy but in warm weather or over a long period of time will drain off and lose some effecttiveness. When re-installing the filter element in its housing, a coating of thick grease at the contact points will help to insure a good seal and prevent any leakage around the edges.

The exhaust system on a bike is something that will go a long time before it will show any signs of trouble. Actually on an engine that is kept

up to its peak operating level at all times the exhaust system should last forever. The main constituents of the exhaust gas are carbon dioxide and water. The carbon dioxide is harmless (not so for carbon monoxide) but in long exhaust systems that don't get a chance to thoroughly warm-up, the water vapors will condense and bring about rusting from the inside. This is what happens to Grandma's car that hardly gets used but needs a new muffler every year but doesn't happen to Uncle Joe and he puts on 50000 miles a year. This is one problem that seldom occurs on a motorcycle. The exhaust system is short enough that even a short trip will allow enough time to heat all the plumbing and keep it dried out.

The major problem encountered on bike exhausts is the accumulation of oil on the two-strokes or on a heavy oil burning four-stroke. The multicylinder two strokes with large mufflers for small cylinders are the ones most likely to cause trouble. The temperature required to burn off oil is much higher than that required to boil off water and the small cylinders of the multis just don't put out enough heat to raise the temperature of those big shiny mufflers. Consequently, over some period of time the baffles in the mufflers will become caked with a hard coating of carbon and tar and the holes will begin to close up. The symptom here is a generally ratty running engine and a very smoky exhaust. About once a year is a good time to dismantle the mufflers and give them a good cleaning or even replace the baffles with new ones. About the only way to clean two stroke mufflers that look like they have been paved with asphalt on the inside, is to burn the stuff off with an acetyline torch and then scrub them with a wire brush.

The causes for a badly 'coked-up' exhaust lie in the type of oil used, the fuel-to-oil ratio and the type of riding. Read Pepe Estrada's chapter on 'Lubrication: 2 Stroke & 4 Stroke' to get some idea of what to expect from various types of oils and make sure your injector pump and control are set properly to achieve the right mixture. Your service manual will tell you how to do this. As far as the type of riding you do, long, high speed touring will result in less oil deposits than just cruising around town. If your pipes seem to plug up more than necessary even with everything in good tune, try enlarging the holes in

MAJOR TUNING

the baffles by drilling them out about 1/32″ larger. Don't go too big or you'll be ticket-bait for excess noise; it's amazing how a little bit bigger baffle hole will go a long time without clogging and won't increase noise or alter engine operation. Don't overlook the exhaust ports and the first few inches of pipe on both two and four-strokes. These can become caked with residue while the rest of the system is fairly clean and the reduction in size can rob you of quite a bit of power. Make sure the valve is closed or the piston is over the port while cleaning; that stuff won't do any good in the cylinder.

Leaks in an exhaust system can cause erratic running, backfiring and possible overheating in any engine, so be on the lookout for oil or soot at the ports and pipe joints. When installing the exhaust pipe, put a new gasket at the port joint and re-tighten all the joints after running for a short while. Make sure all the mounting points are in good condition and securly fastened, otherwise you may be buying a new cylinder if the exhaust port won't take the weight of the whole pipe. Some exhaust ports are notorious for having pipe connections that won't stay tight under any conditions so keep an eye out for yours and safety wire them if necessary.

DRIVE TRAIN

The drive train consists of the primary chain or gears from the engine to the clutch, the clutch itself, the gearbox and the final drive chain, or shaft, as the case may be. The chapters on 'Clutches and gearboxes' and 'Chains' will be a good guide for repair and maintenance of these vital components so we'll go through just a brief refresher here to hit some of the high points. Although motorcycle gearboxes are of the constant mesh type, they are not true 'synchromesh' and therefore they generate a lot more metal particles to grind away the gear teeth and bearings than do automotive gear boxes. For this reason gearbox oil should be changed about once a year on bikes used exclusively for touring, twice a year for city bikes, four times a year if you're a clutchless shifter or off-roader and about once a month for bikes used in track racing of any form. These are minimum suggested frequencies and if your owner's manual recommends changes more often or you feel a little

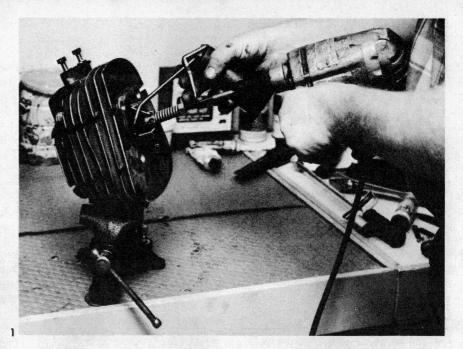

uneasy about it, do it! Oil is cheap.

Separate primary chain cases should have their oil changed about as often as the gearbox and special attention should be given to the drippings for any evidence of broken chain rollers. The primary drive cover should be removed about once a year anyway to check the condition of the clutch and chains should be checked for wear at the same time. Some people advise against it but when it comes to automatic transmission fluid (ATF), consider that it does a pretty good job with clutches and gears that carry a helluva lot more power at higher temperatures than in a bike. One thing for sure, you'll never have a sticky clutch with it.

Once you've ridden a bike for some time it's very easy to get used to all its little idiosyncracies, but if you really want to see a difference in the way a gearbox can shift then dig into the service manual and find out exactly how to adjust the shift mechanism and clutch, and guaranteed, you'll have a slicker shifter than a brand new one. Be careful in adjusting the clutch to be sure there is some clearance between the clutch operating mechanism and the push rods. A tight adjustment will ensure disengagement but a continuous side load on the clutch could bring about overheating of the thrust and mainshaft bearings and that could lead to a blown gearbox.

The final drive chain and sprockets are sometimes a very neglected item and there's really no excuse for it. A lot of street riders don't like to oil the chain because it throws the oil on the

wheel, fender and up their back. Well if that's your problem, Bunky, you don't know how to oil a chain! A dry chain may be clean but it can sure cost you in sprockets, chain and maybe a busted engine. The foaming spray can chain oils are easy to apply and you won't get too much on if you go around just twice, once on the edges of the links on each side. Leave the bike up on the center stand and spin the wheel by hand and give the oil a chance to work in. Then wipe off any excess from the outside with a rag and you shouldn't have any problems. The rear chain should be oiled at least once a week and daily in wet weather; it should never be allowed to run dry or get rusty. The chapter on chains will give you more on adjustment and checking for wear.

WHEELS & BRAKES

Again, it can't be stressed too heavily: keep your spokes tight! Not too tight, and don't make like tuning a harp! The nipples should all be tightened to about the same torque; it was never intended that the spokes

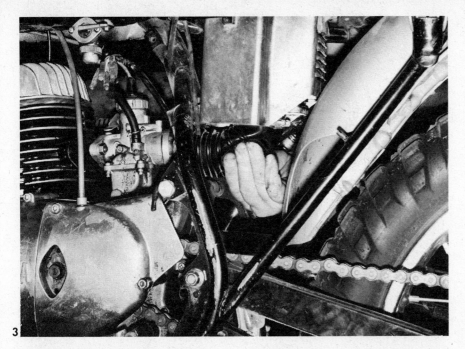

1. With no more than a couple of thousandths wear, new rings will seat right in to a well-honed barrel. Move the hone back and forth to get a coarse criss-cross pattern.

2. A filter should be like new on the inside no matter how bad the outside looks. Heavy grease around the edges will help prevent any sealing leaks.

3. Soft rubber air cleaner hoses should be checked for firmness. Continuous soaking in fuel tends to weaken them allowing collapsing under heavy load.

all strike the same note. The chapter on suspension gives you some tips on how to check for loose wheel bearings and this is fine for an occasional safety check, but at least once a year, and oftener if you're a mud rider, the wheel hubs should be checked to see that there is plenty of grease for the bearings and that the seals are keeping dirt and water out. Actually if this isn't the case you will have found out about it when you do the shake test on the bearings. If you have chronic troubles with bearing wear due to dirt and water the bearings can be replaced with industrial types that have an integral seal built in between the races and come all ready greased, permanently.

Brakes are of course subject to wear just as in any other vehicle so they will need some periodic attention. Most European bikes have riveted brake linings and just about when the adjustment in the cable or rod runs out, the linings are down to the rivet heads. It shouldn't have to be said, but don't try to run the brake lining beyond the rivets, it will only chew up the drums and they are almost impossible to turn out and very expensive to replace. Brake linings are not difficult to replace as can be seen in the illustrations and the cost of the parts is nominal. Complete replacement shoes are also available if you're not inclined to riveting. The Japanese bikes are all equipped with bonded linings but they really don't have any longer useful life than the riveted type. . . . the big advantage is that there are no rivets to ruin the drums. Don't be tempted to get the full wear out of the lining by relocating the brake lever on the cam splines; as the brakes wear further the cam has to rotate further and may have a tendency to get high centered between the shoes and lock up or be slow to release. This can be a very dangerous situation, and the low price for replacement shoes doesn't warrant the risk.

Brake adjustment is a matter of personal preference. Some like 'em tight and some like 'em loose. If you're one of the latter type, don't fall into the trap of letting them get too loose and then running out of full braking power in a tight situation. The hydraulic brakes found on the super bikes are a real boon to the biggies and the disc types are the simplest to maintain. It's hard to generalize about disc brakes because it seems they all have different arrangements of caliper mounting. Adjusting and servicing are covered in the owner's and service manuals. Don't let the friction pads wear too far as the disc rotors are as expensive to replace as hubs.

When reassembling the brakes don't forget to apply a small amount of 'Lubri-plate' to the cam and shoe pivots and to the ends of the shoe return springs, to keep them from rusting. Badly rusted springs should be replaced without question; if one lets go it's a locked-up brake for sure. An occasional drop of oil on the cam shaft between the lever and backing plate will find its way in to keep the brakes working smoothly.

SUSPENSION

The chapter in this book on suspension is very complete in both theory and practice on the care and feeding of shocks and springs. All you have to remember is to keep your eyes open for tell-tale clues on the condition of the parts. Fork seals aren't really leaking until the oil reaches the axle on a day's ride. A little oil around the scraper lip is really nothing to be concerned about. It helps to keep the fork tubes from rusting. An important thing is to keep the oil in the forks clean. Generally, hydraulic forks are pretty well sealed and dirt being sucked in with air is not the problem. Depending on the design of the fork, wear takes place due to the sliding action and the forks become filled with metallic particles that can accelerate the wear at a greater rate. What you're going to have to do is use your own judgment as to the rate of wear by changing the fork oil often when you first get a bike and seeing how long it takes to get the oil filthy.

Dirt is a problem where the seals are concerned. Off road bikes are the most vulnerable but street bikes aren't immune to the grit that gets on the fork legs and then works its way into the seals. For this reason the scrapers that keep the dirt pushed back from the seals should be kept in good condition and if the bike is equipped with accordion boots they must be in top shape also.

The rear shocks are usually so well sealed that leakage is rarely a problem. The thing to watch out for with these is the rubber bushings in the eyes at each end of the unit. The springs at both front and rear may be subject to losing some of their 'sap' so checking their length against new ones isn't a bad idea either. Most important is the security of all the mechanical and attaching parts in the suspension system. The steering head bearings, rear swing arm bushings, front fork yoke clamping bolts

MAJOR TUNING

and the rear shock bolts should all be checked for condition and tightness at not too infrequent intervals.

FRAME

That maze of tubes, gussets and brackets called the frame or chassis is the thing that holds it all together but is seldom given much attention because it is thought of as not doing anything. Just because you don't see any moving parts on the frame doesn't mean that it isn't flexing its muscles. Everything in the frame structure is subject to bending and vibration as long as the engine is running or the bike is moving. Most of the time the deflections in the frame elements are very small such that they return to their normal state without apparent effect, but these deflections are of a continually repeated nature and the effects of fatigue will show themselves given sufficient time. The time it takes for this to happen will vary depending on the type of riding you do; the faster or rougher, the sooner things will happen. This is where the good thorough wash job and a long sit-down and look-see can pay off in stopping the damage before it goes too far.

The most critical points to look for frame damage are where the steering head is met by the main tubes, the engine mounting plates or brackets, the rear swing arm pivot mounts and gussets, and the junction of the top rear section with the forward section. Pull the tank, seat and side covers and squat down with a flashlight in hand and start gazing into those dark corners and recesses. It's really amazing what all those bits and pieces do; try to visualise what is happening as you bounce along and you'll get some idea of the punishment that things are taking. Look for cracks in areas right next to the welds; this is where the metal is most affected by the heat of the welding process and the stresses are greatest where loads are transmitted from one part to another.

The main frame isn't the only thing that gets a lot of gaff. The battery box, gas tank mounts, muffler brackets, air cleaner supports, oil tank hangers and every piece that holds another in place suffers the torment of engine vibration and may give up at any time causing further damage. There have been cases where things like the ignition coil or the horn bracket on some bikes crack off in just a few miles of

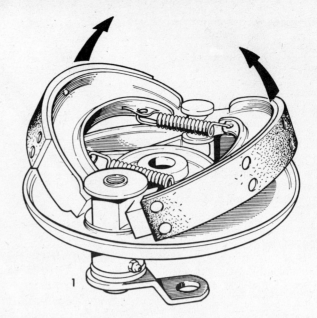

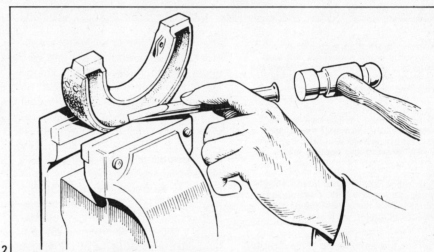

high speed running at a constant speed. A good general rule to help speed the process of looking is that anywhere two parts are held together by welding, nuts and bolts, or any other means is where failure can occur.

Another important thing to look for that will eliminate a lot of rattles and noises are worn rubber bushings and grommets that are used in the mounting of many parts to protect them from vibration damage. Such attachments usually have a shoulder bolt or bushing to prevent over tightening of the cushion. Don't ever attempt to override these devices or overtighten unbushed cushions, and if any of them begin to crumble with age or wear, replace them with new ones. They are very inexpensive and if you don't think they do any good, try going without, you can shatter a gas tank, license plate or whatever in no time at all. See the chapter on 'Chassis' in this book to get a rundown of the various types and what they do.

CONTROLS

Ever give a quick pull on the clutch or twist the throttle and have nothing happen? Broken cables are something that should never happen to someone who spends a lot of time preparing for a big outing on the bike and expects to get his money's worth. Broken cables seem to be chronic with some people and others seem never to have the problem. Although they seem to be something that should naturally suffer a lot of wear because of the way they are made, cables will last indefinitely if properly installed and cared for. Cable routing is an art that has been mastered by very few, even the factories do a poor job in many cases and the cable replacement market prospers from it. You don't have to be a part of it though, just make sure those cables are running the easiest way. The ends of the cable are where they seem to break most often and that is because they are routed such that there is a strain on the cable as it approaches its anchor point.

As long as the cable makes a straight run from its end point so that the inner wire is not rubbing on the edge of the outer sheath or any of the hardware outside, it will not wear out. Cables are also limited in the tightness of bending they can stand so, the bigger the bend radius, the longer it will last and the easier it will operate. This is the test of a properly installed cable: under full load there should be no appreciable drag or binding because of the cable. Dirt and lubrication are other factors in cable operation that should be considered. Off-road bikes suffer the most from

1. Tugging at the brake shoe springs really isn't necessary. Shoes may be removed very easily on most bikes as shown here. Clean thoroughly and lube before re-installing.

2. Rivetted brake linings are easy to replace with the proper tools. A sharp cold chisel and punches of various sizes are a good tool investment that will find wide use.

3. When rivetting on new linings, start in the middle and work toward the ends. This minimizes creep and hole mis-alignment. Brass rivets come with lining and are easy to drive.

4. Tachometer and speedometer cables should be cleaned and lubed annually. A light coat of high-temp grease will not 'migrate' to the bottom. Too much grease can foul the instruments.

dirt and extra care should be taken to protect cable ends from its intrusion. Lubrication should be made an annual affair with routine of overnight dripping. Some of the newer cables have a nylon lining in the outer sheath and require very little oil.

Other types of controls don't require much attention but there are a few things to watch for. If your throttle has an unaccountable bind, make sure the entire assembly isn't pushed onto the bar such that the inside of the grip is rubbing against the end. The throttle should be removed occasionally for a good cleaning of the bar and inside of the grip body. Apply a very thin film of grease and re-install, and make sure that dirt isn't finding its way into the handlebar through chewed up ends of the grips. The rear brake pedal should be checked for wear in its pivot, and rod joints will wear pretty rapidly if the bike sees much mud. Make sure the rear brake rod isn't rubbing against some part of the frame or swing arm. Handlebar squeeze levers can contribute a lot of friction and an occasional tear-down and cleaning plus a drop of oil will make them feel like new.

ELECTRICAL/INSTRUMENTS

The chapter on electrical systems will give you a good run down on theory and trouble shooting, and your biggest problem is in keeping the wiring in good condition. Plain old wear is a big problem with wiring. Vibration, rubbing and chafing, and just flopping in the breeze can do more damage and cause more trouble than you can shake a stick at. The plastic insulation and harness sleeves used nowadays is real good stuff as far as weathering and resistance to oils and chemicals, but it still has to be tied down and tucked out of the way. The transition from the handlebar/front fork area to the main frame is where the wiring takes the worst beating. Make sure there are loops as large as possible in the harness so that when the bars are turned, the wires will not be kinked. Also see to it that the wiring isn't being pinched in the fork stops or between the tank and forks. Corrosion in the connectors can also be a problem, and poor grounding of the various accessories will make for erratic operation. Be on the lookout for loose connections too, check that battery regularly and it will have a long life.

Speedometers and tachs will give very little trouble if they are mounted super soft to keep that real hard engine vibration out. The cables should be greased about once a year, and their routing should be given the same care and attention as control cables and wiring.

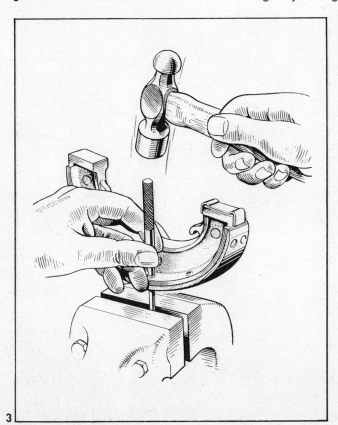

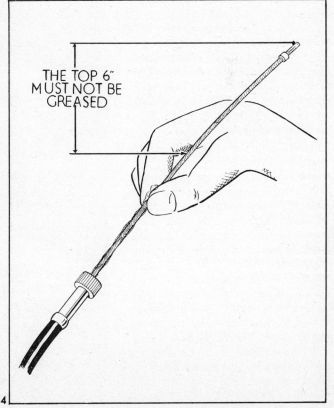

THE TOP 6" MUST NOT BE GREASED

PRESSURE CHECKING TWO-STROKES

A quick and easy test for locating those performance-robbing air leaks
BY DAVE HOLEMAN

The two-stroke motorcycle engine is indeed one of the simplest of engine designs. Conversely though, it is extremely sensitive to air leaks. The two-stroke is reliant on both pressure and vacuum in the combustion chamber as well as the crankcase chamber to run. The pressure provides combustion and forces the fuel charge up to the top end. Vacuum is necessary to draw in the raw fuel and air from the carburetor. While the combustion (cranking) pressure may be up around 150 psi, the crankcase vacuum/pressure will only be from three to six psi.

The pressure and vacuum figures are actually quite critical. Each particular engine is designed and engineered to run best at a certain cranking pressure and with a precise amount of vacuum/pressure from the lower end. The slightest variation from factory figures will result in poor performance that will become increasingly worse as the engine is run. The pressures and vacuum are controlled by airtight fits of the head to cylinder, cylinder to crankcases, case halves to each other and sealing of the protruding and revolving crankshaft ends. Other areas that must be sealed off to ensure maximum and trouble-free performance are the carburetor fit to the cylinder, spark plug seat, compression release (if you use one) and any oil injection fittings that your machine may have.

Briefly, what we are going to do is seal off the intake and exhaust port of the engine and fill the combustion and crankcase chambers with a slight amount of air pressure. Any leaks will be traced and sealed. We will perform this on a piston port engine (Yamaha Enduro) and a rotary valve powerplant (Kawasaki F8-250). With a slight amount of air pressure (only six pounds is necessary, more than this can damage seals or gaskets) inside the engine any or all seals or gaskets not providing an airtight fit will leak. Locating the leak can be done by ear or by applying some soapy water (liquid dish soap is best) to parts or areas that may not be holding pressure.

Once the source of a leak is located, the cure is usually nothing more than a new gasket or seal.

The type of bikes we used for testing are the ones most commonly plagued with air leakage problems. Single-cylinder dual-purpose or dirt bikes have by far the greatest problem with air leaks as compared to street twins or triples. This is probably because they are used more on a year-around basis and they are tinkered with more than street bikes.

Pressure checking street twins or triples is seldom necessary and involves having all the cylinders sealed off at the intake and exhaust to find any leaks. The cylinders cannot be checked individually as the labyrinth seal used between the individual crankcase chambers will not provide a seal unless the engine is running. Therefore should you desire to check a twin or multi you will need sealing plugs or gaskets for each cylinder although the single pressure and gauge unit is all you need. You simply have to pressurize all the cylinders which will occur as you pump up any one of them.

After installing the pressure checking kit equipment to the engine, the squeeze bulb should be used to pump up 6 pounds pressure, no more. Ideally the needle should maintain the six psi reading for six minutes. If you are testing a new engine, odds are it will hold. But if you're testing a used engine, odds are it just won't stay at six pounds for six minutes. A rule of thumb is that a good used engine shouldn't lose more than one pound of pressure in the first three minutes. Any good used engine will have a slight, very slight, pressure loss. The time when the engine definitely needs attention is when it loses any more than a pound pressure in the first minute. An engine that doesn't lose a pound of air pressure within the first minute but won't hold six pounds for three minutes is borderline and will naturally grow worse the more it's run.

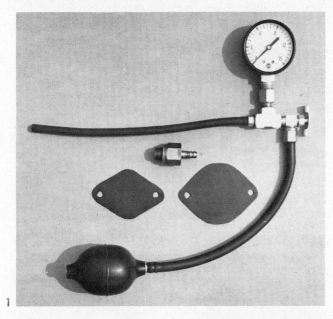

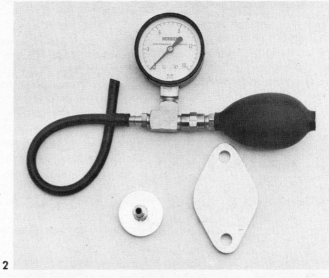

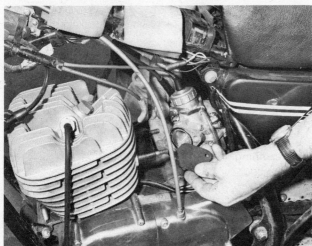

So what does all this mean? If the engine won't hold air pressure it naturally has a leak somewhere. The next step is to locate the leak. Start from the top and work down. If the air leak is really bad you may likely hear it and be able to locate it by ear.

If the pressure drops, the first item to check is the testing equipment. Check the hose fittings and the intake and exhaust seals as these will leak if not cared for and installed carefully. Other things to remember are any particular engine symptoms that were apparent just prior to checking.

The first place to check is at the base of the spark plug(s) and if you have a compression release, there also. At this point it's time to bring out the can of soapy water mentioned earlier along with a small paint brush to apply it with. The object of applying the soapy water is that it will bubble where any air leak may appear making it easy to find visually.

If the spark plug or compression

release leaks, first make sure they are properly tightened but not over-torqued. If this doesn't stop the leak, clean the plug hole seat and install a new gasket. If the leak still persists it's time to remove the head and have the seat(s) resurfaced by a machinist with a flycutter. If the compression release body leaks it may be time for replacement if the leak cannot be fixed.

Before you remove any engine parts continue checking for leaks as it's quite likely that there will be more than one. The next place to check is the cylinder head. This may require laying the machine on its side to permit application of the soapy water so you can make a visual inspection. Any leakage here means resurfacing the head and cylinder with emery and a flat plate and installing a new head gasket.

While you have the machine over on its side, apply the soapy water solution to the bottom of the cylinder

1. The piston port kit for the Yamaha Enduro from Victor Products consists of a squeeze bulb, lines, air gauge, shut-off valve, sealing gaskets and spark plug filler spigot. Air gauge will show leaks as a pressure drop.

2. The Kendick pressure checking kit is like the Victor unit except this one has an automatic inline air pressure shut-off, ball check valve. Other parts for each kit are available for most all two-strokes upon request.

3. The first step in installing the pressure kits is to seal off the carburetor with the gasket or plate included. Don't overtighten bolts.

4. The exhaust port seal is next. Removing the gas tank makes things easier to get at. Install the spark plug filler firmly.

where it seals to the crankcases. A leak here can lead to serious engine damage. Installing a new gasket and possibly machining the bottom of the cylinder should remedy any leaks at this point.

The only other exterior checks that can be made are the carburetor and manifold and any oil injection lines

PRESSURE CHECK

that lead to the intake or lower end bearings. It's not unusual for bolt-on type carburetors to be warped from over-tightening. The same holds true for the manifolds. Surfacing them with emery on a flat plate and torquing to the proper specs cures this problem. With rotary-valve engines, the valve

SYMPTOM	PROBABLE CAUSE
1) Hard starting, low compression or spark plug bridging	Poor spark plug seal Leaking head gasket Leaking compression release Porous head casting
2) Oily spark plug, unusual smoking, gearbox oil loss	Leaking crankshaft/gearbox seal Blown crankcase gasket or seal Porous crankcase casting
3) Sudden power increase, unusual power surging, pinging or pre-ignition, white spark plug reading, seizure or holed piston	Intake manifold leak Oil injection line air leak Loose and/or leaking crankcase seal Porous casting(s) Bad spark plug seal Defective compression release Leaking head or base gasket Blown ignition side crankshaft seal

cover/manifold can leak where it fits to the engine or be porous. Not enough can be said about keeping a close eye on the oil injection lines and fittings. A loose fitting or banjo bolt can easily slip by the scrutiny of the best of mechanics. This also means

checking the fittings at the oil tank as well the engine.

Probably the most common air leakage problem is with the crankshaft seals. The crankshaft seals receive the lion's share of the responsibility of sealing, especially considering that they are subjected to continual wear from the spinning crankshaft. In fact, while going through the steps of pressure checking for pictures with Mike Harper at his Victor Products shop we found that the DT-1 Yamaha had a leaking magneto-side crankshaft seal. Though only a minor leak it would have led to serious engine damage in relatively little time.

Most all two-strokes will have one of the crankshaft seals (usually the clutch-side) retaining the crankcase pressure while keeping out the transmission oil. When this seal starts to leak the engine will not only suck in transmission oil, but it will also blow pressure into the gearbox cavity. Through a combination of oil being inhaled by the engine and lubricant being blown out under pressure, the transmission can be drained without the rider's knowledge. A dry transmission won't last long! Indication of clutch-side seal leaking is hard starting and poor performance combined with black, oily spark plug readings. In extreme cases the exhaust will smoke heavily. If no exterior leaks can be found and the engine won't hold pressure it's possible that this seal is bad. During the pressure testing tests remove the transmission oil filler cap

and listen for any gurgling in the oil indicating a pressure leak into the gearbox cavity.

While the engine will begin to start and run poorly when the transmission seal is gone, the magneto-side seal can produce entirely opposite results. The magneto-side seal will suck in air from the vacant area in the ignition cover and blow out some fuel mixture

1. Now pump up the squeeze bulb until the gauge reaches six psi, no more. Too much pressure can damage seals or gaskets. A well sealed engine should hold six psi for six minutes. A loss of one pound in three minutes is a borderline case. Losing more than a pound per minute is a bad leak.

2. If you have a leak, check the kit fittings first by ear. If you can't pinpoint the leak, apply soapy water to any suspected area. A leak will show up as bubbling soap suds. If this doesn't show any leaks lay the machine on its side and apply soapy water to the head and base gasket areas for air pressure leakage.

3. Commonly the leak will be the crank seals which can often be detected by ear. Gurgling sound indicates a leak.

4. To ensure that the leak is a seal, apply the soapy solution to the crank seals directly and watch for bubbles.

5. Kit for the rotary valve Kawasaki engines is complete and fits all single cylinder models. The installation is about the same except there is no spark plug removal as pressure is pumped through the exhaust port.

6. It may take three hands to check the rotary valve engine as the intake sealing cork pops out easily with full pressure. It's important to scrutinize for possible porous rotary valve castings. While the side covers are off, make sure the oil lines are tight.

1

2

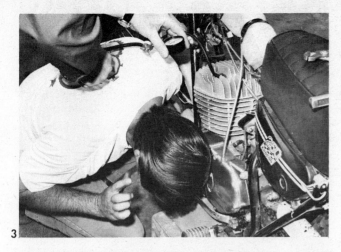

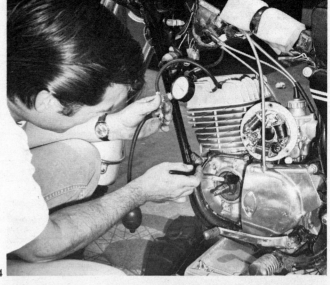

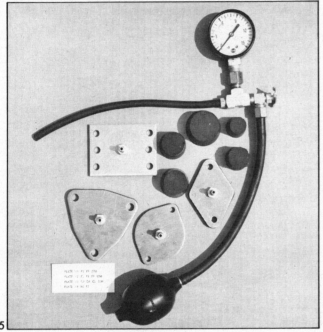

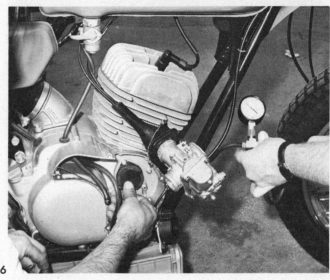

also. When this seal goes or begins to leak the performance may increase due to the leaner fuel/air mixture. Accompanying this in later stages, pinging and pre-ignition may occur which indicate extreme leaning of the fuel/air mixture. This can be further verified by unusually white spark plug readings all of which will certainly mean engine seizure and/or a holed piston in some cases (including our Yamaha DT-1) the leak on this side of the engine can be detected by ear along with visual signs of fuel (oil) leakage into the magneto area.

In some cases the crankshaft seals can be replaced without disassembling the engine, but generally it means removal and splitting the cases to install new ones. Needless to say, if one seal is gone the other is probably about due so it's best to replace both while the engine is apart, along with other seals and gaskets.

The only other source of air leaks is from porous castings, though it is unusual. This is usually the most difficult leak to find. If all of the aforementioned checks have been performed and the cause for the engine not holding pressure can't be found, only one step is left. At this point it's time to pull out an old washtub and fill it with a soluble liquid (cleaning solvent or kerosene is best) and immerse the complete engine assembly. Just like checking an inner tube in water for a puncture, any leaks will immediately appear as air bubbles coming to the surface. In extreme cases, leaks such as porous castings have to be located in this manner. If you're lucky, a porous casting can be cured with a quick heliarc weld. If not, casting replacement is necessary.

All of this may sound like a lot of time or a lot of work, but this is seldom the case. As we found out during the testing procedure with the Yamaha DT-1, the location of the leak was found in just a matter of minutes by listening and using soapy water. For-

tunately in this case the DT-1 seal could be replaced from the outside so replacement was also quick and easy. For any two-stroke, particularly dirt bikes that are a year or more old, it's probably about time to check and be sure the engine is airtight. A few dollars and less than an hour's time can save you the cost of a complete engine rebuild. The Victor pressure checking kits are available from your local Yamaha or Kawasaki dealer. The Yamaha piston port kit is around $17.00 depending on the model and type of machine. The Kawasaki, rotary valve, kit is around $26.00 and fits all their single-cylinder models. The Kendick (Chatsworth, California) pressure checking kit is for piston port machines and runs from $12.00 to $18.00 per kit depending on make machine and can be ordered from your dealer or obtained by mail from Kendick. The cost of any one of the kits will pay for itself many times over each time you locate a leak.

TWO STROKE RING & COKE

You can do it quicker and better yourself and save a bundle, too

COURTESY OF MOTORCYCLIST MAGAZINE   PHOTOS BY PAT BROLLIER

Considering the soaring costs of labor in motorcycle repair shops nowdays, it makes good (dollars and) sense to do as much of your own mechanical work as possible within the limits of your ability and workshop facilities. Most owners of two-stroke bikes turn immediately to a motorcycle mechanic when their popper's mileage increases and performance decreases—knowing full well that car-

HOW TO: Decarbon and rering your popper

1. Suspecting loss of power, start with a pressure check. You're in trouble if pressure is under 120 psi. Hold firmly while cranking the engine over.

2. Then you might check for gasket leak by eyeballing between fins with flashlight. Escaping gases will show evidence of same between head and cylinder barrel.

3. Head off, check piston play with fingers by pushing fore and aft. If you can hear it rattle, you may need a rebore. With exterior parts free, remove barrel next.

4. Nuts away, bump or pry cylinder very tenderly up to avoid cracking fin. As it comes up, immediately stuff rags under it to prevent derbis from falling inside.

bon buildup and worn rings are at fault. It's painful to part with the money at "this" time (any time is "this" time), but delay only compounds the situation and eventually results in parting with even more money (which is even more painful) for a complete overhaul.

Actually, there's nothing difficult about doing your own two-stroke ring and coke job if you have a modicum of patience and the ability to follow the instructions found in the factory shop manual. Of course some factory shop manuals have clearer instruction than others. For this reason, it's nice to have a competent friend to help you through the first one. We can think of few more competent than the instructor of Los Angeles Trade Tech's School of Motorcycle Mechanics, Pat Owens. Pat formerly handled the tuning chores for the Triumph's Racing Division.

So with Pat Owens supervising, let's follow L.A. Trade Tech students Mel Hale and Ken Dickenson through the 34 easy steps to peak two-stroke engine performance. 🎥

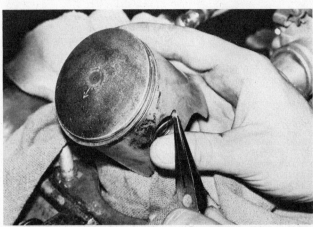

5. Lift out circlip from one side of piston, again being careful broken pieces don't fall into crankcase. Circlip is to prevent piston pin shift and wall scoring.

6. From other side, gently tap pin while firmly bucking far side by hand to prevent bending rod. Note small arrow on piston top faces toward front of bike.

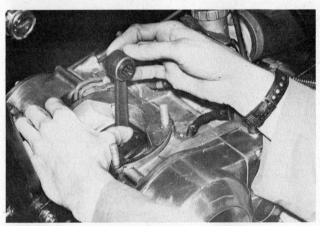

7. Now check for rod lower-end play on crankshaft. Side play is of minor consequence, but up and down play in connecting rod is another story.

8. Check top-end needle bearing for any sign of flaking, grooving or failure of case hardening on rollers. Fit in small end should be snug in race, but not tight.

9. Determine amount of vertical play between ring side and piston groove. If it's more than .005, think about new piston. Also look for scoring and chips.

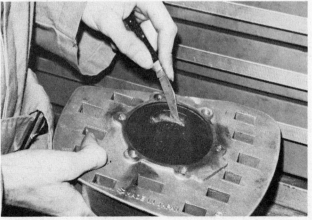

10. Average pocket knife has just the right contour for scraping carbon off head. If you prefer rotary grinder, take it easy around outer lip where it seals.

HOW TO: Decarbon and rering your popper

11. For final touch, shine with emery paper. Then, scrub exterior of head and barrel to remove baked-on mud and oil. It makes a difference in engine cooling.

12. Don't forget the ports. If powered wire brush is not handy, a fine texture of emery cloth equally well. Also check carb-to-manifold and gasket alignment.

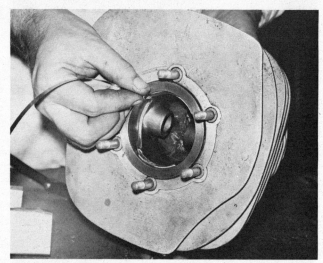

13. Next two photos show cylinder taper check. Since piston has cam-grind (wider front and rear) and taper (wide bottom), invert it in bore with pin boss in . . .

14. . . . . normal transverse position. This gives measurement at tightest relationship. Check at top of barrel then 90° to pin boss. Difference should be less than .003.

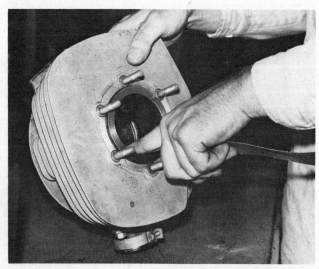

15. Let's assume bore wasn't over .003-in. and all we have to do is rough-up bore with #150 emery cloth using Figure-8 motion to remove glaze, help seat rings.

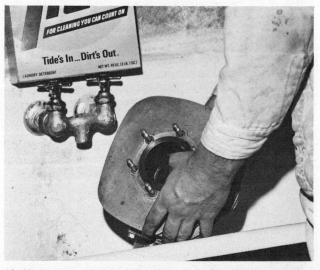

16. Now a word from our sponsor: cleaning emery and metal dust from bore with gasoline isn't good enough: lengthly sudsing with Tide followed by oil bath is!

17. With everything washed and well oiled to foil rust, slip a new piston ring into the bore of barrel from bottom. Mouth of barrel is beveled so chance of breaking ring . . .

18. . . . is slight. To ensure that ring is square in bottom of bore (where ring closure is tightest), push ring down (about 1 in.) with piston head as shown.

19. Now reach in with a feeler gauge and check the piston ring end gap. Check specs in factory shop manual (if none is given, around .012-in. will be okay).

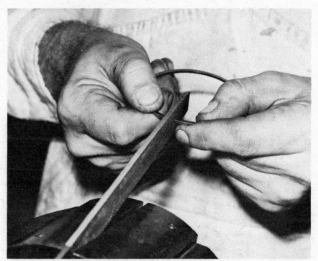

20. If gap is too small, lock file in vise and give it this shot. Go easy! It shouldn't take more than a couple thou. Fitted too close, they'll seize when heated up.

21. Rings can be fitted by hand, but cheap ring expander is better. Be sure ring locating pin in piston hasn't fallen out. Rotating ring can snag in port!

22. Make sure ring is installed with major relief at top so it will properly contour itself around alignment pin. Otherwise it may bind and break in barrel.

TWO STROKE RING & COKE

HOW TO: Decarbon and rering your popper

23. If piston isn't pinned, look for a small initial "R" on ring (indicating top). Oil piston pin and install on rod. Don't forget circlip securing pin.

24. Here's a closer look, and a final reminder to fit piston with arrow in forward-facing direction. Pin is offset to control slap. Hence, concern about location.

25. There are eight different ways this cotton-pickin' gasket can go on and look deceptively right. Careful! Trim any overlap that may exist around transfer ports.

26. Oil everything generously before it is put back together. We're going to emphasize this in a minute regarding oil pressure head in line from pump to cyl.

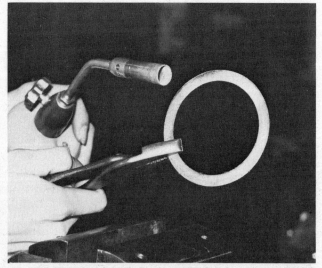

27. With barrel in place, heat copper head gasket to bluish tint, then quench in water to renew. When cool, put on head, button up according to torque sequence.

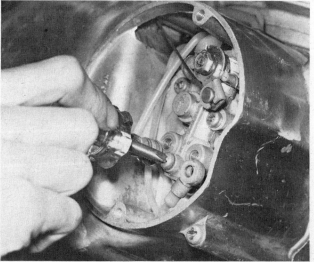

28. Suzuki oil pump feeds two lines; to crank and intake port. Remove Phillips screw from pump body to ensure oil head. Bleed air bubbles; replace screw.

44 • Motorcycle Repair Manual

29. Now disconnect banjo fittings (both of 'em) from pump outlets. Reverse banjo bolt in banjo and fit an appropriate 6mm nut to make it oil tight so we can . . .

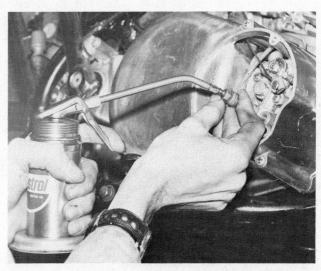

30. . . . force oil into the line with pressure oil can to pump oil into both lines and up to the engine so there will be no pause in oil delivery on fire-up.

31. When you are satisfied the lines are completely full, replace their respective banjos to proper outlets and tighten securely. Now check pump control . . .

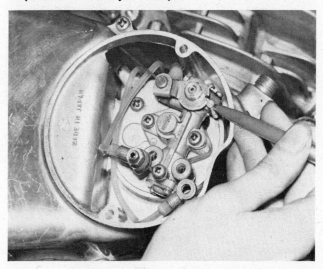

32. . . . before firing engine. Hold throttle wide open (engine off) and see if two stamped aligning marks meet exactly. If they don't, adjust at outside of case.

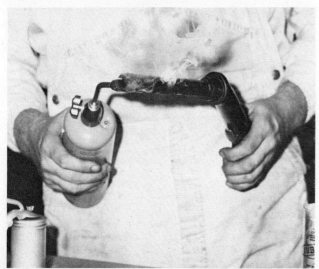

33. With engine all buttoned up, it would be a good idea to burn off excess oil and carbon inside the muffler tube with a small propane torch as shown.

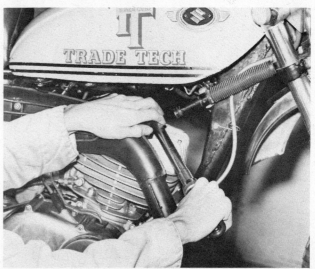

34. After bike has been thoroughly road tested and brought up to operating temperature, then allowed to cool, take final torque on cyl. base and head in sequence.

TWO-STROKE ENGINE REBUILDING

Simple and compact, the modern two-cycle motorcycle engine is a dream to work with

Motorcycles lend themselves to an inordinate amount of fiddling by amateur mechanics when compared to a car. One projection as to *why,* is that everything mechanical is exposed to view and not hidden under a protective layer of sheet metal. In the ''Good Old Days'' prior to World War II, a motorcyclist had to exercise equal parts of brawn, courage, patience and mechanical aptitude. A leisurely ride often led to major roadside repairs and few garage mechanics knew anything about bikes.

Nowadays the tinkering and rebuilding is usually done for sport rather than out of necessity. Many manufacturers, like Yamaha, have sophisticated, reliable machines that can be ridden thousands of miles. Among the two-strokes built around the world are a variety of bikes from, super-simple 70cc two-stroke singles to massive 750cc three cylinder models with water cooling and an electric starter.

HOW TO: Overhaul Your Two-Stroke

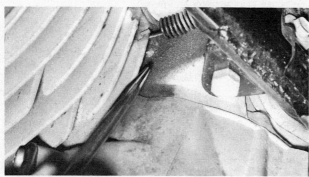

1. Remove the exhaust and intake systems first. Before pulling off the exhaust pipe remove the retaining springs.

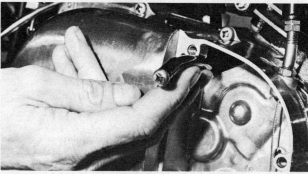

2. Engines with oil injection systems should have the pump removed and the inlet and outlet lines plugged.

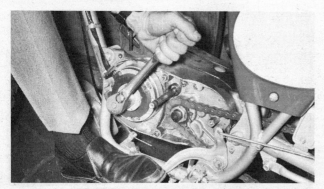

3. A simple method to remove flywheel or clutch nut is to lock the rear brake. This keeps the engine from turning.

4. Don't try to remove flywheels with anything other than a factory puller. Hodaka puller fits most Japanese magnetos.

5. Some engines require the use of a shock puller to break the seal of the flywheel from the tapered crank end.

6. The magneto backing plate will come off after flywheel's removed. Set the backing plate and wires out of the way.

Unfortunately, most weekend tinkerers are unaware that even the simple two-stroke requires more than elementary wrench twisting when it comes to a major overhaul. The two-stroke engine has progressed by leaps and bounds over the past few years. The introduction of automatic lubrication has eliminated the necessity of pre-mixing gas and oil, increased reliability and longevity and helped to wipe out exhaust smoke. But with the virtues comes added complexity and a new need for special attention during an overhaul. Now even some small two-stroke singles, like the Yamaha 70cc street bike, include such sophisticated items as a built-in electric starter.

The motorcycle is still basically a simple machine to work on when compared to the standard automobile, but don't get the mistaken idea that a complete overhaul is just an easy matter of taking it apart and putting it back together again. Today, most motorcycle repairmen are specialists in their fields. You will find that a Yamaha mechanic is best suited for working on Yamahas, and Honda mechanics on Hondas, and on down the line. The reason for this is that these large manufacturers now offer service schools that deal with the specific problems and characteristics of their engines. The shop mechanic must have the theoretical knowledge and skills necessary for working with close tolerances. It is possible for the backyard mechanic to do much of his own repair work, but major overhauls including disassembly of the crank should be done by a professional. If the overhaul is done correctly, the result will be an engine that is capable of living out a life as long as that of the original engine. If the job is done incorrectly, the consequences could be in hard starting, knocking noises, plug fouling and an owner who is firmly convinced that the only way to

7. Be sure the transmission oil is drained, then remove the cover. Plan on using a new gasket and oil.

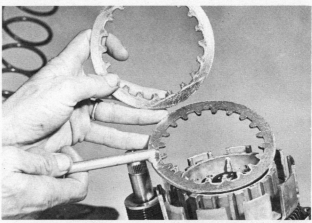

8. You can buy or make your own clutch holding tool. It's the quickest and safest way to remove it without damage.

9. Before you remove the clutch hub nut, be sure to flatten the locking tab. Jamming the gears is not recommended.

10. Removing the clutch on most Japanese machines will expose the shift mechanism. Don't loosen the eccentric screw.

11. One of the handiest special items is this 12 x 12-inch working stand made of two-by-fours for engine case work.

12. With externals removed, the head and barrel are next. Power driven wrenches are fast but can over-torque.

TWO-STROKE

go would be to buy a new machine. Actually, the engine well might be rebuilt better than new if proper techniques are followed and close tolerances are kept.

In many instances, repair of a specific portion of the engine—such as cylinder honing, boring and wrist pin replacement—can be done while the engine is still in the frame. An extensive overhaul requires the engine to be removed from the frame. All wiring must be disconnected, the exhaust pipe and fuel lines disconnected, and linkages and all obstructions removed. Unless you are familiar with the mechanical intimacies of the motorcycle on which you intend to work, it is a good idea to purchase one of the many excellent shop manuals available on the market for your particular machine. Otherwise you should disassemble the machine with extreme forethought, marking any parts that you feel you cannot replace accurately during reassembly. A marked strip of masking tape on all electrical wires will readily identify their location. Most new machines have wires that are color coded to simplify reassembly procedures. For instance, a yellow wire reconnects with a yellow wire, red to red, etc.

Prior to removing the engine from its frame you can simplify the coming teardown work by constructing an engine stand. This stand can be made

HOW TO: Overhaul Your Two-Stroke

13. After the head is removed lift off the cylinder. Be sure to cover the crank opening to catch broken rings.

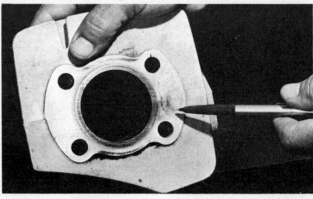
14. Inspect the top surface of the cylinder for leaks, gouges or cracks. Occasionally the sleeve will move up.

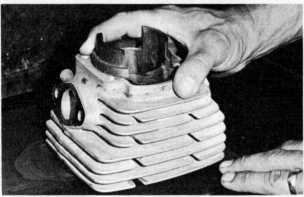
15. It's always a good idea to hand lap the surface to insure a leak-proof seal of both cylinder and head.

16. Just a few strokes on some emery paper laying on a flat plate will give the cylinder top a perfect surface.

17. The wrist pin should be a thumb press fit coming out and going in. Don't damage the bearing by driving it out.

18. When installing the new piston, the pin fit should be snug, not minus clearance. Be sure the clips drop in groove.

very simply of sections of 2x4-inch or 2x6-inch wood nailed together in a 1x2-foot box, and is essential for your working on the engine in the most efficient manner possible. With the engine out of the frame, careful disassembly can now take place. A novice mechanic should note that whatever comes off the engine first will be the last to be reassembled. Unless care is taken, you can misplace some simple but very important small pieces, such as nuts or brackets. Small jars or boxes are extremely helpful in keeping together parts from a specific area. For instance, bolts that hold carburetors in place should be cached in a sealable container and marked for future reassembly. During disassembly note the sizes and number of the screws or bolts involved, and positioning of any irregular pieces such as oddly-shaped gaskets or hinge bolts. Haphazardly destroying an engine piece-by-piece will result in a basket case that will cost more money to put together than if you had taken the complete engine to a professional mechanic to begin with. Any mechanic will tell you that it is far more difficult to try to reassemble a "basket case" than it is to work from scratch in a methodical manner.

Any group of parts or major components should be cleaned of grease or oil as they are removed from the engine. The cleaner you use can be one of the many solvents available at

19. Carefully inspect the needle bearings, bearing cage and rod bearing surface for flaws. Replace if in doubt.

20. If there's a lot of miles on the engine, piston scuffing will be normal. Galling indicates a seizure and reboring.

21. Checking the bore diameter and taper requires an inside micrometer to be exact. Check bore roundness also.

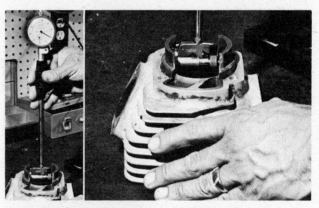

22. A reading from the bottom and top gives amount of taper. Over .002-inch means rebore to next oversize.

23. Always size a new piston by measuring here. Don't rely on measurements stamped on the top of the piston.

24. Piston to bore size will vary. Clearance for 100cc may be .0015-inch, 250cc .0025-inch and 400cc .003-inch generally.

TWO-STROKE

auto supply stores. This may seem unimportant for an engine that will eventually again receive oil in the crankcase, but misplaced dirt or debris can cause serious mechanical difficulties. A small speck of dirt, for instance, could cause leakage between gaskets. It is common knowledge that dirt can rapidly destroy bearing surfaces and shorten the life of any engine.

All this cleaning may seem like unnecessary extra work but no part can be accurately inspected if it is either dirty or greasy. Obviously, a badly damaged part need not be superclean to verify the need for discarding, but most failures are generally small and difficult to see at their onset. It must be remembered during inspection that continual workloads on any mechanical assembly will eventually lead to a failure of that part. Locating areas of potential failure is one of the keys to successful engine rebuilding and the primary reason most professionals will submit suspect parts for a magnaflux inspection. Magnafluxing is a relatively new technique to motorcyclists and is used in locating fine-line cracks that are invisible to the naked eye. Components most eligible for magnaflux inspection usually include the crankshaft, connecting rod and, in the case of the four-stroke, the camshafts and rocker arm assemblies.

HOW TO: Overhaul Your Two-Stroke

25. Check piston clearance at the top also. Run the feeler gauge and piston 360 degrees around the bore diameter.

26. If you can save the old piston and bore be sure to remove all carbon and sludge. Will increase heat dissipation.

27. It's always best to replace rings. Cleaning the ring grooves is easily accomplished with sharp broken ring.

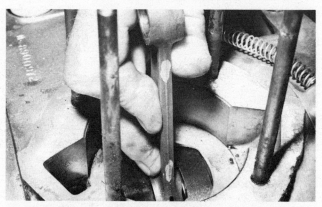

28. Condition of the big end is checked by trying to move the rod up and down while holding it against the flywheel.

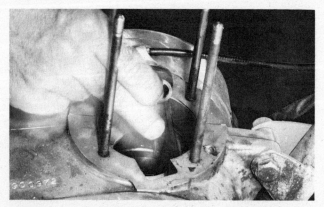

29. If there's no up and down play, check for recommended side play. If it exceeds factory specs, rebuild the crank.

30. Most Japanese engines that split vertically will require a puller to separate the cases without damaging them.

Next in line of suspicion is any point where metal-to-metal contact is evident. Some degree of wear is normal and expected in any engine. A good shop manual will give upper and lower limits of wear to help the mechanic determine when replacement is necessary. Premature or excessive wearing of any component is a good indication that the oil supply is inadequate. Here the mechanic must suspect that the oil pump is not functioning properly or requires adjustment.

In any area, minimum wear will appear as a polished surface such as found in the cylinder bore. A surface blue from excessive heat is also a good indication that there has not been adequate lubrication.

The basic tools required for accurate measurements are a dial indicator, feeler thickness gauges and an inside and outside micrometer. The standard micrometer is used for linear outside measurements from .001-inch or better. For convenience sake, a

micrometer can be obtained that gives measurements in increments of millimeters. Most Japanese motorcycle companies now indicate both American and metric measurements in their tables and specifications. An inside "mike" is generally used for measuring the distance between two inside parallel surfaces such as a cylinder bore. When measuring the inside of a cylinder it is advisable to take several measurements in different spots to allow for any irregularities in

31. Once split, lift the loose case half off slowly and watch for any shims that might be on the crank or gearbox.

32. Remove the transmission only if necessary, although now is a good time to check all the trans bearings, bushes.

33. Engines that split horizontally are a snap to split, but more critical with torquing specs and lock pin alignment.

34. If you take out the trans, inspect the gears and shafts for galling and check the shift mechanism for chips, burns.

35. Many engines require a puller to push out the crankshaft as well as pull it back into the bearing race.

36. Don't make the fatal mistake of leaving out shims and thrust washers. Buy an exploded view drawing, follow it in detail.

TWO-STROKE

the bore diameter caused by excessive wear. Feeler gauges are inexpensive, highly accurate tools that should be part of any mechanic's tool box. They come in a variety of sizes and shapes ranging from a thin wire to a flat surface used for different types of measurement. During an engine overhaul, the feeler gauge can be used often to measure piston-to-cylinder clearance, ignition point gap,

spark plug gap and rod end play.

One of the first checks that should be made is measuring warpage of the heads. Most cylinder heads are subjected to rapid temperature changes that could cause warpage if the changes have been drastic enough. Aluminum alloy heads and crankcases are more subject to distortion than those of iron. A warped area between the cylinder head and the cylinder can usually be spotted quickly. Look for a darkened area

caused by blowby. This type of warpage can be easily corrected by resurfacing the head on a flat surfacing stone, using emery cloth and a mild lubricant such as light oil or water. To check for distortion, lay a straight edge across the surface of the head and slide a feeler gauge between the surface of the head and the straight edge. Repeat this measurement lengthwise, crosswise, and diagonally to determine if the head is distorted or not. If distortion is excessive the

HOW TO: Overhaul Your Two-Stroke

37. An engine with lots of miles will show excess wear on seal lip to metal parts. This thrust washer is worn out.

38. While the engine is down and apart it's always best to replace all O-rings with new parts. Cost is minimal.

39. Rotary valve engines will generally show wear from the spinning disc. Install a new disc, resurface manifold.

40. Always replace the crankshaft seals while the engine is apart. Their cost is small and they'll insure long life.

41. Regardless of engine size, hydraulic press is required to split flywheels and install new bearing, rod or pin.

42. If any play at all can be felt between rod and bearing replace the bearing. Oil generously when reassembling.

head should be milled by a competent machine shop to retrue it. An alternative is to replace cylinder and head.

Because of the soft metal used, threaded holes in the cylinder head or the crankcase can easily become damaged if care isn't taken. Normally, a tap can be used to clean away rust and excess metal or dirt. If the threads have been damaged beyond repair it is far simpler to drill an oversize hole and use a thread insert such as the "Heli-coil." The use of these inserts is especially helpful in the repair of damaged aluminum alloy case or head castings. The inserts are usually made of a strong steel. It should be remembered that *some* distortion and mismatching is standard practice where fastening two metal surfaces together. This mismatching helps keep the components from vibrating loose under excessive and hard usage. However, if the distortion is *too* great the threads could slip, causing damage to soft metal surfaces. To counteract this condition, it is advisable to countersink any hole that is to be threaded.

The greatest amount of wear usually found in an engine is in the cylinder bore, followed by crankshaft bearing surfaces. If the engine being repaired has many miles on it, a ridge will usually be formed at the top of the cylinder where the rings have reached the highest point of contact. This ridge can be removed by honing. Occasionally, the original pistons can

43. Inspect side of the rod surfaces and thrust washers. If old bearings or race are seized to rod, replace both.

44. Most difficult of all cranks to reassemble is triple. Special jigs are required for cranks to measure runout.

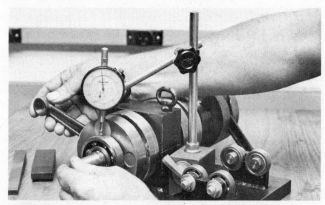

45. With the special crank jig, runout can be measured with dial indicator. Set D.I. at low spot of runout.

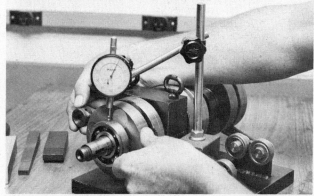

46. Spin the flywheels 180 degrees and the highspot is read. Preferably take the reading off the bearings, not crank end.

47. Using a wedge opposite the low spot, and with a gentle tap it will begin to straighten crankshaft alignment.

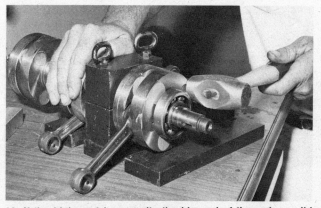

48. If the high spot is opposite the big end of the rod, a solid nudge with a brass mallet will do the trick.

TWO-STROKE

be re-used in the rebuild job if new rings are used and if the cylinder has been honed. The honing operation also serves to remove any minor scratches and to give the new rings a good "bite" for reseating. It is best to check your set-up against the owner's manual to see that piston and cylinder clearance is not excessive. Unluckily, a piston pin may have slipped from the piston and cause

considerable damage to the cylinder wall. If the cylinder wall cannot be bored to a larger size, then it is necessary to replace the cylinder liner. This operation is both time-consuming and critical, and could conceivably be really expensive. It is wise to check into the cost of purchasing a complete cylinder as well as into the advisability of replacing the liner. If piston seizure has been the problem it is best corrected by a minor honing job. The honing will remove the ex-

cess alloy material that has accumulated on the cylinder wall. Recently, some mechanics have found that a diluted solution of acid can be used to remove the alloy without damaging the cylinder wall. If acid is used to remove the alloy it is advisable to run the hone through the cylinder. This is to provide the new rings a suitable surface on which to run.

Boring the cylinder is relatively easy for an experienced mechanic. The cost is usually in the range of less

HOW TO: Overhaul Your Two-Stroke

49. Also check horizontal flywheel alignment. Tapping the wheel(s) as shown on the high spot lines things up.

50. Check flywheel alignment in the same manner as runout. With twin and multi cranks, a specialist is worth the cost.

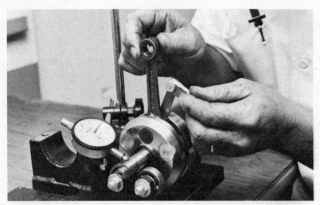
51. Single cylinder cranks are much easier. After pressing together first measure flywheel-to-rod clearance as shown.

52. Check for runout and flywheel alignment the same as with the multis. Always use a soft brass or lead hammer.

53. If desired, the runout may be checked without bearings installed. A drop of oil keeps D.I. from chattering.

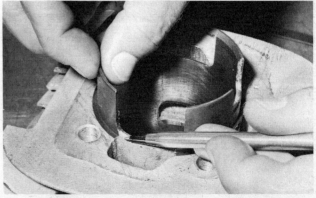
54. Always inspect to see if the steel sleeve has slipped up or down in the cylinder. Machine surface if necessary.

than $10.00 per cylinder. (A bargain when compared to the amount of work that it would take the amateur to do the same job) A cylinder should always be honed following any boring operation. This is done to bring the cylinder to a final correct diameter. The proper surface for a cylinder wall is not extremely smooth. The rings will not seat if the walls are initially too smooth—compression blowby will surely result. Also, a too-smooth cylinder may get scored from lack of lubrication. The cylinder wall should feel smooth to the touch and will look like it has a satin finish with cross-hatch patterns. If done by a professional the honing operation is usually included in any rebore job. Following the boring job it may be necessary to chamfer the lower edges of the cylinder bore to facilitate the replacing of the rings.

Generally speaking, crankshaft bearings will outlast pistons and rings several times over, so replacement may not be necessary. Roller bearings in the rod big-end will permit the rod to rock sideways to a slight degree, therefore there must be some side clearance. But with the rod held firmly to one side, gripped near the bottom, there should be no perceivable up and down play. The ball main bearings should turn freely with no side play and be virtually silent if oiled. Checking of crank bearing condition is something that should be left to the professional if replacement is re-

55. Well equipped dealers will have professional boring bars. Cost for one size over should be $5.00 to $10.00.

56. Be sure the steel liner is honed if a boring bar is used to ream out the sleeve. Boring leaves rough surface.

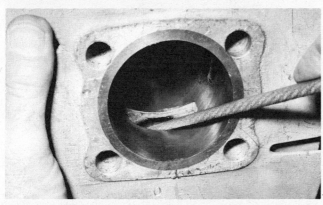
57. Use a fine rat tail file to chamfer the horizontal port edges. A sharp edge will break the piston rings.

58. Repeat the chamfering process wherever there's sharp edges. Wash cylinder in soap and water before replacing.

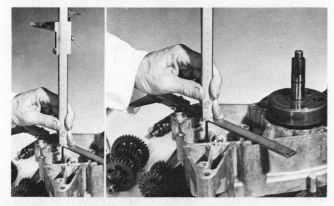
59. Before reinstalling the transmission, especially Japanese, measure case width for gear assembly shimming.

60. Now measure the gear assemblies and subtract the difference. End play shouldn't exceed .005- to .007-inch.

TWO-STROKE

quired, the pro's equipment and facilities will afford the best job. "Splitting the cases" often requires special tools; replacing the rod big-end bearing means pushing the crank pin out of the flywheels with a hydraulic press. When reassembling the crank you will need a special fixture for a dial indicator alignment check of the main shaft sections.

Connecting rods themselves rarely suffer any damage unless there has been piston seizure, extensive breakage, or the engine has had super-hard use. If the rod is removed for crank bearing replacement it should be examined to see if any bending has taken place. Straightening of two-stroke rods *can* be done, but generally their unit cost is low enough to justify replacement for safety's sake.

Just as important as the "hard parts" in a two-stroke are the "soft" seals and gaskets. A leaky crankcase in a four-stroke will leave a puddle on the garage floor, but in a two-stroke it can effect engine operation to some degree, even to the point of repeating any damage which may have required the overhaul. Crankshaft seals should be replaced any time an engine is

HOW TO: Overhaul Your Two-Stroke

61. Clean the crankcase surfaces with putty knife and solvent before assembly. Don't scratch or gouge surface.

62. Always apply a good motorcycle gasket sealer before placing case halves together. Keep it out of innards.

63. Clean all the hardware before reinstalling. Use only impact driver or torque wrench on screws and bolts.

64. If you didn't move the shift linkage eccentric screw, everything should line up without readjustment.

65. Measure ring end gap with feeler gauge. File ends until correct factory recommended clearance is obtained.

66. Make double-sure the rings are right side up and match up with locating pins in piston. Lightly oil rings.

dismantled, and the seal running surfaces should be carefully checked for wear. Mating surfaces of the crankcase halves should be checked for cracks and nicks and thoroughly cleaned prior to assembly. Most crankcase joints do not use gaskets, but sealants such as Yamaha Bond No. 5 or Permatex are a must to insure proper sealing. Cylinder base gaskets and other paper gaskets are ''best held in place.''—their sealing will be assured by using a rubber cement such as Gasgacinch.

So there it is in a nutshell. The simplicity of a two-stroke makes it easy to overhaul on paper, but the work itself is something else. Study that service manual carefully and don't hesitate to call on your dealer for help. Remember, patience and neatness are your best assets in the garage. While you're at it, you may be interested in doing a little super-tuning on your engine so have a look at the chapters on ''More Power'' and ''Two-stroke Hop-up.'' Refer to the chapters on carburetion, electrical, and tune-up for tips on keeping your bike in top running condition. In addition to saving some money, doing your own work can both be fun and a lot of satisfaction. So Enjoy!

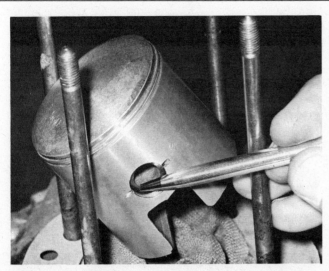

67. When replacing the wrist pin circlip be triple-sure it fits in its groove. Spin with needle-nose pliers.

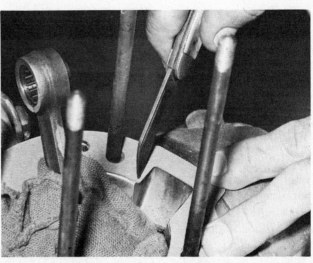

68. If the cylinder base gasket is a bit large inside, cut it to fit ports and sleeve with a sharp pocket knife.

69. Place woodruff key with outer edge slightly up to ease flywheel installation. Some engines need Loctite on shaft.

70. Don't force the flywheel on a tapered shaft. It should fit smoothly. Sharp tap with hammer will seal on taper.

71. Get that flywheel nut on tight. To insure it staying in place Loctite on the nut is a good idea for insurance.

72. Not enough can be said about following torque specs. Proper tightening will insure good sealing and no leaks.

Z-1 TOP JOB

This Kawa ring and valve job is typical of most cammers
BY ERIC RICKMAN

The first clue you will get that your bike nees a top end job will be a compression loss when you are doing a tune up. At least that is the way we found the situation. If you don't make a compression check the bike will let you know by oil consumption or smoking exhaust and mileage loss. Our Kawasaki Z1 is serial number 27, and after 30,000 trouble-free miles we ran a compression check just for the heck of it. We were surprised to find the compression down to 82-74-78-85 psi. The service limit is 85 psi. Actually the bike was running fine, but with this book coming up we decided to use old faithful as a guinea pig for this story. We could very well have run another 20 to 30 thousand miles before having to do this top end since these engines will run well into the 60,000 mile range before this job is really necessary.

Don't be intimidated by those dual cams, sprockets and timing chain when you peek under the head cover on your DOHC machine. We must admit to being a bit dubious about tearing into things, but in retrospect we find that it was a snap. The Japanese engineers have given a lot of thought to making things as idiot proof as possible by marking everything very clearly.

Obviously you are not equipped to do the cylinder boring and the valve work; these will have to be done in a shop. The greater portion of this job is taking things apart and putting them back together again; a time consuming job, and since time is money, this is where you can save a bundle.

Anyone with even a modicum of mechanical ability and a minimum of tools can do this job. The engineers designed the engine so this whole job calls for only two sockets, a 10 and 14mm. You will also need a set of feeler gauges, a couple of screwdrivers, a Phillips and straight blade, plus a few other miscellaneous tools you should have already if you do any work at all on your machine. You will have to have a couple of special tools, a torque wrench is an absolute necessity, along with a shop manual

HOW TO: Rebuild a cammer

1. With the gas tank removed, and the side covers off you can get to the carbs. Remove the 8 hose clamps.

2. Remove air box assembly, and clean up the spilled battery acid. Unit at center is crankcase breather.

3. Slide complete carb assembly out on right side to disconnect throttle linkage. Slip cables off quadrant.

4. Use a 10mm socket to remove cam cover. Note the engine is very accessible and very easy to work on.

and a valve hold-down tool (available from your dealer). It is vitally important that all fasteners be torqued to specifications given in the manual, it's far too easy to overtighten things and strip bolts and studs out of the aluminum cases—a very expensive happening. If you know how to read a micrometer, a 1 in. mike would be nice to have, although the valve adjusting shims are already marked in millimeter sizes.

We arranged to have M.T.C. Engineering of South Gate, Calif. do the machine work for us, so we rode the bike over there and hauled our tools along to avoid having to run back and forth with parts and pieces. Owner Ken Tipton specializes in high performance equipment for road racing and drag bikes. He also has oversize kits for your street machine, how about a 1400cc kit for fast touring? You can ride to the strip, turn a quick 135 mph in the quarter, and then ride back home.

Wash your engine down thoroughly first, paying close attention to the stud openings between the cylinders around the base of the barrels. Wash with high pressure and then blow out with compressed air. This is where dirt accumulates, and it will fall into the engine when you lift the barrels.

Remove the gas tank and side covers to clear the field of action. Loosen the hose clamps at both sides of each carb. The carburetor assembly will pull free of the head, and can be pulled to the right side for throttle cable access. Disconnect the cable bracket from the carb assembly and then slip the cable tips from the throttle shaft quadrants. You can now slip the airbox and intake manifold assembly out of the frame if you wish. Next comes the engine. Remove the exhaust pipes and the tach drive cable from the front of the head, then take the head cover off. The cam chain idler sprocket is removed next, then

we're ready to remove the cams. Careful! The idler stands have rubber spacers under the feet, so don't drop 'em into the engine. Look at the cams and bearing caps, the cams are marked L and R with the exhaust cam having a worm gear cut into the shaft for the tach drive so you can't get 'em back wrong. The bearing caps are each numbered (with an arrow pointing forward), so you can't go wrong here either. Unbolt the cam bearing caps slowly, a few turns at a time so the spring tension on the cam is relieved evenly. This is important! With the bearing caps off (watch the dowel sleeves), lift the chain and slip each cam out of its bearing saddles. Note that the number in bearing saddle under the cam corresponds to bearing cap number—good engineering. So far all you have needed is a 10mm socket on the engine. Pull the 1 and 4 spark plugs so you can reach the small head bolts under the plugs. Re-

5. Cam layout reveals excellent engineering. Remove cam chain idler sprocket, don't lose fiber footpads.

6. Remove cam tensioner assembly from back of engine. Keep dirt from falling into engine, it's murder.

7. Release cam bearing caps at both ends of cam at the same time, slowly and evenly; cam is under load.

8. Bearing caps are marked, you can't mix 'em up. Slip cams out, drop chain into engine. Cams are marked.

Z-1 TOP JOB

move these bolts, then switch to a 14mm socket to remove the head nuts. Observe the large copper washers under the head nuts and don't lose any of them. Head should now lift off easily after a couple of raps with a soft hammer. Be careful! Aluminum nicks and scores, and fins break off much too easily.

Lift out the timing chain guide sprockets at the front and back of the chain well, being careful not to drop the little rubber shaft-retaining blocks into the engine. You can drop the timing chain into the engine, and remove both the inner and outer portions of the chain tensioner assembly at this time. Keep track of the alignment dowel sleeves that are over the studs at the front corners of both the head and barrels. They will have to go back in the same holes. The barrels are usually cemented pretty tightly

to the case and will require some judicious prying and hammering with the soft hammer to get loose. Once they are loose, they can be lifted straight up and off the pistons.

Now you will see why we suggested cleaning the engine first.

A good deal of dirt will fall out of the stud openings. Just do your best to keep as much as possible out of the engine, and use a rag to wipe out any that you can reach. Stuff the case openings with rags to keep things from falling into the engine, then pop the wristpin retaining circlips out of the pistons. A sharp pointed tool inserted in the small pin opening notch will do the trick. Wristpins should push out. If not, use a punch and tap lightly to get 'em out. Remove the single chain guide roller from the center of the crankcase, remembering the little rubber blocks. Use a chain breaker to break the cam chain and lay the loose ends out to the front and rear

of the engine. If the chain falls into the case, it's a hassle to get it out.

Okay now everything is apart. Look into the chain well opening between the barrels. There should be a chain guide shoe in the front portion of the well. Don't panic, mine broke off and fell down inside the engine a long time back with no harm, and it seems this is a regular happening. In any case, this guide and the fiber tensioning rollers should all be replaced. Now you are ready for clean up time. Scrape all the gasket flanges clean without getting anything into the engine. Take the head and barrels to your local cycle shop to get the reboring and headwork done, take the cams and bearing caps too.

At 40,161 miles, these cylinders had exactly .004-in. clearance between the pistons and side walls. This represents about .002-in. wear in the cylinders. The pistons showed almost no wear at all! In fact the machine marks in the skirts

HOW TO: Rebuild a cammer

9. After disconnecting exhaust headers, tap head with a soft hammer, and pry carefully to lift off easily.

10. Note locating dowel tubes over small bolts at each end of cylinder head. Be sure to replace upon assembly.

11. Remove chain guide idler sprockets and tensioner assembly. Don't drop shaft retaining blocks in engine.

12. Grooves in rear of barrel assembly are due to lack of proper chain tension maintenance. Adjust often!

were still visible. The rings wore out first and caused the compression drop. It is a shame to have to bore the barrels .010-in. oversize for this small amount of wear, but that is the first available stock oversize piston. We are wearing the engine out faster with the boring bar than by riding the bike. The exhaust valve stems showed no wear whatever, while the intakes showed .0002-in. wear. The guides and valve stem seals is where the wear occurs. This tiny amount of wear, and the cleanliness of the inside of the engine is attributable to the use of Valvoline SAE 50 four-stroke motorcycle oil and regular 2000 mile changes of both the oil and filter. Suggest the use of a multi-viscosity oil such as a 20/50 SAE. Straight 50-weight tends to hang up the starter clutch on the first cold start, but everything is fine after the engine warms up.

We suggest you plan on replacing all the top end rubber parts.

Rubber tends to get hard and brittle from the heat, and will give you trouble eventually if you reuse the old parts. This includes the carb holders, vacuum plugs, tach drive seals, and head plugs.

M.T.C. Engineering replaced the valve guides with their own high performance guides made of a better material and are a tad longer to give better stem support. The valves were ground and reseated at the same time the new guides were installed. New valve stem oil seals will have to be installed at this time too. The shop will check for tired springs, etc.

The new valve clearances can be set on the workbench—and this is why you brought the cams along. With the head resting on spacer blocks to keep the valves from striking the bench, the cams are installed and the caps torqued down slowly and evenly. Rotate the cams in the running direction only (top forward). As each lobe points directly away from its valve, take a feeler gauge reading between the heel of the cam lobe and the top of the valve stem cup. The book calls for .002/.004-in. (.05/.10mm) clearance. Each valve stem cup has a shim in the top of the cup about the size of a 25¢ piece. These shims come in graduated sizes from 2 to 3mm in .05mm steps (which figures out to .002-in. steps). (.05X.04 = .002) multiply millimeters by .04 to get inches.) Shim thickness is marked on the back of each shim in millimeters, so this is where some trick figuring will have to be done. If you are using millimeter feeler gauges, no problem! However, if you are using American standard feeler gauges you will have to do a lot of figuring unless you have a micrometer handy. Pep Boys here in Calif. has a neat set of feeler gauges marked in both thousandths and millimeters. There is a small notch in each cup to permit you to pry the shim out, but the oil

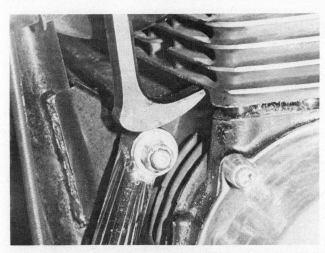

13. Tap barrels with soft hammer, and pry gently to get 'em off the case. Remember; fins break very easily.

14. Wash engine and blow out stud holes first. Keep dirt out of engine. Replace the center guide roller.

15. Valves have automotive type springs and keepers, with added cam bearing cup and adjusting shim on top.

16. Road racer Pat Beacom of MTC removes valves in the conventional manner. Any shop can do this job.

Z-1 TOP JOB

film will want hold it in the cup. We give you all this information because you will have to check the valve clearances after the first hundred miles of running your rebuilt engine. You can do the valve setting yourself with a dealer purchased Valve Lifter Holder, (part #57001-109), which you can purchase cheaper than paying the dealer to check and reset the valves. You can loosen and lift the cam to do this job, but it's a hassle. If you have to make a choice, always go to the wide side since valve gap closes as the valve seats into the head.

Now is the time to decide if you want to get racy, or go the stock route. M.T.C. has overbore kits and hot cams available through your dealer—how brave are you? Always have the new pistons in hand before boring the cylinders. Stock pistons vary slightly in size in our case we got one piston .001-in. larger than the other three. Daryl Collins, "Barrels by Daryl" bored one cylinder .001-in. larger and marked the piston accordingly. He gave us a .002-in. wall clearance job; a little on the snug side for street riding. Okay, now we are ready to put things back together. First order of business is to check the piston ring end gap in the bore to be sure someone didn't mix the rings up back in Japan. A too-tight ring can ruin the whole job and checking takes only minutes. Push each ring into a cylinder bore with a piston head to get it square in the bore, and check end gap with a feeler gauge. It should be between .008/.016-in. (.2/.4mm). Now install the rings on the pistons. The oil ring (wide-grooved ring) goes first. Spread ring with your thumbs and slip over the piston. Not too wide, rings are cast iron and will snap if stretched too far. The next ring is the scraper ring, and has a notched groove around one outer edge (the notch goes downward). The top ring or compression ring can go in either side up—it's chamfered on both edges. Note that the pistons have an arrow on top which should point forward when piston is on rod. Install circlip in wristpin hole that will be away from you when piston is on rod. Position piston on rod and squirt oil in hole and press wristpin in place. Install circlip to hold the pin and check the circlips very closely, since a tiny goof here will blow the whole job. Be sure you have rags stuffed in the crankcase! Remember the old adage, "if it can fall in, it will." Now install a new chain idler roller in the center of the chain well opeing. Be sure the little rubber retaining blocks are firmly in place and use gasket cement to hold them if necessary. Rotate the engine until the two center

HOW TO: Rebuild a cammer

17. TLC, Pat taps guide, installs bolt, drives bolt from underside to remove guide without deforming head.

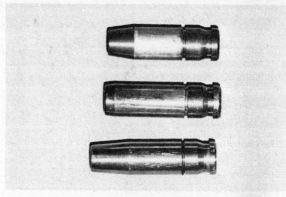

18. Stock intake at top, with stock exhaust center. MTC guides are better material and longer, bottom.

19. Heavy carbon deposit on back of valves indicates stem seals are shot. Stems showed very little wear.

20. After new valve job, valve clearances can be set on the bench. Rotate cams in running direction only.

pistons are at TDC and slip a hammer handle or wood block under a piston skirt to hold them in position. Use a large hose clamp as a ring compressor. Set the ring gaps opposite each other, top and bottom gaps at the back with the middle ring gap at the front of the piston then install the hose clamp after applying plenty of oil to the rings. Tighten the clamp down tight, then back off until it just slips on the piston. Position the clamp as low as possible while still holding the top ring compressed. Use plenty of rubber-type gasket cement on the barrel base flange and be sure to install the base O-rings around each barrel. Now install the gasket and give it a good coat of cement, too. Oil the bores and you're ready to slip the barrels over the pistons. Lower the barrels over the studs and square the center pistons up so the tops just enter the bores. Then press the barrels down gently

and the pistons should slip in easily. Remove the hose clamps and wooden block, and rotate the engine enough to bring the end pistons up enough to get the hose clamps on. Locate the clamps so you can reach the tightening screw to remove the clamp after the barrels have moved down over the top of the pistons. Push the barrels down farther until they engage the rings on the end pistons. Remove the hose clamps and push the barrels down the rest of the way. Be sure you have the alignment dowels in place over the front engine studs.

You will have to thread the old chain ends up through the barrels before they will seat on the case.

M.T.C. uses a heavy-duty timing chain, D.I.D. #219 roller chain on all their drag bike and road-racer installations to take the added load of high lift cams and heavier valve springs. This chain has a tensile

strength of 2700 lbs. and will wear forever in a street bike. This chain is endless, and must be broken and rejoined to install on this job. A Honda 450 master link part #14410-283-000, is used to join the ends of the new chain. To install the new chain, wire the end to one end of the old chain, pull the old chain out and it will pull the new chain in at the same time. Riveting the new master link in place properly is of vital importance. If this link lets go at speed, the cams will go out of time allowing the valves to strike the pistons and each other— totally destroying the engine in a split second. Support the link on a flat piece of metal then have a friend buck up the back of the link with another piece of heavy metal. Use a square-tipped drift punch and upset the tips of the pins. Get a good head on each pin, so the side plate can't work off and let the chain part. Install the chain guide

21. Take reading with lobe up, or pointing away from valve stem; at heel of cam. Set at .004/.006-in.

22. You can unbolt bearing caps, or use this tool available from dealer to hold cup down. Lift shim out.

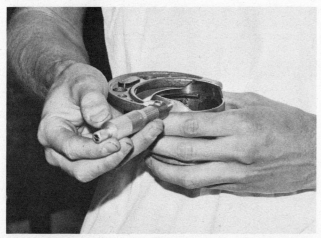

23. Shop will mike new pistons and bore to fit. Book says, .0025/.003-in. wall clearance. Pistons vary.

24. Barrels are checked for roundness, wear and taper with a bore gauge. Barrels had only .002-in wear.

Z-1 TOP JOB

sprockets in each end of the chain well between the center barrels, and at the same time install the chain tensioner assembly at the inside of the back of the barrels. Be sure you have a new guide roller here, too. Watch those little rubber blocks that hold the shafts in place. Be sure a new chain guide slipper is in place in the front of the chain well also. All these rollers and guides keep the whip out of the cam chain. Now you are ready for the head, be sure the alignment dowels are in place and apply a liberal coat of cement to both sides of the head gasket then drop the gasket in place and lower the head on top of it, after fishing the new timing chain through the center of the head. Install the large copper flat washers and the acorn-type head nuts along with the two little bolts at the outer ends of the head.

Torque the head nuts down to 25 ft.-lbs. a few turns at a time following the bolt-tightening pattern accompanying this story. The little bolts are tightened to 105 in.-lbs. With the head down tight, rotate the engine until the left-side piston (#1) is at TDC with the ignition marks lined up in the breaker point case. This will now be the firing stroke for this cylinder and the cams are timed to this crank position. Slip the exhaust cam into position in the front-bearing saddles, note bearing numbers in saddles and get proper bearing caps with their alignment dowels positioned over cam. Exhaust cam has the tach drive gear cut in its shaft, and has L and R marks so you can't get it in wrong. Note timing illustration accompanying story. The cam sprocket is bolted to a triangular cam flange: Place the single bolt point of the flange forward so the bolt hole centerline is just level with

the cam cover flange. Tighten the cam bearing caps down slowly and evenly against the valve spring tension until you have reached 105 in.-lbs. The intake cam is installed next, with the single bolt triangle of the cam sprocket mounting flange pointing to the rear and just level with the cam cover flange. This cam has L and R markings too. Left is to your left when sitting in the saddle facing forward. Tighten the bearing caps down as before, with the arrows pointing forward. Pull the cam chain up tight in front and wrap it over the cam sprocket keeping the cam in position. This removes all slack between the cam and crank sprocket. Drop chain in place over the intake sprocket. To get proper timing between the cams, start with the first pin above the cover flange in front and count back 28 pins in the chain, the 28th pin should line up with a 28 mark and arrow on the side of the intake

HOW TO: Rebuild a cammer

25. Press ring into bore with piston top. Check end gap, should be between .008/.016-in. No less!

26. Slip wrist pins into pistons on rod ends, be sure circlips are in solid. Use hose clamps to hold rings.

27. Use chain breaker to break timing chain. A new chain is a must, if it breaks you loose the engine.

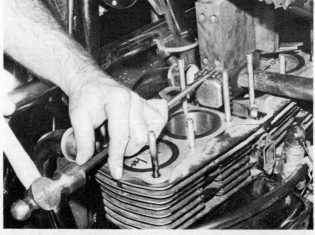

28. Break new chain, thread into case, and use a Honda 450 master link to join. Pein the pin ends over good.

cam sprocket. The last top side operation is to install the chain guide idler sprocket between the cam sprockets. Tighten it down to 105 in.-lbs.

Squirt lots of oil on each cam lobe so you won't have a dry start, and install the cam cover with plenty of gasket cement. Oh yes, here is where we use a racer trick. Install the little rubber half circle head plugs backward, with the open side out. There is a little lip on the closed side that works more efficiently as an oil seal if it is on the inside of the cam chamber. Tighten the cover bolts down to 70 in.-lbs.

Use plenty of gasket cement and next install the chain tensioner at the rear of the barrels. Press the tensioner shoe all the way back against the spring and lock it in place, then install the assembly on the barrels. Release the tensioner shoe so it can move forward and

take all the slack out of the timing chain then relock it in place. Chain tension should be checked at least every 1000 miles, you can't overdo this. Release and lock tensioner with engine turning over on the starter momentarily, this will get all the chain slack out.

Install the tach drive gear after installing a new shaft seal and O-ring in the carrier boss. In retrospect, it would be easier to install the carb holders on the head before it is installed on the engine. Use a light coat of cement on the mating flanges—an air leak here would be hard to find.

With the carb holders in place you are ready for the carbs. Slip the airbox and intake assembly in place first, then slip the carbs in place. They will push into the holders snugly so be sure you have the hose clamps in place first. Tighten the clamps both front and rear, connect the throttle linkage and be

sure and get all the slack out by using the adjustments at the bars. Slip in a set of plugs and connect the wires being sure you have the firing order correct (1-2-4-3). Last but not least, install the exhaust pipes with new gaskets and you're ready to fire her up after the tank and side covers are in place.

Take it easy for the first 100 miles (not over 50 to 55 mph). Don't hold a steady cruise, vary the throttle setting to let the engine cool occasionally. After the first 100 miles you will have to recheck the valve clearances (cold) and retorque the head. Check timing chain tension frequently, and change the oil and filter after the first 500 miles. The new parts are wearing in and you must get rid of the metallic particles.

If you did everything right, it should run like a watch and not leak a drop. '''*LET THE GOOD TIMES ROLL!''*'

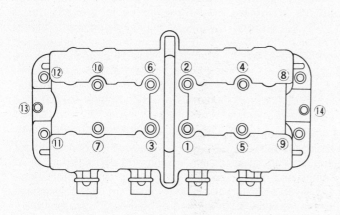

29. Install head gasket (wide metal flanges up), torque head in sequence. End bolts 105 in.-lbs. Others 25 ft.-lbs.

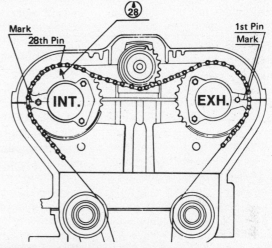

30. Set #1 piston at TDC with timing marks lined up, install cams and time to cover flange as shown.

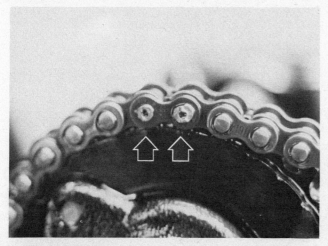

31. Master link (soft link) pins are peined over good. This is critical, lose the chain, you lose the engine.

32. The 28th pin from first pin above cover flange on exh. cam will align with mark on int. cam sprocket.

FOUR-STROKE ENGINE REBUILDING

A complex and involved task can reap financial savings, but rebuilding requires close attention to details, patience and lots of time spent with your nose in a service manual

BY JOE MCFADDEN

The motorcycle engine is a rather precision device, having been developed over the years by competent, dedicated individuals to a degree of sophistication found in no other production form. Indeed, many of the technological developments in the horsepower art were pioneered by the developers of motorcycles. Naturally, such a device is *not* going to respond very well to being zipped apart and thrown back together again like a lawnmower or tractor engine; with a dib here and a dab there to obtain final tuning. One degree; one thousandth of an inch too little or too much can make the difference between "go or blow."

In this article, we are going to discuss the correct procedures and techniques to use in overhauling a four-stroke engine. More important, probably, we are going to mention the many pitfalls which the neophyte motorcycle engine rebuilder encounters, and how to avoid them or overcome them; and we use the term "neophyte" advisedly, for no matter what your mechanical "savvy" with boat, automotive or jet engines, if you've never before tackled a motorcycle engine, cocksureness will leave you in trouble.

If, on the other hand, your mechanical experience is more limited, don't be discouraged. If you are possessed of no more than one thumb on each hand, are willing to spend some time *reading*, and can follow written directions, you can do just as good a job, if not better, than a pro. For those of you who have had previous mechanical misfortunes with the motorcycle engine, we advise you heed the words of this humorous but sadly true American maxim: "When All Else Fails, Read The Directions."

If, on the following pages, you don't see any pictures of your particular engine, *don't go away*. The methods of working on the four-stroke engine are common to all, as construction and engineering similarities abound.

However, if the following procedures or directions differ with those of the Shop Manual written for your particular machine, stick with the manufacturer's advice. Bear in mind, though, that some shop manuals become outdated regarding specifications, especially with newly developed engines. When this happens, your dealer receives service bulletins; if you advise him of the model, year and serial number of your machine, he will gladly inform you of how best to update it. You see, engines built with out-dated parts or superceded instructions cause him anguish too. He doesn't want to reap the spurious profits of selling you a second hundred dollars worth of parts; not when it's going to cost him a sale at trade-in time.

ORGANIZING THE JOB

Start out right, it will save you a lot of time and grief. Advance planning reaps many dividends in any type of mechanical work; lack of it is time consuming, wallet-leaning and exasperating. The following items are essential prerequisites to ensure a first-rate job.

A clean, well-illuminated working area with a sturdy, uncluttered workbench will start things off right. Ventilation should be adequate, but not excessive. Breezes blow dust and dirt particles into open crankcase mouths and other delicate areas, a no-no if ever there was one. Be sure you have a fire extinguisher handy, even if it's only one of the small ones available as a motorcycle accessory. Additional—and inexpensive—safety items should include grounded plugs for power tools; goggles for use in grinding, drilling, chiseling and power wire brushing; pot-holder gloves or welder's gloves to prevent burns when handling heated parts; sturdy work shoes or boots and a sufficient number of suitably strong containers in which to store and carry parts. Such items as crankshafts, cylinder barrels and heads tend to obey the laws of gravity, especially when stored in soggy-bottomed cardboard boxes.

Appropriate washing containers for parts rinsing and degreasing should be immediately at hand. Metal baking pans are convenient, the shallow ones for containing recently disassembled, still oily parts, deeper types (three-

inch or so) for rinsing or cleaning.

Solvent is definitely preferable as a cleaning agent. It is much safer than "Brand-X" gasoline, being far less flammable and easier on the lungs. Five-gallon buckets (with tight fitting lids) about ⅔ full, are ideal for degreasing the "heavy stuff" like flywheels, cylinder heads, crankcases and the like. Clean grease cloths, or reasonable facsimiles thereof, are a necessary adjunct. Avoid using rags or cloths which shed lint and threads.

TOOLS AND EQUIPMENT

Few weekend mechanics can afford the elaborate, time saving equipment found in most shops, but a vise is practically a must. Ditto for at least a quarter-inch drill motor. A small bench grinder can be very helpful, but you can work around it.

Good quality hand tools are essential, needless to say. The tool kit which may have come with your bike *isn't* sufficient to do an overhaul. You should have the appropriate standard tools, American, Metric, or British Whitworth, depending on the make of your motorcycle. Don't try to work around this by using American size wrenches on Whitworth or Metric bolts and nuts. You will only succeed in rounding off some rather expensive—and not always available—hardware. (Don't let those metric allen screws sneak up on you.)

Assuming you don't own a power impact wrench, buy one of the hand impact tools and the necessary bits. They are available as an accessory item at most motorcycle shops and many tool dealers. Again, these will prevent damage to primary, timing cover and other screws and perform well. Without one you will be unable to remove many screws and nuts; items which *must* be on tight to prevent oil leaks.

Assuming you *do* have a power impact wrench to work with, a word of caution: Over-zealous application of torque to mild steel screw heads causes prompt decapitation of said items, which then necessitates the painful Ezy-Out treatment.

If you don't have a shop manual *buy one!* The rider's manual doesn't cover engine overhaul and is generally geared to the tool kit under the saddle. The shop manual outlines each operation of the overhaul, along with factory recommendations for accomplishing it with a minimum of trouble. We advise you to read through the whole manual before beginning the job, then consult the individual sections, specifications and diagrams prior to doing the operation described. In so doing, you will be able to "stay out of the woods," as the expression goes.

Listed in the workshop manual for your machine are, no doubt, a variety of special tools to assist in the teardown procedure. You can usually purchase all of these tools at your dealer, or he will order them for you. Happily, we can do with only one or two, so read *carefully* to determine which are absolutely necessary for disassembly; they're usually expensive. Gear pullers can generally be bought or borrowed from automotive parts houses. Clutch hub pullers are usually cheap enough to purchase, and are necessary if your engine is British. As an alternative to buying the tools required, you can dismantle the engine as far as possible, tote it down to your dealer and have his mechanic remove them. The charge for this is usually minimal. Our advice along these lines is this: If you plan on repeating the overhaul, whether on your own bike or on a friend's, buy the tools you need. Their cost will be more than covered by the labor dollars you are saving, and will save delays and legwork in the future. Moreover they retain their value well.

You may not be equipped to handle such things as boring, valve seat grinding, etc. Find out who handles this work, and be sure of their reputation for competence. Some auto machine shops are well acquainted with motorcycle components, but if you aren't sure, consult your dealer. He is either equipped to handle these chores, or has access to the people who can.

An overhaul can be accomplished at times for less than $50.00, but can run into several hundred. Motorcycle parts are expensive, and so is machine work. If you can't afford the parts *don't tear the engine down.* Parts may become lost or damaged from lying around, and you can wind up with a "basket job." Even a knocking, oil belching engine is worth more together than it is in pieces.

Patience is one item that is cheaper to own than to be without. Don't plan on working fast, unless you're a flat

1. **Start out right by getting a factory service manual. Read through it before you start tearing things apart. Pay particular heed to sequence of teardown and need for special tools.**

2. **Be prepared for the task at hand. The enormous array of parts in a Honda Four requires a large work area and equal size shop bench.**

3. **Ask your mechanic friend about the 'tricks' of the trade. Holding a Honda cam chain with some safety wire keeps it out of the engine innards.**

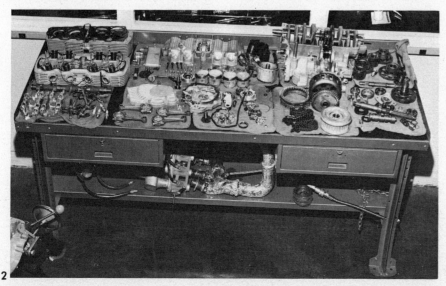

2

3

FOUR-STROKE

rate mechanic with a lot of experience—in which event you shouldn't need to be reading this. Take each phase of the work slowly, and don't get ahead of yourself. Keep your surroundings tidy, and your work organized. Check and double check every procedure; take nothing for granted, avoid short-cuts and leave nothing to chance. If you find yourself becoming disgusted or exasperated at any point, wrap the job up until you're in a more cheerful frame of mind. Disgruntled mechanics do sloppy work and sometimes wreak havoc! It's your motorcycle, don't let it down.

ENGINE REMOVAL

You can make things easier at the outset by spending a little time and effort on cleaning the machine before you even start. A can of Gunk, a brush, hose and some rags will take a lot of grease and muck off. The bottom (underside) of the engine should receive particular attention. This done, drain *all* the oil from the engine and transmission. If the primary case contains oil, drain it.

The gas tank and exhaust pipes can now be removed. If possible, drain the gasoline and refill the tank with solvent. Otherwise, it is just as well to leave the gasoline in, and store the tank in a safe place. Be certain the gas taps aren't leaking; if they are, place the tank in such a position that they are above the level of the fuel. Empty gas tanks contain dangerous vapors and are prone to rust formation as a result of condensation. Exhaust pipes can be wrapped in paper and hung up out of the way to protect their chrome finish. Old coffee cans or paper bags are a convenient method of keeping the assorted screws, nuts and bolts separated. Label the containers. Outer engine cover screws, nuts, and bolts should not be mixed. Left side set in one container, right side in another. This will save a lot of inconvenience on reassembly.

The carburetors are the next order of business. Remove them (after draining) completely; don't leave them dangling from the throttle cables, they bruise easily. Wrap in paper wadding and store them in a small cardboard box. Disconnect the clutch cable if necessary, coil it and tape it to the handlebars. If the speedometer/tachometer cables

connect to the engine, treat them in the same manner. The engine wiring harness is next. Disconnect it. Coil the harness and tie it out of harm's way to be certain it won't become chafed or cut during the removal process; this can cause confounding electrical problems later. The section of the harness leading to the frame should also be pulled up and tied out of harm's way. If your engine has a remote oil tank, drain it and remove the lines where they connect to the tank, unless they are easily accessible from the engine connections. Note: Examine the oil line connections carefully; make a mental note of which line hooks to which connection. If your memory sometimes fools you, buy a small notebook, and jot things down as you go along. Make diagrams of items which might confuse you on reassembly. They *may not* be illustrated in the shop manual.

Upper motor mount brackets are the next to come off. Keep the assorted nuts, bolts, washers and brackets together. Spacers and brackets can be assembled back to the bolts, and the nuts threaded on part way. This will keep them together and sorted. It is sometimes more convenient to remove cylinder heads prior to undoing the lower motor mounts and final removal of the engine (this notably on British vertical twins). Before undoing any of the nuts and bolts, however, remove the rocker caps (Triumph) or cover (BSA). Rotate the kickstarter slowly until both intake valves are in the closed position. You may now remove the small nuts and bolts from the rocker housing to the head (Triumph), followed by the two large long bolts. The object is to take the pressure of the valve spring off the rocker box. Failure to

do this, and removal of the large bolts first, will almost surely cause stripped studs or threads. On the BSA, this procedure permits the mechanic to depress the rocker arm at the valve with a large screwdriver, after which the pushrods can be easily removed. Repeating the procedure on the exhaust will facilitate removal of the rocker shafts (after pushrod removal). The object of the technique is to prevent damage to engine parts. Short-cut operations save minutes in disassembly, and usually provide hours more work on the way back. Whether or not these procedures are applicable to your situation, they should make you more aware of the importance of thought and common sense when you do run into "it don't wanna come off" situations, and there is no shop manual to consult.

If you have removed the head assembly, treat it with TLC, as they are expensive. Tag the pushrods to indicate which valve assembly the pushrod came off, and which end of the pushrod was up, in the case of Triumph and some others. This is best done with the inexpensive packages of colored tape found in auto parts supply houses. There are five different colored rolls, and they sell for around $1.00 for all five. Jot down your coding system in your notebook. And do yourself a favor: Don't throw the

1. If you aren't going to be splitting the cases a rag under the piston keeps broken rings and the like out of the crankshaft big end. Saves them for visual inspection.

2. Make sure all the oil is drained out before complete disassembly. At this point a large, clean work area aids sequential storage of parts.

3. Prior to re-assembly clean all the parts and place in position for inspection. Look for missing pieces.

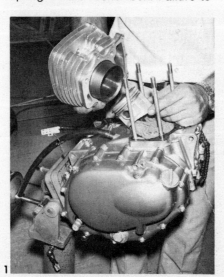

pushrods in the bottom of a big box, then pile the cylinders and heads in on top of them. Abusive treatment like this causes them to bend, and is a common happening.

With the removal of the lower motor mounting bolts and brackets, the engine is almost ready to come out. There remains but chain removal. Disconnect the master link, and with the machine in neutral, gently pull on the top run, at the same time feeding the bottom run through to prevent snagging on any projections. Be careful of the brake switch harness which may be in jeopardy of losing a bit of its insulation. Now connect the master link and its clip to either end of the chain. Since your hands are pretty nasty by now, it is as well to clean them and the chain together in the solvent bucket. A thin coat of clean, heavy oil on the chain will discourage rust. Wrap in heavy wax paper, and file it away.

Well, it seems like we finally come to "hoist 'er out"? Sorry about that. There are a couple of minor details to tend to. Clear all tools from the floor area. If there are any oil drippings about, clean them up, or you may look like Willie Mays sliding into your shop area. With a big hunk of unyielding engine cradled around your neck. We daresay such a happenstance could delay the overhaul proceedings.

Humor aside for the moment, safety is an oft overlooked consideration, but one we feel is important enough to bear mention. In view of this, we would recommend you obtain help in

lifting the engine out of the frame, especially the "big incher" types. Regardless of the fact that you may be able to lift twice the weight of your engine, four hands are better than two in this case, if for no better reason than to prevent chipping the paint. Note: Check your shop manual before lifting the motor out. Some examples will only come out one way. Others can be lifted out from either side, but the manual will advise you of the easiest method.

DISASSEMBLY

With the engine resting on a bake pan on the work bench, wipe your hands clean, sit down with a cup of coffee and the shop manual, and peruse the paragraphs dealing with disassembly. Take note of any left-hand threaded engine nuts, and identify their location. Left-handed threads are a maker's added insurance against loosening. They are *not* rare. Failure to observe this point, of course, results in rounded bolts and nuts, damaged tools and skinned knuckles. Note and adhere to the maker's recommended sequence. Generally, the procedure goes like this: Small cylinder head studs and nuts come off first. Main headbolts are then undone a bit at a time, working around in the inverse order of torquing. This helps prevent head warpage. If you are removing the heads on the bench, you will need some help in holding the engine. Failing the presence of any volunteers, secure an engine plate to the most convenient

(usually front) through bolt. Clamp the other end of the bracket in the vise, and you are ready for some wrench operation.

With the head(s) detached, collect the associated hardware and clean same immediately. Package and label. Follow this procedure all through the job. Remove, clean, package, label, and put away. You will be rewarded for your efforts when reassembling.

Overhead-cam type machines require special care in their disassembly. Hondas are chain driven, and as a matter of course pose no spec-problems when the well-illustrated manual is consulted and heeded. Some ohc machines use spacers to control the end play and backlash in their geared shaft drives. It is essential that these be refitted precisely as they came out. These spacer shims can be "miked," their thickness and location noted on a simple pencilled diagram. Then they can be placed in an envelope as insurance against loss. The diagram and notations will facilitate reassembly.

Regarding unit construction type engines, the primary drive gear can be removed next. Don't remove the cylinders yet!! Nicks and scratches on the connecting rods will result as the engine shifts to and fro during the goings on of timing gear removal. If your machine is alternator equipped, remove the stator, then the rotor (round magnet attached to the crankshaft.) The stator output harness exits the primary via a hollow bolt extending from the left hand case wall. The normal tendency is to pull the harness wire back through this piece. This works great for a while, but the metal bullet connectors at their wire ends—there are three—will not come through simultaneously. The correct method, of course, is to unscrew the hollow bolt by gripping it on the hexagon portion which is difficult to fit a wrench on at times. Vise grips won't hurt it if clamped lightly on the hex portion. When this bolt is removed (right-hand thread) the wire ends come right on through the larger diameter hole, and the assembly comes off. Stators are delicate, expensive and most likely back-ordered two months, so handle gently. With the crankshaft end nut removed, the magnetic rotor will readily come off, though at times may need a bit of urge, applied with a pair of levers from behind. Place the magnetic rotor inside the alternator stator when stor-

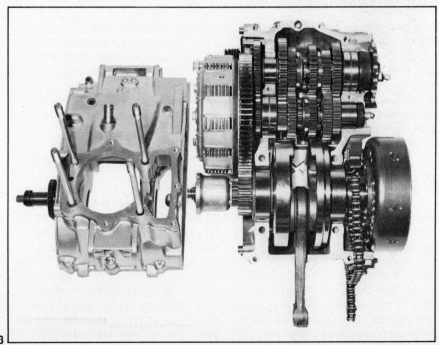

3

FOUR-STROKE

ing. This will keep its magnetic force field from decaying during storage. A weakened rotor field will produce an undercharging symptom. The only way to correct this situation is a new rotor.

The engine sprocket occasionally needs the aid of a gear puller, and care must be used to prevent damaging the crankshaft internal threads.

The clutch assemblies in the type engine we are discussing are simple enough to remove. Follow the directions there. One word of caution (again): Don't ever try to extract the inner clutch hub with anything but the factory puller. This tool is fairly inexpensive and can save you a lot of misery, even if you were to use it only once.

Dismantling the timing side is easy, generally speaking. The late British twin distributors require a special bolt to break them loose from their taper, but a ⅜ × 26TPI bolt can be threaded into the end (following removal of the narrow hold down bolt), given a sharp tap with a plastic mallet or piece of wood, it will break loose from its taper and the timing cover can be removed. Big twin Harley procedure is essentially the same, but a bit less hairy. The timing cover can be removed quite readily, exposing the complete timing apparatus—cam, breather, distributor drive, oil pump drive, etc. With regard to the latter, never remove the Harley oil pump without removing the driving gear and shaft as well. The driving gear is a slip fit on the shaft, retained by a small circlip and a small Woodruff key which transmits the rotational force from the gear to the shaft. It is possible for this shaft to drop through the driving gear, allowing the Woodruff key to fall out. Upon reassembly, of course, the oil pump would be inoperative. Goodbye engine!

With few exceptions, four-stroke engine manufacturers prefer to locate the oil pump on the right-hand side of the engine, driven in one fashion or another by the timing gears. Although the oil pumps are of different types—gear or ball and plunger style, mainly—treatment remains the same. Dismantle, inspect, wash thoroughly in clean solvent, re-assemble after coating the components with oil, wrap and box. The exception to this rule is the BSA oil pump. If the BSA oil pump looks and feels (rotate the tach drive shaft) sound, immerse in sol-

vent, air blast, apply oil and put it away. If you take it apart, you may wind up with a Pandora's Box on your hands.

The ball/plunger type oil pumps are reliable, easy to service, and simple to check. Push the plungers downward into the body, holding your thumb over the inlet (upper) holes. Aim the pump away from yourself, for if all is well, oil will enthusiastically shoot from the bottom outlet holes. Maintaining thumb pressure on the inlet holes, slowly withdraw the plungers. When they are almost at the end of their maximum travel, release them, when they should "snap" back down due to vacuum. If they fail to do so, either plunger to body clearance is excessive—replace the whole unit—or there is dirt obstructing the ball valve seat(s), which can be corrected. The ball-and-plunger type pump is inexpensive, but gear-type units can be very costly. The most exorbitantly priced oil pump on the

market, however, is a worn or defective one. This type likes to "eat" engines. Don't make the mistake of feeding it.

Timing gear on the British Twins requires special extractor tools to remove. The Triumph cam gear wheels can be removed by use of the Z-89 Cam Gear Puller tool; if the cams themselves aren't going to be replaced, nor their timing changed, they can be left mounted in the cam gears. Don't try to remove these gears without the factory puller. You will damage the casings and bushings. The price of the tool is about $22.00, complete with adaptors, and fits the three-cylinder models marketed by both BSA and Triumph, in addition to all Triumph twins, regardless of the year. The cam gear retaining nuts on these are of a left-hand thread; the crankshaft nut is a right-hand thread. A puller is available to remove the crankshaft pinion gear, but although its use is advisable, it can be gotten around.

BSA cams are also a keyed fit on the gear, and may, like the Triumph, be left mounted in the event the cam is not going to be replaced. The small, usually tight fitting Woodruff keys on the camshaft ends should be removed with the aid of a pair of six-inch diagonal cutters. In removing the retaining nuts from the timing gear, the left-hand side of the crankshaft may be held with an adjustable wrench, on

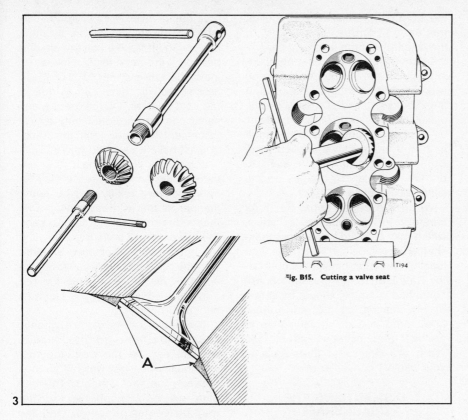

Fig. B15. Cutting a valve seat

1. Take an inventory of the engine parts before you start repairing and replacing. Sometimes you will find the solution to a mechanical problem came from a missing shim or washer.

2. Visual inspection of the valves can tell you how each cylinder was performing prior to teardown.

3. Valve reseating can be done with special hand tools if necessary. A pocketed valve can mean new seats.

4. Not enough can be said about proper valve and head repair. Cleaning and polishing can add horsepower, improve cooling and insure longer engine life. Crack or flaws will stand out also.

the splined portion. Check your shop manual carefully and closely with regard to these procedures. If you don't have, and don't wish to purchase the special extractor tools required, the cases can be split, taken to the dealers and the cam wheels removed there.

Now, remove all engine casing nuts, bolts, and studs. It is a good idea to keep them together with their washers by threading the associated nuts loosely back onto their corresponding bolt or stud. Not only will this prevent their confusion later on, but it will also save time when cleaning.

Lifting the cylinders off is a straightforward enough operation, requiring only removal of the base nuts. Keep these together by stringing them all onto a piece of wire. Rotate the crankshaft until the piston(s) are at top center before lifting the barrels.

When the bottom of the piston skirt appears at the bottom of the cylinder, position a couple of rags around the rod; if you intend to split the cases, this will prevent damage to the rod surfaces. In the event you are only doing a "top end job," the rags will stop metal particles (such as broken ring fragments) from getting into the "lower end."

Occasionally pistons are seized in the bores, and the barrels refuse to budge. This situation is a bad one at times, and generally calls for experienced hands, as improper technique in removal will cause expensive damage. We assume, however, that you are aware of your own limitations, in addition to the price of a new cylinder assembly. In light of this, we advise the *judicious* use of force. Before using force of *any* nature in this predicament, heat the cylinder barrels

thoroughly, using a propane torch on the fins. Try to heat evenly, keeping the flame moving, and working all around the outside of the cylinder. Don't try to heat the inside of the bore. As the cylinder warms up, squirt generous quantities of a penetrating oil, such as WD-40, into the bore. Continue this as you heat, if possible until the top of the piston is completely covered, the idea being, of course, that the cylinder will expand a bit, enabling the oil to seep down and help free the piston. Following this treatment, and before the cylinder cools, run the crankshaft end nut onto the threads, and use a wrench, ratchet and socket, or breaker bar to rotate the crankshaft, freeing the piston. If this effort bears no fruit, have a friend place a piece of suitable wood or other soft material on the top of the piston. A hammer may be vigorously applied to the wood by your cohort, while you exert pressure on the crank nut. Naturally, this is assuming that the piston is in an "after top dead center" position, or you'll be rotating in an upward direction while he's banging down, in which event you'll need to apply your torquing efforts to the left-hand side crank nut, providing it is of a right-hand thread.

It is essential that you avoid using levers, screwdrivers or the like to pry the barrels up. The damage which these items inflict on the machined crankcase mouth surfaces causes oil leakage at this joint. Similarly, hammering on the fins with anything harder than the palm of your hand is not recommended.

With the cylinders removed and cleaned in solvent, examine the bores very carefully, together with the piston skirts. If there are any marks or galling on the areas below the wrist pin holes on the skirt, or above them, on the ring lands, the possibility of a bent rod or excessive crankshaft end play must be investigated. The latter will be discussed in the section dealing with cranks. Rod bend can be detected by the use of a special slotted steel surface plate, or a pair of dead flat parallel bars placed across the crankcase mouth and positioned perpendicularly to the wrist pin. Rotate the crank to bring the bottom of the piston into contact with the bars. Rod bend will be indicated by the gap on either side. An alternative method is to remove the piston, reinsert the wrist pin, and repeat.

One of the leading causes of bent

FOUR-STROKE

rods is mishandling during piston removal, since they seldom bend during normal service. To prevent this happening, we recommend these techniques: First, remove the circlips, using small needle-nose pliers, or a screwdriver of the jeweler's type. Pry carefully—if of the spring wire type—partially blocking the wrist pin hole with the thumb of one hand to prevent the circlip springing out and getting lost. Seeger-type clips, (internal locking ring type) are easier to remove: insert a pair of needle-nosed plier tips into the holes in the ears, squeeze together to contract, and pull out.

If there is a possibility the pistons will be reused, mark them accordingly so they'll go back into the same bores. (Note: some pistons are of the offset wrist pin type. These are usually stamped on top with an arrow indicating the front. It is a good idea, regardless, to make a mark on the front side of the piston crown so there will be no mistake in reassembly.)

Now, push on the wrist pin with your fingers; it may be a loose enough fit to come out in this manner. If not, using a propane torch, heat the piston on the top, moving the flame about in a circular pattern. With the piston warmed up, the pin should be an easy push out; if not, have someone support the piston solidly on one side, and a few taps on a drift with a plastic mallet should produce results. Never use more force than is necessary, as hammering can easily bend a rod. Wrist pin removal tools are available for tough cases, but are really seldom used, even in shops.

SPLITTING THE CASES

With the pistons now off, we are ready to split the cases. Check carefully to be sure there are no studs or bolts remaining which would prevent the cases from parting. Triumph twins have two small screws located just below the cylinder base surface surrounding the tappet guide block opening, which must be removed. It is worth mentioning that these screws are left out when using the 48-inch kits marketed by Webco, Inc. as they prevent the larger barrel flange from passing through, and may damage the cylinders.

In most instances the cases will part readily, when held six inches above the work bench (or a wooden block) and brought down sharply, striking

the left-hand crankshaft end against the bench. If this doesn't do it, thoroughly heat the left-hand case in the vicinity of the main bearing housing, and repeat the procedure. In no event should a hammer be applied to the crankshaft end. A heavy plastic mallet may be used in stubborn cases, or a piece of wood held to the shaft end, and sharp blows applied to it. Do not use screwdrivers or levers to pry the cases apart; gouges on the seam faces cause oil leaks.

When the cases separate, look carefully for any spacers or shims which may be used to control crankshaft end play. Be certain to note their location, and don't mix them up! Harley-Davidson bearings, which are contained in cages, should be immediately cleaned, coated with grease, and stored in such a manner as to prevent them being mixed or lost. Wash the cases out thoroughly at your earliest convenience.

DISMANTLING THE CRANKSHAFT

Sandwich-type crankshafts, such as the Harley-Davidson and single-cylinder types, which have roller bearing big ends, are no job for anyone without equipment and experience; this chore is best "farmed out" to a competent person. Rod shake can be checked, but should only be done after thoroughly cleaning the "big end" bearing, lest the oil hide a bit of play—which it will. Either immerse the whole assembly in solvent, or use a squirt can containing solvent. Most assemblies call for some side play in the rods (verify this in the manual), but any "up and down" shake indicates the need for servicing. Be extremely cautious when handling the crankshaft assembly, as a

hard bump—even against wood—can cause misalignment of the flywheel halves. Squirt fresh oil on the big end bearing if the need for service is not indicated. Leaving the old oil on these assemblies will cause pitting, due to the acid content. Corrosion of these items can be corrected only by replacement. If all is well with the crank, at least have it checked for run-out.

Some later singles have a plain-bearing big end, and these may be serviced very easily, in the same manner as the twin assemblies. Dismantle the rods, taking care to keep the rod nuts and bolts together, and the bottom cap assemblies together with the rod which they came off. It's a good idea to reassemble the rod after removal, screwing the cap nuts back up finger tight.

The plug at the end of the flywheels, situated on the right-hand wedge section, can be removed, together with the flywheel bolt which is located between the two journals. The end plug—one on Triumph, two on BSA, may be center punched. Drill the center punch marks with a ⅛-inch drill bit to a depth of ⅛-inch. Rarely, if ever, will a screwdriver loosen them; the use of an impact wrench is called for, if only the hand type, together

1. Pay particular attention to the condition of the valve train. If many miles are on the machine camshaft(s) and drive system will wear out.

2. Retaining clips for the piston pin must have good spring tension and fit in their grooves. Remove all carbon and clean the ring grooves.

3. Check inside the piston for signs of fatigue or small hairline cracks if they are to be reused. Clear oil holes.

4. Replacing the small end bushing can be done with a socket or large tube, nut and bolt and new bush. New bushing drives out old while seating itself. Can be done in vice also.

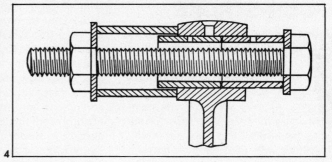

with a "drag link bit." The sludge trap within will, no doubt, be loaded with some nasty looking muck; and can be withdrawn by use of a hooked rod or a large "E-Z out" extractor. Clean every last bit of sludge out of the trap, but don't reassemble as yet, for if the crankshaft must be ground to an undersize, and undersized rod bearings used, it will have to be cleaned again to remove metal particles, and finally blasted through with air pressure, along with the oil passageways.

MEASUREMENT AND INSPECTION

All moving parts must now be checked closely for wear. This is where the inexperienced mechanic frequently comes unknowingly to grief, and often re-uses parts which "don't look too bad," but will cause knocks and rattles. The crankshaft journals should be carefully miked, working around the journal to be sure it is not out of round—a thousandth or so may be all right, but go by the manual. If you are measuring yourself, check and double check all readings. You will at least need to know what size the journals currently are, so you can obtain the correct size rod inserts—don't reuse the old ones regardless of what they look like, it is poor economy. In the event machining of the journals is indicated, expect to pay about $10.00 to $15.00 for the service. BSA twins and singles have a bushing fitted on the right-hand side of the crank. The diameter of the journal at this point should be measured; if need be, it too can be ground to an undersize, though this is not a prevalent condition until the machine has seen many, many miles.

All bushings in the crankcase should be checked, paying careful attention to the BSA right-hand main bushing. Wear at this point will cause a noisy engine, and poor oil pressure. All measurement readings should be written down as they are taken, and compared with factory specifications.

Cam bushings should be checked with a telescopic snap gauge and micrometer, the cam bearing journals checked, and the difference will be the clearance. Wiggling the cam inside the bushing is a poor method of checking, as even a good fit will show some sign of "wiggle." Ball and roller bearings should be examined for roughness and pitting. Wash them in clean solvent, holding them in a horizontal position while rotating the inner races back and forth. Finally, air blast them, and if they are all right, apply a coating of fresh oil.

Camshaft journals should show no signs of galling or scoring; the lobes should show no signs of "flats," which would call for replacement. Tappet feet may evince slight signs of wear, but any cracks in the material on the feet again indicate the need to replace. Check the tops of the tappets—if they are ball shaped (e.g. Triumph, BSA) look for flat spots, as even the smallest of these will wreak havoc with pushrod adjustments later on. Harley-Davidson favors the roller tappet; feel for any up-and-down play, evidence of which necessitates replacement of the bearing. The tappet itself is reusable providing there is no serious wear or damage to the cupped tops. Place the tappet in the guide block, and feel for "slop." The clearances here are only .001-inch or so (check the book). Accurate measurement requires the use of an expanding ball type gauge or a telescopic snap gauge and a one-inch micrometer. Measure the tappet bore in the guide block, and the tappet stem. Overlooking these items will mean differences in the cam timing, and a noisy, inefficient motor.

Working our way up, as it were, examine the pushrod ends for chipped cups, cracks, flat spots (if the ball type), and bend, which may be determined by rolling the pushrod on a dead flat surface, such as a piece of glass. Needless to say, any sign of the above mentioned deformities will require replacement.

The cylinder barrels must be measured with an inside micrometer. Measure the base of the cylinder first, in the front to rear plane, i.e., at a 90-degree angle to the wrist pin, since this is where maximum wear occurs. Note the reading at the bottom. Invert the cylinder, and take a reading just below the ridge at the very top. Read again, ¼-inch down from that, writing the readings down as you go; repeat the readings every ¼-inch for the first inch, as this is the area of maximum wear in the cylinder. Subtracting the bottom reading from the maximum diameter read at the top gives the amount the cylinder is "tapered." Allowable taper varies from make to make, so consult your manual here. Measure the piston skirt with an appropriate outside micrometer at the points shown in the photos. Measure the inside micrometer with the outside micrometer, to give the piston clearance accurately. Subtract the skirt dimension reading from this, and the result, of course, is the clearance. Whether or not the old pistons can be reused, or if boring is necessary, may be determined by consultation with your private "expert," namely the shop manual. Remember that excessive piston clearances cause the piston to tilt at top center, cocking the rings and exposing them partially to the fury of the combustion.

You should be placing all the worn out or bad parts together, and listing them as you go along. Oversized pistons are obtainable at your dealer, and if boring is needed, you will need to take the new pistons together with the cylinders to the machinist you select. It is advisable to take everything that needs machining, e.g., crankshaft, cylinders, heads, and so forth, together. This will save you legwork, a necessary and time consuming part of any overhaul.

Try to obtain all your parts in one trip. You will need your list for this to make matters easier for you and your dealer's parts man. Don't forget to write down the year, model, and

FOUR-STROKE

serial number of your machine, to enable them to help you better. It is a good time to check on any possible modifications while you are parts shopping, so you may update your engine, thereby adding to the reliability of your machine. Take all the engine seals and special lockwashers with you, so they may be correctly replaced in your parts order. It is inadvisable to reuse these items, as their cost is not high. Don't forget to obtain all new gaskets, cylinder head gasket included. Most manufacturers provide a ''Full Overhaul Gasket Set.'' Jointing compound can be obtained from your dealer, or he can recommend the right type for use on your motor.

BUSHING AND BEARING REMOVAL

If your measurements have indicated some bad bearings or bushings which will need to be replaced, you may have your dealer perform this chore for you. If not, the following instructions will tell you how to do it.

In the case of ''blind end bushings,'' such as the timing cover bushings in Harley-Davidsons, and the left-hand cam bushes in the BSA and Triumph, a tap will be needed, together with a suitable bolt of the same thread. These are usually obtainable from used tool stores, surplus outlets, etc. Tap the bushings to be removed, heat the engine crankcase in an oven at 400 degrees for about 20 minutes. The hot case can be placed on the bench, and the bolt threaded into the bushing. Clamp the head of the bolt firmly in your bench vise, and, using a plastic mallet, tap the case away, leaving the bushing and bolt in the vise. Repeat as necessary. The new bushing, which can be placed in the freezer compartment of your refrigerator while the case is heating, can now be driven in carefully. Be sure to line up the oil feed holes. If the old bushing was a loose fit in the case, some Loc-Tite ''Bearing Mount'' can be used to coat the outer diameter of the new bushing prior to installation. This will prevent the new bush from becoming loose in its housing.

Ball bearing mains will either fall out or tap out very easily once the case has been given the heat treatment. The outer races of the two-piece roller style bearings, however, will require drilling three holes in the case, 120 degrees apart, and in line with the

edge of the race. After heating, a pin punch can be applied alternately to the race through the holes, working it out in easy stages. At any rate, under no circumstances should you ever drive a bearing or bush out of a cold case. You will gall the housing and cause looseness between the bearing and the housing. If this is already in evidence, apply Loc-Tite Bearing Mount, and keep your fingers crossed. Peening the metal at the bearing edge will also help retain a bearing in a loose housing, but we don't recommend this on a good fitting setup.

A frequently overlooked bushing in the unit construction engines is the fourth gear bushing in the transmission. The gear must be removed to replace this bushing, but if it is worn, it is advisable to do it now. This is the one that causes all that oil to drip out of the transmission housing when the motorcycle is parked on the side stand.

Pre-1963 Triumph motorcycles have an oil feed bushing in the timing

cover. It should be checked, and replaced if necessary. Overlooking this will cause lower end problems and ''wet-sumping,'' which means oil blowing all over the place due to an overloaded lower end. One result of this is usually hours spent trying to find out what's wrong with the ''darn oil pump,'' when the only thing wrong with the oil pump is that it just can't keep up with the ''flood'' from the high pressure at the bushing. These bushings are supplied in undersize, allowing the nose on the right end of the crank to be machined to suit. Alternatively, the bush can be reamed out if the crank end is in good shape.

Having replaced any bushings, consult the manual. They may have to be ''line-reamed,'' a dealer operation. These reamers are very expensive. Cam bushings in practically all engines require line reaming after replacement. This assures proper clearance and alignment and prevents stress.

When dealing with the clearances in your engine, don't be taken in by the ''loose ones go fast'' bit. You are not building a racing machine (presumably), and loose fits will only result in a noisy, short-lived engine. However, follow the factory standards. You will obtain no more out of your motor than you put into it.

CYLINDER SERVICING

If your cylinders require boring (prices for which range from $5.00 to $10.00 per ''hole'') you may want to finish hone them to suit your own taste. Boring usually leaves a razor sharp edge at the top of the barrel.

This must be dressed off with a small file. Left on, it will cause pre-ignition, as will any sharp edge in a combustion chamber.

Honing can be done with a medium to fine grit set of honing stones. Don't clamp the cylinders themselves directly into a vise. An old metal bracket, or suitable jig, should be bolted to the cylinder base stud holes, or other convenient place, and then clamped into the vise. Use kerosene or solvent while honing, keeping the cylinder as wet as possible. Use steady even strokes, about 50 per minute, and keep the hone moving up and down while it is in the cylinder. When stopping to check, always stop at the end of a stroke, with the honer blades partially protruding from the cylinder. Now they can be squeezed together with one hand, and the assembly pulled out with the other. Never drag the stones out of the barrel. A nice, even cross-hatch pattern should be left on the cylinder bore, with no deep scratches in evidence.

After honing, wash the cylinder thoroughly in hot soapy water. Cleaning in solvent after boring or honing only serves to embed fine metal particles in the bore. After thoroughly drying the cylinder with a soft cloth, smear or spray a thin film of oil on the new surface.

Before putting the cylinders away, check the ring gap. This is done with the new rings. Place one at a time in

1. Plan on needing precision measuring instruments. An inside micrometer will be required to measure cylinder bore size for piston fit.

2. Crankshaft care is critical. Keep journals covered with oil film to protect from damaging corrosion.

3. If you aren't sure of what you are doing take the crank to a competent dealer for repair. He will have all the right tools and inside dope. Hold tolerances recommended by factory.

3

the base of the cylinder in which it is to be used. Square up the ring in the bore using the bottom of the piston. Check the gap with a feeler blade. Your service manual will give the recommended ring gap, but a good rule of thumb is to use .005-inch for every inch of bore. If the gap is less than desired, a thin file clamped in a vise will rectify matters quickly. Hold the ring carefully between the thumb and forefingers, press gently to the file, and stroke. Cut on one stroke, and release pressure on the back stroke. Check frequently in the bore, and try to keep the ends as even as possible. If you go a bit too far, don't worry; loose end gaps are far better than tight ones. Clean the ring ends of filings before placing in the bore to check. Keep the rings sorted to prevent their being eventually mounted into the wrong bore. And be very careful when handling the rings, particularly the oil control rings. They are brittle and can break very easily.

In the event you are going to use your old pistons, they should be decarbonized, and the ring grooves cleaned. The best way to do this is to have them "glass blasted," or "vapor honed." Both terms describe the same process, which is similar to sand blasting, but incorporates the use of minute glass beads. This process is inexpensive—about $1.50 per piston—and will leave them in "like new" condition. The vapor hone treatment leaves no gouges in the critical ring grooves, nor scratch marks on the piston crown. Lacking this, an old ring can be used to clean the ring grooves of accumulated carbon. Be sure you don't damage the ring lands by taking metal along with the carbon. The old wrist pins also should be checked in the event they are going to see further duty. If they are "blued" in the areas where they enter the piston, they should be replaced, as this means they are soft.

The wrist pin bushings in the rods can be checked at this point, by use of "feel," or preferably, a telescopic gauge and micrometer. Measuring their inner diameter, and comparing to the measurement of the wrist pin will give the clearance. Ordinarily, this is in the vicinity of .001-inch or so. Any "rock" felt on the wrist pin when placed in the rod, would indicate the need for replacement.

Replacing wrist pin bushings is a job best left to the "shop," but "if you gotta," the procedure is thus: Mount the rod body in a vise, wrapped tightly

in a rag. With the new bushing ready to go, obtain a socket, which will fit around the wrist pin bushing, and more than accommodate its length. Run a long, threaded bolt through the socket. Heat the end of the rod well with a propane torch; when warm, position the wrist pin in the rod bushing, so its end is just flush with the edge of the rod bushing. Place the new bushing on the portion of the wrist pin which is protruding. Position the socket on the other end of the rod, being sure its edges are not going to foul the wrist pin bush as it comes out. Run the bolt through the socket, wrist pin and bushings, so that its end protrudes beyond the new bushing. Place a flat washer over the bolt end, thread a nut onto the bolt end, and begin tightening the nut down on the bolt. It will force the new bush in, and the old bush out into the socket portion. The wrist pin will maintain the alignment of the new bushing as it goes in. Wrist pin bushing removal tools may be purchased at your dealer, and are reasonably priced.

After fitting the new bushing, final reaming may be necessary, along with drilling a hole at the top—in most instances—to assure lubrication. Most auto machine shops can hone the pin bushings to a precise fit for a reasonable charge.

SERVICING THE CYLINDER HEAD

The most important performance component of the engine, is the cylinder head. Regardless of how well done the engine is from the "head gasket down," the condition of the head, and the manner in which it is serviced can mean the difference between a smooth running or poor performing engine. Cylinder head maintenance is where most inexperienced mechanics fail. Haphazard work will result in poor performance. Since the head, per se, is relatively uncomplicated, it pays to be attentive to every involved detail. To start things off correctly, a tool can be fabricated out of some ½-inch round stock and an old spark plug. Knock all the guts out of the spark plug body, taking care not to damage the threads. Place the tool into the degutted plug body, and weld up. These tools are also available over the counter as an accessory item. A valve spring compressor—$6.00—is a must. The type marketed by Triumph-BSA dealers will take care of

FOUR-STROKE

most heads, including the Harley-Davidson, though H-D has their own, more expensive—but better—unit.

Thread the head holding tool into the spark plug hole, and clamp the end of it tightly in a vise. Never clamp the head in a vise or you will damage it. Position the compressor tool with its yoke on the valve collar, its bolt point on the valve head. Tighten it up till it is firmly in contact with the valve collar. Slowly tighten a bit more, and observe the collar to stem area. If the tool seems to be tightening with no indication of the collar compressing, assist matters with a sharp whack on the end of the compressor tool. This should free the keepers and collar, and the tool can be screwed down further till the keepers have enough space to come out. If you were to continue compressing the tool on a stuck collar/keeper assembly, you would bend the tool arbor.

A pencil magnet is handy for withdrawing the valve keepers, once the collar and spring assembly is compressed. Use small strips of plastic tape to keep the keepers paired. With the keepers withdrawn, release the spring and collar assembly, withdraw the valve, and repeat the procedure on the other valves. When all the valves have been removed, inspection and measurement may be immediately undertaken. Examine the valve stems for galling, and measure them with a one-inch mike. Most British valves are .309-inch on the stem. The ball gauge must be used on the valve guides, although extreme wear can be felt by wiggling the valve in the guide. Mike the ball gauge, and subtract the reading from the valve stem. Consult the manual to see if you are within factory tolerances. If the clearance borderlines on the maximum allowable by the factory, replace the worn valve guides and the valves if necessary. By the time valve stems are worn any appreciable amount, you can count on replacing the guides. Now examine the valve faces. They may need to be machine faced. Be sure there is enough material on them to allow facing without leaving a razor edge. If not, replace the valve(s).

Having determined what will be needed partswise, the best way to clean the head is the glass beading (vapor honing) process. In lieu of this, chip the heavy carbon deposits away carefully, with a screwdriver blade.

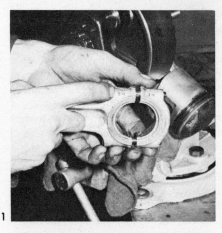

Try not to gouge the aluminum. Finish the job with a soft wire brush and drill motor. Clean the ports well, and particularly around the valve guides. Additionally remove the carbon from that part of the guide which protrudes into the port. If you try to drive the guides out without doing this, you will ruin the valve guide bore; just like driving a rat-tail file through.

Place the clean head in an oven, give it the 25 minutes at 400 degrees routine, then remove. You will need a valve guide punch to drive the guides out, and the preferred method is to have someone hold the head with heavy rags or welder's gloves while you drive the guides out. This will prevent shock damage to the spark plug threads—where the head held in the vise with the tool. The new valve guides should be installed immediately. Having them on ice or in the refrigerator while the head is heating will help matters. However, if the old valve guides were very loose coming out, oversized valve guides will need to be fitted. If the old valve guides were already oversized, they will of course need to be replaced by ones with a larger outside diameter. Oversized valve guides may be distinguished by small rings machined into their upper section. As a rule, each machined mark indicates .001-inch oversize, but in some instances represents .002-inch over. Your dealer can advise you on this.

New valve guides necessitate grinding the valve seats to true the seat to the guide, making them concentric. This requires an expensive hard seat grinder, which relegates this chore to a shop.

With the seats reground, and the valves faced (or replaced with new ones) the head may be secured in the vise with the head tool. Use valve grinding compound, and lap each valve to its seat individually. Apply

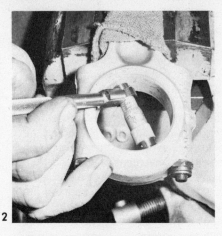

1. Connecting rod and cap must be kept paired. They should be numbered or punched for coding. If not plan on doing it. Identifies side of cap.

2. Before replacing babbitt place cap on rod and torque nuts to factory specs. Measure with inside mike.

3. Keep your working area spotless during crankshaft work. A torque wrench, preferably reading in both foot and inch pounds, is an absolute necessity.

4. Before assembled pre-lube all parts with oil film. Pressed together crank assemblies will require truing to eliminate excessive run out. Will require centers or 'V' blocks.

small dabs of fine grade compound to each valve face in turn, place the guide in position, and with a lapping tool, rotate in a back and forth manner to cover 180 degrees. If, for one reason or another the valve lapping tools available don't work out too well for you, place an eight-inch long piece of PVC or rubber tubing onto the valve stem and, using the flats of your hands to oscillate the tubing, continue with the lapping process. Remove the valve now and then, clean the compound off with a rag, and observe the seat. A thin grey line should appear, and should be even throughout. Continue lapping as needed to obtain this effect. As each valve is lapped to its seat, label it to prevent confusion. After all of the valves have been lapped in this manner, wash all traces of grinding compound out of the ports, and air blast dry or use soft cloth for the purpose.

Valve spring pack, or the seated height of the valve spring, which controls its tension, is normally thought to be in the realm of speedwork. However, it is just as important to the stock motorcycle.

Install each valve, in its turn, and assemble the collars and keepers, using the inner spring only. British motorcycle owners can use a carburetor slide spring for the purpose.

Measure the distance between the underside of the upper collar, and the upper face of the bottom collar. Compare this to the data in your manual. If it's not contained in the manual, consult your dealer. If the ''pack length'' is excessive, check the hole in the valve spring collar where the keepers abut. If it is worn, or enlarged, it will need to be replaced. Generally, the surplus height is from the seat having been ground. Valve spring shims of the appropriate thickness can be obtained to correct the situation. In the case of Triumph-BSA, the discs from Bendix bicycle brakes turn the trick. If you are fitting an oversized valve to compensate a pocketed valve seat, you may be a bit shy on spring height. The difference will have to be machined off the valve stem, where the keepers abut.

Regarding the matter of valve springs, these are certainly due to be replaced by the time the machine needed an overhaul, but their tension can be checked on a spring tester. The book gives free length specifications on the springs, but this is by no means a definite indication that they are good. If in doubt, replace. The best bet for new valve springs for British models are the S&W, marketed by Webco. They are a progressive-wound spring, and must be installed with the close wound coil to the bottom. Additionally, they may require a valve spring pack different than stock, in which case shimming is in order. Specifications for the model are included with the springs.

After determining the appropriate shimming required, assemble each valve in turn. Don't neglect to lubricate the valve stems. With the head all together, wrap it carefully, and store it away from dust, grit or dirt.

CRANKSHAFT ASSEMBLY

Having ascertained the needs of the lower end, the flywheels hopefully are ready to go. If they were machined or balanced, they will need to be super-clean. The new rod inserts should be at hand, and ready to go. If there were any nicks or scratches inflicted on the rods, they can be polished out. The rod nuts and their special nuts should be in good shape. On older models with many miles, they are inexpensive to replace considering their importance. Place the new inserts in the upper and lower rod sections. There is a small recessed portion in rod and cap, with a correlating raised section on the back of the insert, to retain these in position. The notch on each should be opposite the correlating notch on the mating portion.

Carefully, and with clean hands, smear a thin film of heavy viscosity oil on the journal. Place the rod bolts in position in the upper rod, taking note of the offset heads at the top, which must be positioned at 90 degrees to the rod. Before placing the upper section in position on the journal, make a final check of the rod insert. Is it seated properly? Is there any lint or dirt specks on it? If so, rectify. Place the rod down on the journal. Hold it firmly in position with one hand, bring the bottom rod cap and insert assembly into position. These usually have dots, to ensure they aren't put on wrong. Make sure the section with the center punched dot aligns on the same side as the mating dot on the aluminum upper portion of the rod. You may have to tap the cap gently with a plastic mallet as the bolts are a snug fit. When it makes contact with the journal, thread the nuts onto the cap bolts. Ratchet them down to about five ft.-lbs. of torque: just ''wrist tight.'' There are two procedures of assembly from this point to assure correct tension. One is to ''mike'' the bolt stretch to a .004-.005-inch figure (check your manual) the other is to use a torque wrench. Torque each side five ft.-lbs. at a time. After each increase, check the rod to be sure it is still rotating quite easily on the journal with no sign of ''drag.'' From 28 to 32 ft.-lbs. will take care of most. With the rod finally torqued, it should still be quite free to rotate on the shaft (journal) with no drag other than the minute amount caused by the heavy lubricant. If the rod locks at any time during the proceedings, remove it and check the journal all around for nicks or other abnormal markings. The rod inserts also can possibly be in error. Example: Undersized inserts for a standard journal. Don't ever file the rod caps or be tempted to ''scrape'' the insert bearing; you will come to grief. Hopefully, all will be well, and the procedure may be repeated on the other side. Reassemble the cleaned sludge trap. Use Loc-Tite on the flywheel bolt between the rod journals. Be sure you torque this bolt to the recommended figure, normally circa 45 ft-lbs. Replace the sludge trap plug. If the slot in it is gouged or in bad shape use a new one, to make future removal easier. Impact it tightly, and center punch it at the seam to prevent the possibility of it coming loose at any time.

Now is the time to install any seals which mount in the crankcase. A slight chamfer on the aluminum case edge will expedite installation. In case the seal is of the lipped spring type, assemble with the spring facing the pressure side, or the highest pressure side. Left-hand crankcase, main seals face the lower end and crankcase, as naturally it contains far more pressure than the primary. If you have knife- or file-chamfered the seal housing edge, you will have to clean out the metal filings, then wipe or air blast (the latter preferable).

Before assembling the crankcases new bearings and/or races will have to be installed, a process which is practically the reverse of dismantlement. This of course, assuming that you haven't already done so. Place the left-hand case down, and insert

3

4

FOUR-STROKE

only the crankshaft. Run three or four through bolts in and tighten securely. Now, check the crankshaft end play.

The manual gives tips on this. A simple jig can be made up to accomplish the job. Excessive end play can be measured, noted, and corrected by the use of an appropriate size shim, placed between the flywheel and the crankcase. Insufficient play may necessitate the removal of an existing shim. This is common with BSA, especially when a new right-hand main bush has been fitted. Triumph doesn't ordinarily require it, but; if the need is apparent, do it.

Harley-Davidson lower ends are best farmed out to a competent dealer with the equipment to do the job. You can, however, change the pin bushes if necessary. Even most dealers farm out crucial machine work, so don't try to do a job yourself if you don't have the experience or equipment.

Harley-Davidson end play should always be checked. There is no guarantee that it will be all right as is, or that it was correctly accomplished in the course of the last overhaul. Shims adjust H-D end play also.

The clean, left-hand engine "half" (case) should now be laid flat, and preferably supported in a crude 2x4-inch wood block jig. Coat the seam with jointing compound. There is no gasket on this junction. Don't coat the compound on, use sparingly to obtain a thin, even film on both surfaces. This will prevent "squish" dribbles on the inside of the case.

Harley bearings should be assembled with heavy grease, and, noting the location of the thrust washer, placed in the crankcase. Insert flywheels, assemble the right-hand bearing, lube, and install the left-hand case. Assemble through bolts and tighten.

Assemble British models in the same manner, with the exception that the cam(s) must be installed. Triumph and BSA have a crank breather disc and spring combination, which is placed at the bottom of the Triumph intake cam, and in the single left-hand cam bush common to the BSA. The spring mounts inside the disc, and the flat part of the disc faces down, toward the primary side of the bike. This disc has two "ears" or tabs, which engage slots in the camshaft to provide drive. Squirt oil into the bush and on the cam. Insert the cam, with the driving slots aligned with the disc's

ears. In the event the cam is still attached to the camwheel or sprocket, rotate the latter to achieve a close "eyeball" alignment. Lubricate the bearings, airblast all the oil passageways, and check the air tightness of the sump pickup tube in the right case (blow through the bottom of the tube, cover the hole at the oil pump mount where the pressure is blowing out, then suck on the tube. It should be positively air tight).

Assemble the right hand case. We should mention that late ('63 up) Triumph owners, who may have fitted a cam of more radical specs, should ensure that the exhaust cam contains the small slotted disc which drives the tachometer. If not, fit one. They are very inexpensive.

With the right-hand case in position (a slight assist with a light plastic mallet may be necessary) tighten the securing bolts immediately. If the upper end is not to be assembled right away cover the crankcase mouth.

CYLINDER ASSEMBLY

Check the rings before assembling. Most have a tapered, or beveled inside edge, which always faces the top. This taper, or bevel if you prefer, allows high pressure combustion gases to pass behind the ring, and force it outward against the cylinder wall. Chrome rings, when provided, are fitted to the top land alone.

Piston assembly is the reverse of removal, including heating the piston when necessary. The wrist pin bush, piston bosses, and pin should be smeared with oil before assembling. If you are replacing the pistons, and using a set of forged aluminum ones, it is imperative that the wrist pin

clearance in the pistons will be checked; these call for a loose fit. Check the specs which came with the piston assembly; they will detail the involved elements. In assembling the cylinders, you should use ring compressors. Here are a few assembly hints: Space the ring gap openings 120 degrees apart. Place the top ring gap at the furthest point from the two main sources of heat, namely, the spark plug and the exhaust valve. In the Triumph, as an example, the top gap faces the inlet pushrod cover. BSA top rings face 7:00 o'clock on the right-hand side, and 5:00 o'clock on the left-hand side, looking down at the bores. The theory is to keep these gaps to the coolest part of the cylinder. Despite the "rings spinning" theory, this method has worked well for us over the last 10 years. Lubricate the piston skirts, and install the base gaskets, lightly coating them with grease. Install cylinders.

The rest of the reassembly is straightforward, and outlined in your shop manual. With your bits and bolts clean and assorted, you should have a minimum of trouble. The best policy in reassembling is this: Don't hurry. Timing side may be assembled as per directions. Triumph owners can benefit immensely from "degreeing the cams in," or "cam tuning" as it is called. This process enables the Triumph owner to precisely set the timing on both cams, via the three keyway cam gears make this possible. Consult your dealer.

In reassembling gears to keyed shafts, be certain the gear or wheel will fit with no problem. Due to "pinch," the back edge of the key slot may have to be relieved a bit with a small file. Keys should fit well in the

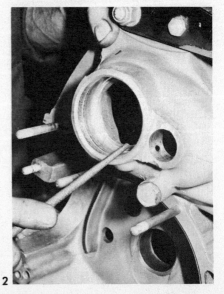

1

2

shafts, and be tapped down firmly into position. If they are hard to get on, lightly sand the edges of them, as the more tight fitting examples tend to expand when initially removed.

PERFORMANCE PARTS

Pistons: When fitting higher compression pistons in place of stock, run the piston clearances a little looser. Higher compression means more heat and heat causes seizure. The timing must be retarded because combustion efficiency is higher, and combustion is quicker. The object is to reduce the negative work on the piston, as well as provide maximum combustion. It is especially important to time both cylinders, or at least check the timing on both. If one is correct, the other advanced, the advanced side can cause just as much trouble as if both were advanced.

Valve-to-piston clearance will have to be verified. This is important, particularly if the cam profile has also been changed.

Carburetion has to be enriched to accommodate the higher compression. A lean fuel mixture causes seizures and "holed" pistons.

1. Engines like the Honda Four necessitate installing the crankshaft in the engine prior to rod replacement.

2. Replace all case bearings or bushings while the engine is apart. Cheap insurance. Smooth all cavities where burr may occur when old bearing is pressed out Clean filings out of cases.

3. Be sure that oil passage holes are in perfect alignment prior to installation. After pressed in clean out passages and de-burr. Pre-oil bushings.

4. Double check work by torquing to factory specs and checking clearance with Plastigage. After tightened make sure assembly will turn by hand.

Cams: Longer duration, higher lift cams are going to require head work. The valve train should—and in cases must—be lightened to reduce inertial loads. They also require different spring pack techniques, to increase valve spring control. Additionally, clearance must be checked between the lower side of the upper collar, and the top of the valve guide. There is a possibility of the collar striking the guide; this will bend pushrods, and break rocker arms. Different pushrod adjustments will undoubtedly be called for. A free flowing exhaust system, of the right length and diameter will be essential, or the increase in valve lift and height will be wasted, if not a detractive factor. "Bigger" cams can require larger ports, valves and carburetion before they can become worth their salt. Remember that with modifications of this nature, you are narrowing the usable power range, and placing the power band further up in the rpm range. Factory cams of late model machines generally provide all the power you will ever be able to use. Follow the directions in the manual and this article, and you will have a superbly running machine.

FINAL ASSEMBLY

The carburetors should be boiled clean, reassembled, and installed, with preliminary adjustments. The oil tank, which should have been flushed, can be mounted, and the correctness of the oil line installation verified. Fill with the appropriate oil.

A half pint or so can now be poured in the lower end. In the British bikes this can be done via the rocker covers by filling the rocker housings on both sides. Harley Davidson products have a timing plug on the left-hand crank-case, through which oil may be poured. A half to a full teaspoon of oil may be poured into each cylinder through the spark plug hole. Gently rotate the kick starter to help some of this oil film on the cylinder walls.

With the gas tank installed, and the timing set, we are ready to start the engine. The battery may require charging. Verify the correctness and tightness of all ignition connections which should be checked, along with an examination for frayed wires.

When the engine is fired, it is going to smoke until the pump catches up with the excess in the sump.

Immediately check the return in the oil tank. This should take place within 30 seconds, otherwise, check your oil line connections, and try again. Run gently at first.

During the first 200 miles, you should baby the machine, but don't lug it. At the 250- to 300-mile mark, an oil change should be performed. Also, and more important, the cylinder base nuts should be retightened. Doing this requires readjustment of the valves.

Repeat the oil change at 700 miles, and again at 1000 miles, at which time a tune-up is in order. Carburetion will have been reset at each oil change interval. Plug readings should be taken from scratch to final break-in. A good idea is to take a compression reading when the machine is first started and warm. This should be noted for reference, and checked every 1000 miles or so.

Having followed the outlined time consuming procedures, you will *not* have to cross your fingers hoping your engine will run. It will. And it will run well and this is the reward of building your own motor.

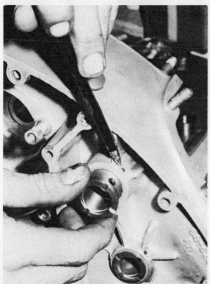

3

4

LUBRICATION: 2 STROKE & 4 STROKE

Regardless of what type of machine you own, its life depends on the correct use of the proper lubricants

BY PEPE ESTRADA

Few subjects have been so ignored in motorcycle publications as the ones we'll discuss in this article. Friction and lubrication is a universal subject. There is no part of the earth that is free of it. There is very little that man does to which it doesn't apply. Every area of mechanics relies on friction. Every machine needs lubrication. But for some reason this subject has been taboo for writers who treat other motorcycle subjects.

Physics is another subject that has been ignored, but rightly so, because physics and mathematics are beyond the scope of motorcycle publications, as is chemistry. We're going to treat the subject of friction and lubrication in a common-sense, useful way. Did you know that the highest possible friction between metals always occurs between two *highly polished* metal surfaces rubbing together? Did you know that friction between metal surfaces will be *reduced* if the surfaces are roughened up slightly? But not too rough. Did you know that surface friction is *lower* with a thick oil than with a thin oil? Did you know that friction *decreases* with faster speeds? That is to say, there is less friction at a high speed than at a low speed. Did you know that friction is a process of converting mechanical energy into heat energy? Did you know that high friction between metal surfaces is very similar to a welding process? Did you know the difference between the *real area* of contact and the apparent area of contact? When you look, for example, at one flat metal on another flat piece of metal the real area of contact between the two is actually but a tiny portion of the apparent area because only the high spots of one side touch only the high spots of the other side across the interface. These tiny spots of real contact are called junctions which join together in plastic formations that resist motion between the two surfaces.

The modern study of friction is barely 20 years old. It started in earnest during World War 2 when an-swers had to be known because of the urgency of the world situation at the time. We were fighting a war. Practical solutions, not classroom answers were needed. Ancient ideas have been modified and modernized in the past 20 years. Also, radioactivity has proved a valuable tool in determining the wear of materials. For example, radioactive pieces are assembled and then run. The highest resulting contamination of an oil will be with radioactive particles from the parts that are wearing the most.

GOOD OILS

Electron microscopes have come a long way in the last 20 years. Some 100,000 magnifications are now possible. It's important to be able to see what metal surfaces really look like up close—real close. Good oils and greases yield better looking surfaces after service. Poor lubricants can actually destroy rubbing surfaces in seconds.

It's not exactly easy to design a good oil. There are many steps along the way. Many oil additives are touchy since you're dealing with chemicals that prefer only certain combinations for best results. In this respect, an oil designer is like a superb chef (or should be).

Oils are classified four ways: Mineral, vegetable, animal and synthetic. Mineral oils are derived from petroleum crudes. Technically, these petroleum products fall in a category of chemicals called the saturated aliphatic hydrocarbons. The crude is refined by several methods into many divisions of light and heavy liquids. The light ends boil easily and become fuel fractions, while the heavy ends become lubricating oil and tar fractions. Ordinary pump gasoline is about 90 percent fuel, leaving 10 percent residual oils and heavy ends. The oil in gasoline serves to lubricate the upper walls, rings, and intake valves. A straight mineral oil is usually a high purity paraffin with no additives.

Vegetable oils are derived from present day plants. Examples are soybean oil and castor oil. Castor oil is often used because it forms a strong film on iron and steel surfaces. It also does not thin out too drastically at 210°F. However, it oxidizes badly

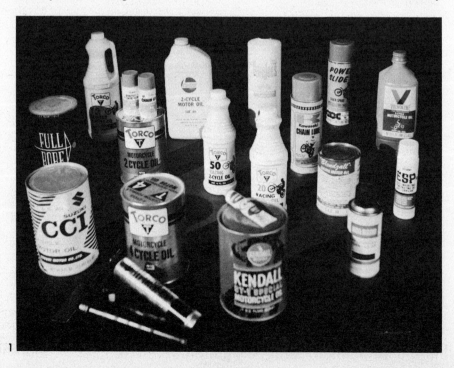

and often doesn't like blending with other oils. It seems modern day petroleum oils have put castor-based oils in the old rumble seat. Animal oils are quite useful, especially in gear lubes. Sperm oil has excellent anti-wear and high EP (Extreme Pressure) properties. It is used in most limited-slip differential lubricants. In fact, new applications for deodorized sperm oil are still being found. Does that sound fishy?

Synthetic oil is man-made. It is usually Polyalkylene Glycol based. Its chemistry is such that it is not highly reactive. This means synthetic oil does not easily oxidize, form sludge or leave carbon deposits. On the other hand, these oils lack EP resistance, form no absorbed film and exhibit only medium anti-wear properties. However synthetic oil is excellent in cosmetics, hydraulics, and as special solvents. Some synthetic oil compounds are advertised as being "non-greasy" or "dry," as opposed to "greasy kid stuff" which uses petroleum oil or jelly.

Some two-cycle engine oils are of the synthetic variety. There are practically no combustion chamber deposits. The exhaust is clean also. However, you should run about 13.0:1 premix ratio and open up the jets a little if you plan any hard running with these oils. For the remainder of this article, we'll be referring strictly to mineral oils because they make up 99 percent of all the oil sold in the world. So let's take a look at some of the properties of mineral oils.

VISCOSITY

By viscosity we mean the rate at which a fluid will pass through an orifice. The word viscosity when applied to oils has several synonyms: grade, weight and thickness. They mean about the same thing. A grade is a specific range of oil viscosity between

certain temperature limits. For example, the viscosity of 30 weight motor oil must fit definite specifications at 0°F, at 100°F, and at 210°F in order to be called 30 weight motor oil. These rigid specifications are actually state laws in most of the U.S. However, 80 weight oil could very easily be called a 30 weight oil because the two viscosity specifications are quite similar. The big difference in the two is the additive package of each oil. The 30 weight is designed for engines. The 80 weight is designed exclusively for gear boxes. A 75 weight gear oil has about the same viscosity range as 10 weight motor oil. So don't let the numbers fool you. Gear oil viscosity specs are on a different scale than the motor oils. In motorcycle gear boxes we strongly recom-

mend you use 80 weight gear oil rather than motor oil.

The load carrying ability of any oil is directly affected by the viscosity. A thin oil cannot resist high loads as well as a thick oil. For this reason it's vitally important to possess sufficiently high viscosity at high temperatures when an oil needs all the help it can have. A multigrade oil is one that fits the viscosity range of a light weight at 0°F but also fits the range of a heavy weight oil at 210°F. Such oils are very good in winter climates. Viscosity is an oil's best friend. Without it, oils would be squeezed out immediately and vaporized by high frictional heats. However, it does no good to have more viscosity than we need. Proper viscosity depends on loads and temperatures of the job.

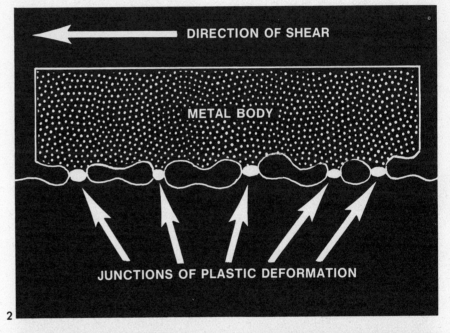

DIRECTION OF SHEAR

METAL BODY

JUNCTIONS OF PLASTIC DEFORMATION

2

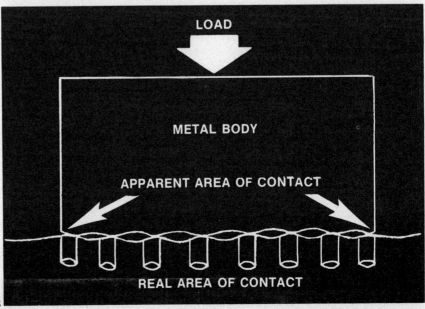

LOAD

METAL BODY

APPARENT AREA OF CONTACT

REAL AREA OF CONTACT

3

1. There is a reason for all of the different types of oils. Each one is best for its intended job.

2. Schematic of a metal body sliding on a metal surface. Only parts in contact are high spots (called junctions), which join like pieces of clay. As the body moves, junctions are broken and reformed. Friction heat is created at these tiny, but numerous high spots.

3. A microscope reveals that the real area of contact is a small percentage of the apparent area between two pieces of metal. The real area increases as smoothness of surfaces is improved. A polished surface would have the most real area of contact.

LUBRICATION

Oil companies keep a close eye on the viscosity of their oils. This is done in a saybolt bath which is a small tank containing warm mineral oil. The bath is precisely regulated at 100°F or 210°F. A sample oil to be tested (about one ounce) is put in a small graduated curved glass container. This container is then placed in the bath and allowed to warm up to the bath temperature. When it does warm up, the curved container is tipped over so the oil specimen inside flows from one end of the tube to another. The seconds are counted that it takes the oil sample to flow between graduations. At 100°F, a 40 weight motor oil must take 700 to 900 seconds to flow between graduations. Sound like a lot? Well at 210°F the same 40 weight oil takes only 70 to 85 seconds. Each of these seconds is an SUS or saybolt universal second.

Can you appreciate that viscosity drops radically due to elevated oil temperatures? The viscosity of water, if tested in a saybolt bath would take only about 15 SUS at room temperature. That's mighty thin. We've included SUS charts for you to check out oils of various weights. Notice that 90 weight gear oil is similar in viscosity to a heavy 40 weight motor oil. Also that a heavy 20 weight oil is nearly a light 30 weight or that a heavy 50 weight is almost like a light 60 weight oil. Weights range from 5W (5 weight wintergrade) all the way to 250 weight for the thickest tropical-grade gear lube. Oils come in many colors and grades. At a mixing station you can see how the various stocks, as they're called, are combined to produce some desired oil ready to be packaged or canned.

To start with, bright stock is a refined paraffin oil of about 150 weight. The best bright stocks are the purest (generically) and naturally most expensive. Neutral stock is a highly refined oil of about 5 weight viscosity. Again, the best neutral stocks are the purest. Mixing neutral and bright stocks together yields base oil stocks that will become our many motor oils and gear lubes. A 60 weight racing oil is mostly bright stock. A 20 weight oil has mostly neutral stock in it.

Then comes the additive package. What do we want? A gear lube? OK, such a package could contain sulfates, chlorinated stocks, phosphates, and lead stock. But an additive package for a motor oil would never contain sulfates or chlorinated hydrocarbons. Such chemicals would damage an internal combustion engine. However, diesel engine oil packages must contain silicones for anti-foam, oxidation retardants, anti-rust, *zinc-phosphates,* and *polymers.*

Polymer stock is a terribly "gooey" substance. A polymerized oil takes less bright stock and more neutral to achieve the same weight oil. But there are several important differences. A polymerized oil is not so thick at lower temperatures. That's good because it tends to retain viscosity at high temperatures. That's very good. But it may oxidize at a high rate which is very bad. Polymerized oils require special additive packages to offset the oxidation problem.

Multigrade oils lose thickness sooner than non-polymerized oils. In other words if you use a 10/30 weight oil for 500 miles then test the SUS viscosity, you'll find it has dropped to perhaps a 10/20 weight. This drop is due to repeated shearing of the polymer stock. Of course, all oils tend to drop viscosity with normal use but multigrades drop a bit more. The way to fight this characteristic is in careful selection of base stocks, expressly for multigrade use. Remember the meaning of the word paraffin: "slight affinity." Polymerization raises the activity of hydrocarbons. If an oil is over-polymerized by an inexperienced individual, it cannot tolerate high temperature operation because of the resulting oxidation.

Oxidation is slow death to lubricating oils. When our pure hydrocarbon molecule picks up an oxygen molecule it ceases to be a lubricant. It becomes a particle of sludge or tar. Whatever it becomes—it is no longer useful as an oil. Prolonged oxidation of a lubricant produces real abrasives besides the sludge, gums, acids, jelly, and tars. Oxidation products are called carbines, carboids, and carbides. Carbines are fully soluble in oil

RANGES OF SAE STANDARD SUS VISCOSITY

WT.	ZERO°F.	100°F.	210°F	
5W	4000 MAX.			
10W	6000-12,000		35 MIN.	Winter-grade motor oils
20W	12,000-48,000		40 MIN.	
10	6000-48,000	150-270	40-45	
20	48,000-85,000	270-400	45-58	
30	85,000-125,000	400-700	58-70	
40	125,000-250,000	700-900	70-85	Motor Oils
50	250,000 MIN.	900-1600	85-110	
60		1600-2100	110-130	
70		2100-4000	130 MIN.	
5W-20	4000 MAX.		45-58	
10W-30	12,000 MAX.		58-70	Multi-grade motor oils
20-20W	48,000 MAX.		45-58	
20-40	85,000 MAX.		70-85	
75	15,000 MAX.		40-48	
80	100,000 MIN.	400-800	48-75	
90	200,000 MIN.	800-1500	75-120	Gear oils
140		1500-4000	120-200	
250		4000 MIN.	200 MIN.	
80-90	200,000 MAX.		75-120	Multi-grade gear oils
90-140	300,000 MAX.		120-200	

COURTESY OF VALVOLINE OIL COMPANY

SUS AT OIL TEMPERATURE

WT.	60°F.	90°F.	120°F.	150°F.	180°F.	210°F.	240°F.
10	700-1400	220-390	100-160	60-82	47-57	40-45	36-39
20	1400-1700	390-600	160-250	32-130	57-80	45-58	39-48
30	1700-3000	600-900	250-400	130-180	80-110	58-70	48-55
40	3000-4500	900-1500	400-500	180-250	110-130	70-85	55-63
50	4500-8000	1500-2500	500-800	250-370	130-200	85-110	63-77
60	8000-13,000	2500-3000	800-1000	370-450	200-240	110-130	77-90
70	13,000-40,000	3000-7000	1000-2000	450-750	240-300	130-140	90-95

and account for the dark color of oils after use. Carboids are only partially soluble and fall out of oil when it's cold or inactive. Carbides are fully insoluble and form sludge deposits in the bottom of the crankcase and in crevices. As you might guess, carbides are abrasive. All of these products are the result of heat, oxidation and time. If the oil is changed frequently, along with the filter, the carbines and carboids would be removed before they can progress into carbides. But drain the oil hot, not cold. Don't go more than the recommended miles between changes; we don't care what the salesman told you. He wanted to sell that machine, and his boss wants you to bring it back for repairs and buy another motorcycle from them in a few years. Believe it!

If an oil is heated past about 150°F, the rate of oxidation doubles for each succeeding 15 degree rise in temperature. And if the oil is agitated with hot air (as in the crankcase), the rate nearly doubles again. We state most emphatically: The worst damage to an oil is entirely due to heat and infrequent oil changes. What we're coming to is this—buy a good oil and use it for what it was intended. Follow the manufacturer's advice. Don't mess around with it by adding anything unless you are a lubricants engineer and being paid for it. There is absolutely nothing you can do to improve a good oil. You can only lower its load carrying ability by playing with it. A good polymerized oil is a tricky thing to perfect. Fortunately we have some pretty good oilmen in this country. So our modern oils really have it. They flow freely at moderate temperatures without losing it at 210°F. They last for long periods of time or for several thousand miles of stop-and-go-traffic.

We should add that cold oil is quite dangerous if you were a motor. You see, cold oil is sluggish, like glue. One cold start is harder on an engine than many hours of running. Imagine the oil pump trying to draw that cold oil out of the sump. Only as much oil can enter the pump as atmospheric pressure can force into the intake side! For this reason *never* rev a cold engine. Take it easy until it's up to temperature. If the pump is turning too fast for the oil viscosity, then cavitation occurs. The oil will foam. Instead of sending liquid lubricant to the bearings, you'll pump mostly oil vapor.

ADDITIVES

Detergent or non-detergent? That is the question. All good oils must contain ZDP. That's the same ingredient that at once aids detergency and load carrying ability. We cannot do without some detergency. Some so-called non-detergent oils are actually "low-detergent" oils sold at a lower price. Some lucky Texas oils were phosphated by mother nature and stored underground for our use. They are sold as non-detergent only because little or nothing has been added. Such an oil bears no label on the can, just a plain top. But avoid the impression that all unlabeled oils are good. They are mostly not. A better word for detergency is dispersency.

The way dispersency operates is to raise the solvency of the oil and keep sludge particles such as carbines in solution and carboids in suspension. Some of the dispersent additives are Barium and Calcium sulfonates and alkylpolyamides.

The two ways that load carrying additives operate is through active film adhesion or through a heat seeking chemistry. Chlorides and sulfides are of the former type. They develop very strong films on metal surfaces. Metallic phosphates are of the second type because these fantastic mole-

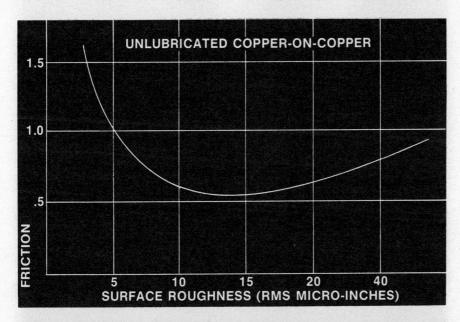

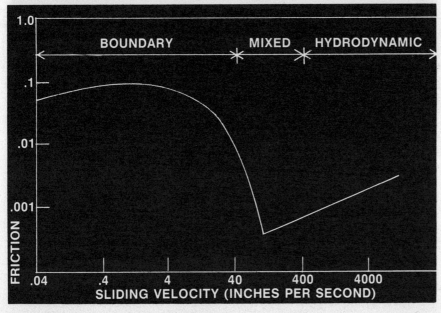

1. Graph showing friction difference between flat polished surfaces and rough surfaces. Friction level is lowest between 10 RMS and 30 RMS. Steel and other metals exhibit test results similar to this graph of copper.

2. This is the relationship between sliding speeds and friction. Boundary conditions are due to more junctions being formed at low speeds. As speed picks up there is a hydroplane effect which causes separation of rubbing surfaces.

LUBRICATION

cules automatically find the hot spots of actual contact or junctions and form a flux on them like a soft powder. This flux formation is much softer than the parent metal and so it begins to dissolve into the oil as rubbing friction continues. That's good. Phosphates are such good heat seekers that all good oils contain them. Yes, and even good gasoline too. It's a good cleaner as well as an upper cylinder lubricant. If it weren't for EP additives, the junctions would break as rather large debris particles and cause scoring.

SPECIAL USE OILS

The labels ML, MM, MS, DG, DM and DS appear on the tops of oil cans. What do they mean? In order, the initials represent: motor light, motor moderate, motor severe, diesel general, diesel moderate, and diesel severe. The labels also indicate what general type of additive package is in the oil. ML oil has a light package while DS carries a complex package of anti-foam, EP, dispersent, polymers, anti-wear, rust inhibitors, corrosion and oxidation inhibitors.

There should be a special class of additives used only in two-cycle engine operation. This is because of the special difficult conditions of two-cycle operation. The worst possible thing you could do to a two-cycle engine is use an automotive oil intended for four-cycle engines! No such oil can cope with the heat and deposit problems of any two-cycle. We'll discuss these problems at length.

Soon, if the present trend towards rotary engines continues, we'll be seeing special oils compounded to better fight the particular lubrication problems of rotary engines alone. Along these same lines, you cannot use gear oils in any kind of engine. They would be extremely corrosive to pistons and bearings. Furthermore, gear oils lack some of the ingredients needed to protect against combustion products. Nor should engine oil be used in gearboxes or motorcycle forks. Engine oils are low in high temperature phosphates and have no sulfides that gears thrive on. Generally gear oils need high EP chemicals not in motor oils.

Fork oil is a mixture of paraffin and naphtene oils to protect and control seal expansion. It also needs anti-foam and other special additives not

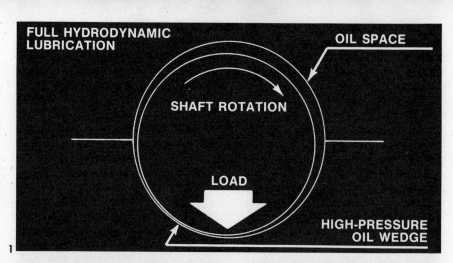

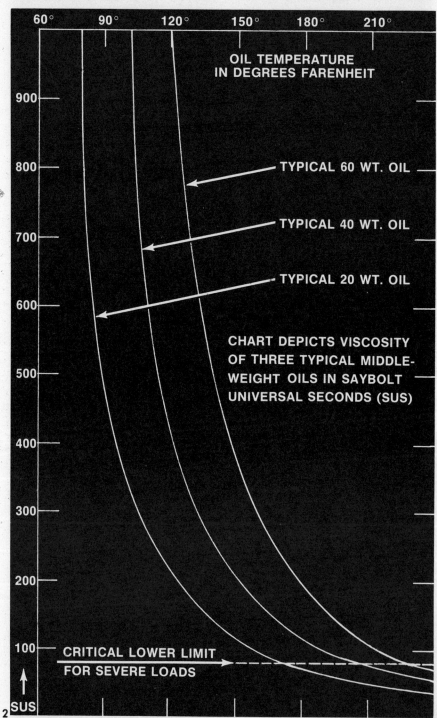

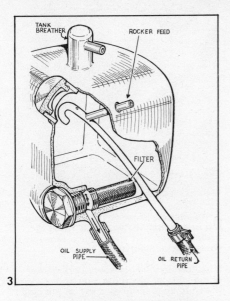

1. The lower left section of the shaft doesn't actually touch the bearing, thanks to a high pressure oil wedge that is constantly being drawn between the shaft and the bearing.

2. Graph showing viscosity losses due to heat. Thickness of oil is determined by its use and how hot it is going to get. Thicker oil is best for heavy duty or racing because of higher viscosity at temperature. Multi-grade oils contain polymerized stock to be thinner when cold, thicker when hot.

3. There is also a screen on the crankcase drain of these dry-sump oil systems. It should be cleaned at every oil change.

4. Screens like this (from a Ducati) are found on most Hondas too. They keep unwanted "junctions" from forming in the engine.

found in motor oils. Motor oils are not all the same, are they? So a poor motor oil could well ruin an expensive set of forks. What's a good motor oil? Only your chemist knows for sure.

It should be clear by now that of all the oil stocks and available additives around that many of them are not compatible when mixed together. That is, the result is a poor lubricant, if indeed you could call it that. And it doesn't take much to turn a good oil sour, sometimes as little as a few drops can do it. Never mix oils yourself. Never combine oils of different labels, even if they're made by the same company. Throw away a used filter. It's an obvious contaminant.

Racing oils are a special breed. If properly blended, the very best stocks went into their manufacture and rigorous laboratory testing is conducted to guarantee quality control of the end product. It's normal for racing oils to have a different (less complex) chemistry than street motor oils. The emphasis in a race oil is on EP, oxidation

resistance, high temperature viscosity, anti-foam, and compatibility with nitrated fuel. Did you know most oils form an explosive mixture with nitromethane? The wrong oil stock used with nitro and "kaboom" goes the combustion chamber rather than proper combustion. An interesting way to test your oil if you plan on running nitro in a drag bike is as follows: Soak a cotton ball in nitromethane then soak it in your sample of motor oil. Then move it to a safe place and light it from a distance using a match on the end of a yardstick. You may have an explosion which is bad, a shower of sparklers which is poor, or perhaps a blue flame which is good.

Racing oils are only suited for the race track. They are one-day oils, intended for a short glorious life rather than a long life in mediocrity. Besides, you'll only form gums and varnish in your street engine if you pour in race oil instead of the necessary street oil. Save the heroics for the strip. The same goes for two-cycle street oils versus racing oils except that the danger is more real in bikes. Race-type two-cycle oils are intended to be premixed about 40.0:1 gasoline-to-oil ratio. The 50 weight racing oil is unnecessary for street use and is sometimes hard to find. Proper street two-cycle oil is 30 weight stuff with cleaners and dispersent additives to combat deposit problems. Street oil is mixed about 16.0:1 by the injection system which has to be lubricated.

TWO-CYCLE OILS

It would be easy to tell you to follow manufacturer's recommendations about motor oils, but we cannot. Bike designers are not oil designers. Fol-

low the recommendations of a good two-cycle oil manufacturer and you can hardly go wrong. This means knowing the people who make your brand of oil.

Another reasonably good way is to buy oil products packaged and labeled by the bike maker for his bike, or by the car maker for his car. But just as there are good bikes and poor bikes, there are good oils and poor oils. So we've listed some recommendations for you at the end of this article.

We hope you've understood the message that two-cycle engines are tougher on oils than other types. Yes, and they are tough on gasoline, too. We suggest that you do not buy no-lead or low-lead gas for any two-cycle. We also suggest that you buy your gas from a relatively new, well maintained gas station. Too many old stations have rusty tanks part full of water, dirt, sand, and plain crud. In a four-cycle engine most of this passes thru the engine causing little harm, but in a two-cycle there is serious crankcase contamination and combustion deposits elsewhere as a result of dirty fuel. Furthermore, low-lead or no-lead fuel does not give clean operation in a hot two-cycle which actually needs premium fuel.

In recent years the political movement for cleaner air has resulted in numerous smog control systems, the most efficient of which, envisioned for cars of the future, will not work effectively in the presence of lead. Ironically, lead itself is not a major pollutant; it is removed from gasoline only because it tends to erode the thermal systems and coats the catalyst in the catalytic reactors of smog devices.

Many companies are removing or reducing the lead content in gasolines due to increasing public pressures. No-lead or low-lead fuels are "in" on the political platform. Unfortunately most engines do not like non-leaded gasoline. In fact, more lead is being used today because the driving public wants decent performance and it is buying more premium fuel than ever before. The real danger in omitting lead from gasoline is to the two-cycle engine. In fact, it's disastrous for the bike owner who innocently purchases no-lead gas because he'd like to contribute less pollution into the atmosphere. The sludge and varnish that quickly forms in the crankcase and around the rings will eventually produce excessive blowby and exhaust smoke. That's not progress.

LUBRICATION

Why does all this happen? The answers came from the president of Torco Oil Company, Bob Lancaster, who has devoted a great deal of research into the two-cycle lubricating business. Bob calls the two-cycle a "reciprocating blow-torch" quite distinct from its four-cycle cousin. When lead is withdrawn from gasoline the octane rating (needed for good anti-knock characteristics) takes a sharp nose dive. So for better anti-knock at low cost, chemicals related to the aromatic family are put into the pump gasoline as a substitute for lead. These added low-boiling stocks are not highly refined. That is, they are not pure generic chemicals. They are perhaps closest to generic Benzene, Toluene, and Xylene. Pure Benzene would be an excellent fuel additive but it's too expensive for the oil companies. Benzene is a fine racing fuel. It burns cleanly and exhibits an octane number above 120. Unfortunately, Benzene like all the aromatics, is not so cheaply refined into a pure state as is octane which is a paraffin.

Keep in mind that low-boiling fuels are quite volatile and have better anti-knock ratings for one main reason—they burn faster in the combustion chamber. Low-boiling fuels vaporize and ignite more readily in cold weather. Generally, the more fuel that completely vaporizes, the cooler becomes the charge. Today's pump gas is about 10 percent oil which is OK. However, the more oil you have in this kind of fuel, the more you have the following—slower combustion, less vaporization, more knock, more tar and sludge deposits.

Watch out. We're not saying oil in the fuel is bad. Only that too much oil and not enough fuel can bring about detrimental results to proper engine operation. The crankcase of a two-cycle is very hot and acts like a "still." That is, it boils (vaporizes) the light ends in the gas right away for transfer to the combustion chamber—leaving the heavy ends in the crankcase. There is no significant sludge problem if the light ends don't leave residue or tars on evaporation. The problem with the low-lead fuel is it does leave residue. Low-lead stuff doesn't always evaporate cleanly nor does it burn "clean" and may gum up the exhaust also. Premium fuel is best for two-cycles. It evaporates well, has good anti-knock, burns "clean," and leaves a sanitary crankcase.

1. Regular oil changes (while oil is hot) will insure that oil "worn out" from oxidation won't let your engine down at some crucial moment.

2. A "sanitary fill" in some dark corner of the yard, or along the side of the house to keep termites away, is the best place for this mess.

The amount of oil and gas you should put in a premix two-cycle engine is determined by what weight of oil you're using. A 30 weight oil calls for a fuel/oil ratio from 16.0:1 to 24.0:1, but 40 weight oil needs a ratio from 24.0:1 to 32.0:1 while 50 weight oil likes a ratio from about 32.0:1 to 48.0:1. Injection oilers in two-cycle engines like 30 weight two-stroke oil best unless the manufacturer recommends something different. In addition we can vary the injector pump stroke via throttle setting.

Another ratio, the air/fuel ratio is affected by the amount of oil in the fuel going thru a two-cycle. Yes, the air/fuel mixture is enriched automatically when you run a "drier" fuel/air mix if there's more burnable fuel in the gasoline. Too much oil shows up in a two-cycle with "wet" plugs and an oily exhaust.

Heat is the biggest danger to a two-cycle which could seize the piston within the cylinder. Some years ago, friend Eric Rickman discovered this one day after a long hard run on his overloaded Yamaha when he backed off the throttle too quickly. In a premix engine, when you chop off the throttle you stop the lube oil, too! The instantaneous cooling of the cylinder around the piston combined with the lack of oil produced a wavy 100-foot skid mark and one shook photographer! Injection oiling systems prevent such things from happening. However, two-cycle racers prefer to mix their own.

CONTACT=FRICTION=WEAR?

Somebody occasionally says, "oil's oil." Such a statement reveals a fundamental lack of knowledge about lubricants and the friction process. Any amount of EP testing soon shows how different oil samples yield a wide spectrum of test results. If an oil film could completely prevent contact between rubbing surfaces, then there would be no need whatever for addi-

tives. No contact—no friction—no wear. It's that simple. But complete separation between metals rarely occurs.

It's definitely true that lubricants must fight friction, however a little bit of friction is necessary for the lubricant to do its job. An excessive amount of friction creates tearing, galling, and eventual destruction of the rubbing surfaces to produce a great deal of surplus heat energy. It appears the primary function of oils and greases is to protect rubbing surfaces and by staying between surfaces to wear-proof them against the damage of sliding or rolling contact. Friction is not equal between surfaces of different materials. For example, the characteristics of steel-on-steel are different than those of steel-on-copper or copper-on-lead or wax-on-brass. Frictional characteristics naturally vary depending on the exact lubricant between different kinds of materials. Some lubricants are more effective than others in reducing friction while some are better in reducing wear. One of the most valuable properties of oils is their ability to clean and cool rubbing surfaces.

We will be discussing boundary conditions and hydrodynamic conditions. By definition, a boundary lubrication condition is one where there is some metallic contact even with a lubricant present. The most destructive boundary condition is a low-speed, high-load situation where surplus heat is being generated. An ideal hydrodynamic lubrication condition is where there is no metallic contact occurring because of high surface speeds with perhaps light loading. We

3. Periodic adjustment of the pump will keep two-stroke auto-oilers from smoking up the atmosphere and fouling plugs.

4. Check the lines to see that they're clear. Replacing opaque lines with transparent ones lets you check oil flow while under way.

are most likely to have a boundary condition with too thin of a lubricant, whereas a high viscosity lubricant such as a gear oil would tend to develop a hydrodynamic condition. It is important to realize that oil additives such as phosphates, sulfates, amines, and chlorinated compounds are used to protect against boundary conditions. Additives reduce surface tearing and encourage "healing" in order to reduce wear.

In a boundary situation many, many junctions are constantly forming, bending, generating and absorbing heat energy, perhaps shearing off whiskers as wear particles, and re-forming new junctions. A good lubricant reduces friction to about 10 percent of the unlubricated value. Junction density (the average number of junctions per square inch) could be many thousands or many millions of junctions per square inch. Modern frictional studies prove that friction greatly depends on the total number of junctions existing at a given instant and on the average strength of the bond at each junction. Very flat, very smooth or polished surfaces have the highest junction densities and will score easily and severely. Scoring is the most destructive kind of wear. A lubricant is supposed to encourage normal wear which is an extremely gradual process of material removal. There is nothing that can stop wear altogether. Slowing wear is not difficult for a good lubricant so long as the surface finish and choice of materials reflects good engineering.

The following surface conditions would tend to develop high junction densities—extreme smoothness, a

polished condition, surfaces of equal hardness, super-clean surfaces free of oxide film, surface temperatures near the melting point, a very slow rubbing speed, high applied loading. If two or more of these high-friction conditions were prevalent at the same time, the two surfaces would weld together and seize totally.

It is often curious to discover that a friction member (like true love) never moves smoothly. Its motion is quite jerky, even at high speed or rpm. The only time a clutch or *brake* is smooth is when it's full on or full off. In other words, friction between members moving at different speeds always causes an almost imperceptible change in speed of both members (a shuddering or vibration). You see, if junctions are constantly forming and reforming, their number is changing and so friction is changing from one millisecond to another. The result is a grab-release situation.

FLUID FRICTION

We should mention a few words about fluid friction which we sometimes call viscous drag. This fluid friction is greater with high viscosity oils and naturally less with lower viscosity oils. It's easy to see that very high fluid friction would tend to slow down the mechanism that it is protecting. However, fluid friction is very much overrated in motorcycle or automotive use. The real enemy that lubricants are supposed to fight is metal-to-metal contact in a boundary condition. Any attempt to substitute a very light oil to reduce fluid friction becomes a self-defeating measure because you are then going to substitute a great deal of metal-to-metal friction in place of a slight amount of fluid friction. In other words, if you have a high load situation such as in a race machine you must reduce metal-to-metal contact in order to deliver the highest amount of horsepower to the rear. The way to do this is almost

always with a higher viscosity lubricant. Viscosity must match the load. Remember, the real enemy is metal-to-metal contact.

The problem of using too low of a viscosity is particularly troublesome in two-cycle bike engines where fuel dilution is such a problem. In the first place, gasoline has no business in the crankcase of an engine, any kind of engine, but in a two-cycle we're pretty well stuck with it. This means that oil chemists must be part magician in order to provide enough good lubricant to protect the bearings, pistons, rings, and other sliding parts in a two-cycle engine. Bob Lancaster of Torco Oil Company has commented that the problems in designing a good two-cycle oil are truly staggering.

Sometimes liquids can exhibit the characteristics of a solid body. Watch a flat rock skipping across water. The water acts like a solid surface so long as the rock is moving rapidly. When the rock stops, it sinks. Similarly, a rapidly rotating shaft in an engine bearing "skips" on an oil film wedged between the shaft and the bearing. This only happens during hydrodynamic lubrication. Friction under hydrodynamic conditions is the lowest possible anywhere because there is zero metal-to-metal contact. No junctions exist. The only drag is viscous from the oil itself. The measured friction on the shaft is only 1/5 to 1/2 of one percent. Hydrodynamic conditions are due to very high shaft speeds on a film of high-viscosity oil. The oil clings to the shaft so that it is continually being drawn (wedged) between the shaft and the bearing. Absorbed films due to additives aid this action greatly. But if the shaft speed slows down or if the oil viscosity drops for any reason such as heat, there will be an immediate reversion to boundary conditions. The best ways to maintain hydrodynamic lubrication are (with a near-polished or "micropolished" journal, a nitrited crank is best (high surface hardness), use of fine steel wool on the bearings (slightly roughened to reduce the number of junctions), use of 50 weight or higher racing oil; finally, never lug your motor.

Hydrodynamic lubrication is not restricted to only engine bearings. The principle applies to most mechanisms being lubricated. Piston rings sliding on a cylinder wall ride a film of oil like circular Hawaiian surfboards. Gear teeth in transmissions and rear ends trap quantities of oil between

LUBRICATION

meshing teeth and so resist metallic contact to a great degree. That's why 140 weight gear oil is preferred in an automotive racing differential. Present day gearboxes seem to be inadequately designed for racing. We see a large number of boxes whose gears have "frozen" on their mainshafts. The reason is insufficient flow of oil on the mainshaft and around the inside of the gears. Hydrodynamic lubrication needs lots of cool oil.

FRICTION COEFFICIENT

We've talked a lot about friction and now we'll discuss the coefficient of friction. Friction itself is a complex process that takes mechanical energy and converts it into heat energy. However, the coefficient of friction is a convenient way of measuring friction mechanically. Look at a 100-pound block of wood sitting on a flat surface. Ask yourself, how many pounds would it take to drag that block of wood slowly a short distance? Well, it would take 20 pounds of steady pull if the coefficient of friction between the wood and ground surface were .20.

A 100-pound block of rubber lying on very smooth asphalt might require 95 pounds of pull. Hot rubber would of course require a pull more than the weight of the rubber, or over 100 pounds. So you see,

$$Cf = \frac{pull}{weight}$$

There's a natural tendency to exaggerate the importance of a low Cf. EP is far more valuable. The misleading factor about Cf is that it is taken under low-load circumstances. Only the weight of the test body is pressing down on the junctions. The heat generated is low and the extent of plastic deformation is low. The amount of welding taking place is also low. Compare this situation with one where 50,000 or 100,000 pounds are pressing on one square inch of rapidly moving surface such as in a differential. What a comparison! This high-load situation is what EP is all about. That's why hypoid gear lubes need lots of EP additives. Palmitates, sulphates and phosphates are some effective EP (or anti-wear) agents which may not necessarily exhibit a high lubricity (low Cf). High viscosity oils using active agents such as chlorinated hydrocarbons yield both a high EP and high lubricity.

1

Low Cf means high lubricity. This is indeed valuable in testing because so much can be learned from Cf figures. Wear rates of different materials usually do correspond with lubricity figures in most cases. It is known that the least wear occurs with a very hard surface riding on a very soft surface. The Cf is low, with or without oil. Lubricity is a tool we cannot do without. The things we've learned about what materials wear best together have come from Cf figures and microscopic photography.

A remarkable thing impresses all researchers in the field of friction and lubrication. It's the strange fact that friction surfaces somehow know best how to finish themselves towards a condition of least friction. Surfaces that are too smooth try to roughen-up slightly for easier sliding. Surfaces that are too rough try to smooth themselves for less friction. You could perhaps compare the phenomena to that of water seeking its own level. The smart engineer is one who prescribes a surface finish that the metal likes right from the beginning. That way during break-in, the surfaces will not have to undergo a drastic lapping-in situation which of course leads to scoring. If the roughness of the finish is out in left field, there is simply no hope. Also besides surface roughness there's the question of what finish pattern is best. The only answer for that is the crosshatch pattern which has proved itself for many years. We like it on cylinder walls, bearing inserts, shaft bores, valve

guides, and bearing races. Research Brush Company in Los Angeles has an excellent line of finishing brushes.

Wetting is something related to lubricity. It's the ability to penetrate and work into tight places. Metals are not so dense on their surfaces. Lattice structures of cast materials such as iron and aluminum are relatively weak. Their surfaces are actually porous. But all metals have oxide coatings that are susceptible to wetting agents. Amos Corgiat, now Vice President of Valvoline Oil Company once donated a wetting additive sample for us to test. We found that overnight the oil had crept 10 or 12 inches up a previously dry steel rod that was left sticking out of the container. That was amazing, to say the least.

GREASE

The word grease is reserved for lubricants in a near-liquid (plastic) state. A grease is a mixture of some lubricating oil and a thickener or soap. Grease bases like lithium, sodium, potassium, calcium, or barium will determine the basic physical characteristics of the grease. The physical make-up of a grease tells us where it can be used. But it's the oil in the grease that does most of the actual lubricating. A good grease is 60 percent oil.

Greases have their additives, too. There are zinc oxides, graphite, molysulfide, teflon and lead. These are filler ingredients, not actually in solution. These fillers are sometimes good boundary lubricants where sliding

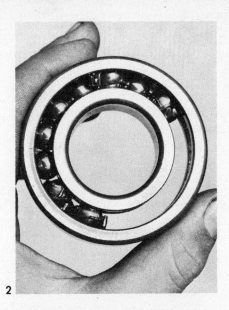

1. The best of oils cannot stand up to constant overrevving. Honda twin crank self-destructed with dirty old oil.

2. Regular oil changes can help you avoid disaster. Crankshaft bearing cage of Ducati disintegrated. Owner discovered shavings and broken pieces during oil change, escaped complete destruction of engine.

speeds are low. The best common load carrier is perhaps a mixture of zinc-oxide and lithium grease.

Sticky greases are necessary where some lubricant must cling to an awkward surface, such where the use of oil is impossible. It's still the oil which bleeds out of a grease that provides lubricity. The body of a grease acts like a reservoir for the oil held within. Most greases are intended for anti-friction bearings (ball or roller) or special cases of low-speed sliding conditions, since there is a distinct difference between low- and high-speed lubrication. And there is an even greater difference between rolling friction and any kind of sliding friction. The job of lubricating a rolling condition is one heck of a lot easier than lubricating a sliding condition.

Never use a grease in place of an intended oil. Greases may be fine in wheel bearings, but they would not be good for assembling bikes or engines for racing purposes. Nor should you ever mix greases of one type with another type due to the chemistry of the inorganic base compounds. Clean your parts thoroughly and avoid all chlorinated compounds when working with greases of any kind. Chlorine plus grease makes salts which are abrasive, such as sodium chloride or lithium chloride. Also, keep nitro fuels away from greases.

We cannot overemphasize that overfilling with grease (more than 1/3

to 1/2 full) leads directly to lubrication failure. An excessive amount of grease churns and creates a great deal of heat. Greases require room to expand and move around so that the oil in the grease can circulate to where it's needed. Use only the proper amount of grease.

Greases are graded by a *penetration* tester. A very heavy grease takes a lot to be penetrated. That would be a grade 6. A grade 0 grease is very oily and is easily penetrated.

We feel that lithium grease has the best advantages for motorcycle and automotive uses in cold wet weather or hot and dry. Lithium grease is especially good if it contains zinc oxide as an additive, along with a high EP oil mix and is corrosion inhibited. Valvoline X-All is one such grease. It's white and is often called white lead which is a misnomer.

In case you've run your bike through deep water or continuous rain, it'd be a good idea to repack your wheel bearings. A little water does not really harm good grease if you change it regularly. The additives in the grease (and in the oil in the grease) can't live forever. They deplete and require changing like anything else. In fact when the oil content of a grease drops to about 50 percent, the grease quits lubricating because not enough oil can bleed out of the thickener to give adequate protection.

"MIRACLE" LUBRICANTS

Since World War 2 we've heard a lot of bally-hoo about solid film lubricants such as graphite, molybdenum disulfide, and teflon. Some salesmen for these products really have silver tongues. The claims they make are pretty unrealistic. At best you'd be lucky to not damage your bike or some of its expensive parts. These "miracle" substances actually can interfere with good lubrication if you have a decent oil or grease. They can coat the metal surface, preventing the oil additives from reaching the surface in order to react with it. Solid films of graphite break down at relatively low frictional temperatures by changing allotropic form into a kind of carbon. Molybdenum disulfide disassociates under friction to raw molybdenum metal and sulfur gas which is highly acidic. It has been well known that most solid-film chemicals will lower the EP of a good oil. The reason the dry-films became well known is that they seemed to raise the lubricity

of straight mineral oils. But we've seen that mineral oil alone is not enough. Nor is lubricity a critical factor without also considering EP.

Please don't go away with the impression that graphite is altogether bad because in some specialized circumstances it's quite good, such as in the presence of water vapor or at cryogenic (extreme cold) temperatures. Without some moisture present, graphite (in all its forms) is no lubricant. In a vacuum such as space, anhydrous graphite (without water) becomes a substance that does not shear easily and would freeze a mechanism. Mixed with an oil, graphite and moly particles (no matter how finely ground) are at best only slightly soluble.

The one very successful dry-film or solid-film chemical is a phosphate coating called Parko-lube or Parkerizing. This is the familiar dull black material on all new flat tappet camshafts and gears. This process is great for protection during break-in and it combines very well with oil additives. In short—it works.

Another workable solid ingredient is lead. It's good in gear lubes for hypoid rear ends which generate appreciable heat and require the highest EP lubricants possible. Such lubricating oils are called SCL for sulfur-chlorine-lead. But watch out never to use an SCL oil in some gear box that contains copper alloys like bronze or brass. SCL decomposes these metals. But it is truly beautiful in all-steel bike components. You can make your own SCL lube by squirting some of Ashland's Chain-Life into fresh gear oil. Never mix Chain-Life and grease.

Lead additives in gasoline do more than resist knock. They lubricate exhaust valve stems and seats for much longer life. Lead in fuels helps the rings and cylinder walls, too.

Oils most certainly do wear out. It isn't obvious when it happens, at least not to the average motorist. Oxidation takes its toll. So does additive depletion, which is the gradual usage of the load carrying agents. When the additives are gone, what's left besides contaminated mineral oil and oxidation products? Do you want good results? Change your oil and the filter no more than every 2000 miles and you'll go a long way. And check your bike air filters too. We've seen reports of *lava* deposits(!) being mistaken for carbon deposits in two-cycle engines. It seems rock dust gets thru those air filters too easily if you're careless. 🏍

CARBURETORS AND FUEL SYSTEMS

Climb aboard for a fantastic voyage through the world of venturis, jets and atomizers

BY DAN COTTERMAN

Some years ago, I lived next door to a fellow who worked on wrist watches for space monkeys. In his off hours my friend invented things, and he was good at it. The only trouble was he didn't know when to stop. A masterfully conceived mechanism, revealed to my admiring eyes a few days earlier, would inevitably be embellished beyond recognition. The final unveiling would expose a spiny growth of bolt-ons and te- diously machined mysterioso whose dimensions had managed to exceed every boundary of practicality. The spur for tampering with the well enough that should have been left alone probably grew from the inven-

MIKUNI

1. Mikuni spigot mount carburetor has become most popular mounting method. Access to main jet is through cap on the bottom of float bowl.

2. Flange mount model has main jet access in handy holder in side of float bowl. Both have different chokes and venting system.

3) Trio of "sliders" disassembled to show profusion of parts not present in "guillotine" carburetors which are discussed in text.

CARBURETORS

tor's passion for creating something that would fulfill numerous requirements.

Save for the fact that the carburetor as we know it today is the result of carefully controlled evolution, it might well be as big as a medicine ball and twice as heavy. In no other aspect of engine performance is so much demanded of so little. Without respect to its size this little device is called upon to instantly cater to the engine's constantly varying demands for different proportions of air and fuel.

Necessity has demanded that it become a thing of sophisticated ingenuity. The fact that carburetor designs run from simple to complex should take nothing from our realization that their inbred sensitivity to an engine's running requirements makes them equally sensitive.

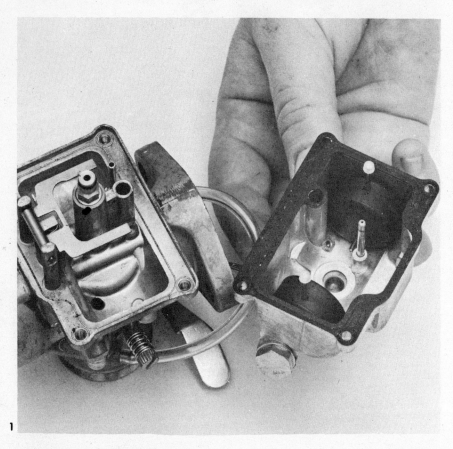

1

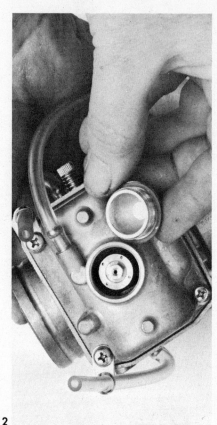

2

3

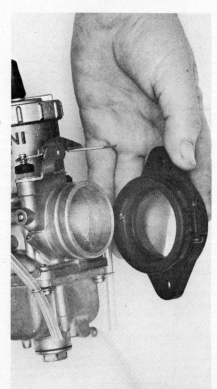

4

Understanding the fundamentals of carburetor operation will be of tremendous value when we're faced with the challenge of analyzing problems. Quite basically, our concern is with a metering device. Fuel must automatically be measured into a venturi, an air passageway through the car-

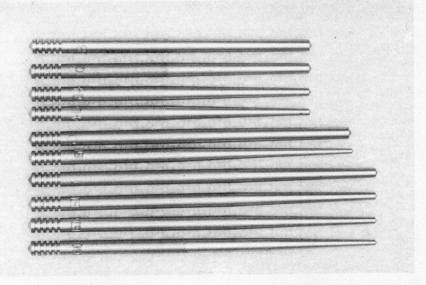

1) Fuel bowl at right has dual floats which actuate forked valve lever. "O" ring is fitted to main jet (left center) to minimize leaks.

2) Here is bottom-up look at spigot type Mikuni with easy main jet access through underside of body—a good feature on competition machines.

3) Mikunis for bikes exposed to rough riding may have baffle surrounding main jet as guard against fuel slosh which results in engine starvation.

4) Here's the rubber flange spigot employed by Mikuni and others to insulate carburetor from damaging effects of engine heat and vibration.

5) Main jet needles must relate to size of jet orifice as well as height of carburetor. Each has adjustment "notches" cut around top end.

5

6) Intake side of carburetor shows slide fully closed, as with engine at normal free idle speed. Here is where idle and pilot jet adjustments affect running.

7) Throttle is now turned on slightly causing slide to rise. Engine is still being fed by pilot jet system at this point.

8) More throttle equals more engine speed as slide is drawn higher. Here slide cut-away is still a factor, but main jet needle setting begins coming into play.

9) This is how slide position might look at highway cruising speeds. Job of metering fuel is dependent upon both needle setting and main jet size.

10) Full-throttle position raises slide up and out of picture. Now main jet size is a real factor in performance.

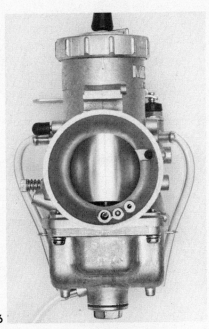

6

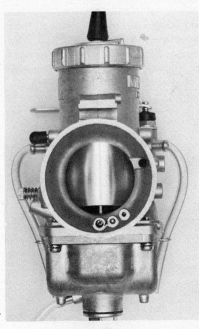

7

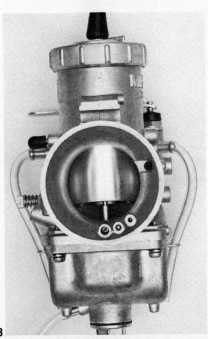

8

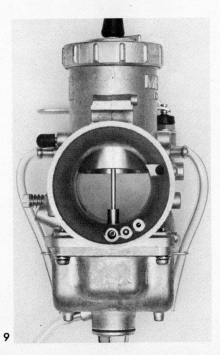

9

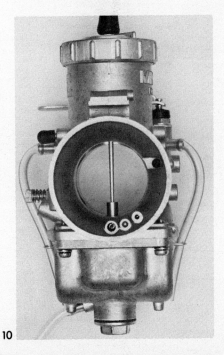

10

CARBURETORS

buretor body, where it can become atomized and drawn into the engine cylinder for combustion. The foregoing would seem to profoundly oversimplify the supply of a combustible vapor to an engine. However, we will soon note that some of the best motorcycle carburetors available today are, indeed, profoundly simple!

I mentioned the engine's constantly varying demands for different proportions of air and fuel. A few seasons back Shell's "Answer Man" told us that the optimum air-fuel mix for an engine, just cruising easy, was about fifteen parts of air to one part fuel. He was, of course, directing his statement primarily to automobile owners, but the same ratio applies to motorcycle engines. Let's go a little further. Using that 15:1 ratio as a basis for comparison, we find that a mixture approximately twice as rich is needed during engine starts and, furthermore, that each of the several conditions of engine loading and speed will de-

2

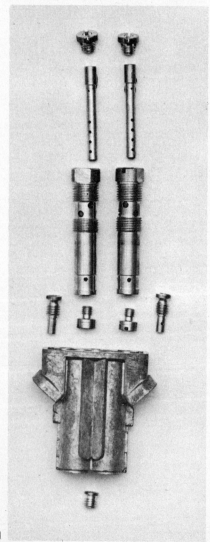

1

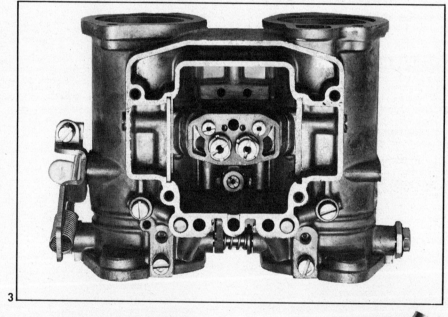

3

4

5

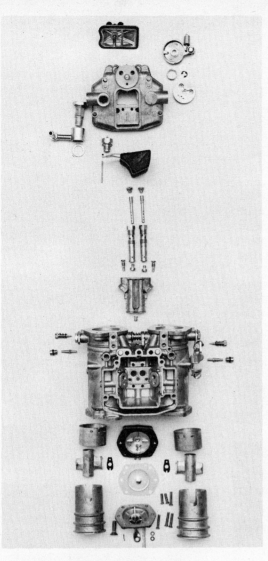

6

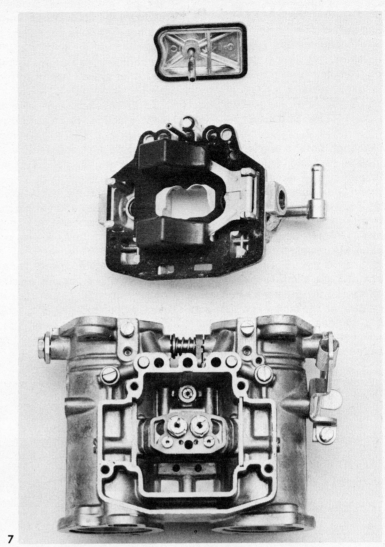

7

1) Comprising Mikuni Solex "jet set" are these matched nozzles, jets and brass inspection cap screws. Jet block is seen at bottom of photo.

2) Here's the "racer's edge" for your Mini Enduro, the twin throated Solex shown here intact. Note throttle linkage, wingnut access on top.

3) Looking down the well as Solex is viewed from topside. Jets and nozzles at center can be removed by means of slotted heads. Idle set is on left.

4) Thatch of Mikunis includes this butterfly-diaphram pumper, cut away here to show venturi, butterfly valve and multiple diaphrams in bottom.

5) Same snowmobile pumper as in previous photo, this time showing linkage, outside adjusters and throttle valve fully open to actuate plunger.

6) From the top: inspection cap, float assembly and main carburetor assembly. Note presence of intervening gaskets, outside adjustment screws.

7) If you thought the Mikuni slide carburetor had a lot of parts, dazzle your orbs over this Mikuni Solex of the Weber side-draft type for cars.

8) Variation of Solex has different throttle linkage and topside assembly. Jazzy chrome stacks help add that fast appearance. O' Solex mio!

8

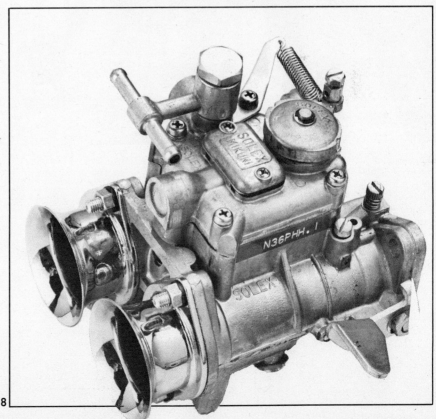

CARBURETORS

mand still other degrees of richness. Complicating matters even more is the variance of air-fuel combination requirements imposed by substantial changes in altitude.

THE SLIDERS

Although not the simplest, the piston-valve or "slide" types are among the oldest and most dependable. Certain individualities notwithstanding, this type would include the bulk of carburetors now being manufactured by Amal, Bing, Dellorto, IRZ, Keihin, Mikuni and a couple of others I may have neglected to mention. Each of these involves the supply of a progressively greater air/fuel mixture through the facility of a slide and a tapered needle that go up together as the throttle is "dialed on." As nearly infinite and controllable as it

may be, the tapered needle being gradually withdrawn from the orifice of a main jet does not satisfy the requirements of the engine at idle and low engine speeds. For this purpose a pilot jet system has been incorporated.

To follow each stage of slide carburetor action we must first picture the engine at idle. In this condition the throttle is closed and the slide is held only slightly open by means of the physical stop provided by adjustment of the throttle stop screw which projects upward at an angle through the side of the carburetor body. At this point, the tiny pilot jet is doing the metering. As the throttle is turned to raise engine speed moderately above idle the volume of air is no longer dependent upon the adjustment of the throttle stop screw because the slide has been lifted to a point where the "cut-away" on one side of the skirt provides a larger

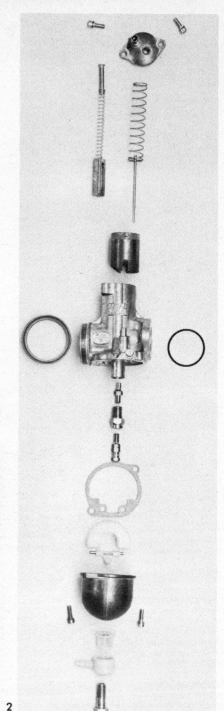

AMAL

1

2

3

4

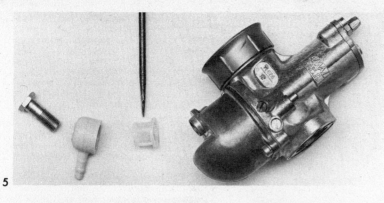

5

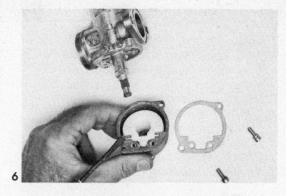

6

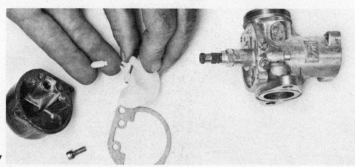

7

8

1) Amal carburetors have found world wide acceptance on European machinery. They have seen few changes over the years. These shown are British Amals.

2) "Exploded" concentric reveals about 15% fewer parts than Mikuni version. Complete gasket sets and overhaul kits are available separately.

3) British Amal slide-type carburetors are, L-R: Mono-Bloc, Grand Prix (with satellite fuel bowl) and latest improvement known now as Concentric.

4) Another view of Amal threesome. Note differences in float bowl locations. Concentric, far right, is best. Late bowls now have main jet access.

5) Pictured beneath Amal Concentric are metal "banjo" bolt with single banjo and fuel filter gauze. Latter must be inspected and cleaned often.

6) Concentric float bowl removed to show tiny "toilet-seat" float and pivot. Re-install very carefully.

7) Here's why: Small forked tab on pivot end of float must engage slot on end of float needle. If not, a spate of fuel will flood carburetor.

8) "Stab" crimp holds part of pilot idle system in Amal body. Concentric body casting is made to be drilled and tapped for use on left or right.

9) Pointing to small copper clip used to position main jet needle in slide. Clip in top notch = lean operation, bottom notch = rich running.

10) Concentric jet block is removed, top, as screwdriver is poised to adjust idling mix at pilot air screw. Larger knurled screw is slide stop.

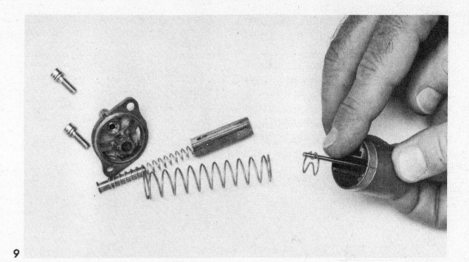

9

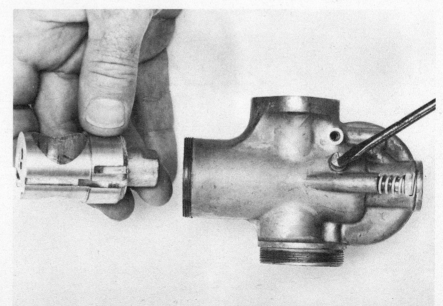

10

CARBURETORS

opening to the venturi. This intermediate stage finds the supply of fuel from the pilot jet augmented by the initial traces of spray from the main jet as that tapered needle I mentioned a minute ago is lifted with the slide to begin its withdrawal from the hole in the main jet. Now we can follow the progressive rise of the slide as the throttle is turned on a little further and see that the general state of carburetor "tune" will be primarily influenced by the position of our tapered needle and its relationship to the hole in the main jet. Please note that it isn't until about three-quarter throttle is reached that the size of the main jet becomes a factor in tuning. There is a tendency among many riders to start changing main jets when their problem exists in some other stage of carburetor operation.

You might find more difference than agreement among the several makes of slide-type carburetors. The operation principle is about the same for all. The differences start stacking up when you look at details of construction. Dellorto, for example, uses a square slide in their center-bowl models, now widely used on Ducati and Moto Guzzi machines. The advantages, according to A.J. Lewis who now heads the service depart-

1

2

1) This is the flanged end of the Concentric that bolts to intake manifold. "O" ring fits into machined groove, provides airtight operation.

2) All together now, a final look at Concentric cautions us to be careful when turning velocity stack or air filter onto these fine threads.

3) Venerable Amal Mono-Bloc disassembles easily, reveals about as many parts as Mikuni slider. Float bowl is at side, can cause mixture changes.

4) Mono-Bloc "O" ring seal is shown at left, while screwdriver points to filter gauze used to clean fuel as it enter float bowl from topside.

5) Side-mount float bowl of Mono-Bloc is seen here with float, float needle and small pivot bush removed. Metal float needle also available.

6) Mammoth Amal Grand Prix is expensive version with remote float bowl to provide large volume of air-fuel mixture for racing. Count the parts!

7) Grand Prix models, intended primarily for competition, are designed for quick, easy access to main jet. Jets come in larger sizes for alky.

8) For more sophisticated and quicker tuning in pits, Grand Prix has externally adjustable float level. The float is a small brass vesicle.

9) A big slide for the Grand Prix holds adjustable needle at side with small spring clip to hold setting. Note largeness at needle's lower tip.

10) Grand Prix velocity stack screws off. Tab on flat strap engages notch in ring, secures stack while other end helps hold top cap on carb body.

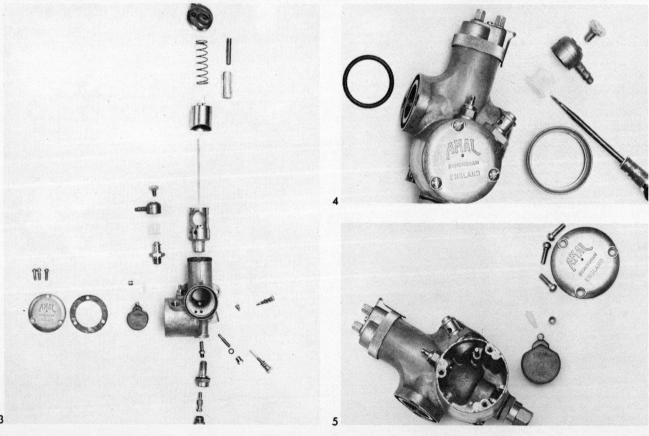

3

4

5

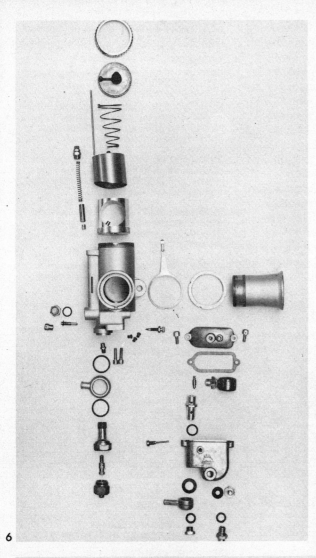

6

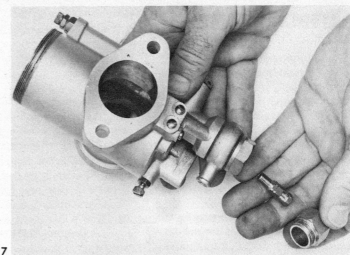

7

8

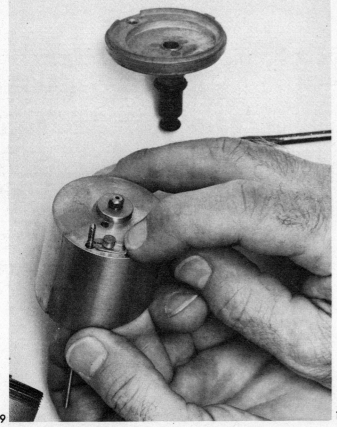

9

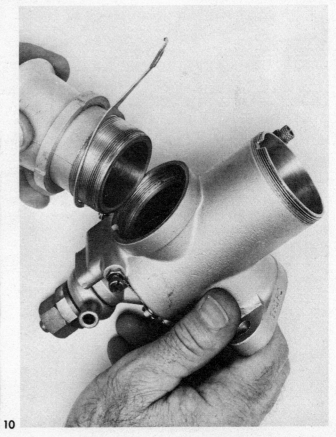

10

CARBURETORS

ment at the "Duke" and Guzzi western headquarters, include easier slide action—which has to mean less sticking—and vastly increased slide life.

New Hondas with slide-equipped Keihin carburetors have attempted to create a situation of more positive up-and-down slide movement by innovating a dual-cable system. The idea is that one cable pulls the slide up and the other pulls it down, depending on which way the throttle twist grip is rotated. This may be the breakthrough that will finally take slide action out of the yo-yo category by giving the rider positive two-way control. It also may eliminate the need for using solid brass slides, simply because they're heavier and, for that lone virtue, seem to return better. Of course, an aluminum slide in an aluminum carburetor body is supposed to be bad, but mere brass plating usually is sufficient.

There was a lot of talk about slide replacement, perhaps as often as each year on dirt bikes. Bob Nicholson of Ossa stresses this necessity by pointing to the fact that a piece of the skirt of a badly worn slide can sometimes be drawn into an engine with resulting top end damage.

An interesting and original feature of the IRZ slide-type carburetor is its incorporation of duality. Dual fuel line feed to the float bowl, dual air adjustments to the low range stage and dual needles for smoother stage-to-stage acceleration. The two needles, slightly different in length, are intended to offer phase graduation without performance flat spots sometimes encountered with less developed systems. The problems with adjustment of a carburetor of this type are not with the design, but with the tinkerer who doesn't know adjustment procedure. At this juncture we might well

1) Dual needles, jets, adjustments, etc. of IRZ carburetor pose challenge to both Mikuni and Amal Grand Prix for array of parts. However, system is okay.

2) Not a leaky float bowl, cutaway is made to show IRZ's metallic float, float needle and tickle-button assembly. Also fuel intake and filter.

3) Reverse side cut away shows IRZ's slide, pilot air intake system (T-shaped channel), plus dual needle and jet set-up in lower chamber.

4) Say, "IRZ!" Looking down throat of carburetor offers clue to double needle function. Adjustments easy to get to. Note bolt-on bottom cover.

5) Assembled and ready to go, IRZ is smooth, trouble-free unit if you take time to learn how to adjust it. Follow manual, one stage at a time.

IRZ

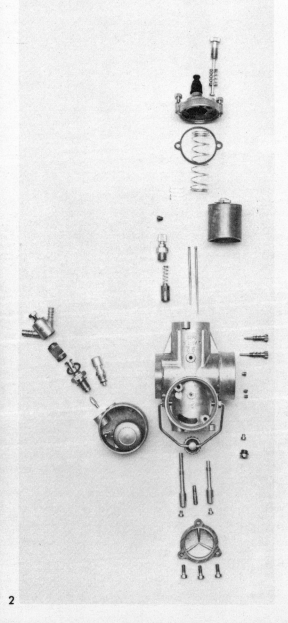

1   2

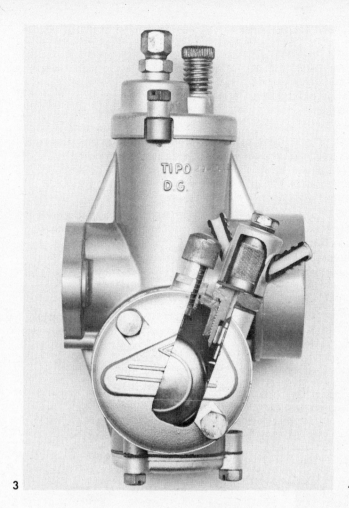

3

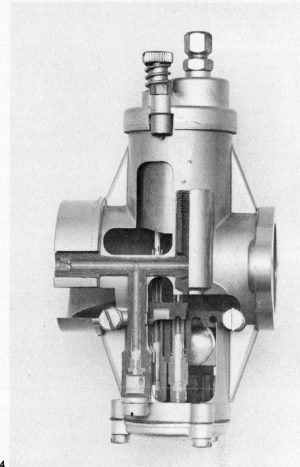

4

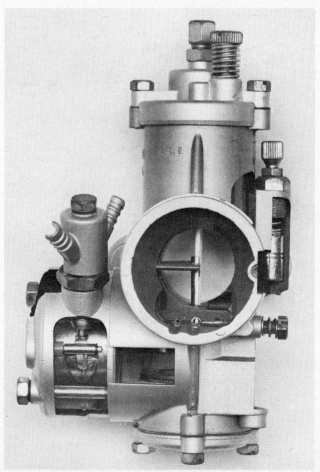

5

6

CARBURETORS

remember that stage-by-stage adjustment is invariably recommended with any carburetor, starting with low speed and working up. If, as we have noted, the amateur tuner begins by changing the main jet when his difficulty actually exists elsewhere, he should heed the warning of Bultaco's Tom Patton who observed that a change of main jet might act to alter flow characteristics in other jets throughout the carburetor. Don't let the need for a minor adjustment in one of the low-range stages trick you into getting everything out of shape.

I also questioned Patton about the differences between Spanish and English Amals. You might coax a part or two to interchange, like maybe a slide, but for all intents and purposes you'd just as well think of them as different brands. The metering systems are different throughout and a different set of values has been assigned to the main jets. In the Spanish Amal, the level of the float is adjustable by the interchange of a number of different float needles.

Comparing carburetors also will reveal a number of variances in the way float bowls are attached and in their relationship to the venturi or "throat" of the unit. Triumph's Bob Ellison commented that the "concentric" design of recent years has proved most efficient because it spotted the bowl in line with and directly beneath the throat. The earlier "monobloc" carburetors featured float bowls located to the side. If, for example, the bowl was on the right, leaning the motorcycle to the right as when accelerating through a long, sweeping bend in road racing, would cause a too-lean mixture. Conversely, a similar maneuver to the left would produce an opposite effect. Sensitivity to acceleration and deceleration likewise is minimized with the concentric float bowl location.

Inside the float bowl we run into another difficulty that seems to exist to some degree in many situations where extremly rough riding is done. Here the problem can be intermittent engine starvation that is caused by fuel "slosh" within the bowl. Mikuni's response has been to incorporate a bell-like baffle into the bowl while Bing carburetors feature a screen and Amal suggests that the main jet access plug on the bottom of their late float bowls will extend up inside far enough to provide sufficient baffling to counteract slosh. Still another maker suggests that if the float is the right weight it won't get to shaking

BING

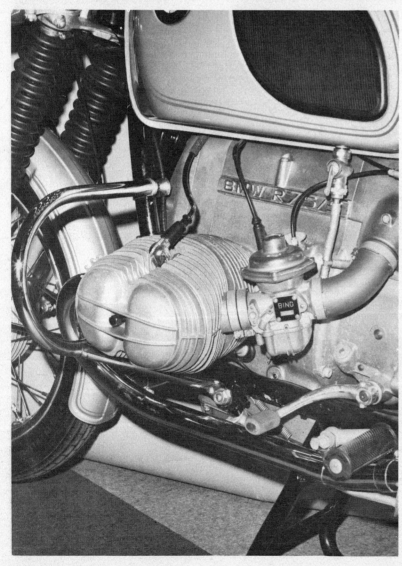

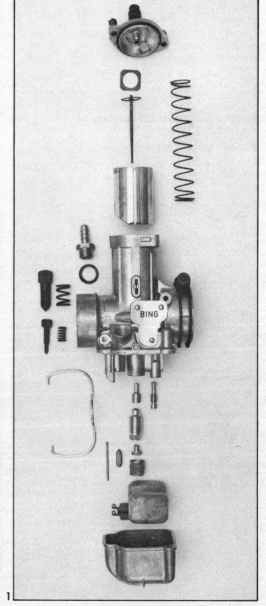

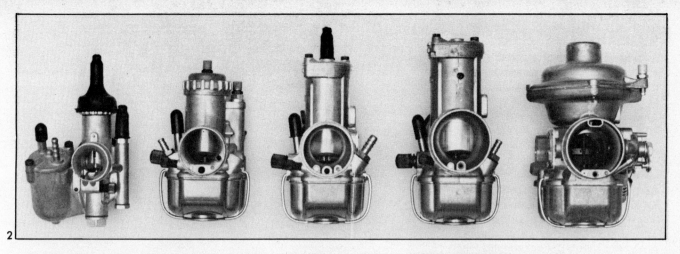

1) As long as we're counting parts it is fair to observe that Bing comes with only nominal assortment of components. Has baled bowl like the IRZ.

2) Bings crop up like Crosby's sons as line-up includes small side-bowl, three manual sliders and diaphram pumper-slider for BMW at far right.

3) Bing's changeable spray-bar vaporizers enrich mix through mid-range. L-R: Richest, 30° slant for 125 Maico, slightly rich and longest and leanest.

4) Bale is swung aside to reveal recessed bowl gasket and dual floats. Of special interest here is screen baffle around main jet to quell slosh.

5) Bing appears as quality unit with this engine-side look at spigot-and-clamp manifold attachment set-up. Carb can be tilted for bowl access.

6) Size extremes are evident with this view of small vs. large sliders. Small side bowl on carb at left compensates for inclined angle mounting.

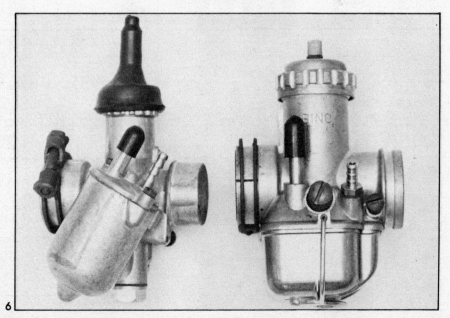

CARBURETORS

around in rough riding and create a situation that would necessitate the use of baffles. At its worst a problem of this sort would be limited to special situations so if it hasn't happened with your bike don't worry about it. If it has, be assured that something is being done at the factory level.

For all its woes with sticking and wearing slides and float bowl problems, the piston valve carburetor remains one of the most flexible types available today. I've already mentioned the variety of float needles that

1) Dell Orto spotlights careful and elaborate machine work on their aluminum air cleaner adaptor and velocity stacks. Each fills a performance need.

2) Robust Italian Dell Orto racing carburetors top a pair of so-called "square" sliders used on Moto Guzzi and Ducati motorcycles.

3) "Square" slide can be seen at top of photo just under large slide return spring. Slide is said to give much longer wear, improved performance.

4) Here's that big racing model, somewhat similar to Amal Grand Prix. Note integral float and needle, left. Dual float bowls sometimes are used.

DELL ORTO

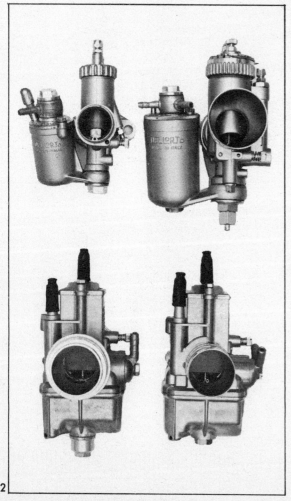

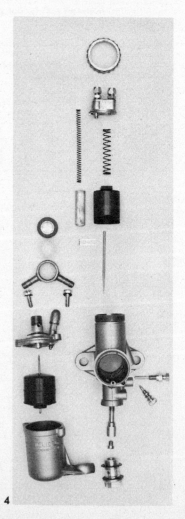

was talked about by Tom Patton and, as I remember, Barnes Enterprises has an adjustable float needle. Main jets can be had, at least for Amals, in an assortment of sizes that run the scale from gasoline to alky. Pilot jets are replaceable, also in different sizes. Slides, too, come with various amounts of cutaway so that they can be suited to the average altitude of the locale in which a motorcycle is to be used as well as to suit other conditions of operation. Finally, the tapered main jet needle has a set of notchlike grooves near its upper end that provide still another means of adjustment: The higher the needle rides, the richer you'll run. Pay attention to factory recommendations with respect to the positioning of this needle as well as other adjustments and jet sizes throughout the carb.

THE GUILLOTINES . . .

At least two carburetors now on the market are using a sort of up-and-

1) **Vacuum pulses from engine make these two Keihins work. Left is "no-diaphram" type for Honda 450 while model on right fits 350 street models.**

2) **Keihin assembly reflects simplicity of concept, is typical of manually operated sliders in line. Main jet and holder are seen under body.**

3) **In same left-to-right order are 450 and 350cc Honda carbs, open to inspection. Effective seal of large "O" ring, left, is quite critical.**

KEIHIN

1

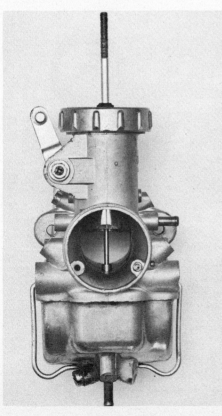

2

3

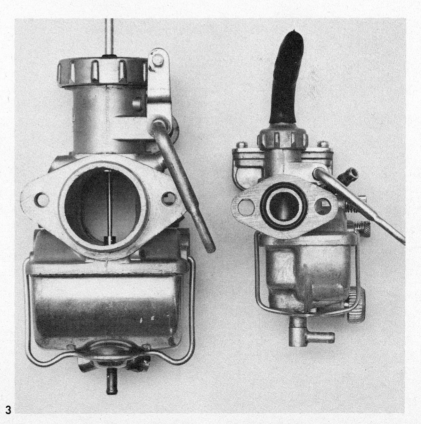

CARBURETORS

down slide that resembles a guillotine. These units, the Lake ''Injector'' and the Posa-Fuel, embody the simplest possible approach to delivering a combustible vapor to the cylinder. A first-impression glance at one of these things when it's disassembled and spread out for photographing immediately gives you the feeling that something is missing. You'll see no bulbous castings with cavernous throating, no bowls or baffles or bells or cups, no diaphragms, no floats and float needles . . . most of it isn't there, but it works!

The idea for operation seems even simpler than the carburetor itself. Gravity drops the fuel to the carburetor in the same old time-tested way. A needle, which has been flattened

1) Traction berms on top cap of our carburetor remind us to ''hand tighten only!'' Never, never use a wrench: An overtightened cap warps carb body.

2) We get a closer look at nomenclature of Keihin for Honda 350cc CB and CL street bikes. Off-road 350 SL uses simple manual slide-type carb.

3) Extremes in size are emphasized as we also notice ''O'' ring flange seal on smaller carb. Model at left combines flange and spigot systems.

4) The lid's off both the 450 and 350 Honda carbs and you can see both slides with flexing diaphram on right. Slide on 450 is of gravity return type.

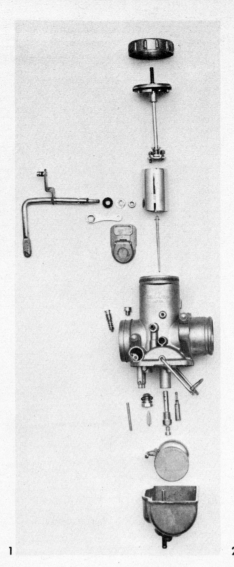

1

2

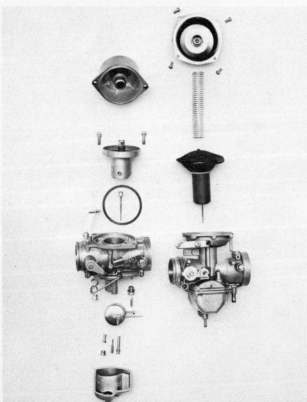

3

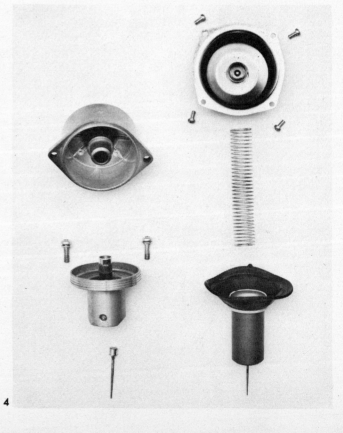

4

on one end, moves in an orifice in such a way as to control the amount of fuel that is drawn into the cylinder. The throttle is turned, the cable lifts the "blade" and engine speed increases accordingly.

What apparently happens obviously is more exciting than talking about how these "guillotines" work. For example, a letter of testimony addressed to the maker of one, the Posa-Fuel, states, "The performance of our machine over a track ridden only the week before was nothing short of fantastic." The writer, parts manager for a western Chevrolet dealership, goes on to indicate substantially better throttle response—especially through the mid-range—and a marked increase in power. Another testimonial for the Lake product extols such

BENDIX-ZENITH TILLOTSON

1) Twin-butterfly, venturi type Bendix-Zenith carb (top) has now replaced auto-diaphram Tillotson on big H-D. Both have accelerator pumps.

2) Tillotson at left has "bullseye" venturi, no fuel bowl, while Bendix-Zenith is less exotic carburetor, representing a return to basic carbs.

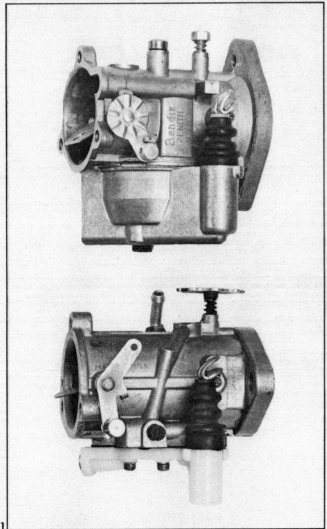

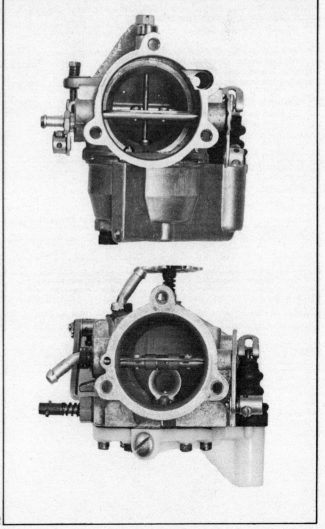

1

2

CARBURETORS

benefits as a surprising increase in power and performance smoothness.

Full instructions on how to get along with your "guillotine" come with either make. Actually, there isn't much to it since the adjustment is so easily accessible you can virtually effect richness changes—such as might be necessitated by a substantial change in altitude—as you ride along. Getting along might also include such thoughtful details as not forgetting to turn off the tank petcock when you arrive at your destination and not letting anyone ding around with your throttle grip when the engine isn't running. It's easy to see that a gravity-fed carburetor with no float-needle shutoff provision would tend to flood with a little playful grip twisting.

There's nothing in anybody's rule book that tells us motorcycle carbu-

1) The Bendix-Zenith as fitted to new H-D 61 and 74 cu. in. models is updating of old Linkert idea with the exception of its accelerator pump.

2) B-Z for H-D has discharge tube extending into fuel bowl. Tube takes fuel up to both idle and high-speed circuits. Accelerator pump at right.

3) Zooming in for macro-shot of accelerator pump plunger, we see three holes at top for adjusting plunger's stroke. How fast do you want to go?

4) Clip on end of needle valve engages tab on float assembly in B-Z carb, shown here with pivot pin out. Discharge tube is at center of float.

5) Tillotson from underside with metering needle and lever removed for inspection. Diaphram exerts pressure on lever to meter fuel into venturi.

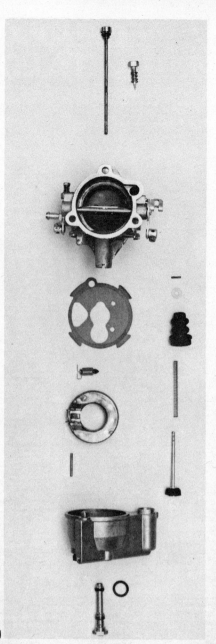

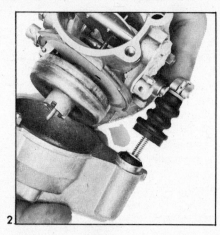

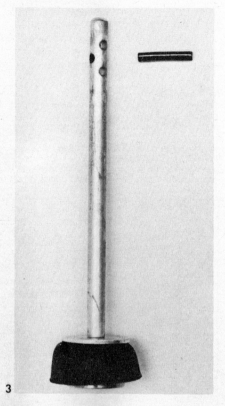

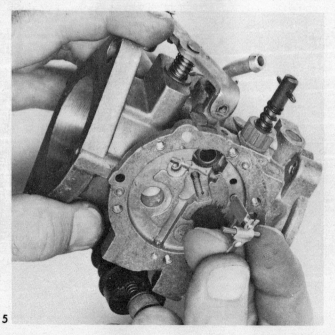

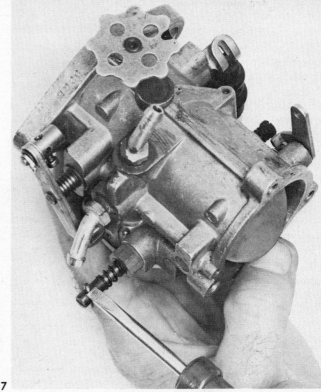

6) Flower shaped disc atop Tillotson controls idle mix adjustment by regulating fuel through idle discharge port. Adjust by ⅛th turn increments.

7) "Big T" has T-bar fingertip adjustment of main fuel jet. Tube on side is inlet with vent tube on top.

8) Bottom cover of Tillotson is off for shot of diaphram. Cylinder for accelerator pump is integral with cover. Butterfly is in open position.

9) Mag-charged twin "shovel Head" Harley big-inch engines are fed by a pair of out-sized butterfly-type S&S carburetors for custom applications.

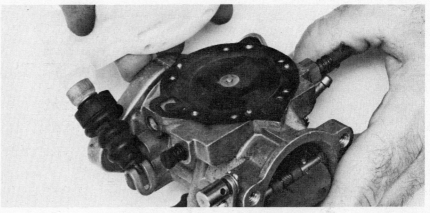

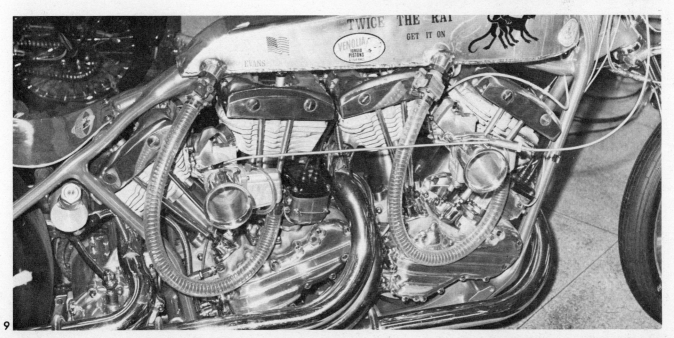

CARBURETORS

retors have to use air intakes that are controlled by slides. The old-time stove-pipe flue was successfully controlled by a pivoted disc for years; maybe that's when they first called it a "butterfly." At any rate it does the job admirably and actually is used to help introduce some refinements into jetting. In this application, the disc can be used, not only as a means of controlling air volume, but also as a means of controlling minor jet orifices as its edge moves back and forth along the inner surface of the venturi. Jet emissions for smooth stage-to-stage transition during acceleration can thus be released into the main-flow to the engine or withheld, all according to what optimum engine performance calls for.

Butterflys are where you find them, which is just a way of saying that carburetors having this flat, pivoted disc venturi control are of different types. Principally, the types would include carburetors with float bowls and those which had no bowls but, instead, took advantage of a diaphragm. Since the bowl type is the simplest we'll take a look at it first.

Names like Linkert, Bendix-Zenith and S&S come up when you approach bowl-bearing butterfly carburetors. The Linkert, of course, is associated primarily with Harley-Davidson a few years back and actually has

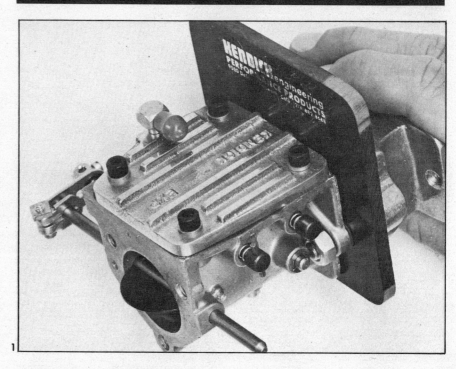

1) Machined, non-conductive shield isolates carb from engine heat. Vibration not as great an influence on this carb with no fuel bowl and float.

2) Custom Kendick carbs provide a look at pumper type (right) and non-pumper on left. Simpler model on left, the "EXP," supersedes pumper.

3) No-bowl diaphram carb, left, is compared to a couple of bowl-type pumpers. Simpler version is said to be free of fuel pressure inside chamber.

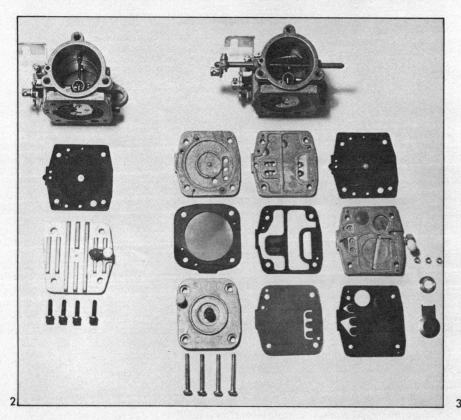

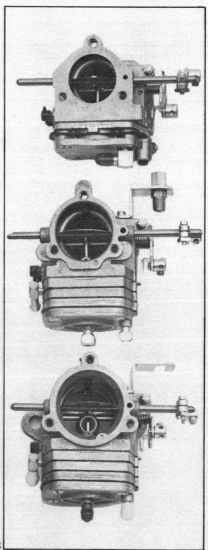

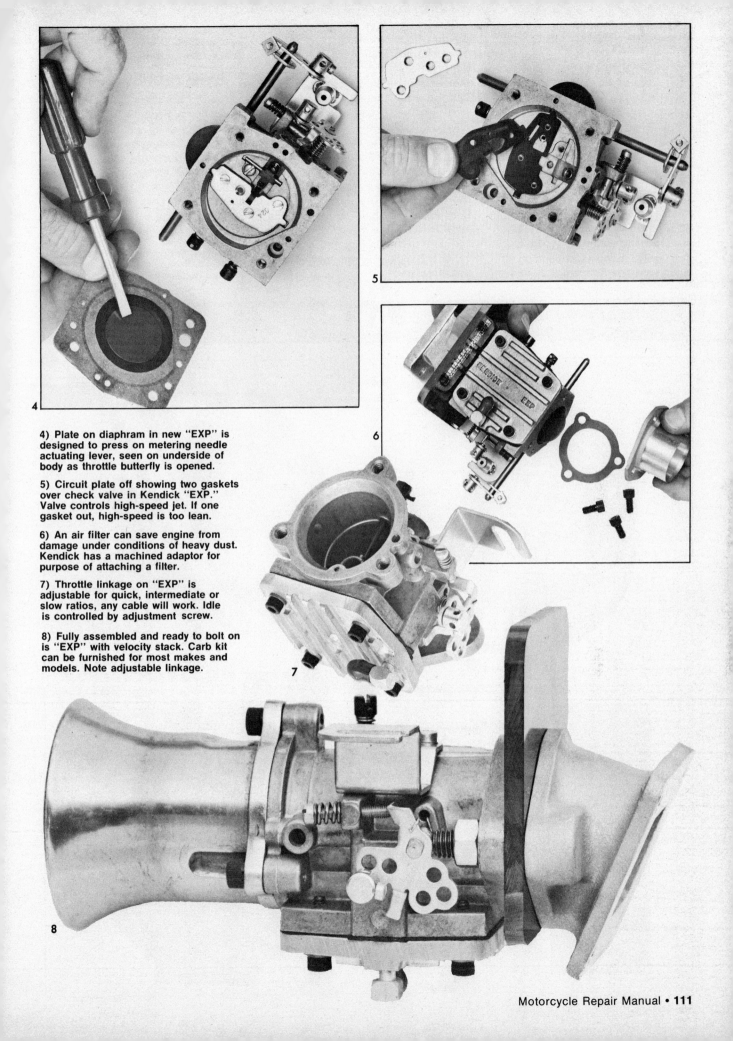

4) Plate on diaphram in new "EXP" is designed to press on metering needle actuating lever, seen on underside of body as throttle butterfly is opened.

5) Circuit plate off showing two gaskets over check valve in Kendick "EXP." Valve controls high-speed jet. If one gasket out, high-speed is too lean.

6) An air filter can save engine from damage under conditions of heavy dust. Kendick has a machined adaptor for purpose of attaching a filter.

7) Throttle linkage on "EXP" is adjustable for quick, intermediate or slow ratios, any cable will work. Idle is controlled by adjustment screw.

8) Fully assembled and ready to bolt on is "EXP" with velocity stack. Carb kit can be furnished for most makes and models. Note adjustable linkage.

CARBURETORS

two butterfly discs, one to act as a choke, the other for throttle control. High- and low-speed needle adjustments angle in from the topside of the Linkert and present a quick and easy means of adjustment. The S&S is similar in concept, if not in detail, to the Linkert. The main difference lies in the former's greater bowl capacity and larger throating for special application on some of today's maximum horsepower Harleys.

A little more detailing can be found on the big Bendix-Zenith rigs now being employed as original factory equipment on new Harley-Davidsons. The extra attraction here is the addition of an accelerator pump to provide that added mixture richness when sudden acceleration is needed. A small, finger-size plunger pump is included on one side of the carburetor. A quick turn of the throttle sends the plunger downward, applying pressure to a small reservoir of fuel which is supplied through a check valve from the main bowl. The extra charge is then forced up past another check valve and into the mainstream of air-fuel mixture traveling through the venturi. The plunger rod, incidentally, has three adjustment holes at its linkage end so the amount of pump stroke can be regulated.

CAME THE PUMPERS . . .

It was inevitable, I suppose, that someone, somewhere would sooner or later come up with the idea that a diaphragm could be acted upon by changes in pressure within the carburetor and, furthermore, that said diaphragm could be counted on to push against a lever that would, in turn, open a valve to the admission

1) Lake assembles and installs easily. Running with or without air filter can be achieved. However, richness of air-fuel mixture requires readjustment.

LAKE

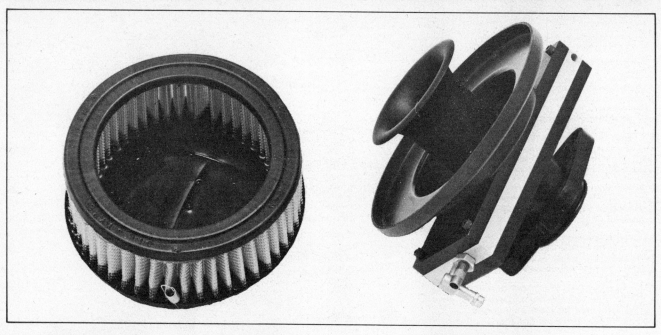

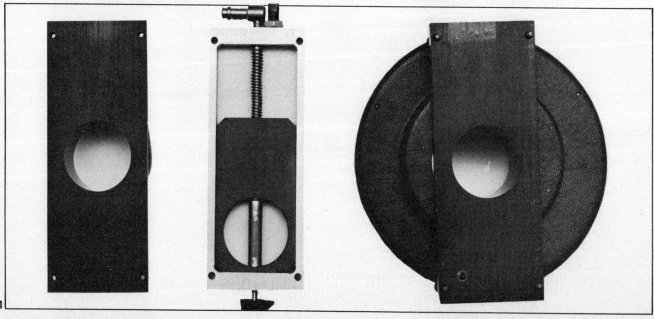

2) Lake's rack and slide are seen with slide in fully closed position. Needle, needle holder and adjustment know have been removed for inspection.

3) Guillotine slide at fully raised position as in full-throttle running. Allows maximum amount of fuel to be metered into mix. Dial knob adjusts.

4) Lake's assortment of needles is not without strange, flattened version at center. Correct needle adjustment at between 9 and 18 turns from stop.

5) Another guillotine carb, this time it's the Posa-Fuel. Larger model can be had with optional idler screw. Polishing also is an appearance option.

6) Posa-Fuel has slightly different adjustment details when compared to Lake version. Also features fully enclose guillotine slide rack casting.

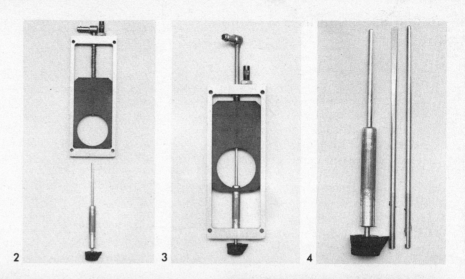

2   3   4

POS-A-FUEL

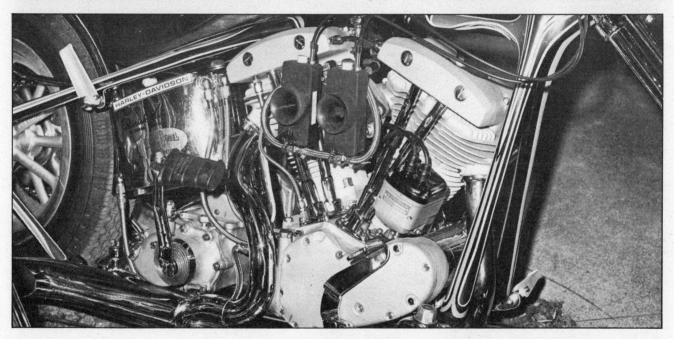

5

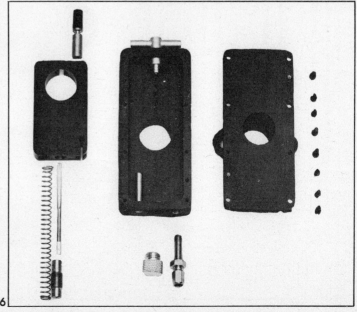

6

CARBURETORS

of fuel, and so on. The idea works and, I might add, it works quite well. Since the intensity of pulses from the engine are proportionate to piston speed, hence the need for more air and fuel, both concept and result seem to have aligned themselves.

Most of the people I mentioned as makers of slide-type carburetors also have in their stable at least one model that features diaphragm pumping. Bing, for all its much-perfected sliders, makes a pumper for the BMW. Mikuni has one that's in use on the Yamaha 650 and Honda puts Keihin pumpers on 350 and 450 models and calls them "CV" (constant-velocity) carburetors. Then, to be sure, there was Harley-Davidson's brief romance with the Tillotson a while back. I had no problems with the Tillotson on my Sportster after I converted the choke to a tickler by dangling a rivet through the atmosphere vent on the bottom side of the diaphragm. A push or two

on the shank of the rivet from beneath would flex the diaphragm just enough to let a little extra fuel into the venturi for starting. The main trouble seems to have arisen from flooding that would take place when a small particle of dirt from the tank would get into the inlet needle seat.

Adjustment procedure for pumpers parallels other carburetors pretty closely. Each model within each make has its personal idiosyncrasies and you'll find that, even within this chaotic framework, each individual motorcycle will react to tuning efforts in a slightly different manner. There is, however, a correct procedure outlined in the particular workshop manual for your bike. That Nth degree of perfection you're seeking usually won't be too far from the general settings recommended by the factory.

SOMETHING SPECIAL . . .

Before we go on to some tips on

tuning and maintenance, there are some special carburetor applications that are worth looking at. Actually, the S&S could have been mentioned here because it's one of those biggies that is capable of supplying the quantities of fuel needed to run super-powered stroker Harleys and other gas locomotives. The custom power boys also are going for the Mikuni Solex, an out-sized, dual-throater taken from the original Weber design. Frank Ryan of Mikuni says the people using them on bikes are probably buying them from Datsun dealers, since Mikuni's motorcycle division doesn't have anything to do with their sale or distribution. Carburetors of this type look good on a bike—they can make one look as if it is about to "stage" for an eight-second run, even if it's only parked under a shade tree. For this reason, I would suspect that, while they are doubtless quite efficient, they are equally cherished for their scarey appearance. After all, looking fast is half the fun!

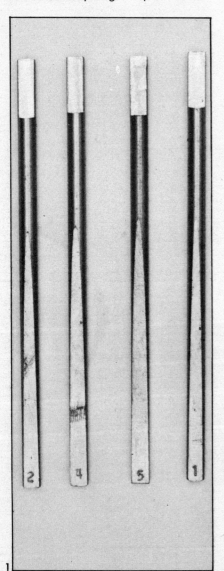

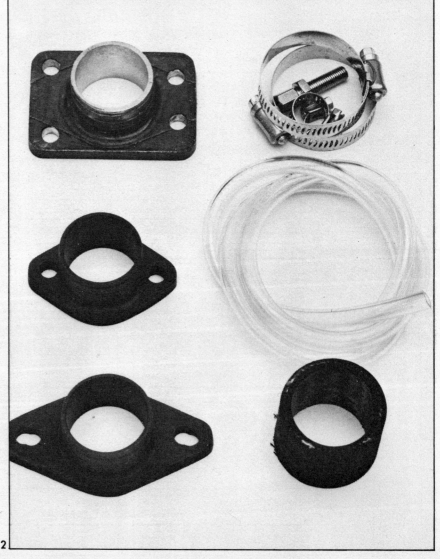

1) Differences in thickness of Posa-Fuel's various jet needles with higher numbered, thinner, needles giving richest fuel supply at high speeds.

2) Flange and air filter adaptors for Posa-Fuel carb kits are shown. Include transparent fuel line, clamps.

3) One of several in-line fuel filters available. Accessories of this type either trap of screen-filter residue in fuel. Use can be recommended.

4) The heavy grease being applied around circumference of this air filter will help form seal, trap dust particles. Element needs oiling, too.

5) Screen filter opened up to show accumulation of sediment from fuel tank. Particles can jam needles and jets in carburetor and cause trouble.

6) Throttle valve and cut away, jet needle and main jet drawings emphasize importance of cut away sizes, needle adjustment notches and main jet size.

3

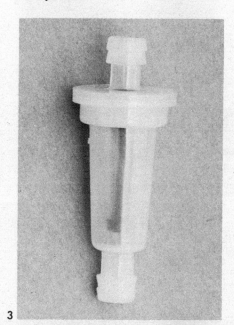

5

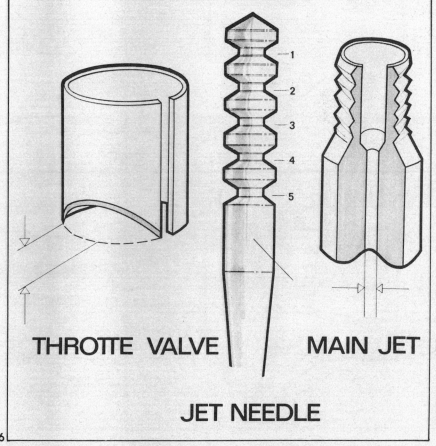

4

6

THROTTE VALVE   MAIN JET

JET NEEDLE

CARBURETORS

The Kendick is distinguished among custom carburetors because it is a simple carburetor that has been redesigned to become even more simple. The pumper model previously offered has had roughly two-thirds of its parts stripped away only to re-appear as a new, improved carburetor called the "EXP." Gravity feed has taken the place of the pumper system. There is no bowl, as such, but there is a valve-controlled metering chamber. Vacuum across the jet, as created by the movement of air through the venturi, actuates a diaphragm which, in turn, moves a needle off a seat and allows fuel into the chamber. The new "EXP" is said to have no fuel pressure in the metering chamber, as with the pumper, with the result that metering at low speeds is less difficult.

We had no sooner set up our photos of the new Kendick "EXP" than Dick Raczuk phoned to say the choke had been discontinued in favor of a "tickler" system. So, if you have a chunk of rubber in your mind, erase the choke disc and imagine a tickler in its place. Three sizes, 29mm, 33mm and 40mm are offered, the latter featuring a "bullseye" venturi so that there's still a vacuum over the main fuel nozzle, even on the low-speed circuit, providing smooth power surge all the way through. A Kendick "EXP" is said to have been set up on a Maico

1

2

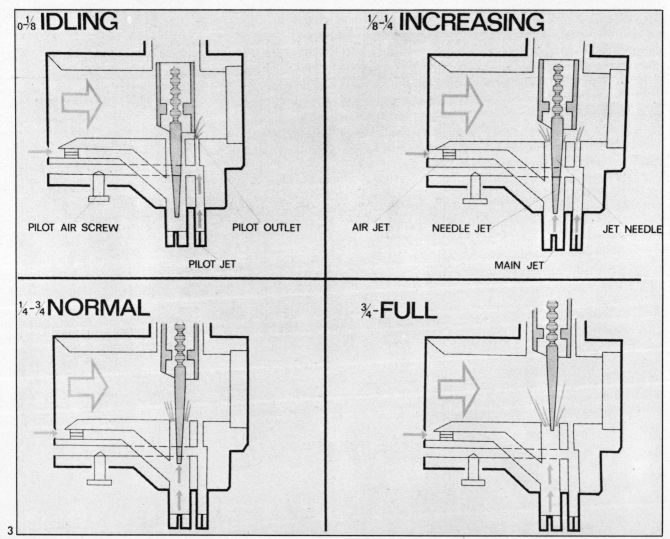

0-$\frac{1}{8}$ IDLING

PILOT AIR SCREW   PILOT OUTLET

PILOT JET

$\frac{1}{8}$-$\frac{1}{4}$ INCREASING

AIR JET   NEEDLE JET   JET NEEDLE

MAIN JET

$\frac{1}{4}$-$\frac{3}{4}$ NORMAL

$\frac{3}{4}$-FULL

3

and run on Axtel's dyno with the result that it pulled a thousand rpm sooner on the low end and added another thousand rpm of pull on the top end! Add to this bounty the extra advantages of claims for instant starting—with the new tickler system—and virtually flood-free operation and the whole proposition begins to look like a pretty fair investment. Like other custom items, the Kendick careburetor comes as part of a kit which is adaptable to your bike. This would

1) Size of cut away can be influenced by altitude at which run is made. Smallest cut offers richest low-speed running. Conversely, largest=leanest.

2) No, this isn't a Harley idle jet! It's a shot through a typical two-stroke cylinder for a look at interesting intake, exhaust and transfer ports.

3) Four drawings show stage-by-stage acceleration cycle of slide-type carb. Principals of function are same, though details vary from brand to brand.

4) Shape and amount of piston cut away in two-strokes is critical to performance and can influence distribution of torque over entire power cycle.

5) Here we see a pair of two-stroke cylinders from the outside. Reed intake port at left, exhaust on right. Pistons don't normally come this high.

include a machined manifold, heat shield, air cleaner adapter and linkage adapter. Raczuk says any throttle cable will work and that a swivel position adjustment lets you have a quick or slow throttle, according to your preference. Get it all together and you'll be able to add a tooth to your countershaft sprocket, the man says.

TAKE YOUR CUE FROM THIS TIP OR TWO . . .

I rambled at length with people in

service departments, manufacturers and mechanics for days before I delved into the text of this report. The following is a boil-down of dozens of carefully scribbled notes on carburetor curioso. Dennis Blanton at American Honda is the one who talked about the twin cable idea on the new Honda slides. He also observed that too many people get all worked up about their carburetor and start adjusting on it before they even take the trouble to find out whether they're

4

5

CARBURETORS

getting an ample fuel supply from the tank. A darned good suggestion! I've seen people push their bike several blocks into my shop so I could take a broom straw and open up the vent hole in their gas cap. They also have been known to fail to check the balance tube between twin carburetors before deciding they need a tune up. Tom Patton at Bultaco brought up the matter of plug reading when tuning carburetors. There's a tendency to take readings after putting around on the street which, in fact, gives little indication of running condition. If it's the main jet you're testing then it'll have to be done after a freeway-type main jet run. The reading should be

taken immediately, not after you've left the freeway and rolled into your garage. An off-white, parched appearance will show you that combustion is involving too much air, go richer. To the opposite, a black, sooty plug will indicate the need to try something a bit leaner. It's that dry, brown look you're after. George Wall of Hercules, with whom I discussed the Bing carburetors, said he noticed that most home tuners tend to back adjustment screws out too far. On that subject, there's always a manual recommendation for just how far to back out that adjustment screw and remember, as I mentioned earlier in this discussion, always tune stage-by-stage, starting at idle and working up. Jim Wismer, one of the Harley-David-

1) Paired reed valve intake system is exemplary of sophisticated air-fuel intake system on current Yamaha competition two-strokers.

2) Here reed valve pair sets pose next to massive intake port. Flexible "flappers" open and close with eng-impulses. Can be replaced if worn.

3) A head-on look at Yamaha reed valve pairs as cylinder, with intake port opening, occupies foreground. Port polishing would help performance.

4) Another type of reed valve assembly is shown along with full manifold and gasket assembly. Reed action pulses work well with pumper carb.

5) Reeds and reed mount are removed from manifold as if to inspect. Reed petals should be examined periodically for signs of fatigue, chipping.

6) Custom reeds are available for replacements. Fiber-epoxy type offered by D-H Enterprises is "digestible."

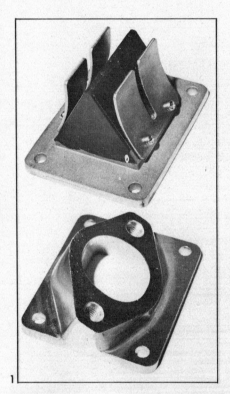

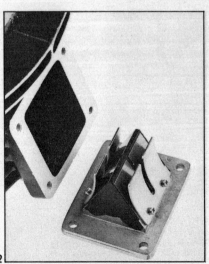

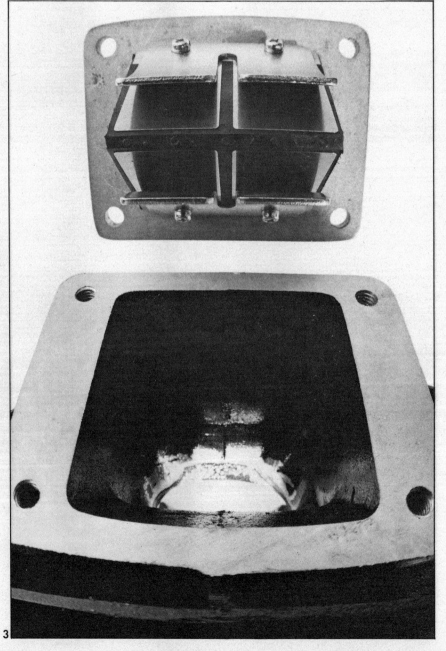

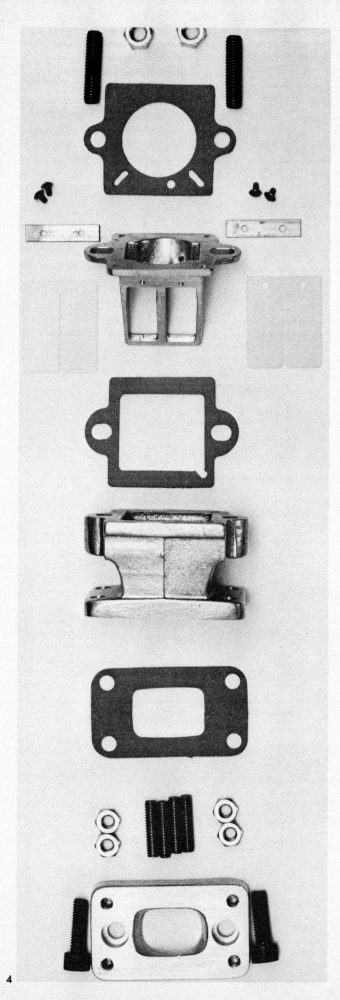

4

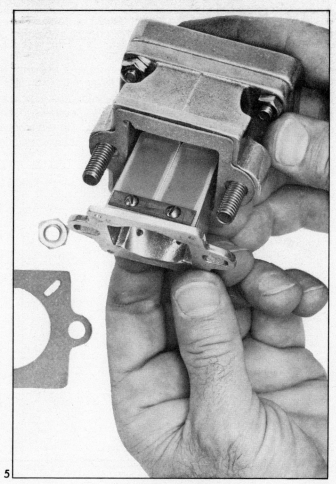

5

6

CARBURETORS

son people I conacted locally, aptly pointed to the fact that even something as simple and inexpensive as the addition of a velocity stack helps. If, however, you've removed an air filter in order to add the stack, bear in mind that you may very well be running somewhat leaner than before and that re-adjustment of the carburetor probably will be necessary. On the subject of air cleaners, I have never found reason to believe that they are absolutely necessary on street bikes. In fact, Jerry Fairchild, a prominent builder and tuner of Class "A" speedway machines for over 40 years, will tell you with great conviction that an air cleaner isn't even necessary on a dirt tracker. To prove his point he has for many years run his Prestwich and Jawa engines with naught but a funnel and screen " . . . to keep out the big chunks." Fuel filtration is another proposition: It's a good idea because dirt and stray flakes of paint can raise hob inside a carburetor. A trick I've used to prevent build-up of rust on the bottom

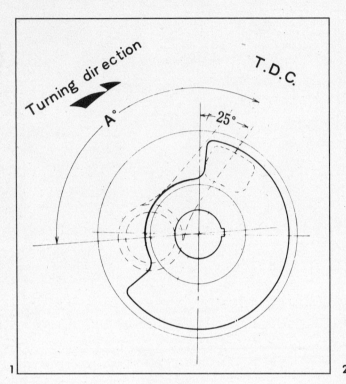

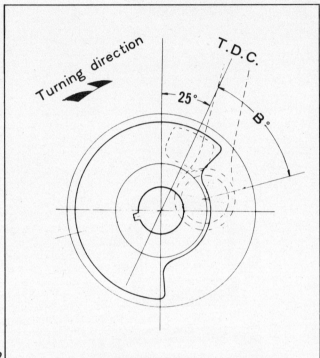

of a gas tank involves dropping in a couple of "00" buckshot. They're too big (about ⅓-inch) to become stuck in the petcock and won't rust. They roll around inside enough to prevent rust deposits without making enough noise to become an annoyance. Finally, don't be caught up in the popular misbelief that installing a set of megaphones on a bike calls for re-jetting the carburetor(s). The idea going around is that megaphones will "open up" the exhaust system and cause substantially leaner running. Maybe so with completely open, true racing megs, but with anti-noise laws being what they are, the truth is that megaphones have become just as restrictive to exhaust systems as orig-inal equipment factory mufflers. In fact, a lot of today's megaphones are even more restrictive than factory equipment! No longer megaphones, most have become inefficient and un-necessarily restrictive mufflers with a sporty exterior. Their use will nearly always cost you a couple of ponies. But, like I said, looking fast is half the fun!

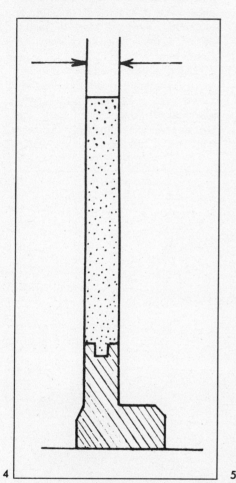

4

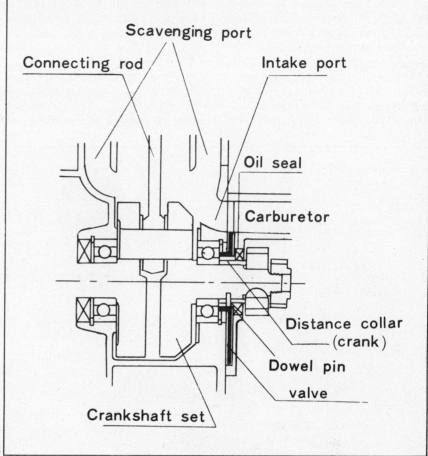

Scavenging port

Connecting rod

Intake port

Oil seal

Carburetor

Distance collar (crank)

Dowel pin

valve

Crankshaft set

5

1) Rotary valve provides timing for admission of air-fuel mix in 2-stroke engines. Here, valve is about to open port to accept air-fuel mix from carb.

2) Intake cycle completed, rotary valve has again covered intake port, readying engine for combustion cycle. Note position of con rod and port.

3) Hilborn injection and Air Research supercharging combined on Honda's exotic 8-cylinder record attempting Hawk. Note air collectors for carbs.

4) Cross-sectioned rotary valve is drawn to show importance of maintaining correct thickness, a condition which should be checked periodically.

5) Bowels of rotary-valve 2-stroke engine shown in blackline detail to indicate relationship between carburetor, intake port and scavenging port system.

6) Snail cage housing for turbocharger holds exhaust driven impeller claimed to turn up to 30,000 rpm. Power loss to drive virtually nil.

6

THE AMAL MARK II

This successor to the Concentric is loaded with interesting and practical features

The Amal laddies have now taken a giant step. They have labored to produce a carburetor that combines the virtues of the earlier products—and more—with none of the vices. From what we have seen the future for Amal carburetor fans is bright. Here is an in-depth look at the latest in British carburetor technology: the Amal Mark II.

The differences between this model and its predecessors are enormous. Indeed, they are so extensive that just about the only parts interchangeable are the carburetor jets. The rest is all new.

Let's start from the top: The Mark II is capped off with a screw-on, self-lubricating top made of plastic (the English call it "Kematal"). It seals neatly and snugly yet appears strong and allows quick, easy access to the slide.

The slide itself is physically much larger than its Concentric counterpart. It is also significantly lighter than the old part. And remember when we mentioned the matter of similar and dissimilar metals in friction? Well, any potential problems in this area have been eliminated by making just the slide in zinc-based alloy while the body it rides in is aluminum. Too, the Mark II weighs but 1.75 lbs., .5-lb. less than the Concentric.

Taking a lesson from Mikuni, the Mark II metering needle is now secured by a circlip surrounded by a holed disc. If you harken back, the Concentric's needle was secured with just a clip upon which would

1

directly bear the throttle return spring. Also, it is important to note that the Mark II needle boasts five adjustment grooves. The Concentrics had but three.

The carburetor body has several interesting features. A Mikuni-type mixture enrichment device (choke) is used. And, for additional tuning versatility, a variety of jets is available. Most contemporary mixture enriching systems meter fuel through a fixed orifice. However, the Mark II uses a jet, and Amal jets are available in sizes ranging from 15 to 70 in steps of five. This enhances the swapability of the carburetor, state of tune, air filtration flow and other factors that confront hop-up artists.

The fuel-sloshing tendency of prior carburetors has been eliminated by locating the float bowl vent outlets (there are two) high on the carb body. In this way, for fuel to now slop out, it must rise well over 2 ins. from the bowl to the vents.

One of the carburetor's most interesting features is its dual pilot circuits. You see, in terms of pilot fuel requirements, two-strokes and four-strokes differ vastly. Generally, the four-stroke, due to the somewhat gentler nature of its intake tract pulses, requires more fuel when running on the pilot circuit. Air speed through the two-stroke's inlet is significantly higher, thus its drawing power is stronger.

In order to cope with this contingency, Amal engineers have incorporated two separate pilot circuits in the carb body. One circuit offers a relatively short, direct passage of fuel up from the bowl. In other words, draws a short, light column

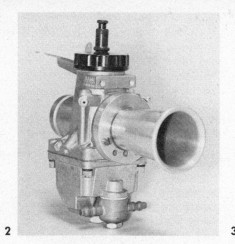
2

3

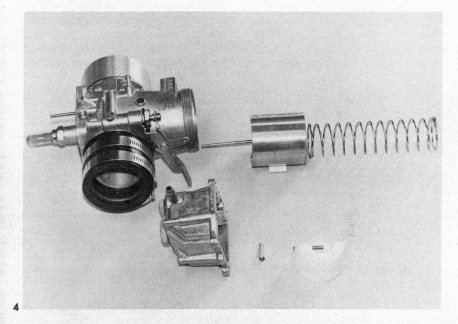
4

5

1. From junior to giant, there's an Amal Mark II for every application. The 22mm bore is the smallest, while tops is the 2000-series 40mm bore.

2. If simple is better, the Amal Mk II has few peers since assembly and disassembly is quick and easy. Note double inlet banjo fitting.

3. Precise tuning of the Mark II is easily and quickly accomplished thanks to well thought out design.

4. The best features of early Amals are found in the Mark II and past problem areas have been corrected.

5. The new needle valve is made of aluminum tipped with Viton for better sealing characteristics and longer life. These Viton-tipped needle valves are also available for early model Amal carbs from Burak.

PHOTOS BY PAT BROLLIER

THE AMAL MARK II

of fuel into the venturi. This circuit is used for a four-stroke's lower inlet velocities.

The two-stroke circuit is based on a much longer passage through the carburetor body, and a longer, heavier column of fuel. So, this passage is used for two-stroke applications. Were you to swap roles of these circuits, the four-stroke would run extremely lean at low speeds while the two-stroke would be plug-soaking rich.

A threaded brass blank is used to plug the circuit not to be used, while a pilot jet of appropriate size screws into the hole of the other circuit.

Amal has also made important in-roads in needle jet development. When the throttle of a four-stroke engine is tugged open a sudden lean condition occurs. One way to cure this and its attending burp, spit or just plain lag is to use an accelerator pump to inject a dollop of raw fuel directly into the tract. But this can be somewhat complicated, so what Amal has done is to develop a needle jet configuration that allows this sudden leanness to be kept to a minimum. The Amal four-stroke needle jet has a larger inside diameter at its pickup (bottom) end than it does at its outlet. Additionally, it is cross-drilled with a tiny hole to allow for better aeration and increased sensitivity to pressure changes. In comparison, Amal's two-stroke needle jet of equal flow capacity is smaller at its inlet and bigger at the outlet. It is not cross-drilled.

An earlier Amal problem has also been cured. In certain cases if the needle were adjusted to its highest position in the slide, the needle could indeed come out of the needle jet, thus sticking the slide WFO. This situation was cured by making the needle jet holder a speck longer so it now cradles the needle securely no matter what its position.

In comparison to many other carburetors, Amal float chamber volume has characteristically been rather small. This has many advan-

1. The needle is now secured by a circlip instead of a simple two-sided clip as in the Amal Concentric. Needle has five adjustment grooves instead of three as in the Concentric.

2. Looking down into the float bowl, the idle mixture jet is on the left and the cold start jet is in a recess at the top of the picture.

3. The screw-on, self-lubricating top is manufactured from a plastic material Amal calls "Kematal."

4. The slide in the Mark II is made from a zinc-based alloy and rides in an aluminum body.

5. Two float sizes are available. The left (smaller) one is used in four-cycle engines while the larger is designed for two-cycle applications.

6. The two needles on the left are cross-drilled for proper fuel atomization in four-cycle engines. The two on the right are for two-cycles.

7. The main jet is the same as in the earlier Amals. Protective filter screen is still retained.

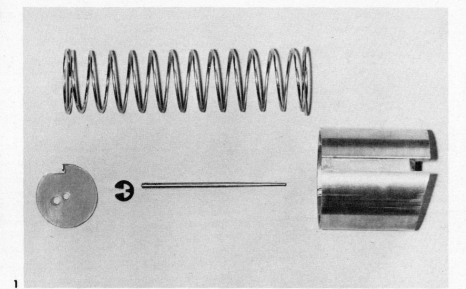

1

2

3

tages, not the least of which is a greater tolerance of altitude changes. However, this situation has also brought the Amal, particularly the Concentric, the criticism that "Amals run out of gas." But this gripe does not bear up under inspection. Largely this problem resulted from motorcyclists swapping around with carburetors and throat sizes and not making the necessary float needle valve compensations. You see, earlier Amals, from sizes 22mm all the way up to 38mm all used the same float bowl. Many individuals would overlook this and so, the gripes. Using the correct

4

float needle jet, however, obviated these complications.

The Mark II Amal still abides by the smallish float bowl precept. Also, it comes with a much larger needle and seat, big enough to make everybody happy. Further, the new needle valve is now made of aluminum and tipped with Viton, a resilient, tough polymer with excellent sealing qualities. (Owners of earlier Amals will be pleased to learn that Burak Bye-Products, 15170 Raymer St., Van Nuys, Calif. 91405 sells a Viton-tipped replacement to fit all Amals.)

For a given float chamber, two floats are offered. Two-stroke carburetors will normally be fitted with the larger float while four-strokes will come with the smaller item, unless otherwise specified.

The Mark II has another interesting feature: adjustable high-speed air bleed. This circuit, sometimes also called the air circuit correction can be a valuable adjunct to the performance-conscious tuner. There are three different jets available.

Mechanics will be pleased to know that the Mark II is also versatile in that it fits right into existing

Mikuni carburetor flanges. Additionally, by the time you read this, Burak will have completed and ready for sale adaptors to fit the units to the 650 Yamaha. Already the carburetors fit Triumphs and Nortons. Further, the Mark II is available as standard equipment on the Bultaco Frontera and the 175 Husqvarna. It is also used on certain production Ossas and Montesas.

Indeed, it appears that Amal has launched a concerted effort to regain its past prestige among motorcyclists, tourers and racers alike. The scope of fine tuning and versatility incorporated in this new design indicates the British company to be dead serious in their efforts to produce carburetors to fit the ever-widening spectrum of motorcycles today. The 2600-series Mark II is available in 22, 24 and 26mm bores. The 2900 series spans 28, 30, 32 and 34mm sizes. Carburetors of 26, 28 and 40mm diameters are of the 2000 series. Prices are $56, $58 and $69 respectively, which is somewhat costlier than most Mikunis, but the innovation, quality and superb engineering exemplified by the Mark II Amal makes it all worthwhile.

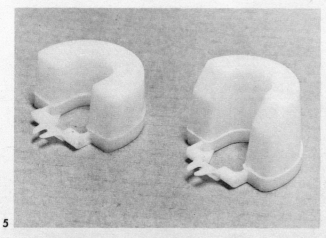

5

6

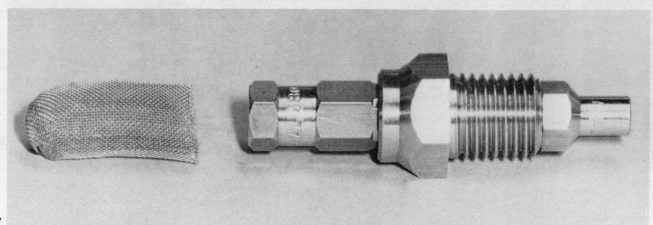

7

WATER COOLING

Some tips on this new and important big bike component

COURTESY OF MOTORCYCLIST MAGAZINE

Not long ago, a patriot rode through the land crying out, "The water-cooled bikes are coming!" Unlike the warning given over 200 years ago of the impending British invasion, not many people paid heed to the cyclist advocating stronger ties with the automobile. After all, they're strong enough already what with electric starters, mag wheels, tubeless tires and automatic transmissions.

Lest we forget, many of the world's first automobiles were air cooled and two of the best still are (Volkswagen's beloved Beetle and the legendary Porsche). It was, in fact, many years before the issue was settled in favor of water-cooled engines in horseless carriages and they became automobiles. If it were not for heat exchangers (radiators) the automobile may well look very different today. And what, pray tell,

would a Rolls Royce be without its distinctive radiator shell?

Water cooling for motorcycle engines has been popular in European road racing machines for many years (CZ, MZ, Maico, etc.) and more recently in the Suzukis, Harleys and Yamahas. The 350cc and 500cc Yamaha road racers have had notable success with their water-cooled two-strokes. Suzuki's GT 750, however, is the first production street bike to incorporate water cooling and it's been followed by Honda's GL-1000 Gold Wing. When these two motorcycle giants lead, others automatically follow, so watch out for the water cooleds!

There is very little difference between the cooling system in an automobile and that found on a motorcycle, but differences do exist and for this reason, mention should be made of them. On automobiles, the pump that circulates the coolant

1

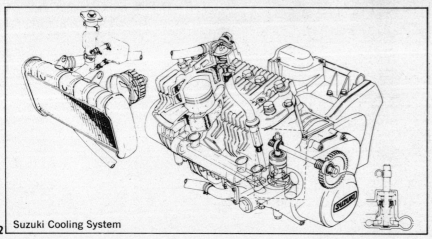

2 Suzuki Cooling System

1. With fuel tank removed, innards and outards of Suzuki water pumper are revealed. Gussetted top tube houses radiator filler neck. Hoses are braided for added protection against bursting, but clamps should be inspected regularly for tightness.

2. This diagram reveals the basic elements of water cooling system.

3. Here we see the radiator (1), fan (2), combination thermostat and flow control valve (3), cylinder block (4), crankcase (5), water pump (6) and radiator bypass hose (7). During warmup, water flows in engine only. Between 82 and 95°C, thermostat opens hose to radiator without closing the bypass valve so water from engine and radiator meet at impeller-type water pump. All the while, a heat sensor on thermostat sends readings to the rider. At 95°C, bypass valve closes and all water is cooled by radiator before returning to engine. Fan automatically cuts in if temp reaches 105°C.

4. Naked lower engine casting shows water pump swirl chamber. Needless to say, regular inspection of gasket between this and mating casting is a necessity. Cooling system drain plug is seen at upper left.

5. Both Honda and Suzuki radiators can suffer squashed fins if subjected to high pressure of steam cleaner. Best bet is scrub first then use 50¢ car wash hose at moderate distance from those fragile fins.

6. Water cooled street machines have a racing heritage dating way back.

is belt driven, on motorcycles it's gear driven. On automobiles, air is sucked through the radiator by a belt-driven fan, whilst bikes being unshrouded with sheetmetal need only a thermostatically controlled electric fan for extreme situations. A very popular aftermarket automotive accessory is an expansion or overflow tank. Honda GL-1000 and Suzuki GT-750 owners will be pleased to know an expansion tank is incorporated into their cooling system (at no extra cost). Motorcycles also have the advantage when it comes

to warm-up since coolant flow is restricted to the engine until proper operating temperature opens the thermostat to include the radiator in the circulation pattern.

Since owners don't encounter fan belt problems and occurences of overheating are virtually nil, maintenance is more a matter of inspection than anything else. Naturally, coolant level is most important and the expansion tank should be checked frequently to make sure coolant level is adequate. Don't be tempted to exceed the 50/50 coolant/water mix. And, use only coolant containing no salt (ditto for the water) as per the manufacturer's instructions. Although distilled water isn't really necessary, if you suspect your tap water of containing too much salt (water softener in the system), then by all means use distilled or steam iron water. Salt acts as a corrosive agent on the aluminum components and you'll find yourself replacing the water pump and eventually the engine if you ignore this fact. Remember, too, that it's the water that really provides the cooling. Ethylene glycol acts as a rust and corrosion in-

hibitor, a lubricant and permits elevated operating temperatures, but the water in the 50/50 mixture is what picks up the heat from the engine and dissipates it through the radiator.

Never, never remove the radiator cap when engine temperature is high: Remember the system is under pressure. Any checking and replentishment of the coolant level should be done via the expansion tank. If, through gross neglect, the expansion tank runs dry, let the machine cool completely before removing the radiator cap.

Radiators collect bugs which can decrease efficiency by restricting air flow. But a shot of high-pressure steam from a 50¢ car wash can bend the radiator fins and really clobber air circulation through the radiator. To get the bugs out of the radiator, scrub carefully with a bristle brush and hot, soapy water first. Then use the 50¢ car wash steam cleaner (but back off) from the back side, keeping the nozzle 18 to 24 ins. away from the radiator. Follow with another scrub-down with the bristle brush. Rinse with clear water under very moderate pressure. Oh yes, don't be tempted to remove the wings on your Honda GL-1000 radiator. They are designed to enhance air circulation through and around the radiator.

Naturally hose clamps, flanges and the like should be inspected and tightened periodically and the hoses checked for cracks and weather checking. Replacement of hoses and gaskets is quite simple.

Don't be afraid of the water-cooled machines. They offer performance, endurance and easy maintenance with only a 20-lb. penalty. And we're sure you'll see their numbers increase.

3

4

5

6

ELECTRICAL SYSTEMS

An understanding of how the juice flows is important to solving trouble-shooting problems. Digest this chapter—it isn't as difficult as you may think.

BY JIM LEWIS

What's the matter, boobie? You say that electricity has you thoroughly confused? You say that the closest you want to come to the electrical system on your motorcycle is when the spark plug needs changing? And that even then, you get zapped by the spark?

Well, cheer up old buddy. It can be explained to the layman in terms and concepts that even the rankest novice mechanic can comprehend. The biggest problem with most explanations is the terminology, the big, unfamiliar words that the electronics-types throw around with total abandon. Most people have a vague idea what volts are and know that amps have something to do with it too. But those words are no longer in popular usage any more. Now it's impedance, electrical potential difference and electromotive force.

Many who try to obtain a better understanding of electricity, become

WIRING DIAGRAM

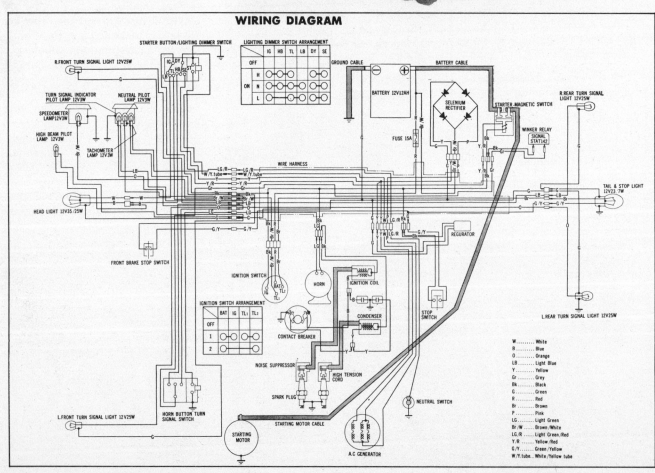

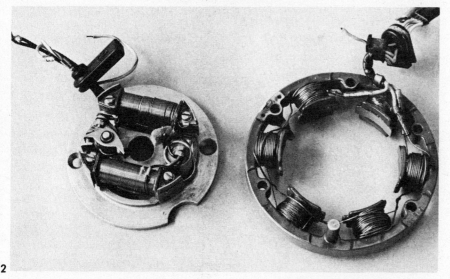

Water is used along with another form of energy (fire and resultant heat) to do that job.

When everything is going right, that's the principle behind most electrical systems on a motorcycle. The battery (water tank) is charged (set up on a hill and filled) and it then supplies electricity (water) for various jobs and is itself replenished by a generator (water pump).

Now that wasn't too bad was it? Impedance, EMF and potential difference weren't mentioned once. Admittedly, it was a very simple-minded explanation and has some drawbacks, but it's a start in the right direction for most beginners. From here, let's move on and talk a bit about electric generators and how they work.

Electricity can be produced a number of different ways. You've probably walked across a wool rug in your socks and then received a shock when you touched a doorknob. It's not likely that you fully realized it at the time, but you were an electric generator and a battery all at the same time. Your socks picked up a small electric charge by rubbing across the rug and it was stored in your body. The entire charge of electricity was released when you touched a metal object. This is plain old "static" electricity, the same stuff that Benjamin Franklin played around with in 1746. It doesn't have much value today for anything except thunder and lightning because it is used up instantly. To be useful, it must be continuous and steady.

Static electricity is made by rubbing two different materials together like silk socks and wool or cat's fur and a rubber rod. There's another more efficient way to make electricity and that's with a magnet and a coil of wire. When a conductor is moved through a magnetic field, an electromotive force or EMF is induced in it. If the conductor forms a loop or closed circuit, an electric current will register on a sensitive meter connected in the conductor circuit. When the conductor is moved downwards, the needle swings in a direction corresponding

so tied up with the unfamiliar words in explanations, articles and textbooks that they soon give it up as a lost cause. Here then, is your chance to take a grasp on the subject without those problems because the whole thing will be dealt with using an absolute minimum of technical words. If you should wish, once you have an idea of what is going on inside those little copper wires, then you can pick up a book at the library and learn the fancy names.

ELECTRICS THEORY

A favorite way to explain electricity is to substitute water for electrons inside the wires. That's a little hard for most of us to sink into our confused skulls, so let's forget about the wires and substitute a complete water system, pipes and all.

We have a water tank up on a hill with water, a means of piping it down to the bottom of the hill and a way of connecting hoses up to faucets at the bottom. We can fasten a number of garden hoses to the valves and lead them just about anywhere we want and do quite a few things with the water. Put a small nozzle on another

and squirt a high stream of water with that one. Use another one to fill a water bed and another to operate the sluice in a gold mining operation.

There are hundreds more things that might be done with more hoses from this tank except that there is a limit to the number of hoses that this particular system can support. That means that we can't have too many connected to it. There's also the fact that the tank would be emptied very quickly if we ran a large number of hoses from it.

Now we have a system of water up in a tank, a pipe that allows us to use it but we know that there's a limit to how much we can draw from it. Let's take one of those hoses and run it over to a boiler. We fill it up and light off the boiler. Steam is produced and we add just a bit more water to keep the level up from time to time. The steam drives a paddle wheel which we connect to a water pump down by the lake. The pump feeds water into a pipe that goes up to the tank on top of the hill. Notice, though, that the force of the water coming out of the hose at the boiler doesn't provide the energy directly to refill the tank.

1. Typical A.C. generator with magnets mounted inside the solid wheel in center. Coils of wire are situated around the circle and connected together for added voltage output.

2. Generator coils can be mounted in such a way that the magnets either rotate around the coils on the outside or rotate around inside the circle.

ELECTRICAL

to the direction of current flow. If the conductor is moved upwards, the needle will swing in the opposite direction, indicating that the current flow is also in the opposite direction.

The amount of movement of the needle will depend upon the speed at which the conductor is moved up and down, and the density of the magnetic field. The same effect can be obtained by moving the magnet in and out of the coil of wire. Induction will again take place and current flows in the wire coil. This time, because the coil consists of several turns of wire, instead of one, the induction will

be increased, thereby giving a greater output. The meter will register in exactly the same manner as before, only in with a greater deflection.

When the coil has been wound round an iron yoke, which concentrated the magnetic field around the wire coil, we have a simple alternator. In the center of the yoke a bar magnet is rotated.

The direction of the magnetic field will change every 180 degrees of rotation of the magnet. The north pole is at the top, but after the magnet has rotated 180 degrees, the south pole is at the top. The direction of current flow in the coil has been reversed. Induction has taken place due to

movement of the magnet and alternating current has been produced.

The sine wave shown is a simple representation of the current output from an elementary alternator. It shows the current during one complete revolution of the bar magnet alternator.

The vertical line represents the current in amperes, which is positive—above the neutral point or horizontal line; and negative below the neutral line. Starting from the left side, this line is divided into 360 degrees, that is, one complete revolution of the bar magnet. From zero degrees the current gradually builds up to its maximum value at 90 degrees; then

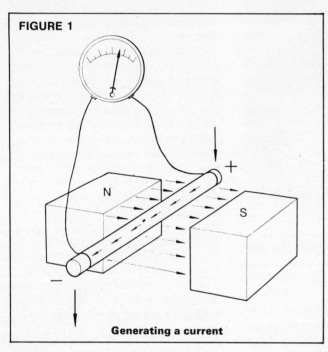

FIGURE 1

Generating a current

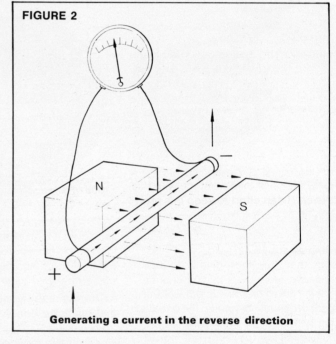

FIGURE 2

Generating a current in the reverse direction

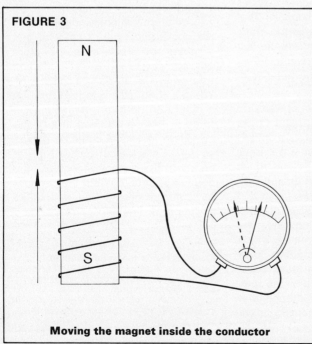

FIGURE 3

Moving the magnet inside the conductor

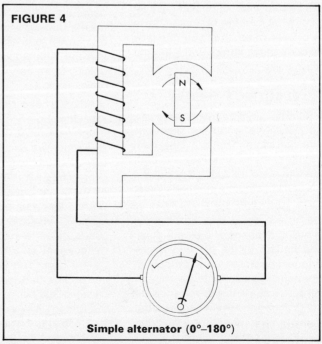

FIGURE 4

Simple alternator (0°–180°)

gradually decreases until it is zero again at 180 degrees, becoming zero again at 360. This cycle is repeated as long as the magnet is rotated.

Alternating current of this type is of limited use. A battery cannot be connected directly to an alternator for charging purposes. A battery can only be charged by DC current. There are two ways of converting AC current into DC: By means of a mechanical switching device and through a solid state rectifier.

DC generators consist of an alternator and the mechanical switching device made up of a commutator and graphite brushes. When the alternator is in the zero to 180 degree phase, the switch is in one position that allows the current to pass through the loop. As the alternator rotates to the 180 to 360 degree phase, the commutator and brushes switch the leads so that they are reversed. This negates the backward flow of current with the result that the current in the loop beyond the switch flows only in one direction as evidenced by the meter which deflects only to one side. In other words, the current is DC.

Wear in the brushes and commutator is the chief disadvantage with this system. In an effort to keep this problem minimal, the brushes, which are the easiest to replace, are made of soft graphite, much the same as is used in a lead pencil. Eventually though, even the brass commutator will need servicing and cleaning.

With the advent of solid-state rectifiers, converting AC to DC was very much simplified. Consisting of four diodes which allow current to pass only in one direction, the rectifier does the job of the brushes and commutator without any moving or rubbing parts to wear out. By proper arrangement of the diodes inside the rectifier, AC current coming into the rectifier is converted to DC.

Motorcycles aren't very complicated as compared to a television or a stereo. Lights and turn signals can run straight off the battery and generator. Ignition, however, does need special attention. The 12 volts common to most of the motorcycle systems isn't capable of jumping the .025-inch gap in the spark plug electrodes. Just 12 volts aren't enough power in that form. Just as water will squirt farther when the stream is made smaller through a nozzle, so will electricity "squirt" farther if its form is altered. The battery's 12 volts is changed into about 20,000 volts. The

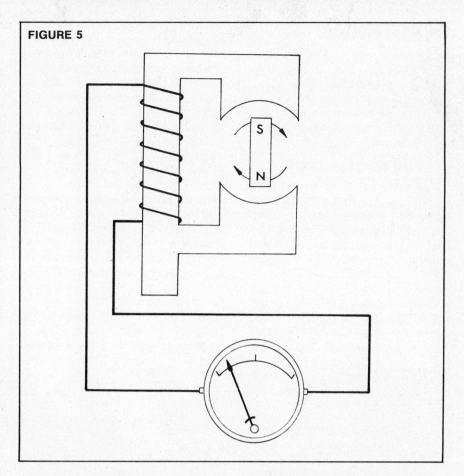

FIGURE 5

total volume of electricity is the same as before but it will now jump the spark plug gap and ignite the gas/air mixture inside the engine.

Converting the 12 volts into 20,000 volts is the job of the high tension coil and it works on the same principle as a generator. A coil of wire sits in a magnetic field that is changing in strength. The magnet, in this case, is an electromagnet which is very handy for this type of a job. It can be turned on and turned off with the result that the magnetic field strength changes without any moving parts. An ignition coil has hundreds and hundreds of loops of very thin wire. This configuration will produce a very high voltage but not much current or volume. (Actually, a greater volume would be preferred, but that would require a larger source of electricity, more than what a convenient-size battery can provide.)

Hook a spark plug up to the coil of very thin wire, connect a 12 volt battery to the electromagnet and then take a look at the spark plug. No spark is visible. Why? Because the magnetic field has to be *changing* to produce electricity and that 12 volts of DC electricity makes a rock-steady magnetic field around the coil.

The easiest way to change this

magnetic field is to simply shut if off. From one instant to the next, the magnetic field disappears. The coil of very thin wire reacts to this change and instantly electricity is induced inside its wire. The 20,000 volts charge down to the spark plug and zap across the gap. Simple and very effective.

If you had been watching when you first hooked up the battery (and if the battery had been a big heavy-duty model) you might have seen a spark at the plug. The sudden appearance of a magnetic field is also a change and that would produce 20,000 volts in the second coil just as the disappearance did when it was shut off. But most motorcycles have small batteries and they aren't capable of creating the magnetic field suddenly enough for the thin wire coil to do its thing. Simply shutting it off is always a sudden occurrence and most bikes operate on that principle.

The electric switch that shuts off the battery's 12 volts to the electromagnet and causes the collapse of the magnetic field is the contact breaker point. When the points are closed or together, the 12 volts flow through the electromagnet. It is a steady magnetic field and nothing is produced in the thin wire coil. As the points open, the

ELECTRICAL

12 volts are shut off, the magnetic field disappears and the coil reacts to produce the 20,000 for the plug.

That's basically how it works. If you want to know more of the details, you might pick up some books on basic electricity at the library.

DC BATTERY COILS

The majority of the motorcycles sold today are of the battery-coil operation. A wet-cell battery under the seat provides the operating current for the entire system, lights and ignition. It provides steady electricity at all times as long as it's in good shape and has a full charge. A battery converts electrical energy into chemical energy which is stored in the lead plates and the acid inside the plastic case. In a fully charged, fresh battery,

this acid (called electrolyte) is a solution of about 38 percent sulfuric acid. When the switch is turned on, electrons flow from the negative plates in the battery to the positive plates to provide the electricity. Eventually, the supply of electrons are depleted and the battery is no longer fully charged. Charging it replenishes the supply of electrons for later use. Test for a full charge with a hydrometer which will measure the specific gravity of the acid. It should be about 1.29 when fully recharged. This will be enough to activate the ignition coil which will produce a hot spark for easy starting. Lights will be even and bright at all engine speeds, including idle. Until fairly recently, most motorcycles manufacturers used DC generators to support the battery and keep it fully charged. On paper, this sounds simple and easy but, as you can guess,

things never work out that well in reality. Motorcycle electrical systems have a problem: The generator produces too much most of the time. The problem isn't solved by using a smaller generator, because it wouldn't be able to keep up with the electrical demands when lights are in use at night.

The answer was to incorporate a voltage regulator. Excessive voltage is either prevented or bled off before it flows to the battery. If it were allowed to pass into the battery unchecked, the battery would soon overheat and deteriorate. This was the problem with some of the British motorcycles in the mid-1960s and the reason they needed battery replacement every 12 months or so.

The principle behind the older DC generator voltage regulators was to bleed off some of the voltage through

1

a resistor. This cut down on the amount of current that passed through to the battery and helped prevent damage.

The resistor was switched into the circuit by an electromagnetic switch which was controlled by the battery. As long as the battery was up to nearly full strength, it could hold the electromagnetic switch on and this would cause the resistor to act on the generator and bleed off some of the electricity. The battery was already fully charged and didn't need the generator's full output.

These older style regulators work very much like an automotive regulator and are very difficult to adjust without exact specifications and without any meters. If you believe that yours isn't doing its job, first check the surfaces of the switch points.

These resemble contact breaker points and they can become corroded. If this happens, the resistor may not be brought into the circuit even though the electromagnetic switch is closing the points. Very, very gently, dress the point faces up with a clean point file or with a narrow strip of #200 wet-or-dry sandpaper. Be careful not to warp or bend the thin metal arms that the point surfaces are mounted on. If this does no good, check for broken wires or leads and only replace the regulator as a last resort.

DC generators have not been used extensively for quite some time. Triumph used them on their twins up until the late 1950s and Harley-Davidson dropped them a couple years ago in favor of the AC generator. Yamaha still uses a DC generator on their 125

Enduro model. The reason for this is that the generator doubles as a starter motor. It is relatively easy to convert any DC generator over to a motor by changing a couple of wires around. Pressing the starter button feeds the battery's current into the proper wires to cause the generator to act like a motor. After the engine is running and the starter button is released, the generator operates in the normal manner and supplies current again to the battery.

The biggest drawback to a DC generator is the commutator and brushes. Generally, anytime a DC generator quits, it is because of the brushes and, occasionally, the commutator. But replacing the brushes is fairly simple. They are held in place by a coil-shaped spring which can be lifted out of the way. The brushes, which are made of graphite; are then free to be removed from their guide slot. Disconnect the wire lead and completely remove the lead and brush from the generator. Slip a new brush into the guide slot, connect the wire lead and set the coil spring into place.

After a long period of operation, it may be necessary to have the commutator renewed. This involves cleaning the grooves between the faces and sometimes smoothing the faces and making them true again. If they are left rough, the brushes will wear out rapidly.

Once past the battery in the system, lights, switches and ignition are usually straightforward. There is little difference in most battery systems other than generator and regulator

2

3

1. Newer Hondas are using a variation on the A.C. generator. Instead of permanent magnets to create the field, electromagnets are employed. Battery supplies current to activate them and the field is constant due to D.C. mode. Since the electromagnets are stationary, the magnetic field must be changed somehow to create the flow of current in the wire coils. This is accomplished by an iron wheel with a zig-zag slot in the side. The wheel is actually two pieces held apart by a non-magnetic strip of metal. The electromagnets affect the two pieces so that one becomes a magnetic north pole and the other a south pole. The engine spins the wheel between the coils and current is generated by the rapid change of north-south magnetism.

2. Lucas A.C. generator has rotating magnets in center of a ring of wire coils. Newer models are encapsulated in plastic to protect them from vibration.

3. Common A.C. generator on many two-cycle motorcycles. One coil supports ignition while the other supplies current for lights and horn.

ELECTRICAL

AC BATTERY COIL

AC (alternating current) generators are very simple. Consisting of little more than a series of connected wire coils arranged in a circle around a cluster of rotating magnets, they have no rubbing or touching parts. There is nothing to wear out such as the brushes and commutator in a DC generator.

But, as you remember in the first section on theory, not as much can be done with AC as with DC current. That was the reason for the commutator and brushes—it had to be converted from AC to the more useful DC electricity.

Then, along came solid-state electronics and transistor radios. By ex-

perimenting, scientists discovered that certain compounds of selenium had very strange electrical properties. They would allow electricity to pass in only one direction. The current could go forward but not in the reverse direction. Other compounds were found to freely pass electricity but only up to a certain voltage and anything over that was converted into heat. Many other unusual properties were found in other substances and soon the electrical designers were dreaming up ways to use these chemicals in electrical gadgets. They put these chemical compounds into tiny metal containers, stuck wires into the proper places and named them transistors, diodes, rectifiers and such. They are very useful things, very small, no moving parts and that means nothing to wear out. Although sometimes the chemical used inside is very expensive, there is such a small amount of it the price isn't high usually. These inexpensive, simple and reliable devices have had a profound effect on electrics and will, no doubt, continue to make things easier in the future.

One of the very first of these new solid state devices to find use on a motorcycle was the rectifier. It allowed the simple AC alternator to be used in place of the DC generator. That meant no more brushes to replace, no more worry about the commutator shorting out.

Rectifiers are made of the chemicals that allow electricity to pass in only one direction. It's like a one-way valve. A rectifier allows the half of the

AC electricity going forward to pass freely. But when it tries to alternate (to go backwards) the rectifier stops it. The end result is DC electricity that comes in spurts. Half of the AC electricity is lost with this type of a rectifier which is called a half-wave rectifier.

There is another type of rectifier which does a better job. You can probably guess what it's called: a full-wave rectifier. This type does everything that a half-wave does but goes a step further. In addition to allowing the AC electricity to pass in one direction, it opens up a new path for the AC in the opposite direction

1. In Lucas system, this capacitor will directly replace the troublesome battery with no alterations or modifications. Ignition will work normally but lights will dim at idle. Complete system is very simple. Principle is something like a D.C. energy transfer set-up. Zener diode must handle all the voltage regulation.

2. One of the first ignition systems to provide a hot spark: the magneto. Completely self contained unit was bolted to flange on engine and driven from crank through gears or chain. Contact breaker points are mounted on end of housing. Lever and cable on handlebar manually controlled the spark advance.

3. Two types of E.T. magneto rotors: inside and outside coil. Inside coil on left has a heavier magnet assembly and this acts as a flywheel. Outside coil is used on racing machines more frequently due to light flywheel effect.

4. Unit on left is oscillator from early Kawasaki 500. This converts the 12 volts D.C. through A.C. to 400 volts D.C. Triggering unit sends signal to SCR for spark.

1

so that it can make a U-turn and join the other half. As the magnets spin past the coils, the north-south-north-south poles set up the alternating plus-minus-plus-minus current. The electricity is jerking back and forth inside the wires. As an example, let's say the rectifier allows the plus current to pass freely. As far as positive electricity is concerned, the rectifier isn't even there.

But when the current tries to reverse, the rectifier crosses the flow with the end result being DC current.

The full-wave rectifier wastes none of the AC electricity and is reliable until the day you hit it with a hammer. There is another advantage with the AC generator/rectifier combination. Voltage regulation is a great deal simpler. Because of the way the alternator coils are situated around the magnets, it's easy to run the wires from the coils up to a switch where they can be controlled before they are led to the rectifier. In this way, any number of the coils can be hooked into the entire system depending on how much electricity is needed. For instance, during the day when the lights are off, perhaps only two of the total six coils are needed. Then, when the lights are turned on, more coils can be switched into the circuit at the same time. This is possible (and is often done) by incorporating a double switch into the light switch. Two separate switches mounted in the same housing and operated by the same knob—one switch to turn on the lights and the other to connect the other coils into the system. Some of the older Hondas, Triumph twins and BSAs used this method of controlling the generator and protecting the battery.

It's a fairly good system, but it isn't automatic like the old electromagnet switch-type regulators. If the battery happens to be low on its level of charge, the rectifier won't do anything to correct this state. It will continue to run the system on only two coils in the daytime. And if the battery is fully charged, a small amount of current will flow into the battery and slowly overcharge it. English machines had a great deal of trouble with this. Chrome on mufflers and paint on the frames of many 1965 models was ruined by battery acid spilling over from overcharging batteries. It takes a very careful balancing of alternator coils and a large battery for this method to work well. When it's balanced right, it's trouble free.

2

3

4

ELECTRICAL

Then another of those solid state gadgets caught the eye of the motorcycle company's engineers: the Zener diode. This little electronic device will allow electricity to pass freely up to a specific voltage. When the incoming voltage exceeds that specific voltage, the diode chops the excess off, converts that into heat and allows the rest to pass as if nothing had happened. A 12-volt diode will ignore anything up to 12 volts. But if 14 volts tries to pass, it will knock two volts off and 12 volts will come out the other side of the diode. Sounds like it would make a perfect voltage regulator and that's what the engineers figured too.

However, it won't take too much excess voltage before it will melt itself. Generally about 10 percent over the rated voltage is the limit, which means a 12-volt diode can take 13.2 volts maximum before it will go belly-up. Most 12-volt alternators will produce something like 16 volts when the engine is operating up near its redline and that's more than enough to sizzle the diode.

It helps to mount the diode in an aluminum plate that has cooling fins built into it. Since heat is what ruins the diode, the mounting plate with fins (a heat sink) will help it pass off that killing heat. It helps even more to mount the diode and heat sink out in the airstream where it has a chance to cool better.

When a diode is added to the alternator/rectifier system, many of the overcharging problems disappear and the battery life is doubled. However, don't operate the bike with a bad battery. The battery (when it's in good shape) absorbs a lot of the extra current produced by the alternator and the diode takes care of the rest. When the two split up the extra electricity like this, both survive a lot longer. Without the diode, the battery will only last about a year. Without the battery, the diode will only last until the revs hit about 4500 and the voltage climbs up to 13.3 volts. For most of us, that means the diode is dead at the end of first gear! Those of you who have already sizzled one have discovered that some dealers charge $21.00 for

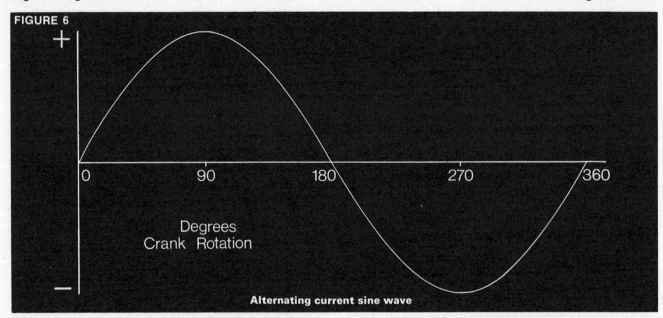

FIGURE 6

Degrees Crank Rotation

Alternating current sine wave

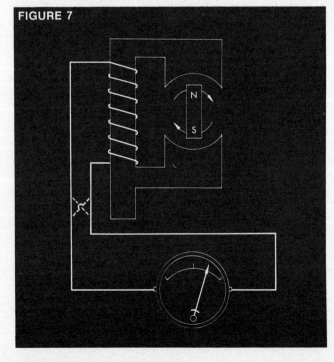

FIGURE 7

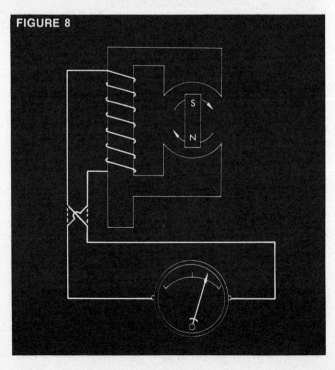

FIGURE 8

a new beauty—and installation is extra. You can save yourself a bunch of bucks by dropping by a local electronics shop. Pick up the heaviest duty 12.3 to 12.6 Zener diode he has or that he can order for you. The tab will be about $2.50. Better take in your owner's manual or a workshop manual (something with an electrical schematic in it) so that the man behind the desk can find you one with the right polarity and so that he has an idea of what you need.

With this type of a system, always keep a close eye on the water level in the battery. Don't let the battery lose its charge and deteriorate because that can ruin the diode. Also, keep the battery contacts clean. If they are corroded, the battery won't get a chance to take its share of excess voltage and pass it to the diode.

Troubleshooting either the DC or the AC generator/rectifier and battery system is not too difficult. Anytime one component in the system fails while the others work with no problem, you can figure that either the part (headlight, horn, turn signal, etc.) is no good or, more likely, a wire has broken or shorted against the frame. It always boils down to finding the faulty wire or replacing the part.

But, if the trouble lies in the power source, then it takes a little Sherlock Holmes thinking. It helps to know what the system will act like when each particular major component fails. When the generator quits or the rectifier is broken, the bike will run on only the battery and as the battery runs down, the bike will run worse and worse until it finally quits because there isn't enough electricity to operate the ignition coils. This state is easy to spot at night because the lights grow dimmer and dimmer. Revving the engine won't have any effect on the brightness either.

How do you know if it's the generator or if it's the rectifier? At this time it's very handy to have a volt-ohm meter. With this meter, the output of the generator can be measured and checked against what the shop manual says it should be putting out.

Alternators don't often go bad but when they do, their problem is generally a broken wire inside one of the coils. This may not stop the output of the alternator completely. It might still produce, but on a much lower level. That's why it's important to have the factory specifications handy when you take the readings with the volt-ohm meter.

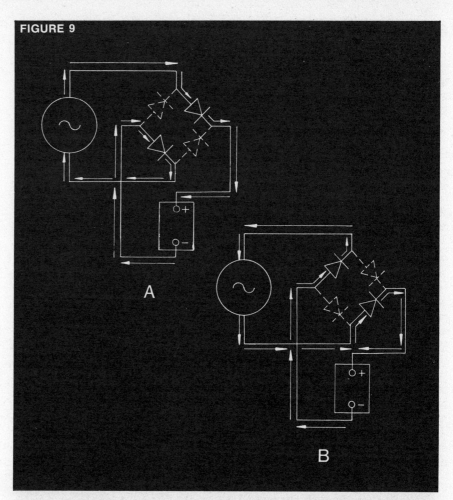

FIGURE 9

A

B

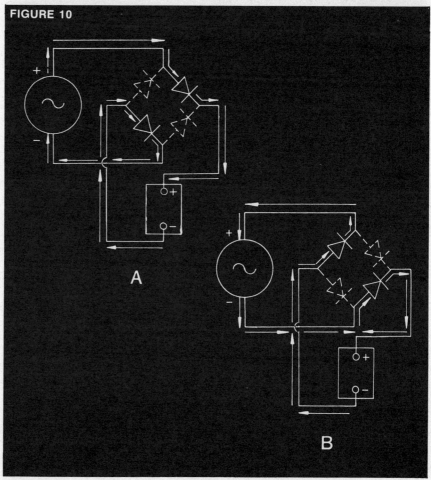

FIGURE 10

A

B

ELECTRICAL

Should the resistance readings be all right (which would indicate that there weren't any broken or grounded wires) but the output is still low, then there is the possibility that the magnets are weak. This is very rare, but it has been known to happen. Extreme heat or dropping the magnets on a hard surface can weaken them as can storing the magnets near another very strong magnetic force. More commonly though, connections will be loose or corroded.

After you've found the generator output high and the connections clean, what then, you ask? Elementary, my dear Dr. Watson—the rectifier, of course. If you wish, you might borrow the rectifier from a friend's machine and put it in place temporarily. There's really not much else that could be wrong if you've been careful with your test procedures up to this point. The only other possibility is the wire leading from the rectifier to the battery.

Suppose the bike is a bear to start and the light always goes dim when the engine is idling. The dimming light indicates that the battery isn't doing its job of providing a constant source of steady electricity. This may be due to a worn out battery or perhaps also due to a blown fuse on some models. Fuses are usually connected in series in the ground wire from the battery. If it blows, this would isolate the battery from the circuit. Some bikes will run like this, but most quit completely without the fuse.

A battery that is always slowly going dead in spite of recharging it in a shop could mean two things: The battery is on its last legs or that the alternator isn't running on all of its coils. In a situation like this, it's a good idea to check the alternator output first before replacing items blindly.

In almost every case of electrical problems, the trouble lies in something small. The major components don't go bad that often. Broken wires, bad connections and somebody's fat fingers stirring up the works sometime in the past are the most common bugaboos. Always work from a factory electrical schematic, work slowly and carefully. Most of all work with your head; think out what could be wrong from the way it acts and go from there.

E.T. FLYWHEEL MAGNETO

Way back in the old days, motorcycle engines ran on completely self-contained magneto ignitions. Everything was encased inside one housing that was attached to a convenient location on the engine. Gears or chain were used to take drive from the engine to turn the magneto and generate the spark. These magnetos worked very well, especially when compared to any other ignition system that was available at that time. They slammed out a 30,000-volt spark that is still envied today. However, reliability wasn't all that enviable. Magnetos had a tendency to fill up with engine oil that leaked past the mounting flange on the engine cases. And the drive train put a heavy strain on the bearings in the magneto and caused them to wear out rather quickly on some models, especially

1. "Black box" unit for generator supported CDI is small and simple. This unit, from Kawasaki 350 Bighorn, contains the capacitor and SCR which controls and supplies the spark.

2. The Bighorn flywheel/alternator rotor. Under the magnet flywheel are the coils for the lights, ignition, and trigger coil. Lighting coil is the largest and the trigger coil above the ignition coil is the smallest.

3. Femsa CDI unit, standard on many European motorcycles, is very simple and compact. This one has outside coils for a light-weight flywheel effect on fast revving competition engine.

4. Unusual magnet arrangement triggers Femsa unit instead of a separate trigger generator as on others such as Kawasaki 500. Note inside coils and heavy magnet wheel for street bike.

1

2

3

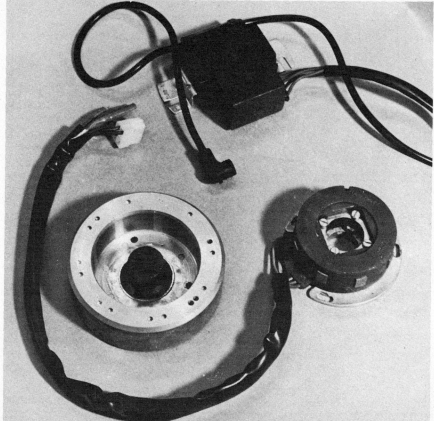

4

those with chain-driven mags. But their very hot spark ensured their popularity for many years. In fact, they are still considered the hot set-up in many racing fraternities today.

But engine designers decided to clean up their creations and move components inside where possible. The magneto's turn came almost last and when it did, the designer split it into two pieces. The low-tension half of the magneto, which is mounted to the end of the crankshaft, looks almost identical to an AC alternator. Wires lead from here to the high-tension half of the magneto which is usually mounted under the gas tank. The Lucas E.T. (energy transfer) system is a good example of this type. It is one of the few systems that produce the voltage for the spark by the sudden *appearance* of an electromagnetic field reather than the disappearance of it. All that is important is a change in magnetic influence to produce the spark. If the appearance is sudden enough, it will do the job.

Of the six coils of wire in the alternator, four are for the ignition and the remaining two support the lighting system. Except for the fact that they operate around the same magnets, they are completely separate and operate independently of each other.

The AC generator serves as the source of electricity for the entire system; there is no battery. Because of the nature of the alternator, the current flow isn't steady. It has high and low spots in the voltage. Each time a magnet swings past a wire coil, there will be a burst of electricity followed by a lull until another magnet swings by.

Lights aren't affected by this rapid fluctuation. They will operate in a normal manner. But the ignition is another story. As you remember, an electromagnetic field is built up around the coil of very thin wire in the high-tension coil. The contact breaker points open and that field changes suddenly which produces the voltage needed for the spark plug. The E.T. system has pulsating electricity and if there is a dead spot in the current occurring right at the moment the points open, there won't be any current creating a magnetic field. With no magnetic field to change, the breaker points accomplish nothing and there are no 20,000 volts and no spark. The rotating magnets in the alternator have to be positioned so that the magnets swing past an igni-

ELECTRICAL

tion supporting coil at the moment the points open. This will ensure that a strong pulse of electricity is in the ignition coil creating a good electromagnetic field. Now, when the points open, that magnetic field will appear and produce a good spark.

This brings up one of the characteristics of an E.T. magneto: It is very difficult to retard the spark for easier starting as can be done with a battery operated ignition. This is because retarding the spark would mean opening the points at a slightly later time than usual and that point in time wouldn't have a strong pulse of electricity for the electromagnetic field. Whereas battery operated ignition is usually set up for about 25 degrees of retard at idle, the E.T. can only take 10 degrees before the spark fades.

English twins running the E.T. have arranged the system so that all four alternator coils supporting ignition feed to the high tension coil that is about to fire. The other coil is cut out of the system and "ignored" until its turn to fire comes around. This means that each high tension coil is fed a heavy jolt of current and it can produce a hot spark.

The E.T. ignition system is very simple and troubleshooting it is easy. There are actually only three components to check out: The alternator, the high tension coils and the breaker points. All of these are relatively trouble free and in the event of trouble, first check the points and then look at all the wire connections. The alternator has nothing to wear out and the wires in the coils don't usually break. The newer alternators are sealed inside a plastic armor and this helps hold everything tightly. Vibration is no longer a problem. The high-tension coils are also sealed in plastic but there has been a small problem with vibration breaking the wire leads where they exit the plastic. It's not usually possible to solder the leads back and the coil must be replaced.

It has been found that the Lucas E.T. is very sensitive to the breaker point gap. If the engine starts missing and becomes hard to start, the first place to look is in the points.

Many of the Japanese bikes, particularly the smaller ones, use an E.T. system. However, they will also use a battery to help the lighting system. The ignition still operates directly from the alternator as in the Lucas E.T. The lighting coils in the alternator are connected to a rectifier which in turn supports the battery. The advantage to this system is bright lights, even at idle. Also, some states now require that the taillight be capable of operating for a minimum of fifteen minutes without the engine running and this is only possible with a battery in the circuit.

Four-cylinder Hondas have an interesting variation on the E.T. system in that only two high-tension coils supply the spark for all four cylinders. Honda's coils have double spark plug leads and two plugs fire from each coil. This necessarily means that both plugs fire simultaneously. The system is arranged in such a way that while one plug is igniting fuel/air in a cylinder, the other plug is firing harmlessly in a cylinder that is on the exhaust stroke. The only disadvantage to this set-up is if one plug is defective and fails, the other plug will not fire even though there is nothing wrong with it.

CAPACITOR OVER BATTERY

In a standard battery/coil electrical system, the battery's role is to provide

FIGURE 11

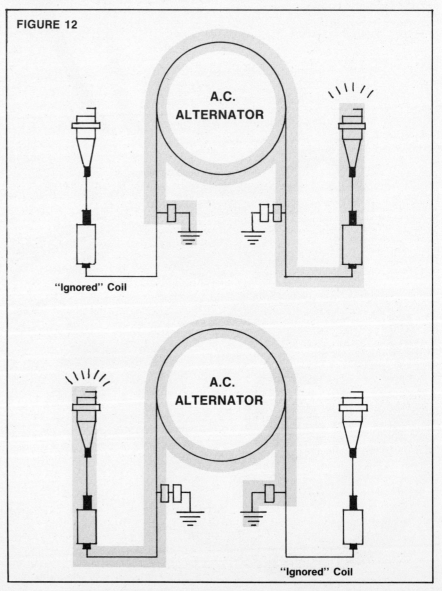

FIGURE 12

"Ignored" Coil

A.C. ALTERNATOR

A.C. ALTERNATOR

"Ignored" Coil

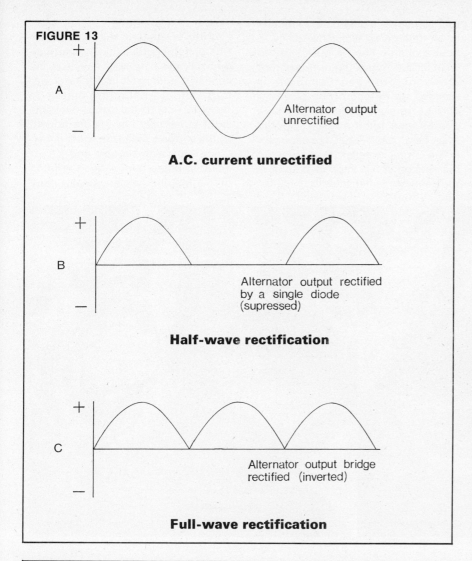

FIGURE 13

A

Alternator output unrectified

A.C. current unrectified

B

Alternator output rectified by a single diode (supressed)

Half-wave rectification

C

Alternator output bridge rectified (inverted)

Full-wave rectification

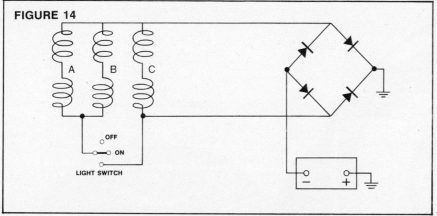

FIGURE 14

A   B   C

OFF
ON
LIGHT SWITCH

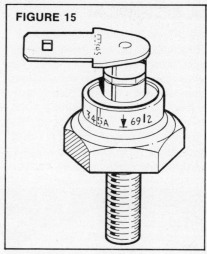

FIGURE 15

circuit would be overloaded most of the time.

The second reason is due to the characteristic bursts of current produced by any generator—it isn't a steady flow but has rhythmic "dead" spots in it. The current flows in a rapid on-off-on-off-on-off manner. Lights aren't affected by this fluctuation in a way visible to the naked eye. In fact, as you may know, household lights flicker in this same way all the time and is not visible.

But the ignition coils may have a problem doing their job with this "on-off" mode. Everything will work as long as the current is in the "on" position. The electromagnetic field can be set up and then collapsed by the breaker points for the spark. But if the current is in the "off" position when the spark is needed, there's a problem—no spark. Normally, this is where the battery would support the system and everything would function in spite of the dead spot.

Here is where the capacitor comes in. It is another solid-state gadget, although capacitors have been around since the ancient days of static electricity. Back then they were known as Leyden jars. Modern capacitors are cylindrical in shape and vary in size from ⅛-inch to more than two inches in diameter. Inside, it looks like a jelly roll made of aluminum foil and a paper-like insulator.

If you connect a battery to the two terminals on a capacitor, there will be a flow of electricity into the capacitor for only an instant and then it will stop flowing. The battery leads can be removed and still nothing happens. But touch a wire across the capacitor terminals and there will be a little zap of electricity. The capacitor holds a charge of voltage inside. A good quality one will hold it for several min-

a steady supply of current. One of its secondary roles is to provide a means of voltage regulation. Any excess current produced by the generator is absorbed by the battery and converted to heat inside the battery. (It is this heat that causes a battery to "boil over" when overcharged.)

Batteries have always been a problem. They are large and heavy in addition to being a nuisance to maintain. Bike customizers and individuals involved in racing have come up with

various means of eliminating the ugly, bulky thing.

One of the more popular means in recent times has been to use a capacitor in conjunction with a Zener diode and, occasionally, some resistors. There are two reasons why the battery usually can't just be removed. The first is voltage regulation. Without a battery, the generator's current would flow unchecked into the system. Light bulbs would blow out anytime a shift was missed and the entire

ELECTRICAL

utes before the charge fades away.

Probably in just about every motorcycle shop in the country, practical jokers have charged up the small ignition capacitors (also called condensors) and left them lying around for unsuspecting souls to pick up. The joker has a big laugh when the victim touches the terminals and is zapped.

Aside from practical jokes, capacitors can serve a very handy function in an ignition system. This ability to hold a charge can be put to use to fill in for the "dead" spots in a generator's output. The capacitor is charged up by one of the bursts of current from the generator. When it comes time for the spark, should there be a "dead" spot, the capacitor in the circuit releases its charge and the ignition coil is zapped in spite of the generator's flat spot. Very handy.

Plus, no battery acid to spill over.

However, there is still the problem with voltage regulation. Straight battery/coil systems may find that the lighting circuit can't take the generator's output without the battery in there to absorb the excess voltage. Light bulbs may have to be bought by the carton to keep the lights going.

Systems with battery and Zener diode to share the overload will find that the Zener alone usually can't

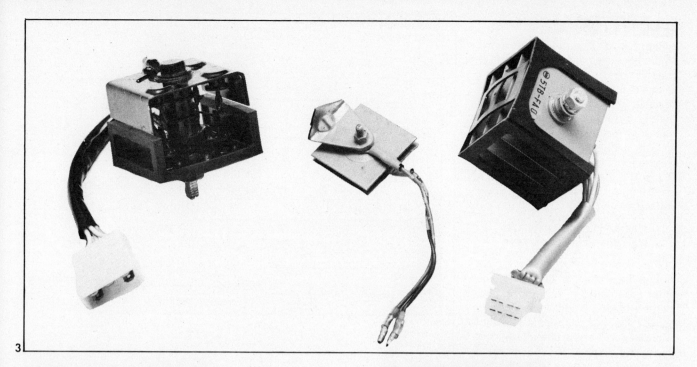

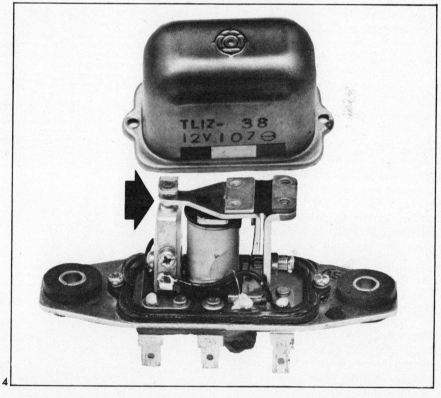

1. Trigger generator on early Kawasaki 500 triple. Three small magnets each spin past a coil which sends jolt to unit "A" under the seat and triggers spark. Distributor on right side of engine switches 30,000 volts to appropriate spark plug. New models have three separate ignition systems supported by a common generator.

2. Yamaha 125 enduro utilizes a combination starter motor/generator. Generator is D.C. type and has commutator and brushes. Two brushes are for starter motor and other two are for generator operation.

3. Two types of Honda rectifiers. In the center is a half-wave type surrounded by two models of full-wave rectifiers. All are very rugged and seldom give any trouble.

4. Battery controlled, electromagnetic type of voltage regulator. Arrow points to contact points which may need cleaning with a point file if corrosion exists on the faces.

handle the overload. Then the same problem as above will come up—bulbs will blow frequently. Most systems will utilize Zener diodes and perhaps a few resistors inside a "black box" to help with the voltage regulation.

Battery eliminator kits have been offered for sale as accessory items for a few years now and this is all that they are, basically. The new Nortons and some of the BSA 500 singles come standard with a capacitor in place of the battery. In the Norton, for example, there is no "black box." The Zener diode normally used in conjunction with the battery will withstand the overload as long as it is mounted in a good heat sink out in the airstream. (Since some states have a "parking light law" which nec-

essitates a battery, all of the connections have been left in place.)

Most people, when they kick start an engine, will rotate it up against compression and then kick it over. This means that the plugs will attempt to fire immediately. Because the capacitor isn't charged up (the engine hasn't yet been spun over fast enough for the generator to put out a good jolt), it is very unlikely that the engine will start on the first kick. There won't be any spark. A very strong person might be able to kick it hard enough

for two revolutions and it could start for him. But the normal man will have to kick the Norton twice to set it running; once to charge the capacitor and again to fire it.

Troubleshooting is pretty easy. It works or it doesn't. There's the possibility that the generator is in phase with the ignition. (That means that a burst of electricity is produced at the moment the points open.) The engine would run under this condition, even with a faulty capacitor. However, it would either idle but throttle would

ELECTRICAL

cause it to die, or run but not idle. This is because the burst of electricity doesn't cover a long enough period of time to fire both ends of the ignition advance and retard positions. If you weren't sure whether the capacitor was any good, you might charge it up with a battery and leave it lying around for some poor soul to pick up but you'd better make sure he's smaller than you and doesn't know any karate.

CAPACITOR IGNITION, BATTERY SUPPORTED

The electronics designers took a look at the capacitor and saw some other advantages in applying it to ignition systems. When a charged capacitor unloads, it does so instantaneously. The entire charge zaps out all at once. They realize that this kind of a zap would do twice as much good in an ignition high tension coil as would the same charge released in a slower manner as in a conventional battery/coil system. It is the *change* in electromagnetic field that produces the spark and if the change is more sudden, then it is more effective in producing that spark.

This was tried and it worked, although nothing really spectacular occurred, so it was decided to increase the voltage going into the high tension coil and set up a bigger electromagnetic field. They were faced with a number of possible ways to increase the 12 volts coming from the generator. One way was to convert the 12 volts DC into 12 volts AC and then run it through an AC transformer. This is the way it was done on the first Kawasaki 500 triple. The DC to AC conversion is done through an electronic gadget called an oscillator. An explanation of how it works is delving pretty deeply into electrical trickery. Rather than confuse the issue here, just let it be understood that the thing does it.

The transformer works on the same principle as the high-tension coil. A changing electromagnetic field produces electricity in a nearby coil of wire. The 12 volts AC powers the electromagnet. Because it is AC, the rapid plus-minus-plus-minus characteristic reverses the electromagnetic field everytime it changes direction. Reversing the field is a change and this produces a current in the nearby coil.

Whereas an ignition high tension

FIGURE 16

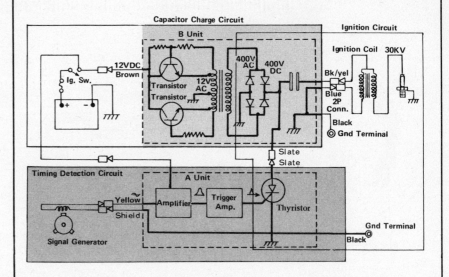

Early Kawasaki H1 500cc three CDI system uses an oscillator in unit "B" to kick the 12 volts D.C. to 400 volts D.C. It passes through an A.C. stage in doing so. Unit "A" is the triggering system. The signal generator sends in a tiny jolt which is in turn amplified (made bigger) and this is fed to the thyristor (SCR). It controls the 400 volts D.C. that generates the 30,000 sparkplug voltage in the high tension coil.

Kawasaki used a distributor to control the firing order. It is a simple switch that feeds the 30,000 volts to the appropriate sparkplug.

FIGURE 17

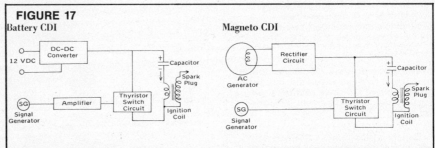

FIGURE 18

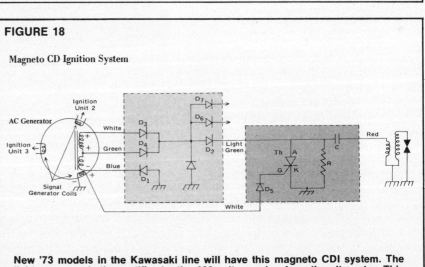

New '73 models in the Kawasaki line will have this magneto CDI system. The light grey area is the rectifier for the 400 volts coming from the alternator. This then feeds the capacitor in the darker area. The signal from the trigger also feeds to this "black box" which contains both the capacitor and the thyristor (SCR). There are three identical ignition units, each with its own capacitor and SCR which supplies current to three high tension coils to generate the spark.

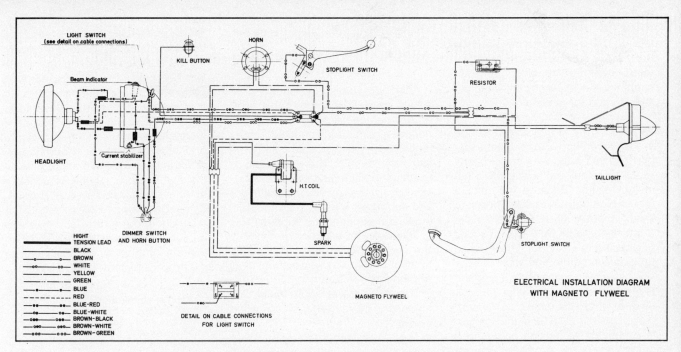

LIGHT SWITCH
(see detail on cable connections)

KILL BUTTON

HORN

STOPLIGHT SWITCH

RESISTOR

Beam indicator

HEADLIGHT

Current stabilizer

DIMMER SWITCH
AND HORN BUTTON

H.T. COIL

SPARK

TAILLIGHT

STOPLIGHT SWITCH

MAGNETO FLYWEEL

	HIGHT TENSION LEAD
	BLACK
	BROWN
	WHITE
	YELLOW
	GREEN
	BLUE
	RED
	BLUE-RED
	BLUE-WHITE
	BROWN-BLACK
	BROWN-WHITE
	BROWN-GREEN

DETAIL ON CABLE CONNECTIONS
FOR LIGHT SWITCH

ELECTRICAL INSTALLATION DIAGRAM
WITH MAGNETO FLYWEEL

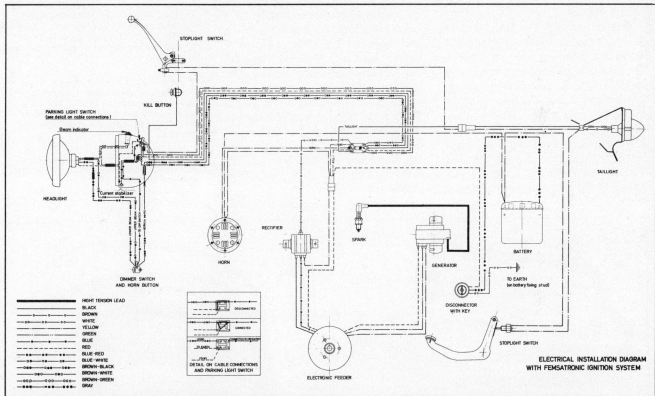

STOPLIGHT SWITCH

KILL BUTTON

PARKING LIGHT SWITCH
(see detail on cable connections)

Beam indicator

HEADLIGHT

Current stabilizer

DIMMER SWITCH
AND HORN BUTTON

HORN

RECTIFIER

SPARK

GENERATOR

TAILLIGHT

BATTERY

TO EARTH
(on battery fixing stud)

DISCONNECTOR
WITH KEY

STOPLIGHT SWITCH

	HIGHT TENSION LEAD
	BLACK
	BROWN
	WHITE
	YELLOW
	GREEN
	BLUE
	RED
	BLUE-RED
	BLUE-WHITE
	BROWN-BLACK
	BROWN-WHITE
	BROWN-GREEN
	GRAY

DISCONNECTED

CONNECTED

DETAIL ON CABLE CONNECTIONS
AND PARKING LIGHT SWITCH

ELECTRONIC FEEDER

ELECTRICAL INSTALLATION DIAGRAM
WITH FEMSATRONIC IGNITION SYSTEM

coil uses the contact breaker points to collapse the field and produce the current, an AC transformer uses the alternating current to change the field and produce the current. This is convenient because there aren't any moving parts to hassle with.

The second coil in the transformer must be made up of very thin wire. If the second coil were the very same size of wire and the same number of loops, the output would be nearly the same as the input, 12 volts in and 12 volts out. By using the smaller wires and putting on more loops, the

voltage is increased. This doesn't really mean that more electricity is being produced, only its form has been changed.

Output from the transformer is 400 volts but it is AC. It now needs to be converted back to DC for the capacitor to be able to work with it and that is a job for a rectifier. As the 400 volts DC comes out of the rectifier, it is fed into the capacitor and held there for the high tension coil when the time comes. A total of 400 volts has a lot of squirting power behind it and it doesn't work well in a contact breaker

system. When the points open, the electricity keeps right on jumping across the gap. No spark at the spark plug.

But the electronic people already had this one figured out. There is a solid state gadget that has an interesting characteristic: It won't pass any electricity, not even a big charge, unless the side of it is touched with a tiny dab of current. It's like a heavy-duty electric switch that is activated by another smaller electric current. Perfect for the job. This gadget, called a thyristor or a silicon-controlled rec-

ELECTRICAL

tifier (S.C.R.), would be used to control the 400 volts stored in the capacitor for the high tension coil. Just touch it with a small current when the time is right for ignition.

The engineers could have used the battery current to activate it through a set of contact breaker points but that involved using the same old parts which were still prone to getting out of adjustment. Because the voltage required to activate the SCR was so small, it would be possible to make a little generator with only one coil of wire and one magnet. This generator would produce one small jolt per revolution. Mount the generator to the engine in such a way that this jolt occurs when the spark is needed, feed it to the SCR and the ignition is complete. No moving parts and a super spark is produced—about 30,000 volts.

This is basically the way the first model of the Kawasaki 500 received its spark. It was a bit cumbersome because of all of the converting going on. This intricacy also makes it nearly impossible for any troubleshooting on the part of the owner. It takes sophisticated test equipment to check it out in the event of a malfunction. About the only thing that can be checked for are loose wires or shorts. If you have a friend with a running bike, you might try switching components until

you come up with one that works. Then go buy a new part at the dealer.

CAPACITOR IGNITION, MAG SUPPORTED

After one studies the battery supported capacitor ignition for a time, an obvious question comes up. Why not use a generator wound with many loops of very thin wire to supply the 400 volts of AC? The end result is exactly the same as using a battery-oscillator-transformer arrangement and that result is achieved without all those components and expense.

This is the only basic difference in the two types of capacitor ignition systems. From the rectifier on, they are the same in theory and principle. The new Kawasaki 500 triples will have this newer style of simplified system.

The strong, hot spark has proved popular for use in two-cycle motorcycle engines because of resistance to spark plug fouling. The Femsatronic unit, used on Bultacos, is typical of those found on competition and enduro machines. Femsa encapsulates the capacitor, rectifier and miscellaneous components in a plastic block along with the high tension coil. It's convenient having everything all in one spot, no clutter on the bike and this simplifies installation but it does make repairs a bit on the expensive side if anything goes wrong.

Bultaco has an unusual triggering

method to fire the spark plug. Whereas Kawasaki uses a separate little generator to create the current for the SCR, the triggering coil for the Femsa is built into the primary ignition generator. The triggering coil is set to activate the SCR whenever a north pole swings by. Normally, generator magnets are placed so that they are oriented in a north-south-north-south arrangement. But this is impossible on the Femsatronic. There would be a number of sparks on every revolution. Femsa goes around this by setting the magnets into the rotor so that there are four south poles in a row and then a north pole to trigger the spark at the proper moment. Some generating

1. Typical starter motor and solenoid. Starter button on handlebar can't carry electrical load to motor. Solenoid is an extra heavy-duty switch, electrically operated by starter button.

2. High tension coil from Japanese motorcycle using E.T. system. CDI coils are identical in appearance and can sometimes be interchanged from system to system.

3. New Honda XL-250 has an "inside-out" alternator. Coils mount in cover and magnet rotor has open side facing outward. No special puller is necessary to work on coils with this method.

4. Examples of accessory capacitor discharge units. Essentially, they are capacitors using SCR firing mechanisms. Battery provides the trigger current.

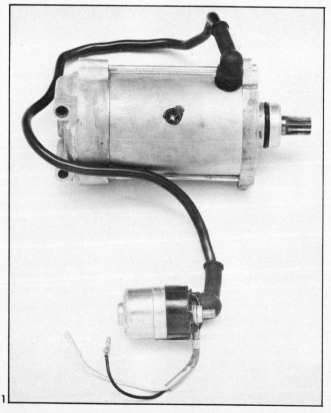

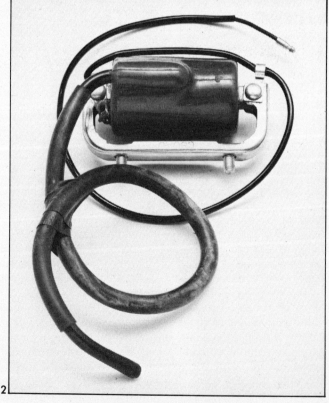

3

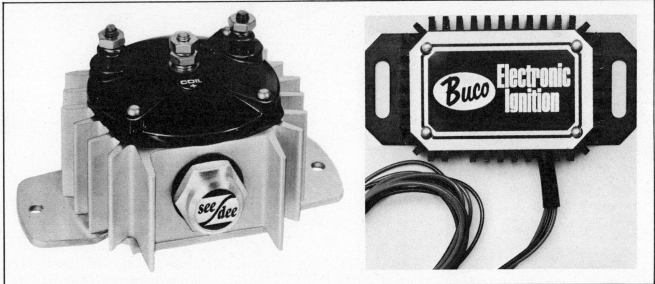

4

efficiency is lost but it doesn't seem to hurt or hamper anything.

Lighting is totally separate from the Femsa ignition system but mounted inside the same generator. The entire lighting system can be removed from the machine without getting into the ignition. This is a wise way to make the electrical system because it ensures a consistent ignition. If the lights operated from the same circuit, it would make a difference whether they were on or off. Compensations would have to be designed into the system to make it work under both conditions. Separate circuits prove much simpler in the long run.

Troubleshooting one of these is very straightforward. Look first for broken wires or bad connections. If it's not that, replace the generator or replace the coil. By using a volt-ohm meter, the generator can be tested to see if it's putting out the required current. This will determine which component is faulty and needs replacement.

It is possible to use the Femsa high tension coil with a normal contact breaker and generator hooked into it. This isn't a better way to run an ignition, it's just one of those flukey things that work out. It is a convenient temporary repair in the event that the Femsa generator is faulty and a breaker point set-up is available.

On some bikes, such as the Kawasaki Bighorn 350, the trigger coil for the SCR is a separate coil inside the generator and it too should be checked for output. If it's bad, there would be no trigger signal and no spark, even if all the other components were in good shape. A simple replacement coil would cure that problem. And they all lived happily ever after. 🏰

CLUTCHES AND TRANSMISSIONS

All the power in the world is useless if you can't put it to work. That is why these vital components deserve careful scrutiny

BY DAN COTTERMAN

I have a philosophy that helps me every time I sit down to fix something. I figure the guy they hired at the factory to put the thing together wasn't any smarter than I am. The fact that he knew a lot more than I do about the particular object I intend to repair doesn't throw me out of phase—not if I can spend some time making up the difference by finding out what I'm doing before I begin.

Making up the difference is what this is all about, not by giving you a bolt-by-bolt description of every clutch and transmission on every motorcycle you might encounter, but by bringing to light many of the things that apply to any repair effort. I'm talking about the little things—the tricks that may or may not be mentioned in service manuals and rider handbooks. Often overlooked by the fellow who undertakes the doing of his own repair and maintenance work, they can make all the difference.

We'll make the rounds through primary drive systems, shifting mechanisms, transmissions and adjustments. Then we'll settle (or render deathless) that old controversy about whether it's a good idea to use automatic transmission fluid in bikes. We'll talk with the people who make the parts and the people who install and repair them, starting with the clutch.

CABLE ADJUSTMENT

Let's attack this thing from the outside. Before you jump to the conclusion that your clutch is a goner or that your transmission won't shift, be sure the clutch cable adjustment is right. I know, it sounds all too obvious, but aren't these the things even the best of us sometimes forget? During five years as a dealer I can remember numerous instances of standing next to a bike while the owner sat there telling me how his clutch was either slipping or not disengaging enough to allow effortless shifting. With the latter situation, the transmission itself would sometimes be blamed. As the conversation went on, it was easy

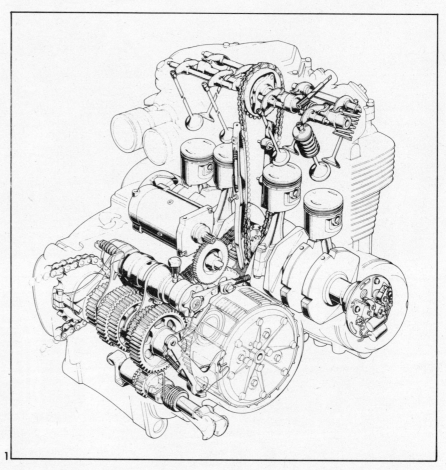

enough for me to glance at the handlebar end of the clutch cable adjustment. More often than not, the problem of slipping could be traced to insufficient "play" in the handle, while balky shifting was usually the result of too much free movement in the handle. Either of these extremes could be remedied by a few quick twists on the adjuster. It was even easier to smile and say, "Try it now," after which the fellow would buzz up to the corner and back to report that everything was working fine.

There is seldom any charge for that kind of on-the-spot service, no matter where it happens to be rendered. The dealer chalks it up to good will and settles for the satisfaction that he was able to do someone a favor. It doesn't become expensive until adjustment is neglected. The slipping clutch wears away the friction surface on the driven plates, glazes them over and causes more slipping. Compounding the situation is heat, which works to warp both driving and driven plates. On the other hand, the clutch that isn't adjusted so as to release properly will make shifting difficult. The extra pressure that has to be applied (due to difficult shifting) can result in misalignment of elements of the shifting mechanism and bent or broken shifter forks.

WORKSHOP MANUALS

Let's say you've done the right thing and have the rider handbook for your particular bike and let's assume you've followed the instructions therein and have carefully seen to the proper adjustment of your clutch. If these steps fail to correct the problem it's time to go inside. Now's the time to really begin making up that difference we talked about a few minutes ago by laying your hands on a workshop manual. Study the job at hand carefully before you loosen the first screw, make sure you have all the tools you're going to need, and continue to consult the manual as you take things apart. Don't, whatever you do, start ripping things apart and tossing them in a box without regard to the order in which they were originally assembled. There's a fair chance that the particular manual you're having to use won't have an adequate drawing to indicate the correct order of reassembly. In the case of many of the older Japanese machines you may be confronted with a grainy photographic reproduction of a clutch or transmission, snapped with a wide-angle lens from some considerable distance, while its components were spread over some colorless background. Mechanical drawings are better, but even drawings are subject to inaccuracies, as we will note in the section on transmissions. Further emphasizing the importance of observing the order of parts as you remove them is the classic situation involving the manual that details the procedure for "unassembly" thoroughly enough. Then, when you turn the page to find out how to put it back together it simply says, "Reverse unassembly instructions." Friends, you haven't lived until you've tried to read Czechoslovakian-English backwards! But, regardless of the flaws you may encounter, a workshop manual is the best way to go when you're doing your own repair work. Just remember to take your time—you might even discover that someone before you has had the thing apart and put it back

1. Sophistication has led to far more complex driveline systems for cycle engines like Honda's Four.

2. Adjustment at the clutch lever should be made with the engine at operating temperature. Normal free play at pivot opening is ¼ inch.

3. Many machines have external access to primary clutch adjustment. Adjustment should be made here first.

4. Your factory service manual should give you the proper free play necessary at external pivot arms. Recommended adjustment is amount of tolerance necessary to prevent slippage, friction.

5. Transmissions using a long crossover pushrod must have play to keep the delicate parts safe from friction damage. Remember to replace ball.

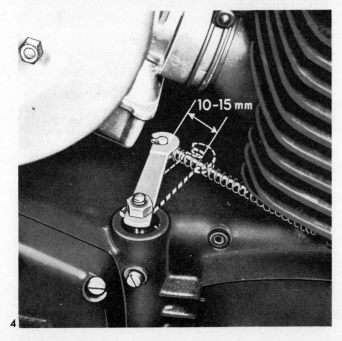

10-15 mm

CLUTCHES

together wrong or, worse yet, left something out.

Going a step further, let's suppose you've taken your clutch apart and that the parts are carefully laid out, hopefully in the order in which you removed them. If this wasn't practical you may even have made a rough pencil sketch to show the order of reassembly, an excellent idea. The question now is what to look for. How do you know whether parts can be salvaged or must be replaced? There are some definite signs.

CLUTCH PUSHROD

We were talking about adjustments so let's take the clutch pushrod first. Naturally, it should be straight, but finding this out is kind of like buying a drumstick: The simplest way is to roll it slowly across some reasonably flat surface, not necessarily the garage floor, but preferably a piece of glass. If it wobbles while rolling you have probably found at least part of your trouble. Look at each of its ends. If either of them is mushroomed, the pushrod should be replaced. It should also be measured to be sure it is of standard length. If your manual doesn't state correct length, take it to your dealer and compare with a new one. A difference of a few thousandths of an inch can be taken up by the adjustment screw, while a sizable difference will make good clutch adjustment impossible.

. . . AND SPRINGS

The books sometimes tell you to measure the length of the clutch tensioning springs. This method is good,

1. While the pushrod is out, trueness should be checked. Windy Briggs of Kawasaki rolls a pushrod over a flat plate. Bent rod must be straightened.

2. Clutch spring screws on Japanese bikes are tightened to bottom. Springs may be color coded. All must match.

3. Using Vernier calipers is best method of checking for collapsed spring. Service manual will give tolerance.

4. Removal of clutch and primary gear nuts is easily done with special tool. Make one from old friction plate.

5. Japanese clutches with helical-cut gears have considerable side thrust. Therefore extensive use of thrust bearings, washers. Assemble in order.

6. Wet, oil bathed, clutches can use fiber on steel or steel on steel plates.

7. Engine thrust has mushroomed tabs. Must be filed smooth or replaced.

but measure also the importance of these little springs against their relatively low cost. If you've any doubts, replace them all. You might even want to take a set of calipers to the parts counter with you and check several of the new springs for evenness of length. I've seen a measureable difference in the lengths of clutch springs right out of the box from the factory, so it doesn't hurt to be sure of going home with a matched set.

Matching the tensions of these clutch springs is also of importance. Uneven spring tensioning will cause erratic clutch action and rapid destruction of the plates. If yours is a clutch that calls for running spring adjustment screws all the way in till they "bottom" it will have been enough that you made sure the springs were all of the same length. However, tensioning the springs on many motorcycles is a matter of careful adjustment. Your workshop manual will tell you how to effect this adjustment, but be sure to check your work by pushing the starter arm through while observing the rotation of the plates with the clutch lever pulled in (disengaged). Uneven spring tensioning will be evidenced by a wobble as the plates rotate. This also is a good technique for checking pre-

liminary clutch adjustment. Pass the starter arm through with the clutch engaged and disengaged. And don't forget to remove all your spark plugs so you won't be working against engine compression.

HUBS AND HOUSINGS

I chatted with Jim Hunter, a tuner of considerable experience when it comes to British machines, and learned something that applies to many clutch repairs, regardless of where the bike may have been manufactured. Hunter was quick to point out the fact that the fellow who installs a set of new clutch plates on his own is usually in such a hurry to get everything bolted together again and back on the trail that he overlooks some rather important steps in the operation. One of these is the cleaning of the spline cuts in the clutch chainwheel. The continual back-and-forth agitation of the tabs on clutch plates in these spline cuts will eventually create little notches. Understand that when either engaging or disengaging, the clutch plate tabs must move laterally along these cuts. If the notches aren't dressed off, as with a scraper or small file, the tabs can hang up on them when you get ready for your

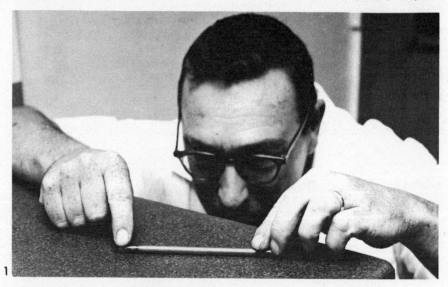

1

2

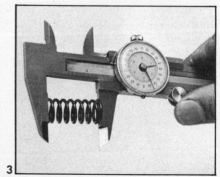

3

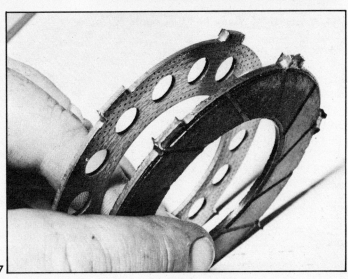

test run and foul up what might have been a good job.

Something else mentioned by Hunter does not apply to all machines, but is infinitely worth passing along. It simply involves some attention to the tightening of three or four screws in the center hub. Particular attention was drawn to British clutch setups. If the tightening of these three or four screws (depending on model) is neglected, more trouble will result.

CLUTCH PLATES

I called Barnett Tool and Engineering for a Q & A session with motorcycling's "Mr. Clutch" and was referred to one of the organization's key men, Mike Taylor. The interview was tape recorded and it's a good thing because it turned out that Taylor expounded information on clutch plates faster than I could have scrib-

bled it down. Our conversation was later transcribed into four pages of handwritten notes. I think you will find the digest of those notes well worth the reading!

I was interested in what material was used for the friction segments on Barnett clutch plates. With one exception, it is a composition material which is manufactured by the Armstrong Floor people. It comes in different grades and is selected by Barnett on the basis of its softness, durability under the stresses of heat, pressure and abrasion and for its resistance to swelling when saturated with oil. There is no difference in the material whether for dry, wet or so-called "oil-bath" systems.

The difference in material comes with dry plates for super-torquers like the Harley-Davidson 74. Plates for these feature a substance more similar to brake lining, a hard-faced mate-

rial that comes from the makers of Raybestos. However, plates with the softer Armstrong material also are available to the 74 rider. It seems to be a matter of personal choice, probably influenced by the way the bike is ridden.

WET VS. DRY

Taylor stated a preference for dry clutches, indicating that plates run in oil tend to stick together too much. "The sticking problem is even worse after the plates become slicked up," he added. I asked about the heat factor in dry-versus-wet clutches and was told that heat was not an important consideration with the Barnett friction material. The only exception, according to Taylor, probably would be found in extreme cases involving intentional slipping or a combination of slipping and heavy loading, such as in quarter-mile drag racing.

CLUTCHES

PLATE INSPECTION

Art takes over from science as we learn that there is no practical value to measuring the thickness of friction-lined driven plates. You can use the thickness method as a means of making a very general decision as to the remaining life of a clutch plate. However, it is much more important to learn to use your senses of sight, touch and smell when appraising the condition of a plate. The severely-burned friction segment will have, very simply, a scorched smell! It may very well look and feel slick and glazed. If extensive slipping has taken place, check both the driving and driven plates for warpage. Warped plates should always be replaced.

The next step is to take a look at those little tabs. You'll find them on the outer circumference of the driven plates and on the inner circumference of the drive plates. If possible, compare them to new plates so you can obtain an idea of what they're supposed to look like. If the wearing is not too severe, these tabs can be filed so that their edges are again parallel. Remember, however, that the now-reduced dimensions of these tabs is going to provide even more room for them to lash back and forth in the spline cuts, thus making a bad situation worse.

But what about the plates that still show an appreciable amount of thickness—with no warping and good tabs? They're a bit slicked up and that's about the worst of it. You have the option of salvaging these plates and saving yourself some money. Begin by thoroughly cleaning each surface. Follow the cleaning by roughing up the surface with a medium-grit paper or cloth, but remember you are just more or less etching the surfaces, either metal or composition, you're not necessarily grooving them. Heavy scoring with abrasive materials will only speed up wear as the plates come together and separate. "Just knock the glaze off," says Mike Taylor. But with this instruction he adds a caution: "Avoid having them sandblasted. If you feel you must sandblast them be very careful because they (the steel plates) can be warped." There scarcely seems to be a need for stating that plates with composition segments should definitely not be sandblasted!

Before I put the question of automatic transmission fluid to Taylor, I asked him about a preference for either steel or aluminum plates. There were some strong recommendations for aluminum. There's the obvious advantage of lighter weight. To that was added a statement that the T2075-T6 aluminum used by Barnett rids itself of heat more quickly and therefore is less apt to stretch and

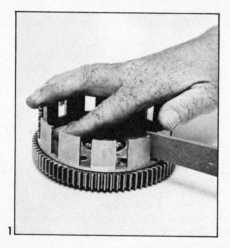

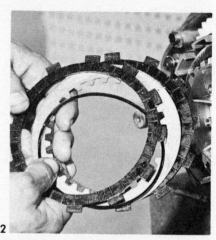

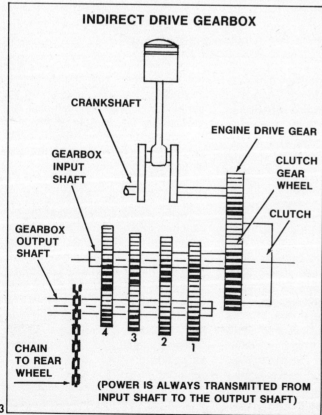

INDIRECT DRIVE GEARBOX

CRANKSHAFT

ENGINE DRIVE GEAR

GEARBOX INPUT SHAFT

CLUTCH GEAR WHEEL

CLUTCH

GEARBOX OUTPUT SHAFT

4 3 2 1

CHAIN TO REAR WHEEL

(POWER IS ALWAYS TRANSMITTED FROM INPUT SHAFT TO THE OUTPUT SHAFT)

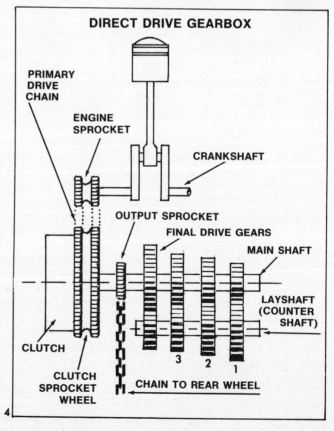

DIRECT DRIVE GEARBOX

PRIMARY DRIVE CHAIN

ENGINE SPROCKET

CRANKSHAFT

OUTPUT SPROCKET

FINAL DRIVE GEARS

MAIN SHAFT

CLUTCH

LAYSHAFT (COUNTER SHAFT)

3 2 1

CLUTCH SPROCKET WHEEL

CHAIN TO REAR WHEEL

warp. It's also somewhat harder than most steels commonly used for clutch plates and, when you think about that, you will see that the tabs will hold up longer. Beefing up the benefits of installing aluminum plates is the fact that they no longer cost more than those made of steel.

ATF, THEN AND NOW

Now, about ATF, is it or isn't it a good idea for use in bikes? Taylor indicated that a few years back it would melt the adhesive that held the friction segments on the metal. In that way it caused real trouble. In still another way it might not have been quite the thing for those earlier bikes with sleeve bushings in their innards. Now,

however, with ball and roller bearings in use and a new adhesive that won't give up, ATF is all right. As far as use with Barnett plates, Taylor states emphatically, "We recommend it!" "In fact," he continued, "we sometimes have calls from riders who say, 'I just put in one of your clutches and it won't work.'" The upshot of these complaints is usually that the customer has used too heavy an oil and it is causing the plates to stick.

We'll come back to the subject of ATF in a few minutes. Right now, it's time to look at a couple of other aspects of Barnett plates as compared to the stock, factory variety. The Barnett plate is a product whose design and manufacture has been

dedicated to durability and the ultimate minimization of that age-old bugaboo, slipping. The slightly softer friction material, special phosphate etching on all metal surfaces and greater contact area seem to accomplish the desired effect. Because of the increased clutching properties, Taylor indicated that heavy-duty clutch springs are not recommended with Barnett plates.

TRANSMISSION TALK

I still had slipping clutches on my mind as I began my conversation with Hodaka's Mike Hamilton. I wanted to learn something about Hodaka's ball-lock shifting system. Fortunately, I learned more than I had expected. Maybe it should first be realized that the Hodaka transmission has to be turning in order to shift. If the bike is standing still, it must be rocked back and forth to make the necessary gear changes. This is, to a limited extent, true of most transmissions. While most constant-mesh transmissions have the power transferred through the clutch, to a mainshaft, thence by gears that are moved back and forth by shifter forks, to corresponding gears on a countershaft, the Hodaka ball-lock has a series of 20 balls that are moved by the shifting linkage to bring about gear changes. The balls are thrust by a ball receiver so as to index into whichever gear is selected. The ball receiver is on a control shaft which moves inside a countershaft with 20 holes in it. On either side of the ball receiver you'll find a coil spring. These springs are designated, "Control shaft spring, left," and

1. Clutch housing gears can serrate. Filing should correct unless severe.

2. Rubber O-rings push oiled plates apart when stuck together from suction. Good idea to replace them if cracked.

3. Indirect drive transmission must transmit power from input to output shaft in all gears. Sprocket external.

4. Common with British is direct drive design. Minimal power loss in top gear. Sprocket between clutch and gears.

5. All Hodaka models have crankshaft-mounted clutch. Good for torque inertia but impedes high speed disengagement.

6. Barnett clutch at top arrests problem of plates 'welding' together.

7. De-glazing cork friction plates with emery on flat restores adhesion.

8. Burnt cork plate can be saved sometimes by de-glazing. Acetone clean first.

CLUTCHES

"Control shaft spring, right," so if you're assembling one of these units, be careful to install in the correct left-right order. Hamilton wanted Hodaka do-it-your-selfers to know the importance of paying careful attention to those two springs because they can tend to collapse. However, if the springs are at fault and shifter adjustment is not possible, you can remove them through the right side by taking off the right cover, then the primary gear and clutch. Nothing to this point will have offered much resistance, not till you come to where you have to remove that little snap ring. This is where you can spend a couple of hours pricking away with a pocket knife or an ice pick and probably wind up wounding yourself. The preferred alternative is Hodaka snap ring tool (#909524). The current price is $7.29—fairly heavy, but not when you think of the grief it can save you by turning a frustrating hour or two into a two- or three-second operation! Once the snap ring is out, you can pull out the shaft and get at the springs. They're probably inexpensive, so it sounds like a matter of automatic replacement rather than measuring, checking tension and all that. You might also want to check the ball receiver while you're in there, just to be sure everything's right.

SLIP A BIT—SAVE A LOT

We were on the matter of minimizing clutch slip with Barnett plates when Hamilton came forth with the revelation that the Hodaka plates are meant to slip, just a teensy bit, when gear changes are made. The idea is to take some of the shock off the gears. The same holds true when the bike comes to earth again after sailing some distance through the air. Now, anyone with a small, high-revving motorcycle can perk up and pay attention. Take a small screamer and let it take off the crest of a jump without shutting down the throttle. According to Hamilton, rpm's can climb very rapidly, say to 2500 . . . perhaps five times as high as a larger machine (like a 250). The result can be a substantially heavy shock to the gears in the transmission and rear chain. The calculated "give" in the Hodaka clutch works to spread these impulses over a longer period of time. While this is happening, the shock of sudden gear changes and rear wheel landings have been distributed over several gear teeth, instead of being soaked up by just one or two. Consider the proportions of that small bike transmission and remember it isn't the hairy piece of machinery you get with a Harley 74 or a Norton Commando!

SHIFTY, EH?

We talked about getting information from the people who make the parts and those who install and repair them. Steve Kolseth seems to qualify in all three categories and had some commentary on shifters for the Sachs, DKW, Penton and the newly imported Monarch (all use the Sachs/DKW engine) motorcycles. This group's shifters, whether four- or six-speed, are of the same design. The idea is similar to the Hodaka, except that one spring is used, instead of two. Also, instead of balls, a long "T" bar engages the gears. Kolseth was not, however, specifically referring to Sachs shifters, which seem to have had some shimming problems (in one degree or another) for some time. He was talking about a replacement shifter set-up called the Koba Kit, which sells for just over $40.00 and can be put on in two or three hours by anyone with a moderate amount of mechanical ability. There is a claim for the elimination of all false neutrals along with other advantages.

As far as shimming with the Sachs setup is concerned, the advice was to "Start with the shift mechanism at the case and shim it on out from there. There are three or four different spots where you can put shims. With four or five different thicknesses available through dealers, a guy can get everything about perfect. The idea is getting everything as tight as possible without binding up."

A MULTITUDE OF SHIMS. . .

"A necessary evil" was about the most consistent comment that came in response to questions about shims. Bob Snow and Mark Rosendahl were two more knowledgeable people I talked to. In this instance, their qualifications included several years' ex-

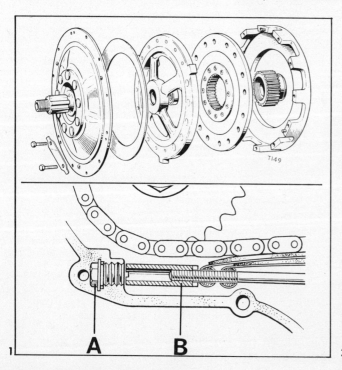

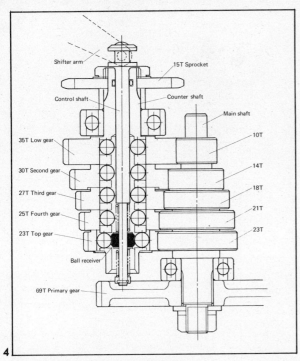

Labels on diagram 4:
- Shifter arm
- 15T Sprocket
- Control shaft
- Counter shaft
- Main shaft
- 35T Low gear
- 10T
- 30T Second gear
- 14T
- 27T Third gear
- 18T
- 25T Fourth gear
- 21T
- 23T Top gear
- 23T
- Ball receiver
- 69T Primary gear

4

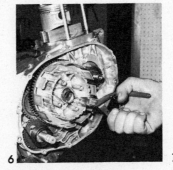

5

6

7

1. Triumph Trident uses single plate dry clutch. Works well. Primary chain adjustment is screw; lifts follower.

2. Spring tension adjustment adjusts plate wobble. Spin with clutch in.

3. Indirect drive transmission has gears constantly meshing; Yamaha 350.

4. Unique ball-lock transmission of Hodaka's is simple. Top gear engaged.

5. Ball receiver pushrod runs inside drive shaft. Pushes balls out when moved laterally to lock gear on shaft.

6. Plan on need for circlip pliers when working on Japanese clutch and gearbox. Enormous Honda 250 single clutch will probably never fail.

7. Transmission end play should be kept around .015-inch. Measure assembled cluster on shaft. Then measure inside depth of case halves. Subtract gear length from case width.

perience in installing and repairing motorcycle clutch and transmission parts. Snow was quick to suggest that most clutch replacements are necessitated by an over-tight adjustment on the clutch pushrod. Somewhere, guys get the idea that the adjustment screw should be tight against the end of the pushrod. Snow didn't say that, I did! This happens to be one of the flukes I've seen all too often. The idea is to run that screw in till it just touches the end of the pushrod, then back it out a little and set the locknut. Be careful, because this is where the locknut can bind up on the screw just enough to carry it back in against the end of the rod, spoiling the adjustment. Note the position of the slot in the screw before you set the locknut.

If possible, put a screwdriver through a box wrench and hold the screw in position as you secure the locknut.

As far as shimming techniques are concerned, both Snow and Rosendahl agreed that the first thing the home mechanic is likely to do is fail to get the original shims back in the way he took them out. Otherwise, it is a good idea to be sure that there isn't too much movement of the gears in a back-and-forth direction along the length of the shaft. You can figure a maximum allowable movement of .004- to .005-inch. The Yamaha 250 is one that was mentioned as occasionally having a jumping-out-of-gear problem which may be cured by proper shim spacing of transmission gears.

MORE ON ADJUSTMENT...

It seems that everyone who has ever worked with or written about transmission maintenance and repair agrees that the great majority of transmission problems can be traced directly back to incorrect clutch adjustment. Regardless of the cause, however, occasionally it becomes necessary to open up the gearbox for the replacement of parts. If such has been your fate, consider what you'll have to be looking for.

LET'S INSPECT THE FORKS

The bending of shifter forks is perhaps one of the most common ills, and knowing when they should be replaced is important. In the first

place, it isn't a good idea to try to straighten a shifter fork and put it back in an otherwise good transmission. Once it's bent, and bent again to get it back to its original shape, it has been weakened and is therefore more liable to break and cause serious trouble. Check shifter forks for signs of discoloration from heat, chipping and pitting while you're about your diagnosis. A worn fork is also a source of trouble and should be replaced. Finally, be sure that the forks move freely on their shafts before you begin to follow reassembly instructions.

... AND GEARS

Gears, too, are subject to diagnostic inspection. Again, as with the forks, signs of unusual wear should be cause for replacement. Gears which work together should be replaced together. It isn't wise to replace a gear and not replace the one it works against. A mismatch is created that will cause the new gear to wear more rapidly, to say nothing of the noise and other difficulty that may result.

It happens that, not knowing simple shortcuts, the inexperienced will often make entirely too much work for himself. Take the Husqvarna, for example. I talked to Imperial Motor Sports, locally, and learned, for one thing, that it's a waste of time to look for an adjustment on the shifter mechanism: There isn't any! Also, according to Imperial, the workshop manual doesn't tell you that you can pull the

CLUTCHES

transmission out of a four- or five-speed bike without removing the clutch. It seems that the guys don't believe it can be done with the result that they never even try. There apparently is no detailed run-down on "how-to" . . . you just do it! Getting it back together was described as a sort of "safe-cracker" technique. "Just tap the cases together, and, as you do so, slightly rotate the clutch and it'll almost always line itself up and go in," I was told.

And take note of this, you Bultaco buffs. When you're putting the shifting mechanism back in a 250 five-speed, look for a circular plate, the one behind the plate that's held in place by three screws. This circular object has a couple of notches for the spring-loaded triggers that take care of shifting. Now, you'll see a long arc and a short arc. Be sure the short arc is at four o'clock. On the 360 four-speed the short arc should be at 12 o'clock. The outside plate on the 360 should have the short arc at six o'clock. There is an outside plate on the 250 but, according to Bultaco, it'll only go on one way. There are reportedly three ways of putting some of these set-ups together, so the tip on position of these arcs is worth remembering.

Also from Bultaco, all five-speed parts books and workshop manuals have a drawing that shows the shifting fork on the right as upside-down. Remember that the fork on the right should have its longest arc on top, instead of on the bottom. So, don't follow the diagram—at least with respect to the position of this one shifter

fork—if you want to be able to get into fifth gear! This is not necessarily a case of bearing down on the Bultaco manuals, I have seen it happen in many others. The reason may be traced back to the fact that the fellow who illustrated the parts wasn't entirely hip to the function of what he was drawing.

When adjusting the Bultaco's clutch springs, they say go in about three full turns, then adjust to where everything runs true. Also, the new Bultaco plates are said to be capable of withstanding abuse without swelling. The plates, alternately steel and cast iron at one time, are now all-steel. This would indicate the absence of any composition friction segments on the driven plates.

TIP ON TRIDENTS AND OTHERS

There is one thing about adjustment of the Triumph Trident clutch that is deserving of momentary attention. The workshop manual, in referring to internal clutch operating mechanism adjustment states: "Very little movement is required in the clutch pullrod to disengage the friction plate, so there must be a clearance of not less than .005-inch between the rear face of the large adjuster nut and the ball bearing in the actuating plate." The foregoing statement is absolutely correct. You take a fagot of thickness gages, pull out the one marked, ".005," and start adjusting. What the book doesn't tell you is that there will inevitably be some tiny amount of space between the threads on the end of the pullrod and the threads in the small adjustment nut when you have loosened it to make the adjustment, and there is no force on the threads

1. Proper shift adjustment and religious use of clutch arrests 'rounding' of male and female gear dogs.

2. Too much gusto with the throttle, popping the clutch and old, dirty oil let this gear seize on shaft, explode.

3. Popular with Japanese is shift cam drum setup for five and six speeders.

4. Honda uses this novel shift plate shifter on their cam drum to eliminate gear jumping in their 100-125 singles.

5. Shift forks must be straight, parallel. Fork on left is bent, must be replaced. Impossible to straighten.

6. Kawasaki uses the more popular cam drum pinned on one end. As shift lever is moved, change arm ratchets drum to move gears laterally.

7. Fork is burnt and worn excessively from improper adjustment. Can also be caused from holding lever up, down.

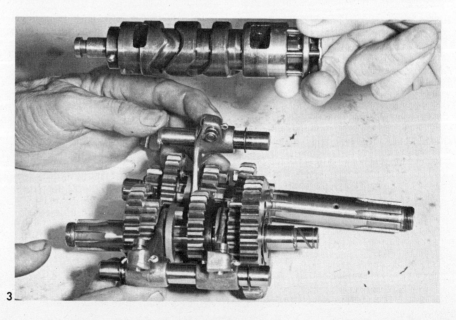

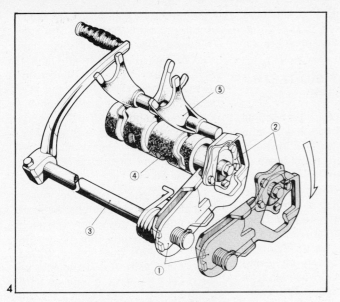

4

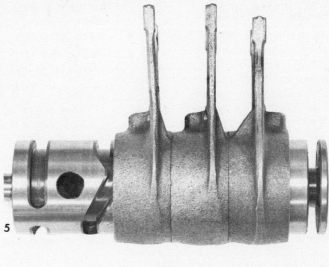

5

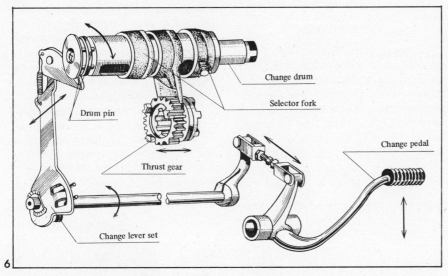

6

Change drum

Selector fork

Drum pin

Change pedal

Thrust gear

Change lever set

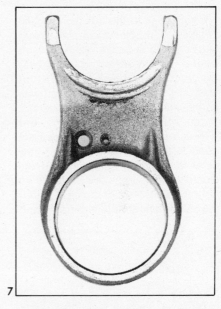

7

in either direction. This slack may amount to no more than a couple of thousandths, but this adjustment is somewhat critical if you want satisfactory clutch operation. What happens if you set the large adjuster nut for the desired .005-inch and tighten the locknut? The slack is absorbed by tightening and you've lost your adjustment. Learn to allow for this discrepancy before you set the locknut and you'll save yourself a lot of grief. The idea of slack in adjustment threads can be applied to other motorcycles and other situations, too. Tappet adjustment, to mention one.

OIL'S WELL THAT ENDS UP ON THE PAVEMENT

Little attention is devoted to primary chain case covers or engine and transmission casings in the average written word on the maintenance and repair of motorcycles. That may account for the fact that so much attention is drawn to those inevitable pud-

dles of oil found under transmissions and primary chain cases on many bikes. A drop or two after a run of some distance is not necessarily cause for concern. However, despite the hardened belief of many individuals, the propensity to puddle is not a calculated engineering feature of certain makes. There is no mystique involved. If everything is right in the assembly, and condition of cases, gaskets and seals is good, there should be nothing more than that drop or two I mentioned.

You say you've replaced the seals, made sure nothing is warped, and that all surfaces are getting maximum contact over good gaskets, and all the screws are tightened to the point of stripping, and she still leaks? It could be you've got an invisible crack somewhere. It can happen that a crack of this sort will escape attention at the factory with the result that even a brand new machine will plague its owner with seemingly unfixable oil

leaks. The chances for invisible cracks in aluminum casings will increase in direct proportion to the age of the bike and the kind of treatment it has endured.

There are at least two relatively inexpensive solutions to the dilemma of invisible cracking. If you were working with a ferrous metal, magnafluxing would be the answer. Aluminum, being non-magnetic, calls for other tactics. One involves a three-step process with the use of something known commercially as Met-L-Check. A red dye is first spread over the entire surface of the aluminum. It dries in about five minutes and is wiped off with a remover, also included in the kit. Finally, the surface is sprayed with a liquid chemical which causes it to appear a pinkish-white. If a crack is present a certain amount of the dye will have worked its way in and will thus have escaped the wiping done in step two. When the last treatment of chemical was administered, in step

CLUTCHES

three, it caused the dye to react and come to the surface. The result is a distinct red line along the entire length of that previously invisible crack. Another die-check method is available through the Mackay people. I have not personally tried this method, but I have known others who did, and successfully. The Mackay liquid (maybe someone else also makes a similar product . . .) is mixed with the oil and will color a crack purple, I believe—so it can be located and repaired. This latter method can be used while the bike is in operation.

ATF . . . RAH! RAH! RAH!

It was back to the question of ATF in bikes as I began my interview with Lee Burch, long-time Harley-Davidson dealer in Whittier, California. His recommendation of ATF, at least in the Milwaukee product, was enthusiastic and without qualification. Burch was specific, though: "Ford ATF is what we use. It is especially good in transmissions in brand new bikes during the run-in period. It lets machine-chips from new surfaces go right to the bottom of the case where it won't be caught up in there among

the gears and do any harm. Anything in the gearbox is liable to be carried up by some heavier oil to where it'll cause extra wear."

TRANNY, WHAT BIG TEETH YOU HAVE!

There was a tip, too. It concerns a lot of people who take the speedo cable off their Harleys. The drive end is removed from the transmission, right in a place where it is wide open to all manner of grit and other foreign matter. The drive mechanism is still turning, even though the cable has been removed. If dirt causes it to lock up, the worm can hop up amongst the gears and the misery of having the fleas of a thousand camels take up residence in your beard will be condensed into a few danger-laden seconds!

ATF CAUTION

I thought more about ATF in transmissions and clutches and wondered about using something that light in a bike that had a system of sharing oil between, say, the primary chain case and the engine. The late Triumphs, among others, are included in this category, so I got in touch with Bob Ellison of Triumph's West Coast operation and asked for a statement.

Although there isn't a gorging spate of oil passage between the late Triumph's lower end and the chain case, putting anything as light as ATF in the chain case is not recommended. Then what about the recommendation for one weight in the engine and another in the primary. The answer came to me this way: "Use a multiple-viscosity oil. Something like one of the better grade 20W-50s will do."

Then what about these rider manuals that recommend 90 gear lube, or 80, and then the guy in the bike shop will tell you to substitute 40- or 50-weight oil? This question prompted my contact with Rob Lancaster at Torco Oil Company. It isn't as confusing when you hear it from someone who knows what he's talking about. Lancaster, whose father, Bob, developed many of the Torco products now in circulation, explained that a different set of weight numbers had been assigned to the gear lubes. That's why you'll find that 80 gear lube will have the approximate viscosity of 30-weight motor oil. Likewise, 90 gear lube might come out about like 50-weight motor oil. But wait . . . they're still not the same. Temperature, it seems, will tend to

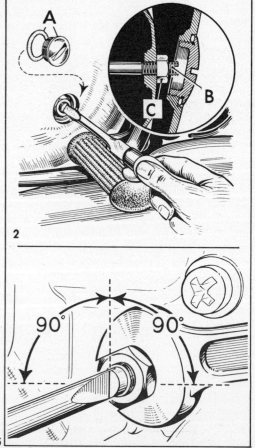

make more difference in the fluidity of gear lubes, perhaps because the makers employ more cross-blending to achieve some specific viscosity. On the other hand, motor oils have more "built-in" cross-fluidity. Some of this is purely rote on my part, but I believe the explanation clears up a lot of misunderstanding about viscosity scales. Stick to gear lube if recommended.

A FINAL THOUGHT ON ATF

"ATF is possessed of some good anti-friction characteristics which should make it recommendable for clutches," says Lancaster. This more or less came as a culmination of remarks that I'd solicited on the stuff. It is generally a good idea for use in the clutch. If the clutch housing also includes your primary chain it shouldn't make any difference, and the same goes for any ball or roller bearings present in the area, although sleeve bushings just might be another proposition. As far as using it in transmissions is concerned, there was some question in the mind of Lancaster about ATF's load-carrying abilities when you consider the sheer pressures exerted between gear teeth. If in doubt about using ATF, use the recommended lube or gear oil until you can qualify its use with an experienced mechanic.

GEAR CHAIN . . . NEW TO BIKES?

Honda used a gear chain on their land speed record attempt bike, probably as much to indicate their faith in it as it was for its reliability. Gear chain is a series of seven or so little plates pinned together in segments to take the place of the links you have come to be familiar with in regular roller-type chains. Gear chain presents a smooth surface from the outside with a gear-tooth inner surface. Then, instead of working between two sprockets, it works between two gears. This is the set-up reportedly used on the new Honda 350 and 500 four-cylinder bikes to transmit power between the engine's crankshaft and the clutch. Most of the Honda people I talked to said it was too soon to know whether gear chain as a primary drive component was going to work out or not. The reason, generally, was that there were not any machines out of their dealerships with really high mileage on gear chain primaries. The four-cylinder 750, incidentally, still uses regular roller-type primary drive. But, getting back to the gear chain, you probably know it has been used extensively on automobile engines for years as timing chain.

We've mentioned roller chain as primary drive and we'll be back to it shortly for a look at some of the things that apply to its adjustment and wear. Right now let's discuss the type of primary drive system that's most likely to be found on smaller machines. This is the gear system where one gear works directly off the end of the crankshaft to drive a corresponding set of teeth on the outer circumference of the clutch housing wheel. These are of two types, helical and straight-cut. Some say that the helical, or angle-cut type, is quieter and smoother for pure pleasure riding. However, when you're after that last available iota of power, the straight-cut variety is definitely preferable. The reason is due to loss of power that stems from whatever minute amount of side thrust loading friction might take place as the slanted teeth in the helicals match up. This, of course, would not be present in straight-cut teeth.

As far as checking for damage or wear on primary gears is concerned, it might be thought of in much the same manner as regular transmission gears. The roller chain primary drive is likely to give a lot more trouble than gears, but permit easier ratio change. For example, not many riders are likely to blame a shaky ride on a worn-out or loose primary chain—no more than they'd blame rough shifting

6

7

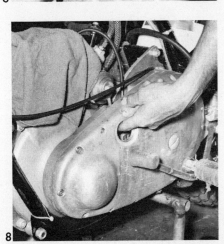

8

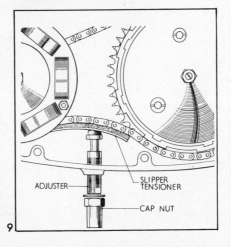

ADJUSTER — SLIPPER TENSIONER — CAP NUT

9

1. Europeans, especially British, use simpler, more trouble free shift plate. Cammed grooves move forks, gears.

2. Also simpler is BSA clutch pushrod adjustment. Tighten, back off ¼ turn.

3. Top of shift fork is deep blue in color from burn after being bent.

4. Cammed eccentric screws are used to move and adjust shift linkage. Turning screw moves linkage up, down.

5. Locking nut holds eccentric screw in place. LocTite recommended.

6. Spring loaded detent rests against serrated cam drum or plate to firmly position it in gear selected, neutral.

7. Some torquer type engines use coil spring shock absorber. Allows sprocket to spin under sudden shock, saves gears.

8. Engines with primary chain drive need regular adjustment. Check play.

9. BSA uses adjustable slipper tensioner to take up chain slop. Older designs require moving gearbox back.

CLUTCHES

on an improperly adjusted primary chain.

Nearly every chain, primary or final drive (new or used) is going to have something of a "tight spot." As long as it isn't too pronounced this isn't going to hurt anything. However, if there is too much difference in the adjustment you can achieve on one section of a chain when compared to another, it is time for a new chain. The idea with any chain is to find where it is tightest before you make the adjustment and set it at that point. As you can readily see, setting the prescribed chain slack on the loose spot would create a dangerously un-even situation when the tight section came around. I have seen entire transmission housings on non-unit motorcycles snapped in twain like a fortune cookie by the type of mistake just outlined.

DON'T KICK IT, STROKE IT!

You may have guessed that the theme of much of what I have written thus far has been devised to keep you from having to open up your clutch or transmission in the first place. Like I said at the outset . . . let's attack this thing from the outside! Maybe "attack" isn't the right word. Neither is "kick!" Kick . . . you see it every-where: kickstarter, kickstart mechan-ism, kick-crank, kick it! Kick is quite possibly the most damaging mis-nomer associated with motorcycle operation. The fan-gear and ratchet-and-pawl components in most bikes are pretty sturdy, but nothing of mere steel could possibly stand up under the brutal punishment to which it is subjected by a lot of riders. I have seen pawls broken, fan-gear teeth knocked off and transmission hous-ings cracked—to say nothing of bro-ken crank arms and pedals—by peo-ple who launch themselves skyward, then come down, muddy boots and all, with kill-vengeance on the starter

1

2

3

4

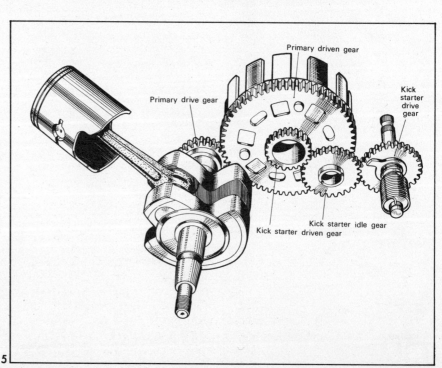

5

Primary driven gear

Primary drive gear

Kick starter drive gear

Kick starter idle gear

Kick starter driven gear

mechanisms of their motorcycles. This is the unfailing sign of a rank amateur. You'll see the experienced rider put just enough weight on that crank pedal to assure correct engagement of the parts inside, then shift his weight over the pedal and come down with a smooth, even stroke. There's a lot less exertion involved and a lot more satisfaction in the long run.

I haven't been able to give you too many specifics. Clutches alone could easily absorb book-length attention, to say nothing of how little can actually be told of the entire power transmission train within the confines of just a single chapter. Instead, my effort has been to help you expand your concept of the things we've discussed and, in addition, emphasize the importance of being careful and using workshop manuals to the best advantage. At the same time I may have over-conveyed the idea that there is a delicacy about motorcycles, particularly primary chains and clutches. If this has been the case, be reminded of the 500cc. J.A. Prestwich and Jawa Class "A" Speedway machines. The primary chain and clutch on these bikes is operated in what you might call an open-air "sand-bath." The only oil the chains ever feel may result from an occasional squirt administered by a tuner between races. On relatively short American speedway courses these exposed components bear the brunt of nearly every conceivable abuse. Clutch bearings may benefit from nothing more than a carefree smear of Vaseline and, at that, only when they're periodically disassembled for cleaning. Otherwise, getting stuffed with sand or decomposed granite to a point of becoming wholly inoperable usually will call for no more than a few sharp raps with a rawhide mallet or a handy two-by-four. Clutches on Class "A" bikes might go a bit further, but you could doubtless figure a primary chain would be worth no more than a total of fifty miles of accumulated circle burning. You've got a lot more going for you if you'll observe the right maintenance and repair procedure.

1. Gear driven primary either straight cut or helical. Straight has less friction, more noise. Helical quieter.

2. Morse Hyvo drive becoming popular with high-hp engines. Quiet, strong.

3. Spring loaded ratchet kick start needs inspection for worn serrations.

4. Kick pawl assembly also simple, but more sensitive. Serrations, pawl wear.

5. Typical kick start drive system goes through starter, idle gear, clutch to primary drive. Shown is Suzuki 400.

6. Speedway bike has external drive and clutch. Sand-bath clutch and chain undergoes severest of punishment.

7. Tachometer drive usually runs from worm gear off gearbox. Care must be taken to install perfectly straight and aligned. Slight cock destroys gears.

8. Kawasaki 350 road racer has special external dry clutch. Multi-plate clutch has less friction drag than internal oil bathed assembly.

6

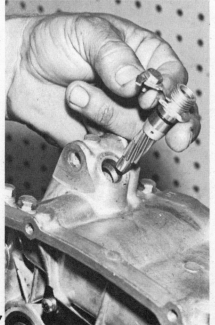

7

8

THE FINAL LINK

With a little knowledge and attention, you can assure many thousands of miles of service from your chain.

BY DALE BOLLER

Although chains are rarely repaired or rebuilt, a good motorcycle repair manual must establish certain truths about these strings of steel which are a common failure in all types of riding. If a mechanic's goal is to ensure the reliable running of motorcycles, he must understand thoroughly these critical driveline components and know exactly how to keep them operable and efficient. No other system within a motorcycle receives the misuse and abuse of the chain systems (primary, cam and drive), so the mechanic must be able to spot improper applications or neglect, then correct the former, communicate to the machine's owner the dangers of the latter and finally explain to him the dos and don'ts of exact maintenance procedures. Study it carefully.

Chains are used in motorcycles where power transmission by gear or shaft is too expensive or technically infeasible. The choice is hardly a compromise, however, since a well-lubricated roller chain provides positive, non-slip drive at an efficiency of 98 percent. The positive mesh between rollers and sprocket teeth minimizes bearing loads on sprocket shafts since the chain does not depend on tension to provide friction drive as is necessary with a belt and pulley. There is also no side thrust.

Other benefits make the choice a wise one: A single chain can drive several different shafts, such as both cams in a 450, or the myriad of shafts within the timing case of the old 750 Royal Enfields. Chain installation is easy and the drive ratio can be altered by changing one or both sprockets. If adequately lubricated, chains don't deteriorate with age or exposure to the elements as rubber belts do. Roller chains are relatively cheap, compact, light and reliable. Due to standards set by the Association of Roller and Silent Chain Manufacturers and by the American National Standards Institute (ANSI), they are interchangeable among brands except on certain Iron Curtain bikes

such as Jawa, CZ and MZ. A properly designed and maintained chain drive has slow, predictable wear and a long useful life—on the order of 15,000 hours of operation or 500,000 miles of riding! These figures are never reached in practice because motorcycle designers choose the smallest chain which will work at all in order to keep the drive as light, cheap and compact as possible. And of course in motorcycle applications ideal operating conditions are impossible to achieve.

There are two kinds of links in a chain, pin links and roller links. *Pin links* consist of two solid pins press-fitted into *sideplates,* or linkplates. These are the wider links. A *master link* is a removable pin link. The pins ride inside bushings which are part of the roller links.

Roller links are more complicated. A tubular bushing is press-fitted in each end of the sideplates. These bushings are usually curl-formed from flat stock and individual manufacturers have their own tricks for making and assembling them. For example, the bushing seam may be oriented toward the middle of the link so tension acts opposite the seam, or the ends of the bushings may be acid-etched to give better bite to the press-fit. The bushing seam on Diamond brand chain has a cutaway shaped like a diamond to

act as a reservoir for lubricant. Fitting loosely over the bushing is a tubular *roller.* This is what contacts the sprocket teeth. Though the roller is free to rotate on the bushing, this is not its primary job. The main task of the roller is to absorb the impact as the chain and sprocket engage. Some chains, in small sizes, don't have rollers and the bushings run directly on the sprockets. These are called "rollerless" chains.

All chains are classified by size in terms of their *pitch,* which is simply the center-to-center distance between a pair of pins or bushings. Common drive-chain sizes are 3/8; 1/2-or 5/8-inch pitch by some varying width—classified by the width of the roller—usually in the area of 1/4, 3/8, 5/16 or 1/2. Most Triumphs use a 5/8 x 3/8 chain, and the Honda Four uses a wider 5/8 x 1/2 chain. Each link (roller link, pin link, master link) is one pitch long and thus the number of pitches always equals the number of links. This number is traditionally specified with the chain closed in a loop, i.e., including a master link. When you ask for a chain with 102 links, you'll receive a length 101 pitches long, plus a master link.

Though motorcycle people almost always refer to chains by their pitch and roller width, as 1/2 x 1/4 or 5/8 x 3/8.

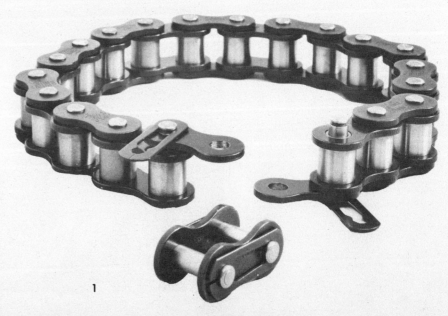

1

Sometimes motorcycle designers want chain of standard size, but a little stronger; or the same size, but a little cheaper. Enter the special, or non-standard chains with non-standard numbering—No. 520, No. 530 or the popular Whitney No. 625, which is a high performance 5/8-inch pitch used by many 750 Honda Four owners. Whatever the number on a special chain, be sure the pitch and roller width is equivalent to that on the chain you are replacing.

Because the ANSI standards go back as far as 1913, they have penetrated throughout most of the world. There is a true metric standard, used on some European bikes (Jawa, CZ, Maico) that have different width and diameter rollers in standard pitch lengths and therefore cannot be interchanged with ANSI chain. New sprockets will be required to fit standard chain, so at the time you buy such a bike it would be a good idea to buy a set of replacement chains...a primary and two or three rear chains.

The accompanying table of chain proportions gives the principle dimensions of No. 35, No. 40 and No. 50 standard chains, the sizes most

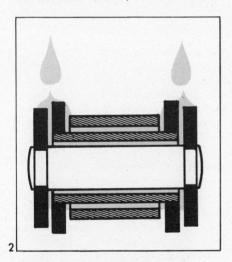

2

1. These small plates, links and rollers of steel must transmit all the power and work load of motorcycles from five to 200 horsepower. Full Bore's chain uses unique master links.

2. The secret to long chain life is getting lubricant where it's needed most. High friction and wear points are between link plates and the roller-to-pin surfaces. As shown here a small drop of lubricant in the right place will keep friction to a minimum. Quantity of lubricant is second to application method.

3. Chains are used to drive the gearbox, camshafts, timing systems as well as rear wheel power train. Thus the single, duplex, triplex and even the dual plate master link.

used on motorcycles. Roller diameter, linkplate thickness and other measurements are all certain proportions of pitch "P". Thus the roller diameter is 5/8's of the pitch, within a specified tolerance. The minimum-ultimate-tensile-strength,

DRIVE SYSTEMS

Sprockets should have at least 15 teeth. This lower limit is set by "chordal action," or changes in link speeds while going to and from the sprocket. This phenomenon becomes increasingly severe when there are fewer than 17 teeth. Chordal action occurs thusly: The effective shape of a sprocket is actually a polygon; a six-tooth sprocket would be a hexagon, an eight-tooth sprocket an octagon, etc. A straight line between the pins of a link setting in two troughs of a sprocket represents one side of the sprocket's overall polygon shape. The center of this line, and therefore the center of the link, is minutely closer to the center of the sprocket than the two ends of the link. As the chain goes around the sprocket, the middle of each link has a different, slower speed than the two ends of the link, which are further from the center of rotation than the middle is, and therefore travel at a faster speed in order to cover a longer distance in the same time. On the other hand, all parts of a link have the same velocity when it is moving in a straight line between sprockets. This means that a sharp change in velocity and direction is required as each link engages a sprocket—which translates into a

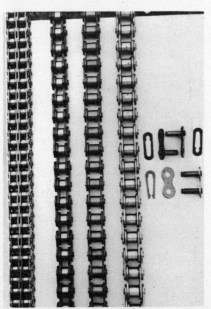

3

sharp impact of chain roller on sprocket teeth and certain wear producing pressure and bearing changes between pin, bushing and It causes a high-frequency up-and-down vibration of the links and, most important, it means that each roller experiences a sharp impact as it engages, and again as it leaves, the sprockets.

The larger the sprocket, the closer is the approximation to a circle and the less is the effect of chordal action since there are more sides (link pitches) to the polygon and thus less variance in distance of the side's length from the center of the sprocket. Directional changes are also more gradual on a larger sprocket. On many motorcycles the output sprocket is too small, causing excessive chordal action and abnormally short chain life. Expect trouble when you see 15 or fewer teeth, unfortunately a common occurence on too many countershaft sprockets. Camshaft drives are another area where the designer may have tried too hard to save space by using small sprockets. Primary drives are usually OK. Whenever you lower a gear ratio, do it by fitting a larger sprocket on the rear, not a smaller one on the countershaft.

Sprockets should have no more than 70 teeth. Since gradual changes in pitch due to wear accumulate as rollers contact increasing numbers of teeth, large sprockets are therefore more sensitive to chain wear. Big sprockets don't cause extra wear, like small ones do, they're just less tolerant of existing wear by an amount given in the section on why chains fail.

Chain wrap is the amount of angle around a sprocket for which the chain and sprocket are engaged. Wrap should be at least 120 degrees, which is 1/3 of the way around the sprocket; otherwise too few teeth are carrying the load. This becomes a problem for high gear ratios and multiple-sprocket single-chain arrangements. Equal size sprockets always give 180 degree wrap, and the wrap will be over 120 degrees if the gear ratio is less than 3.5:1. Chain wrap is adequate on normal motorcycle drives.

Shaft centers are correctly spaced when the distance is between 30 and 50 pitches of chain. When the center-to-center distance

THE FINAL LINK

between the output sprocket and the rear wheel sprocket is 25 inches and a 5/8-inch pitch chain is used, the spacing is 25 ÷ 5/8 = 40 pitches, which is good. Primary drives are often shorter, but not unreasonably so. In fact, spacings around 20 pitches are desirable for pulsating loads like the output of an engine. Very long chains will surge and vibrate, giving a rough drive and shortened chain life.

A *reduction ratio* of 7:1 is the safe upper limit for chain drives. In contrast, a worm gear can give 50:1 reduction. This is obviously a limitation for some applications, but not for motorcycles since the needed ratios are no more than 5:1 and are achieved without resorting to extremely large or small sprockets.

Design power is the normal or average power to be transmitted by a drive system. It takes around 15 horsepower to cruise a motorcycle at highway speeds. This must be multiplied by a service factor to account for uneven or shock loads, pulsating power sources and load reversals. All these are present for bikes. A service factor of around 2.0 is typical, so the chains should be capable of transmitting 2 x 15 = 30 hp.

A three-strand 3/8-pitch primary chain reaches its maximum power carrying capacity at 3000 rpm on the small sprocket. With a typical 25-tooth crankshaft (small) sprocket, the capacity is 11.9 horsepower (which includes the service factor of 2.0).

Dyno tests conducted previously by the *Motorcycle Repair Manual* staff have shown the corrected rear-wheel horsepower developed in high gear at 3000 engine rpm (about 50 mph) by some common machines to be:

BSA/Triumph 750	16 hp
Honda 750 Four	19 hp
Norton	23 hp
H-D Sportster	30 hp

This looks reasonable. These listed powers are for full throttle at 3000 rpm, and it doesn't take anywhere near full throttle to cruise one of these bikes at 50 mph. The 11.9 hp chain capacity is quite adequate here.

The difficulty is that as crankshaft speed increases beyond 3000 rpm the engine power goes up, to the vicinity of 60 hp, while the chain

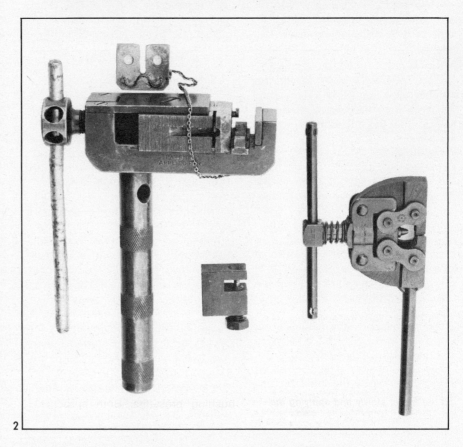

capacity goes down, from 11.9 hp to only 3.2 hp at 7500 rpm. Only THREE horsepower! The situation on the rear chain is similar. At full throttle and full speed a big road bike is pumping twenty times the recommended amount of power through its chains. Is it any wonder the chains don't last 15,000 hours?

But should they last 15,000 hours? Yes, if they are to be used on a piece of equipment intended to run that long between overhauls—like a factory conveyor belt.

FAILURE MODES

Ultimate-tensile-strength, fatigue, wear, corrosion and galling are the main kinds of chain failure. Identifying the cause of failure will help you decide what corrective action to take—if any is possible. Improving a chain to resist one kind of failure usually requires sacrifices elsewhere. There's no free lunch.

Ultimate-tensile-strength measures a chain's ability to carry a steady pull. If the chain is loaded beyond its ultimate strength, the linkplates may break across the pin or bushing holes. There should be visible stretching of the metal alongside the break. A brittle failure—linkplate cracking without visible stretching of the metal—is a sign of defective steel, improper heat treating or embrittlement due to corrosion. Bushings can also fail in ultimate strength as when a loose chain jumps teeth on the sprockets. Unless weakened by corrosion, rollers rarely fail in ultimate strength. Pins may be sheared off between the pin and bushing linkplates or they may suffer brittle fracture in the center. To overcome ultimate strength failures you need a larger chain.

Fatigue-strength is always less than ultimate-strength and is related to loads that are applied repetitively. For example, as the chain moves around the sprockets, the top side is under heavy tension while the bottom side is almost slack; the impact of a roller on a sprocket tooth is another repeated load contributing to fatigue of the chain. Load reversals such as occur when you shift, accelerate, use the brakes, go over jumps and bumps or ride a bike with excessive drive train

1. Impending disaster. Not an uncommon sight is Japanese chain link plates cracked as shown. Caused by improper set-up, the battery vent tube was placed over this chain. Acid corrosion from the battery fumes caused this weakness caught just prior to a very expensive breakage failure.

2. Proper tools make for a sanitary job. Chain breakers range from large industrial link pin removers to a garage size to a special mini-size breaker to fit in your tool kit.

3. Spray lubes for chains have lead to ease of maintenance chores. Spinning the wheel slowly and applying the lube atop the chain lets the liquid roll down the sprocket onto the links.

snatch all add to fatigue.

When you find evidence of fatigue, replace the chain. Fatigue in sideplates usually shows up as a hairline crack that starts at a pin or bushing hole and works outward at right angles to the length of the chain. As the crack grows, its two faces rub together, giving them a burnished appearance instead of the rough, grainy texture found on cracks that happen all at once. Linkplate fatigue failures are due to too small a chain, to high frequency vibrations in the chain even when the average load is not excessive, to worn sprocket teeth or to dirt in the tooth pockets. Enlarging both sprockets in proportion (to keep the same gear ratio) will often help overcome fatigue failures.

Bushing fatigue cracks start on the inner surface of the bushing. Either they progress across the bushing where it contacts the sprocket teeth, or they go part way around it near the sideplates. Causes and cures are similar to sideplate fatigue failures.

The main cause of roller fatigue is the impact of the roller on the sprocket tooth as they engage. Jumping teeth is especially bad; it can be identified by the tooth marks or scuff marks left on the rollers. Roller fatigue is traceable to small sprockets, high chain speeds and lubrication that is inadequate to absorb the impact forces. Bigger sprockets, more lubricant and a thicker or more viscous lubricant will help.

Pins have greater fatigue-strength than sideplates, bushings or rollers. They rarely suffer fatigue failures.

Tight joints are a kind of fatigue failure in which nothing actually breaks. What happens is that the press-fit of the bushings in the sideplates loosens up, allowing the bushing sideplates to rub against the pin sideplates, making the joints stiff. Look for inadequate lubrication, misalignment of the sprockets, unusually high loads or obstacles that rub against the chain such as the chain guard, chain guide, shock absorber or a frame member.

Sprocket misalignment wear is always easy to spot since one side of the teeth will be obviously worn. In bad cases the twisting loads can destroy the chain by breaking the bushing press-fits. Both sprockets should be in the same plane when correctly aligned. Chains are tolerant and careful eyeballing of the rear chain from behind the bike is usually good enough. Check for missing or improperly installed shims on the rear and output sprockets, for a reversed output sprocket (they're not always symmetrical left-to-right), for a bent swing arm, and especially for misalignment of the rear axle in its adjustment slots. If your eyeballs aren't calibrated too accurately, a straightedge or tightly drawn string held along the sides of the sprockets will help you to see if they are in the same plane.

Wear is the one kind of chain failure that must be considered normal and unavoidable. As metal wears from the pins and bushings, the chain grows longer. This process is accelerated by the presence of desert dust, moto-cross mud and pavement particles, but very little can be done to prevent the action of these abrasives.

Eventually a chain will lengthen to where it doesn't fit the sprocket teeth and has to be replaced. You cannot measure chain wear by bowing the chain sideways as many people think, for the amount of bow depends not only on the pin/bushing wear, but also on sideplate wear due to sprocket misalignment and on the initial amount of sideplay built into the chain—which varies considerably among brands and types of chain. To measure wear accurately you must test the amount of elongation, or "stretch" (it's not actually stretch in the sense of pulling taffy, of course).

To measure *chain stretch*, lay the chain in a straight line on the floor and carefully push the links together to make the chain as short as possible. Mark where the ends of the chain are. Now hold one end at the mark and pull on the other to extend the chain as much as possible. No great force is needed. Measure, in inches, the difference in length between the mark and the extended position of the free end. For normal sprockets, this is less than three percent and the chain is still OK. But if you have a giant 80-tooth overlay on the wheel sprocket you can't use three percent since $200/80 = 2.5\%$, which is less. So you must compare the measured 2.59 percent to the allowable 2.5 percent. This shows the chain to be worn out since its actual percent stretch is over the 2.5 percent limit.

Wear is greatly influenced by lubrication. A dry chain wears about 300 times faster than a well-lubricated one! Even a tiny amount of oil can greatly reduce wear. Erratic lubrication allows some joints to wear faster than others which makes the chain longer in some places than in others and prevents you from obtaining a proper slack adjustment.

Corrosion is a failure mechanism that is extremely underrated. Rust will accelerate pin and bushing wear and can cause "stress corrosion cracking," which is related to ultimate strength failure, or "corosion-fatigue failure," which is related to fatigue-strength failure. When corrosion and fatigue are working together to break a linkplate or pin, the telltale sign is often that there are several partial cracks near the main break. Corrosion weakens metal by destroying the surface finish.

Like piston seizures in a two-stroke engine, *galling* should not normally happen, but when it does, it's bad news. Galling means that

THE FINAL LINK

the pin and the bushing pressure-weld together, then are torn apart as the chain flexes over the sprockets. This literally tears chunks of metal from the pin and bushing, causing extremely rapid "wear." Galling can be identified (on a chain you're replacing) by a mixture of bright polished and rough torn spots on the pins—just like a seized piston. Galling is always caused by inadequate lubrication *at the joint*. This can happen several ways:

First, the whole chain may be starved for lubricant because you haven't put any on. Second, the lubricant may be too thin, so that the oil film breaks down under load, allowing metal-to-metal contact. Third, the lubricant may be too thick, so that even though it's all over the outside of the chain it has failed to penetrate between the pins and bushings. Fourth, the loads may be so high that the lubricant is squeezed out from between the bearing surfaces; with a suitable lubricant, this takes loads high enough to cause ultimate-strength or fatigue-strength failures anyway, so the galling is a secondary worry.

Master links are subject to ultimate strength, fatigue, wear, corrosion and galling failures just like the regular pin and roller links. In addition, they have some problems of their own. The master link is a pin link, but with the pins supported by press fit on only one side. This means the master link pins are subjected to a certain amount of bending. To reduce the chance of pin fatigue the cover plate should be a snug fit on the pins. This will support their free ends as well as possible, though not as well as a press-fitted plate. You should have to push the cover plate pretty hard to fit it on. Once in place, the plate is held on by a U-shaped spring clip or "feather" that fits annular grooves in the pins. The closed end of the "U" should point in the direction of chain motion to minimize the chance of it disloging should the chain brush against an obstacle. It is important to tap the master link pins back until the spring clip comes up snugly against the cover plate. Shop around for master links. They vary quite a bit among brands, some having cover plates that fit the pins very loosely; these should be avoided.

Press-fit master links are available for all size chains and are superior in performance, but harder to put on and take off. Since the pins are supported by press fits on both sides, and since there's no spring clip to come off, these master links are essentially as strong and reliable as a regular pin link. To put one together use a pair of Vise-Grips and place an old master link cover plate over the one you're installing: this reduces the chances of bending or nicking the press-fitted plate and allows you to squeeze it down below the ends of the pins. Put paint on it so you can find it again. Don't reuse a press-fit master link. A so-called "endless chain" is actually an ordinary chain closed with a press-fit master link.

Don't resize a chain to an odd number of pitches by using a half-link. *Half-links* are the weakest links. The pin is not supported by a press fit on either side and the dogleg sideplates are inherently weaker than straight sideplates; furthermore, they put a bending stress on the press fit of the bushing, which is likely to loosen. Half-links are in-ferior to regular links and to master links in both ultimate strength and fatigue strength.

To obtain an odd number of links in a chain, it is much better to use an offset link assembly, which is two or more pitches long and includes a second master link. Because the offset pitch is entirely press-fitted, its fatigue strength is greater than a half-link's, and the whole assembly is no less stronger than a master link. Fatigue is the main consideration since the offset assembly behaves like the main body of the chain in other respects. If possible connect the assembly with press-fit master links or fit standard masters with one facing inside, the other outside.

Examining an old chain can tell you which failure modes are most troublesome. If your chains fail by normal wear, there is nothing to be gained by experimenting with chains designed especially for high ultimate strength; these may wear even faster. On the other hand, if you can trace the failure to fatigue cracking, a brand or model of chain designed for superior fatigue

strength may be the answer. Unless you have some idea why the old chain needs to be replaced, you're shooting in the dark.

CHAIN LENGTH

The stock-length chain will no longer fit your bike if you change the size of the output or rear-wheel sprocket, if you mount an overlay sprocket or if you extend the swing arm to improve the machine's handling. How do you find the right chain length to use?

The usual way is to gather a standard chain and a handful of master links, half-links, offset-link assemblies, and short lengths of chain. Armed with a good chain-breaker and plenty of patience you will eventually find some combination of parts that fits. This may take quite a bit of fiddling.

Here's a tip on installation of your new chain. Use the old one, still attached to the motorcycle, to fit the new one on. Simply connect the new chain to the old chain with a master link (you don't even need to add the coverplate and spring clip) and pull off the old chain while

3

1. Keeping proper chain tension is just as critical as carburetion and correct ignition timing. To make correct adjustment (usually 1 to 1½ inches free play) riders full weight should be on the machine. This will compress the rear suspension units and move the rear axle up to its normal running location without play.

2. The most accurate and best way to adjust rear wheel position and chain play is to measure the distance of the rear axle from a constant. In this case we are making the distance from the swing arm bolt to the rear axle equal. Keeps wheel straight.

3. When lubing the chain be sure to get to the link plates on the inside. Bending the spray nozzle does it.

feeding in the new one. It's also much easier to connect the new chain's ends with the master link if the ends are both engaged on the rear sprocket.

LUBRICANTS

Nothing about roller chains is more mysterious than selecting lubricants. Besides the old standbys—oil, grease, wax, graphite—there are dozens of brandname lubricants on the market, each claiming to be the ultimate answer. Most of these proprietary lubricants are careful to avoid telling you exactly what it is that they contain, possibly because they're based on a magical formula of bat's ears, newt's eyes and chicken blood. Evidently this approach works, because most riders either continually change lubricants, always looking for that elusively perfect one, or else they've found the perfect lubricant and stand behind it steadfastly.

To make some sense out of this behavior, the first question to ask is: What is a chain lubricant supposed to do? Well, it has to reduce friction by lubricating the moving joints, primarily the pin-bushing bearing. The film of lubricant formed between the bushing and the roller is supposed to act as a shock absorber, smoothing out the repeated impacts when each roller engages a sprocket tooth and the less frequent but larger impacts of popping the clutch, shifting without using the clutch, or landing after a jump. And the lubricant must protect against corrosion which, for a motorcycle chain, means protecting it against rust. These are the three basic functions a chain lube must perform.

The outside of the roller does not need lubrication to prevent friction because the roller, despite its misleading name, does not actually roll on the sprocket teeth the way that gear teeth roll across each other as they mesh. Sideplates bear against one another where they overlap, but very little lubrication is needed here to reduce friction for the simple reason that in a properly aligned chain there is very little or no sideload to create friction in the first place. So the things any lubricant must do are to reduce friction and absorb shock inside the chain and to prevent rust on the outside of the chain.

The simplest and cheapest chain

lubricant is ordinary motor oil, SAE 20 in cold weather, up to SAE 40 in 100 degree plus temperatures. All chains come from their manufacturers prelubricated—mainly to prevent rust—and oil is the usual lubricant used. Unfortunately there's a built-in conflict. Thicker oil sticks to the chain better and absorbs shock better, but thinner oil penetrates better to where it's needed inside the chain. Also, oil is not the greatest rust preventative. While all good motor oils contain additives to inhibit rust, they can do their job only so long as they resist being washed off the chain. Special rust preventatives will stick more tenaciously than plain oil.

Some old timers insist on boiling their chains in grease, a ritual based on the thin-to-apply/then-let-thicken approach to solving the conflict between thick and thin lubricants. Everybody should try this at least once. It will prove that tending a huge pot of bubbling, boiling, smoking, stinking grease is a pain in the neck. Aside from the inconvenience, a serious, often-overlooked problem is that it is easy to overheat the grease and damage it. Many greases will break down chemically at temperatures beyond the boiling point of water, irreversibly impairing their lubricating properties. Boiling in grease is best reserved as a punishment for feature editors, not as a way of lubricating chains. Don't waste your time.

The first special chain lubes were a combination of a thick oil or grease (grease is just oil thickened with special soaps) and a solvent that thinned the mixture for good penetration when applied, then evaporated to leave the oil or grease behind. This was a great advance over heating the grease to thin it for application.

The recent trend has been toward aerosol cans of brandname chain lubes whose strong point is ease of application and, let's face it, a lot more glamour than kerosene and oil. Ashland Chain Lube has an armlock on convenience with its white foam that clings to the chain when you spray it on, slowly breaking down to fluid and penetrating the crevices. Any spray-can product can be carried on a trip without danger of breaking or leaking; this feature alone may make the aerosol products worth their price.

Some chain lubricants are merely

THE FINAL LINK

dispersions of solid lubricants like molybdenum disulphide, graphite, lead or that new miracle lubricant perfected for NASA and used on space vehicles, tungsten diselenide. Unless they contain rust inhibitors, however, solid lubricants are not very good for motorcycle chains.

Carl Shipman, the proprietor of The Dirt Rider mail-order accessory house in Albuquerque, New Mexico, sells his own mixture of dry molybdenum disulphide and Teflon for you to mix with good old rust preventing oil. He may be close to the answer. Take a look at his 12-page "Chainlube Handbook," which reiterates many of the truths found in this article and explains his lube formula completely.

You may come across industrial chain lubes that carry the idea of solvent reduction to its extreme. These are solvent reduced asphaltum or tar. Intended for large chains operating at slow speeds, these lubes are unsuitable for motorcycle use. Don't be tempted by the notion of a lube that won't fly off. Even in their thinned condition they won't penetrate the small clearances of bike-sized chain and they won't provide adequate lubrication at high operating speeds.

A relatively new, but very promising class of motorcycle chain lubricant is rust preventative spray such as LPS No. 3. The unique property of these materials is their affinity for metal. Each molecule of the "snake oil" has an almost erotic urge to couple with a molecule of strong, hard metal. If you spray snake oil onto a water-wet chain it will actually penetrate through the water in its drive to adhere to metal, displacing the water from the surface of the chain. Once bonded to the metal the rust preventative will resist attempts to wipe it off much better than ordinary oil or grease. The characteristic phrase to look for on the can is "displaces water" or "displaces moisture."

If you wash your bike at a car wash, you can blast the dirt right off the chain with the powerful detergent spray. This blasts the lubricant right off, too, and the chain will start to rust within minutes. If you squirt water-displacing snake oil on the chain immediately—waiting 'till you arrive home is too long—the rust preventative will dis-

place the water, coat the chain, and nary a trace of rust will occur. Regular oil-base lubricants will protect the chain unless washed off, but they will not penetrate through water like the snake oils.

To evaluate any special chain lube ask yourself: How is this product better than SAE 20 oil (rust prevention, ease of application, penetration, etc.)? Is this advantage worth it to me? Unique advantages and disadvantages pop up when evaluating lubricants for your special purpose. For instance the desert rider who is considering a dry lubricant to reduce wear from dust and grit by eliminating oil and its affinity for these abrasives will lose oil's superior effectiveness as a shock absorber between roller and bushing; he'll merely be trading one kind of wear for another. Observations such as this only tend to complicate matters, and unfortunately, no one has the final answer. You must use the criteria presented herein to help you decide which type or brand of lubricant best meets your requirements.

Correct lubrication technique is the essence of chain care. In the

first place, don't depend on a chain oiler if your bike happens to be blessed/cursed with one. All too often, built-in oilers dump too much or too little oil, they plug up without warning or fail to direct the oil where it is needed. Oiler or no, you'll still have to lubricate the rear drive chain manually to do it effectively. The primary chain and cam chain normally run in an oil bath, which is the way all chains are supposed to operate, so we don't have to worry about them.

The most effective place to apply a liquid lubricant is along the upper edges of the sideplates. This allows the lube to work down among the rollers, bushings, pins and sideplates. It's pointless to squirt lubricant on the rollers along the centerline of the chain.

The neatest, most convenient and most effective way to lube a chain with an oil-spout or an aerosol-can plastic-snorkel tube is to raise the rear wheel off the ground by lifting the bike on a shop stand or if you're lucky, merely on its own centerstand. Slowly turn the rear wheel backwards so the chain comes off the bottom of the wheel

4

1. Stretched chain can raise havoc with sprocket teeth. In this case the chain stretch was so great that the rollers overlapped on the teeth (from 9:00 to 12:00 o'clock) and ripped off the tips. Ruined the clutch.

2. This is what excessive chain stretch looks like. The only place the chain is fitting is at 2:00 o'clock. Both chain and sprocket are ruined.

3. More and more machines are going to the use of Hyvo chain for the awesome task of primary drive for superbikes. This multi plate chain runs on straight teeth sprockets, is quiet, super strong and bulletproof. Hyvo chain must run in an oil bath.

4. When replacing the master link plate and clip, place the open end of the spring clip trailing the forward travel direction of the chain. Putting the open end of the clip in the direction of travel invites its getting opened by a bush or . . .

sprocket and moves toward the engine. Now spew the lubricant on the side of the sprocket just above the chain's sideplates. The lubricant will run down onto the upper edges of the sideplates—which is exactly where you want it to go. If you try to spray the edges of the chain while they're in midair between the sprockets, you'll waste most of the lubricant and make a big mess on the bike and floor. Now repeat the process on the inboard side of the sprocket, oiling the other row of sideplates.

You can reach the inboard side of the sprocket through the wheel spokes, not too hard with a long-spouted pump-type oil can, but perhaps a bit awkward with an aerosol can. Here's a trick to simplify reaching the inboard side with a spray can. Take the slim plastic tube off the nozzle and hold it at one end so it slants up at about 45 degrees. Now hold a lit cigarette under the tube about 1/4-inch from its free end. The tube will soften and the last 1/2-inch will bend straight down from its own weight. This leaves you with an applicator tube that bends back on itself at

the end. Putting the tube back in the nozzle, you'll find that you can reach the inboard side of the chain from behind and below the wheel sprocket, and the tube still works OK for the outboard side. Using this method, the hardest part about lubricating the chain is getting the bike on and off the stand.

How much lube should you apply? If the chain throws oil all over the bike—and you—you're applying too much at one time. If you're using a solvent-reduced lubricant, give it a long time to thicken before you ride the bike—like overnight. The best time to lube a chain is just after you've completed a ride. Not only does this give the solvent plenty of time to evaporate, but also the chain is warm and the lubricant will penetrate more freely. The worst time to lube is just before you go riding. After the freshly lubricated chain has set a while, say the next morning, wipe it off lightly with a rag. This will not remove the thin film of lubricant necessary for rust prevention, but it will get rid of the excess lubricant that would otherwise fly off while you're riding.

How should the chain be prepared for lubrication? As we said before, there is always a certain amount of abrasive debris irretrievably lodged in the pin/bushing joint and under the roller; the undesirable effects of its presence are unavoidable short of boiling the chain every 10 miles. External washings under pressure can purge most foreign matter from between overlap portions of the sideplates, the only other place dust and grit is harmful, but this area will only stay clean briefly and the chain must be sprayed immediately with water-displacing snake oil to prevent rust.

How often should you lubricate? Conditions vary so widely that no set number of miles or days is an adequate guideline. You have to adapt the lubrication cycle to the particular conditions under which your chain operates. The type of lubricant you're using, the amount of dust in the air, how fast you ride, air temperature, the power-carrying capacity of the chain, the sprocket rpm, the chain pitch and even the brand of chain influence the length of time a chain can go until it needs lubrication. You have to take all these things into account remembering that the common error is to try to make up for too infre-

quent lubrication by applying too much lubricant at one time.

A properly lubricated chain will never rust. Allowing it to rust is a serious business. The finely-ground surface finishes are destroyed, which means the chain has to break-in all over again after being lubricated. If this cycle is repeated the chain will suffer abnormally fast wear-out. Furthermore, corrosion weakens the highly heat-treated steel, making the linkplates susceptible to corrosion-fatigue cracking. Your chain will be as well-lubricated as you can keep it if you apply a little bit of lubricant frequently enough to suppress traces of oxidation.

You can see why boiling a chain in grease is so inefficient. It's such a messy, cumbersome business you're not likely to do it often enough. Amount of lubricant is no substitute for frequent, properly applied lubrication. The greatest advantage of spray can products may not be their magical secret ingredients, but that the very ease of using them encourages the average rider to lubricate his chain more often. Lubrication frequently enough to keep the rust away—even with bacon drippings—is better than infrequent lubrication with the latest miracle product.

ADJUSTMENT

Proper adjustment is a large factor in efficient operation and longer chain life. Multi-strand or Hy-Vo primary chains wear rather slowly since they are enclosed and bathed in oil. Some are adjusted with slipper followers according to the manufacturer's shop manual while others have no provision for adjustment at all and are replaced when slack exceeds the specified maximum. Cam chains must also receive frequent inspection for proper tension and compensating adjustment if necessary; tensioning devices are usually external, as on Honda Fours, and easy to use. But the heavily loaded—often overloaded—poorly lubricated, and exposed rear chain requires continual adjustment during its short, brutal life.

A tight chain places heavy loads on the shaft bearings, the sprocket teeth and the chain joints, causing abnormally fast wear of all parts. On the other hand, a loose chain vibrates and surges causing exces-

THE FINAL LINK

sive wear and noise, and it snaps like a whip under impacts, possibly snapping itself apart. Proper adjustment treads the narrow line between too tight and too loose.

How to align motorcycle wheels so both are exactly in the same plane and tracking straight should be the subject of detailed explanations. But for some reason it's always passed off by suggestions which range from eyeballing down the top run of the chain to laying a two-by-four along both wheels and juggling the rear axle adjustment until the tires look parallel with the board. Bunkum. In the eyeball method a chain can look straight but the wheel can still be crooked, and in the board method there is no way you are assured the front wheel is pointing exactly straight before lining up the rear one.

Assuming the frame was made in a jig and therefore the front wheel is always aligned properly and the swing-arm pivot axle is at exact right angles to the front wheel, there is a way to assure perfect rear wheel alignment. Simply measure the distance from the swing-arm pivot point to the rear axle on both sides of the machine. When this distance is equal to the millimeter, and it is best to measure from the center of both shafts, then align-

ment is correct. Measuring may be hindered by exhaust pipes or foot-peg mounts which require bowing of the measuring device (usually a steel tape) which of course makes a longer reading. It may be wise to drill and tap the shafts enough to extend their centers with threaded dowling beyond any possible obstructions to accurate measurement. A lot of effort? Not when you consider wheel alignment means even more to handling and safety than it does to the chain.

For years there's been a poorly worded rumor going around about *chain stretch*. A chain operating anywhere near its design load and speed doesn't actually stretch, like a pair of old shoes, but it grows longer as metal wears away from the working surfaces. Only .005-inch of wear on each pin and bushing "stretches" an average chain by a full inch. Recall that a chain is worn out when its measured stretch is about three percent of its length; using it beyond this point invites failure and damages sprocket teeth.

Many riders will remove a couple of links from a worn chain so that they can continue to use it even

after the axle has reached the end of its adjustment slot. If you do this, better take a look at those numbers again. Figure out what part of an inch .015PL is for your bike. Say it's .675-inch. With a properly adjusted new chain installed, measure the amount of remaining axle travel. Suppose it's 3/4-inch, a reasonable amount. This means the chain will be worn out before it develops so much stretch that the axle hits the back of its track as you try to adjust the chain. If the axle travel available when the chain is new is only 1/2-inch, then you can remove two links when you run out of axle adjustments and continue using the chain a while longer, until the total takeup is about .675-inch.

When chain stretch exceeds three percent, the tension is concentrated on only a few sprocket teeth instead of being spread out over many teeth. This wears out the sprocket. The teeth develop an easily identified hook-shape. This hooking increases the effective pitch of the sprocket, so it will quickly damage a fresh replacement chain...again, by concentrating the load on a few rollers instead of

1

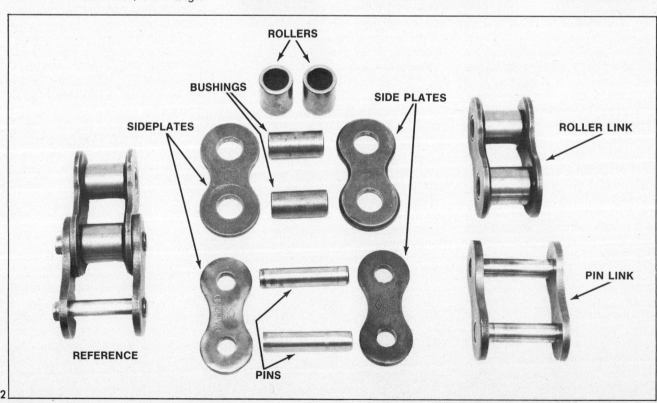

ROLLERS

BUSHINGS

SIDE PLATES

SIDEPLATES

ROLLER LINK

REFERENCE

PINS

PIN LINK

2

spreading it out over many. Under normal circumstances, replacing the chains before they exceed three percent stretch, a set of sprockets will last for from three to five chains—unhardened sprockets with few teeth wear faster. Any visible amount of hooking means the sprocket is worn out. If you try to squeeze more use out of the original equipment chain on a brand-new bike, by removing links as slack forms, you can easily destroy the sprockets with this first chain. From that point on, the misshapen teeth will chew up replacement chains faster than a Pike can munch a Minnow.

Also, never install a new link in a chain that has been appreciably elongated by wear. The pitch of the new link will be shorter than that of the other links, and the resulting shock each time the link engages the sprocket will soon destroy the chain. The shorter link will wear hard on every tooth it contacts and sometimes can set up chain whip.

If you buy a bike new don't indulge the false economy of trying to make the original chain last as long as possible. Often the original equipment chain is not as well made as the replacement chain your dealer stocks in bulk. Replace the chain when axle take-up reaches .015PL. If you buy a used motorcycle, it's safe to assume that

3

1. Shown (middle) is an offset link assembly with master links. This should only be used to make up odd pitch count in necessary cases. Though superior to half link in strength, should be avoided when adjustment will give even pitch count.

2. Exact picture of chain construction will help you understand importance of proper chain maintenance. Top to bottom; rollers, bushings flanked by roller link plates and pins flanked by pin link plates. Individual links at right join to form complete chain link assembly on the left.

3. Unattended chain wear led to the complete destruction of this countershaft less teeth.

the chain that's on it, or a previous one, has been run too long, damaging the sprockets. So when you decide to replace the chain, replace the sprockets, too. At least the small output sprocket, for it takes a worse beating than the larger sprocket on the rear wheel.

Your best defenses against chain failures are frequent lubrication, adjustment for minimum (but never zero) slack and replacement of both chains and sprockets before they're excessively worn. It's bad enough to sit out a race or to find yourself stranded because of a broken chain (Murphy's Law: On any trip, the chain will break at that particular point along the road which is farthest from facilities to repair or replace it.); but the real disaster is for the broken chain to bunch around the output sprocket and destroy the crankcase castings. This can be big troubs. You can buy an awful lot of chains and sprockets for the price of a new crankcase—assuming you can get one, that is. So accept the fact that the rear drives on motorcycles are almost always underdesigned, and the chain and sprockets have to be replaced periodically like tires or brake linings. The life you save may be your crankcase's. On rare occasions a broken chain may even wrap around and lock up the rear wheel. Granted this is not probable enough for you to lose sleep over it, but there still remains an outside chance that the life you save through proper chain maintenance may just be your own.

SPECIAL CHAINS

There are several kinds of special chains which may or may not have advantages for motorcycle applications. Let's take a look at some of them.

Yankee Motor Company, the Ossa distributor, has recently introduced their "Full Bore" line of 1/2-inch and 5/8-inch motorcycle chain manufactured especially for them by Union-Whitney. It has a carefully considered trade-off between wear rate and fatigue strength suitable to the conditions on a motorcycle. The most novel feature is the patented master link. Instead of pressing both pins into one sideplate and slipping a spring-clip retained coverplate over the other end of the pins, the Yankee master link is made in two identical parts. One

pin is pressed into each sideplate, forming an L. The two L's are slipped together and held with two spring-clips, one on each side of the master link. This remarkable design reduces or eliminates bending stresses on the pins. Furthermore, both clips must be removed to disassemble the master link. This increases reliability. It is hard to imagine both clips breaking or being knocked off at the same time. It will be interesting to see how this new master link works out in practice.

The Daido Corporation imports plated chain that is made by a novel, secret process that allows the chain to be plated after assembly. This cuts manufacturing costs and lowers the price to a level competitive with conventional chains. Marketed in Southern California as Superchain, field results have been encouraging. Superchain resists rust very well which leads to long life under the realistic conditions of water crossings, rain, and carwashes.

One final kind of chain should be mentioned even though it is not a roller chain at all. This is *Morse Hy-Vo chain,* a modified version of automotive silent timing chain. Expensive and requiring special sprockets, Hy-Vo has the one great advantage of transmitting high power at high speed through a very compact drive. It's best known application is on the front-engine Oldsmobile Toronado. The same type of chain is in the Honda Four primary-drive system. Its design minimizes chordal action and is well-suited to use with the pulsating drive of a piston engine. A one-inch wide, 1/2-inch pitch Hy-Vo chain can transmit 75 hp at 5000 rpm with a 25-tooth small sprocket. For comparison, a two-strand No. 50 roller chain running at 1500 hp on a 25-tooth small sprocket has a maximum capacity of only 38 hp...half the power with a physically bigger drive. When all else fails on those multi-engine drag bikes and Bonneville record machines, Hy-Vo may be the answer.

Chains are complex mechanisms that need constant monitoring and care to prevent premature failure and ensure long life. Replace them before you reach the borderline of failure due to wear, and before that point, care for them with dedication.

GIVE YOURSELF A BRAKE

If you can't stop, you shouldn't even start

PHOTOS BY ERIC RICKMAN   COURTESY OF MOTORCYCLIST MAGAZINE

All that keen stuff you have hung on your scoot to make it look sharp and go faster isn't going to be worth much if you can't stop quickly and safely when the occasion demands, so pay close attention and we will tell you how to keep those binders in good shape—

they being the cheapest insurance you will ever get.

There are only a few things you need be concerned with: linkage, lining and springs are the basics. It may sound odd, but you needn't worry about wearing the brake lining to the point that the metal por-

tion of the shoes will contact the drum. Long before that occurs you will lock up the brake unexpectedly and buy the farm. Hang in there and we will tell you why.

Most '74 and later motorcycles sold in the U.S. have brake wear indicators as part of our Uncle's

HOW TO: Reline Drum Brakes

1. Before disconnecting cable, lock brake full on and observe the lever location at backing plate. Mark if necessary, then disconnect cables and pull off wheel.

2. Rear wheel and brake assembly will drop out just as easily as the front when rear axle is pulled. Watch out for those small linkage parts; they're easily lost.

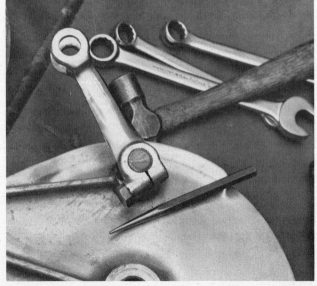

3. It is a good idea to mark the brake lever and brake cam-shaft relationship with a center punch to make certain lever is reinstalled in the same relative location.

4. This front wheel brake is typical of most drum brake set-ups. Be sure to check speedometer grease seal and line up the drive tabs upon reassembly of the unit.

safety program. This indicator is usually a small pointer mounted on the brake lever at the backing plate to show total lever travel, which is limited by brake lining wear. If you have an earlier bike, apply the brake hard and note the brake lever position relative to some point on the backing plate. Disconnect the brake cable, speedo cable and torque arm as necessary, pull the axle, roll the wheel out of the frame and lift the backing plate and shoe assembly out of the drum. Now turn the brake lever to the previously noted position. Take a look at the cam between the movable ends of the brake shoes. As the linings wear, the cam must turn farther each time the brakes are applied, eventually turning too far and either becoming wedged between the shoes, or going over center, preventing it from releasing. In either case, the brakes remain locked full on, and you're in deep you-know-what. Only sufficient lining will prevent this from happening; when in doubt replace the shoes. Next take a look at the return springs; replace any that look weak or stretched. The springs must pull the shoes back away from the drum, returning the actuating cam to center, at the same time pulling the hand lever or foot pedal and cable back to the released position. This takes a strong spring in perfect condition.

Stuff a rag into the axle hole to protect the bearing, then blow all the dust out of the drum/shoe assembly and lift the shoes off the pivot pins. Don't try to remove the springs; if you have a single pivot pin, grasp the shoes at the sides

5. Remember how the lever location was marked on the backing plate (Step #1)? Align the lever with that mark and check location of the brake cam to determine wear.

6. If cam is overcenter (above) or close to it, it is time to install new shoes regardless of how much lining remains. Actually if cam goes overcenter it's too late!

7. Measure inside of drum to check for distortion. If drum is out-of-round or worn excessively (check specs in service manual) the hub must be replaced with new one.

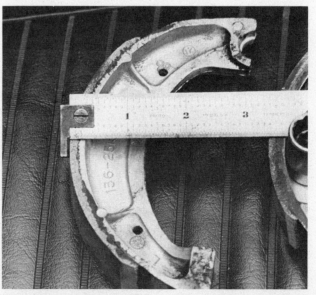

8. Check and record thickness of new linings and compare with specifications in service manual. This is example of bonded and molded linings: rivets are out.

BRAKE

and lift the shoes into a "V" position—they will come off easily. If you have dual pivot pins, remove the locking plate, then it will take a bit of judicious prying carefully and evenly a bit at a time to work them up and off the pins. Turn the brake cam ¼ turn (straight across) to facilitate lifting the movable ends of the shoes.

Take a close look at the brake-cam shaft; does it turn freely? Is it loose in the backing plate hole? If you have been in a lot of water the shaft is usually corroded and turns hard. Tap the shaft out and clean it up on a wire wheel or with emery paper—clean up the hole too. If the shaft has over .020-in. side play, you're going to have to spring for a new backing plate. Apply a light coat of grease and replace the shaft in the backing plate; put a little grease on the brake-cam too. Use grease sparingly as you don't want any to drop off and get on the brake linings. Check the pivot pin(s); they must be clean and given a light coat of grease.

Now look at the shoes. If the linings are badly glazed, have high or hard spots, sand or file the areas smooth. If the shoes are worn unevenly, replace both shoes. When replacing shoes, file the leading edges of the lining to a long taper. Do your brakes squeal? Here is a neat trick—cut a couple of short lengths of rubber hose and slip 'em over the springs. They must fit snugly and they will damp out vibration in the springs, a primary cause of brake squeal, and prevent

HOW TO: Reline Drum Brakes

9. Before reassembly, check movement of brake cam in backing plate for looseness (see text). If cam is too tight, tap out and clean the bearing surfaces thoroughly.

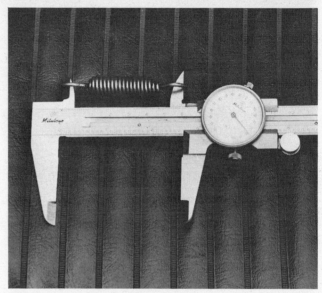

10. It's a good idea to check the length of each brake shoe retaining spring against the specifications in the factory service manual. Replace if stretched.

11. Reassemble shoes to backing plate being sure to apply a thin coating of grease to come shaft, cam faces and anchor pin(s). Don't use too much—a dab'll do it.

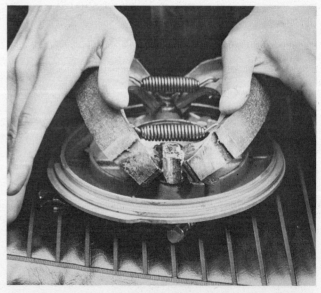

12. Remove and replace single anchor pin brake shoes as shown here. Upon reassembly, install springs first with the ends of the hooks facing the backing plate.

a broken spring from damaging shoes or drum.

Next check the drum. Take some measurements between faces to be sure it is not out of round or warped. The wear pattern will give an indication of high or low spots. Look for a heavy ridge around the outer edge of the drum, indicating excessive wear of the lining contact area. Cover the bearing, and use light emery paper to remove rust or rough spots. If the drum is out of round or badly worn, it's new wheel or hub time.

Okay, now we're ready to put everything back together. With the wheel and axle in place, apply the brake hard and hold it full on as you tighten the axle nut; this centers the shoes in the drum, assuring even braking.

There are too many different brake adjustment procedures to specify a single method here. Suffice it to say the major adjustment should be made at the wheel lever, with minor adjustments made at the bars or pedal. Basically, be sure the brakes don't drag when released

and the hand lever doesn't touch the grip when fully applied. Don't forget to adjust the brake light switch linkage.

Remember! Those super good brakes aren't any better than the cable that makes 'em work. Take a good look at your cables—do they move freely? How are the ends? Are there any worn or frayed spots? When in doubt replace.

That should take care of you as far as drum brakes are concerned. For the care and maintenance of discs, turn the page. ♔

13. It is a good idea to cover the bearing and blow dust out of the drum. A heavy lik at drum edge will be tipoff to excess wear (also grooves). Mike the wear.

14. Big bike rear brakes often have single cam and dual anchor pins. Cotter pins and anchor-pin retaining clip must be removed and cam rotated 90 degrees before removal.

15. With clip removed and cam rotated 90 degrees the shoes are sprung apart and lifted over the cam shoulder parallel with anchor pins. Reverse this to mount.

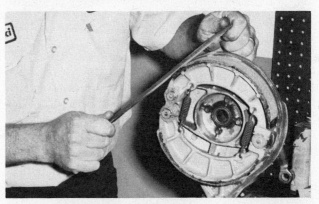

16. To forestall squeeling and chattering, chamfer the edges to a more gentle angle that found on the stock replacement linings. Go easy with that file, too!

17. This big bike has front brakes with dual cams. Replace shoes when lining gets thin. Make certain that linkage is adjusted with the brakes locked full on.

18. Dual leading shoe front brakes are hard to check without removing wheel. Although a bit more complicated than single leading shoe design, they're not tricky.

DISSECTING DISC BRAKES

The easiest to work on and the most important

COURTESY OF MOTORCYCLIST MAGAZINE   PHOTOS BY ERIC RICKMAN

The disc brake will probably require less maintenance than any other single item on your bike, but that's no reason to neglect it completely. As an example of just how trouble-free and long-wearing disc brakes are, I have over 10,000 miles on my Kawasaki Z-1; I took the brakes apart for inspection and photography for this story. Checking against new parts, I found that one puck was worn .055-in., the other .051-in., while the disc had lost only .0005-in. of metal for a total of .1065-in.—less than 7/64 inch of wear. At that rate I'm good for over 50,000 miles before I have to look at 'em again.

Discs have several other virtues; they are self-adjusting, never fade in heavy use, and never fail when wet. In addition, you can brake much more heavily with discs as the transition between heavy braking and lock up is very gradual. They have more feel.

Disc brakes work by pinching a pair of pucks made of brake lining against a revolving disc attached to the cycle wheel. Puck to disc contact area is much less than shoe to drum area in drum-type brakes because hydraulic multiplication exerts much more pressure per square inch against the revolving disc than can be applied to a drum brake.

HOW TO: Handle Disc Stoppers

1. Kawasaki disc brake pads (or pucks) have inspection groove as visual aid to amount of wear. Floater puck (left) is thicker than fixed one (right) to compensate . . .

2. . . . for thickness of floating arm of caliper (now on right side). As you can see here, grooves in pucks give visual warning when it's time to replace those pads.

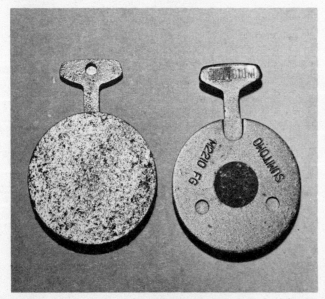

3. Some disc brake pucks have indicator taps to warn of excess wear. These units are Yamaha. If pucks wear down too far, sudden brake failure can occur.

4. Some disc brake pads are bonded to floating arm and don't need grooves to indicate wear since amount of material remaining can be seen easily as in above.

The pinching action causes the heavy pressure to work against itself with the disc caught in the middle. A like amount of pressure exerted outward against a drum would destroy the brake and hub assembly.

Disc hydraulic systems fall into two types, the self-centering dual piston in a fixed caliper, or the single piston type that requires a floating caliper. Master cylinders on the bars are pretty much alike. Yamaha utilizes a typical double piston system in a caliper fixed to the fork leg with the pistons located opposite each other, one on each side of the disc. The pistons apply pressure against the pucks to pinch the rotating disc; since equal pressure is applied to both pistons, the caliper can remain fixed. Honda uses a floating self-aligning caliper with only one piston, the second puck is fixed to the opposite side of the caliper. When pressure is applied, the piston pushes the first puck against the disc, then must pull the caliper and second puck against the opposite side of the disc. This requires the caliper to be free to move. Honda accomplishes this by mounting the caliper on a short swing arm pivoted at the fork leg mounting point. Kawasaki and Suzuki float their calipers on a pair of bolts used to hold the caliper halves together. The piston actuated puck is held lightly in a mounting plate fixed to the fork leg, the caliper bolts are fitted loosely through the mounting plate leaving the caliper free to move from side to side when pressure is applied.

Basic maintenance consists of taking a close look at things when you make your pre-flight walk around inspection before take-off. Look for leaks around the fittings and lines; be sure the hoses are in good condition and the metal lines are fixed to the frame or fork legs so they can't flex, bend or vibrate.

Squeeze the brake lever; it should have a solid firm feel. If it's soft and spongy there's air in the hydraulic line. Take a peek in the master cyl-

5. After removal of the front wheel, the floating puck drops out when brake is applied. To replace, crack the bleed valve, press puck and piston back in place.

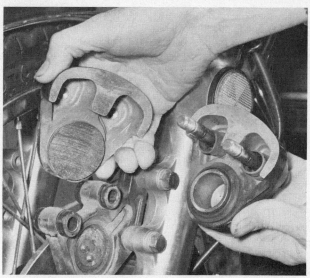
6. Kawasaki floats caliper on fixed arm, one puck floats in arm and the other is fixed to back side of caliper. The piston is hollow.

7. Caliper is self-centering on the brake disc thanks to center piece which slides on the two large cap screws. Hex-head Allen wrench at right is included in tool kit.

8. All boots must be flexible and tight. Discs work well in dirt and water only if the seals are in top condition. Check boots covering cap screws as well.

DISC BRAKES

inder fluid reservoir occasionally to be sure it is full. Check the disc for cracks, grooves and score marks; if cracked, replace, if grooved or scored, pull the wheel and disc, pop out the puck and dig out the offending bit of grit. If things aren't too bad, replace; the puck and disc will soon wear in.

Late model bikes have visible puck wear indicators, earlier models have indicating grooves cut in the edges of the pucks, but you have to peek into the caliper to see the red painted grooves. If you can't see any indicator grooves, take a closer look. Remove the disc by dropping

the wheel. Still no grooves? Squeeze the hand lever a couple of times and the movable puck(s) will drop out into your hand. The fixed puck is usually held in the caliper by a single screw, clip or cotter pin and can be easily removed for inspection. To get the movable puck back, crack the bleed fitting on the caliper and press the piston back with your fingers; close the bleed fitting and slip the puck back in place.

Brake fluid doesn't evaporate, so the master cylinder can't run out of fluid unless there is a leak somewhere, and this is the only way you can get air in the system, other than breaking the line to install

longer fork legs or handlebars. Okay, the lever is soft and spongy— you're going to have to bleed the system to get the air out. First, if you haven't broken a line, find and fix the leak. Then fill the master cylinder reservoir with only the best disc brake type fluid; it could save your life.

The master cylinder must be level in the following operation. It can become air-bound and fail to operate otherwise. Slip a short length of small diameter clear plastic hose over the bleeder fitting and drop the other end into a container. It's a little awkward, but with a full reservoir and the lid on the master cylinder, squeeze the brake lever sev-

HOW TO: Handle Disc Stoppers

9. Particular attention should be paid to brake lines and fittings as well as the brackets securing same to the bike. Discs are trouble-free only if cared for.

10. To check for disc warpage, lock forks and use a dial indicator. Standard is .004-in. If runout is over .012-in., the disc must be replaced with new one.

11. Use a micrometer to check for disc wear. Kawasaki allows a maximum of .059-in. before replacement becomes necessary. This is critical to operation of the system.

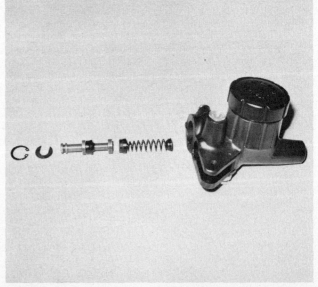

12. Although quite compact, master cylinder units are automotive type. Overhaul kits are readily available from your dealer. Wash parts in alcohol, never solvent.

eral times while holding the lever back against the grip. Open the bleeder valve slightly and watch for bubbles as the brake fluid flows out of the caliper. Close the bleeder valve before releasing the hand lever and pumping it a couple more times. Hold it back, open the bleeder valve and again watch for bubbles. Keep repeating this sequence of operations until there are no more bubbles and the lever is firm and solid. Refill master cylinder reservoir and you're in business. Don't get any brake fluid on your paint job.

If the brake has an irregular pulsing sort of stopping action, the disc could be bent or warped. Check for run out with a dial indicator as per illustration, or slip a feeler gauge between a puck and disc, rotating the wheel and looking for tight spots.

If for some reason you must disassemble the master cylinder or caliper, seal and cup kits are available from your dealer. Use a jet of compressed air in the brake line opening to get the piston out of the caliper; be careful, that piston will fly into the next county. DO NOT use any oil-based solvent to wash the rubber parts. Use clean brake fluid, isopropyl or ethyl alcohol, and don't soak the parts.

Take notes and make sketches if necessary, but keep track of the part relationship so things get back together in the proper sequence. This is a life and death matter.

Be very careful to get the rubber boot seals back in place and don't use old, brittle or worn boots. They must keep dirt and water out of the moving parts. If dirt gets in, the piston or caliper can become scored which in turn will chew up the piston seal causing a fluid leak. Everything must then be replaced. If the movable caliper gets bound up, the pucks will wear at an angle; replace the pucks and free the caliper.

Discs are the simplest and most trouble-free part of your bike. Treat 'em right. The life they save could be yours.

13. To bleed system, apply brake then open bleeder valve. Close valve, release brake and reapply. Repeat until bubble cease. Do not reuse fluid bled from system.

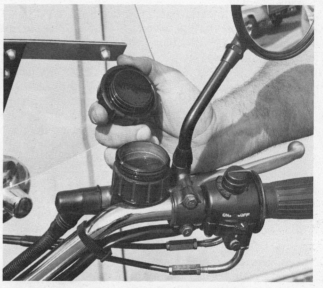

14. While bleading brake system, master cylinder must be full and level. Inspect regularly and top with disc brake fluid only as specified in factory service manual.

15. Practically all big bikes are using hydraulic disc stoppers and conversion units are available for many older bikes. Frequent inspection is important.

16. If one is good, two are better! Kawa fork legs are reversed to bring calipers behind forks. Factory kit provides new dual manifold and master cylinder Mag is Morris.

CHASSIS DESIGN AND CONSTRUCTION

A maze of triangles, welding and steel tubing, but understanding frame design will expedite modification or rarely-needed maintenance

BY DAVE HOLEMAN

Motorcycles, all types, are comprised of a series of components that when all put together provide the power to go and stop and turn corners and absorb bumps. Sounds simple enought, but a new motorcyclist is not a motorcyclist very long before he realizes that some machines do all of these things better than others. And this in spite of the fact that the various components appear identical in function if not in design. Why?

If you are a genuine motorcycle enthusiast who enjoys knowing all there is to know about motorcycles, you have doubtless read many books and magazines covering the subject. Engine theory is popular, and many of the theories are proven by representative examples from the world's manufacturers. Theory tells us that the route to high horsepower is many cylinders. The three, four and six-cylinder engines used in the most successful road racing machines bear this out. Theory tells us that lots of brake lining area is the best way to get a vehicle stopped. The monstrous brakes on those same road racers would seem to indicate that this theory, too, is correct. But what about the chassis? Where do you find the textbook that lays all there is to know before you? If you find one, send a copy.

Because of the fact that a motorcycle chassis, frame and swing arm, has only a few moving parts it should never wear out, require overhauling or rebuilding. The only places where there is any frictional movement is at the swing arm pivot, fork crown bearing surface and rear shock absorber bolt mounts. Here, all that is needed might be a rare replacement of the swing arm bushings should they wear enough to permit the rear fork to move side to side. The fork crown bearing surface is most always a set of races that are pressed into the frame head stock. Again a rare occurance is replacing these races with new

ones should the fork assembly loose in the head stock and adjustment won't take up the slack. That's about it for any moving parts that might wear out.

There are no moving parts in chassis, but the frame of a motorcycle does work. Particularly with tubular frames and swing arms the chassis must flex just enough so as not to give or break. Too rigid a frame will react like it is too brittle and break or crack at its weakest points. Too flexible a chassis will give and bend to the point of collapsing and breaking. In the middle are hairline cracks and fractures that come from borderline design or marginal materials. Naturally these small hairline cracks can lead to disasterous breaks. The most common victims are off road machines and large, high horsepower superbikes. And if you might think frame failure isn't a common problem with

the new superbikes a candid visit to the warranty departments of any of the manufacturers would open your eyes to a prevalent problem.

The problems that do occur with motorcycle chassis are directly related to the work load put on it. Our resident engineer Bill Ocheltree, put the engineering aspects of chassis design into a few well chosen sentences as follows.

"The speed at which a force is applied to a material will cause it to show different strength characteristics. A very rapidly applied shock load in excess of the ultimate strength may not cause failure under certain ideal conditions, whereas a shock amounting to a small fraction of the maximum load will cause failure under more adverse conditions. The actual conditions under which impact failure occurs are so varied that it is difficult to place specific values on the impact resist-

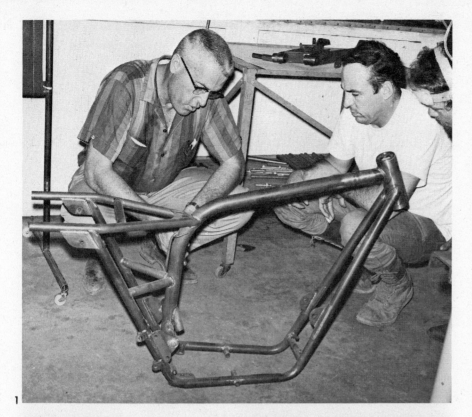

External forces are generally based on acceleration rates in various directions and are expressed in relation to the weight involved in "g"'s. One "g" is an acceleration rate of 32.2 feet per second per second or the acceleration produced by the earth's gravity on a free falling object. The weight of an object is the force it exerts against a scale due to the gravitational pull of the earth. An object accelerating at say 1.5g would require a restraining force of 1.5 times its weight. If an object is subjected to a force 1.5 times its weight, it is said to be under a 1.5g load condition. A motorcycle coming down from a 5 foot high jump takes about 1/2 second to hit the ground and in that time it has reached a vertical speed of 16 feet per second. Now if it takes 1/10 second to reduce the vertical speed to zero, then the bike has been accelerated (or decelerated) at 160 feet per second per second or 5g. Every part on the bike and all the attachments have been subjected to a load equivalent to 5 times their weights for a period of 1/10 second. In some instances this can be considered a shock load especially when something breaks loose. If everything has been designed to withstand this kind of loading, then it is considered normal. If the bike is repeatedly subjected to loads of this nature, then fatigue must be taken into consideration and everything beefed up further.

External 'g' loads are of course seen by the engine at frame attachment points and at the attach points of accessories such as the carburetor and exhaust pipe. The most critical external engine loads are those transmitted through the drive train to the points of attachment such as engine mounts. Rapid clutch engagements, gear shifts or the sudden discovery of traction by a spinning wheel can put tremendous loads on the chassis.

If you were able to wade through that you're ready to dive into design and construction priciples. Periodic cleaning and inspection for these hairline fractures, particularly at welds and junctions, will permit you to repair and arrest a dangerous failure. This is about all you can do, inspect and weld. In some cases reinforcing the frame superstructure or beefing up a swing arm will save you a lot of future grief. Frame breakage and failure isn't prevalant

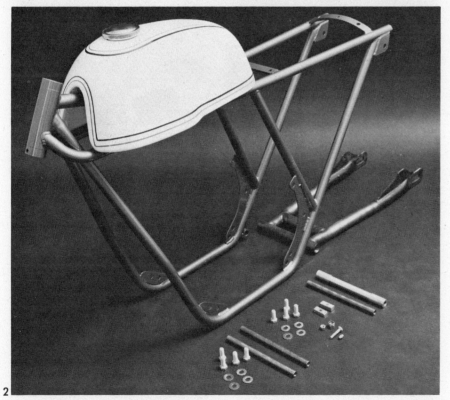

1. Production frames are generally a replica of specialty chassis designed to perform perfectly in competition. Large tubular backbone enhances strength while keeping weight minimal.

2. Specialty chassis kits have become quite popular for many of the Japanese small-bore bikes. If properly designed and engineered, small lightweight tubing will withstand great work loads. Long swing arm has cross brace for lateral rigidity.

ance of various materials. Therefore, attempts are made to avoid or minimize shock loading by absorbing the loads over as long a time period as possible.

Virtually no loads imposed on a moving vehicle can be considered static. The basic loads from which design calculations are made, to determine the strength required are always expressed in dynamic terms.

CHASSIS DESIGN

with most modern motorcycles, but it isn't uncommon either. Don't discount it happening to you. Understanding the construction and design of frames may help you forsee some of the enourmous problems of trying to engineer the perfect chassis.

As with every other component in the motorcycle, frames have undergone considerable evolutionary development over the years. Today, manufacturers are using three types of frame design for production. Each has its own advantages and disadvantages. There are the single and double loop cradle tubular frame, monocoque and backbone styles. By a wide margin, the welded tubular steel type is the most commonly employed.

European and British manufacturers have always emphasized the value of frame design and good handling qualities over engine performance. This has been proven again and again in just about every class of street and competition bike.

No matter what type of frame design comes under discussion, one of the primary factors surrounding its worth (or worthlessness) is its rigidity. In the tubular frame, double and single loop, rigidity is ensured via *trianglization*. The tubes are curved in such a manner, that when welded together, they form a group of triangles concentrating the stress points at the corners. Stresses therefore act upon three points rather than one. An excellent example of this layout on a modern bike would be the triangle formed by the upper rear shock absorber mount, rear axle and swing arm pivot.

Monocoque frames are widely used in various classes of racing cars, but in production motorcycles, their application has been limited to some of the small-displacement Japanese machines. Notables are the Honda 90 and Yamaha 80. Monocoque bike frames are formed of stamped sections welded together at matched seams. They are tremendously strong, can be manufactured by unskilled manpower and lend themselves to mass production quite well. However, they are quite heavy for their size and do not lend themselves to production changes easily.

Banana and backbone type chassis are widely applied by European

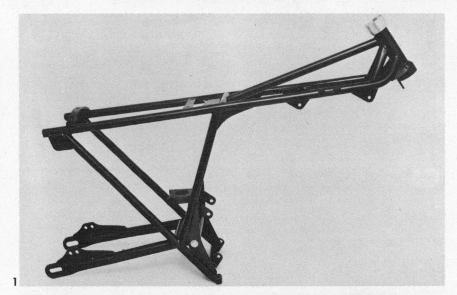

manufacturers, and while they use steel tubing, they are laid out in a completely different manner than the cradle frame. Backbone frames utilize a large-diameter tube originating at the headstock which runs horizontally back to the fuel tank area, then curves downward behind the engine/transmission area. The engine is attached to the tube in several places, forming a stressed component.

Similar to the above is the banana type frame. It uses no support from the steering head to the engine, as with the backbone type. Support is drawn from a formed section which curves downward to the center of the bike, then sweeps back up to the rear. Sections of tubing originating from this primary member support the rear suspension and powerplant. Certain examples of this variety use the power-

1. This unusual multi-tube backbone type frame uses engine as a structural supporting member where attached under headstock, forward swing arm.

2. One of the most incredible frame designs we have ever seen is this Swedish Lito scrambler. Huge thinwall tubing is joined by special castings.

plant as a stressed member, others do not.

Aside from the front and rear suspension, a motorcycle's handling characteristics are governed by the location of the engine, seat, foot pegs, steering head angle, swing arm location and length. Collectively, all these components have a relation to each other in weight distribution and center of gravity.

The center of gravity (CG) is the point on any bike where it would spin like a top if a rod were passed through that point horizontally. CG is controlled by the bias of weight

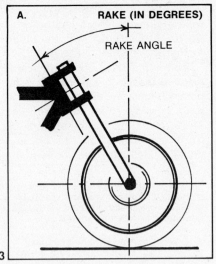

A. RAKE (IN DEGREES)

RAKE ANGLE

3

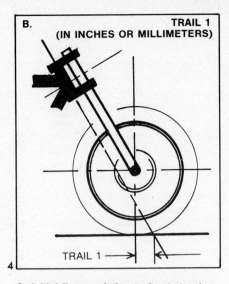

B. TRAIL 1 (IN INCHES OR MILLIMETERS)

TRAIL 1

4

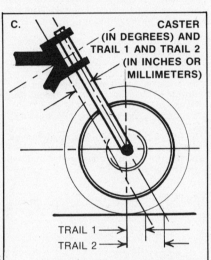

C. CASTER (IN DEGREES) AND TRAIL 1 AND TRAIL 2 (IN INCHES OR MILLIMETERS)

TRAIL 1

TRAIL 2

5

3. Initial figure relating to front steering geometry is rake angle (in degrees). This is measured from the headstock center line to a vertical drawn from the CL of the front axle.

4. Next is a horizontal measurement, trail, calculated by running the headstock centerline to ground level, dropping the vertical axle CL straight down then measuring the linear distance.

5. Caster is the amount of angular difference the fork legs may be from CL of the headstock. In most cases this figure is zero or parallel centerlines.

6. Negative caster angle will produce two trail measurements from verical of the front axle, one from the fork angle the other from headstock CL.

7. Increased caster can often produce excessive negative trail (1) and better tracking but unstable turning.

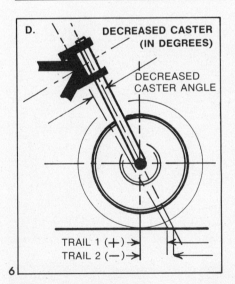

D. DECREASED CASTER (IN DEGREES)

DECREASED CASTER ANGLE

TRAIL 1 (+)

TRAIL 2 (−)

6

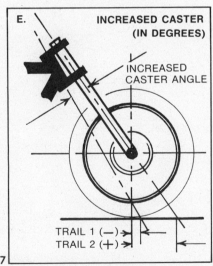

E. INCREASED CASTER (IN DEGREES)

INCREASED CASTER ANGLE

TRAIL 1 (−)

TRAIL 2 (+)

7

supported by each wheel, and the distribution of the locations of masses (engine, oil tank, etc.) from top to bottom of the machine. Relationships between these two factors determine a bike's general handling characteristics.

Most modern bikes have a weight bias varying from 45 percent front, 55 percent rear, to 40 percent front,

60 percent rear. The first set of figures applies to the typical street and road motorcycle, while off-road and moto-cross machinery will be in the 43 percent front, 57 percent rear category. Reasons for this: Road bikes have more components, higher total weight with most of it located towards the front. Dirt bikes have fewer components and lower

total weight. The off-road machine performs better when there is close to 15 percent less weight on the front wheel than on the rear, while the road-goer handles better with a more closely equalized bias and central CG. In terms of weight, these figures could mean 10 to 20 pounds (more or less) on the front wheel.

The center of gravity should be as low as practicality permits. In other words, engine, seat and footpegs should be located as near to ground level as possible. This means that the machine will tend to remain vertically stable. Two exceptions to this rule are trials machines where the rider moves at very low speeds and is turning and leaning constantly to avoid obstructions—and dragster/Bonneville machines which need to travel in a straight line only. The trials machines have a higher than normal CG, while the quarter-miles and record breaks need an extremely low CG.

Let's stick to the conventional motorcycles in this discussion. Naturally, different machines, even in the same class have different CG's, so we must use a common, easily located point to determine the vertical center of gravity. This point will be the centerline of the crankshaft. On most modern road machines, the crankshaft's centerline should be common with, or no more than one inch higher than the centerline between the front and rear axles. In this case, we are referring to bikes above 100cc displacement and/or 200 pounds in weight. A higher crankshaft centerline would lead to top heaviness, while a lower centerline could cause ground clearance problems when cornering. The greater width of the three- and four-cylinder engines makes this problem more acute.

Taller four-stroke engines usually have the CL of the crankshaft overlapping the horizontal axle line. Examples are the Triumph, BSA, Norton and other European road bikes, all of which are considered to be good handlers. Some of the best handling machines of all time were four-stroke singles such as the Velocette, BSA Goldstar and Matchless. Because of the height and narrowness of these designs, their crank CL's were usually below the axle CL—up to two inches below.

Current Japanese practice keeps the crankshaft CL as much as three

CHASSIS DESIGN

inches above the centerline of the axle. This has resulted in top heaviness, mostly in road bikes. It shows up in cornering and at high speeds. Much of the Japanese machinery has a higher weight distribution on the front wheel than British and European bikes.

Small displacement, light weight trail bikes are an exception to the above situation. Their crankshaft CL's are as much as two inches above the axle CL. Handling is not adversely affected due to the fact that these small bikes have CG's in about the same region as larger types. Furthermore, these bikes are not subjected to the high stresses and speeds of other machines.

Now let's discuss another factor that determines CG: Footpeg and saddle position. Naturally, the center of gravity will change with the rider(s) aboard. With a road bike, saddle location plays a very important role here. Footpegs account for only a small portion of CG change, but obviously the rider's weight is concentrated almost entirely on the saddle. Time has proven that the optimum saddle height above ground level is 31 inches. Road racers will sometimes lower their height to as low as 28 inches for improved handling, but any height above 31 inches will adversely affect handling due to an elevated CG.

Saddle height is of secondary importance on the off-road bike. In this case, footpeg position assumes the critical role, the reason being that the rider's weight will center on the pegs when he stands upright. This is especially critical on motocross machinery. Saddle height is still important, though, on other types of dirt bikes, because more time is spent sitting than standing.

Trail bikes are an exception. Here there are no requirements for high speeds or cornering. These machines must be extremely agile at low speeds, therefore they have high engine and footpeg location for extra ground clearance. The footpegs are above the crankshaft's CL and behind the engine and gearbox. This results in maximum weight distribution on the rear wheel.

Now, let's put some of these components together, beginning at the front and working rearward.

First, the fork assembly must be attached to the chassis head stock. The primary consideration at this point is the rake (see drawing 'A'). This is the angle in degrees between the vertical CL of the front axle and CL of the head stock.

This angle does *not* always indicate the angle of the forks themselves. True fork angle can vary if upper and lower triple lamps are not identical, but for the moment, assume that fork angle and rake are identical.

Current road bikes have a rake angle of 26 to 28 degrees. Some Japanese machines are nearer the 26 degree figure, while European and especially British bikes are closer to 28 degrees. On = off road motorcycles and moto-crossers have slightly more rake angle, usually between 28° and 30°.

The other front end dimension which must be determined is *trail* (see drawing 'B'). Trail is the horizontal distance (in inches or millimeters) between the vertical axle centerline (CL) and CL of the head stock. Trail measurements range from 2½ to four inches. Road bikes will be closer to three inches, while off-road machines will be closer to four.

Trail is the most critical measurement in regard to the front end because it determines to a large degree how the front end performs. The greater the trail, the more the front end will "trail" or go in a straight line. The machine with the

1. The brothers Rickman set a new standard in competition and specialty chassis design with their nickel-plated scrambler frames and wheels.

2 One-off frames are commonplace with diggers. Monstrous tubing gives rigidity to lengthly wheelbase. Rake, trail and wheelbase keep this twin Triumph going in straight line.

3. Specialty road racing chassis also one off. Features light weight with maximum strength. Welding is heliarc.

4. Britisher Alf Hagon specializes in dragster chassis for big 'V' twins. Uses backbone idea with engine as supporting member; minimal welding.

5. Location of center of gravity moves with any change of front or rear wheel position. Location changes logitudinally, not in height.

1

2

most trail will have the greatest steering effort. Examples of extreme trail would be four inches in a dragster or Bonneville machine and 2½ inches or less in a trail bike.

There is a second method of finding out the trail of forks. This is measured by finding out the horizontal distance between the centerline of the forks and the vertical line used in the previous trail measurement. This method is used when the upper and lower triple clamps are of unequal, the forks will not be parallel with the head stock CL.

As you can see in drawing C we now have two trail figures, #1 and #2. Trail #1 is the relationship of the frame head stock angle to the chassis and is directly derived from *rake angle*. Our new figure, Trail #2 is the relationship of the front fork assembly to the head stock. And this brings up another new figure, *castor angle* which is the angular difference of the fork assembly to the headstock.

As shown in drawing C, 0 (zero) degrees castor angle is when the fork assembly is actually parallel to the head stock. Most manufacturers use this 0 degree figure as standard by making the top and bottom triple clamps identical. Having 0 degree castor angle insures a constant relationship of trail #1 to Trail #2. This will tell a rider that oversteering or understeering difficulties will be related to *rake angle* and the chassis head stock as the *caster angle* is 0 degrees.

In drawing D you can see the physical results of having a decreased castor angle. This occurs when the lower triple clamp is shorter than the top and pulls the front wheel axle to the rear. The result is an increase in Trail #1, but a decrease in Trail #2. The effect here is to let the front wheel trail or track more than 0 degree castor angle while greatly increasing the steering quickness. Most complete Ceriani fork assemblies come with non-matching upper and lower triple clamps that give a resultant decreased castor angle around one degree. Decreased castor angle would tend to neutralize an understeering condition.

Now, conversely in drawing E we see increased castor angle and the technical results. Increased castor angle-results in a sharp decrease in our Trail #1 figure while stretching out the Trail #2 dimension. Some of the veteran cross country riders used to install what is called a *rake plate* (actually a misnomer, should be a castor plate) to get more fork angle and slow down the steering. While this slowed down the steering it had a pronounced result in making turning sharply side-to-side more instable if the castor angle increased more than two degrees. But some production machines have found a slight bit of increased castor angle was good to slow the steering feel on road bikes. Triumph used 0.48 increased castor angle for many years with their 30.5 and 40 cu. in. road burners.

Rear suspension is equally important in handling as the front, but less complicated. Today, the swing arm coupled with spring-over-shock is almost universal in motorcycle engineering. Angles, dimensions and fixing locations have seemingly become nearly standardized throughout the industry.

The swing arm is pivoted at the rear of the frame and its pivot center shoud be ½- to one inch above the horizontal CL of the rear axle and countershaft sprocket. This permits chain clearance when the

3

4

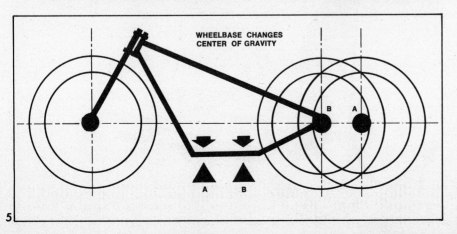

WHEELBASE CHANGES
CENTER OF GRAVITY

5

CHASSIS DESIGN

suspension is fully compressed up-wards.

With the machine at rest, the swing arm should be parallel (see drawing 'F'), or nearly parallel to the ground. When the swing arm angle is correct, the rear wheel is pushed directly upward into the shock absorber when encountering a bump. If the swing arm angle is excessive (see drawing 'G'), however, the rear wheel will be pushed rearwards as well as upwards and the shocks are unable to absorb the full force. The remainder of the force is directed forward to the swing arm pivot, and from there to the frame.

Finally, we must determine the length of the swing arm. This measurement is taken from the CL of the swing arm's pivot and the CL of the rear axle. Here again, we find a common figure near 18 inches. Common exceptions are trail bikes with swing arms nearer to 16 inches and hill climber that can run to 22 inches. The short swing arm causes more weight to be placed on the rear wheel, while the longer arm on

1

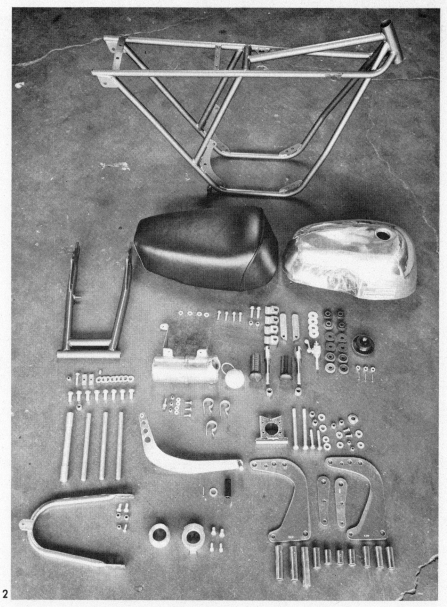

2

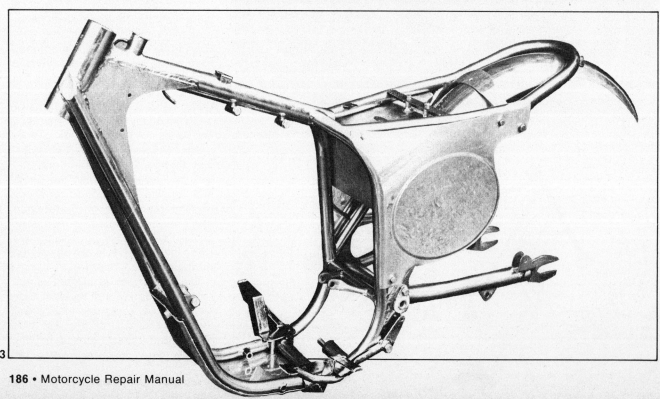

3

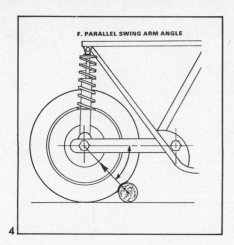

F. PARALLEL SWING ARM ANGLE

4

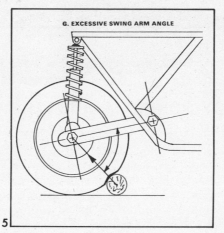

G. EXCESSIVE SWING ARM ANGLE

5

6

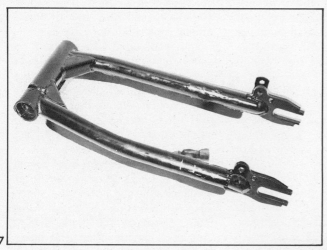

7

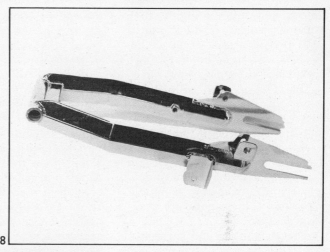

8

1. Some machines, particularly British, use offset (non-identical) triple clamps. Object is to decrease caster angle about ½ degree to quicken steering with minimal harm to trail.

2. Complete specialty chassis kit has all parts less wheels and engine.

3. Rickman moto-cross chassis for four stroke has abundant headstock gusseting. Was one of first bikes to use the tubular chassis members as oil reservoir. Had large capacity, ran cool.

4. Preferred to insure least shock and best pivot angle is swing arm parallel to ground level. Also forces chassis height to be lower to ground.

5. Excess swing arm angle is common with many Oriental machines. Swing arm arm angle places greater shock load on pivot point and axle. Thrust of force makes shock absorber task more difficult and demanding.

6. Best for swing arm pivot point is Oilite bronze bushing between tube steel members with shaft in middle. Oilite gives good lube, minimum flex.

7,8,9. Different needs make for different ideas. Most common is round tube swing arm. Has low material and production cost and provides adequate rigidity. This one has been strengthened with flat steel supports, bottom. Rectangular swing arm is said to be strongest for side thrust loads. Material more costly, hard to bend. Cast aluminum fork offers light weight and low cost in mass production. Still in testing stage, this cast idea may provide progressive step forward.

9

hill climbers is to cause the opposite effect—as much weight as possible on the front wheel.

What we have covered in this section on chassis is not as much theory as experience acquired over many years of practical application and study of motorcycle frame design. Sure, there are exceptions to every rule or practice mentioned and there always will be. The three undetermined factors that determine what combination works best is engine size, rider (size and style) and environment or how the machine is to be used. As it goes today chassis design has reached a point of near perfection. Look at the Yamaha Enduro line that uses the same chassis style for all its machines,

but considerable improvement was seen with the introduction of their special production motocross chassis. Honda's four cylinder bikes have all but identical chassis design, power to weight ratios and suspension units. Yet the 500cc four cylinder model is heads above the other models in handling performance. Why? Was the 500 designed to handle better intentionally? Probably not, it just happened that everything fell together in better proportion.

While we never will be able to completely understand all the relationships of chassis design to handling characteristics, we do have the basics. Some of these cannot be deviated from and become constants. Therefore, the variables such as rake and trail and castor can be studied further to offer a solution to a handling problem. Surely after reading this you will place more emphasis on studying those spec charts when reading road tests or listening to the local racers talk. Now it isn't all Chinese and can have some absolute value to you which is much more than most motorcyclists can enjoy.

WHEELS

Gather 'round and we'll discuss two of the most important components on your machine

BY ROBERT SCHLEICHER

Stop and think about it and you will conclude that the weight of the motorcycle hangs from the spokes at the top of the wheel at any given position rather than being supported by those on the bottom, for although they have great tensile (end-to-end pull) strength, they would immediately bend if even a small portion of the weight of the machine were to be borne by those spokes at the bottom of the wheel. In compression they are relatively weak. And because the wheel rotates when it works, and the forces that are put through it are of a twisting nature, the spokes are angled out from hub to rim in both directions to resist acceleration and braking, approximating a double triangular configuration for maximum strength.

In addition, since the spokes attach to either side of the hub and the center of the rim, another triangulation is formed by the spokes between the extremities of the hub and the center of the rim to resist side loads, which are admittedly much less than those encountered in an automobile because the motorcycle is a single-track vehicle which must bank to corner. The only exception to this arises when a sidecar is attached to the motorcycle, in effect making it subject to the same side-loads as encountered in an automobile.

The spoke lacing pattern, when viewed from the side of the machine, can have a marked affect on the strength of the wheel and its hub. If you have *no* front brake and, therefore, no brake torque loads on the spokes, you can get away with a lacing design where the spokes angle straight out from the hub to the rim so they never cross one another—the wheel experts call this a "cross zero" lacing pattern.

The other extreme of wheel loading arises when the motorcycle is used in rough off-road competition where braking and accelerating torque are often most violent as the wheel hops through the air and bangs into rocks and ruts at full braking or accelerating power. These severe jars really do their best to wrench the spokes right out of the hub. The best lacing pattern for this type of use (or abuse) is to lace the spokes so there is as much of a spoke angle as possible between the hub and the rim. The greater the angle, the more spokes a single spoke will cross over. This results in what is rightly called a "cross three' or "cross four" spoke pattern. Even the best of the ready-to-race off-road machines don't have a spoke pattern where each spoke crosses over four others between the hub and the rim; an expert wheel man may be able to benefit by replacing the stock wheel, using longer spokes and a rim with the spoke holes drilled at a greater angle. The vast majority of production motorcycles, regardless of whether they are intended for street use, road racing or off-road racing, have their wheels laced with the spokes in a pattern where each spoke crosses one, two or three others. This is fine for road use.

The giant drum brakes used on some road racers also affect their spoke pattern in that they reduce the space between the hub (brake drum) and the rim so that there just isn't room for the spoke to lie at much of an angle. A road racing machine will often have only a "cross one" or "cross two" spoke lacing pattern. Because of their lighter weight and power, the smaller machines don't require more than 36 spokes, but there is a financial savings involved over fitting 40 spokes—four spokes-per-wheel on a run of 10,000 lightweights saves 80,000 spokes.

Wire wheel spokes are available in a variety of diameters and materials as well as lengths. The spoke itself may be either the common nickel-plated steel or stainless steel. The majority of the wheel-lacing experts claim that the strength characteristics of each type are practically equal but that the stainless version is superior in resisting corrosion.

Most wheels are laced with spokes having a diameter about

1

2

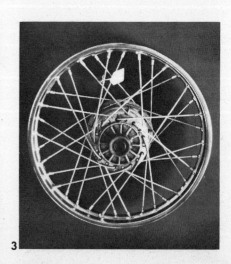
3

equal to steel-wire gauge of 8 to 12. If you are relacing a wheel for use in off-road racing, you'd do well to consider a larger diameter No. 6, No. 8 or No. 10 gauge spoke, particularly for the rear wheel. A road racing machine's wheels are best laced with a smaller No. 10 or No. 12 gauge spoke that will provide as much of its own shock-absorbing capacity as possible.

The long, thin nuts that screw onto the rim end of the spoke are called nipples. You have a choice of nickel-plated steel, stainless steel, chrome-plated brass or aluminum nipples if you're willing to search among the wheel parts suppliers. Most Japanese machines are equipped with brass-spoke nipples but the wheel rebuilding experts prefer nickel-plated steel nipples. Aluminum nipples will save a few precious ounces of weight for the serious road racer. You should always buy matched sets of spokes and nipples to be sure that the threads are precisely the same. Spoke and nipple sets run between 35 cents and 42 cents a piece, de-

1. Understanding various spoke lacing patterns is critical to the selection of proper wheel assemblies. Show bikes rarely used on the road can utilize appealing esthetics of straight pull spokes with no crossing pattern at all. Spokes with high tensile strength and should be installed by an expert. Buchanan's spool hub is shown laced to 21" rim.

2. 'Cross three' pattern is strong enough for drag bikes or flattrackers lacking a front brake. Cross patterns (0, 1, 2, 3, or 4) refer to the number of spokes crossed by another (counting only the spokes on the same side of the hub) between the hub and rim. This cross three pattern of Buchanan has the first cross hidden by the wheel hub flange.

3. Strongest for rim support and even transmission of torque and braking loads through the hub is 'cross four' pattern. First two crosses are hidden but can be found with study. Yamaha DT-1 wheel now has No. 8 spokes.

4. Fitting a larger rim front is one of the common wheel modifications. Here a Kawasaki 100 gets a 21-inch rim with a cross four pattern. Hub diameter and spoke hole location can dictate lacing pattern. Check these out before buying a gob of spokes.

5. Triumph wheel has new No. 8 gauge spokes in 'cross three' pattern. After rim is trued, tire should be mounted and shaved and then the assembly should be balanced. Clamp-on lead weights (left) offset the extra ounces of the valve stem and tire lock. Many handling quirks are blamed on lack of wheel care such as lack of high-speed balancing.

pending on the material. A plated steel nipple usually sells for 12 cents and an aluminum nipple for 14 cents.

It's obvious enough that the wheel diameter must match the tire's inside diameter (i.e. a 21-in. wheel needs a 21-in. tire). What's not so plain is that the width of the wheel's rim must also be matched to the tire's width (called the "cross section" of the tire) which is ultimately determined by clearance within a given motorcycle chassis. The dimension you want is definitely *not* the overall width of the rim, but the width of the area that keeps the tire's inside edge (called the tire "bead") on the rim. The tire and wheel manufacturers have adopted an international standard set of markings for motorcycle rim widths that have next to nothing to do with their actual dimensions. The following chart will give you the rim-width marking that is usually stamped on the rim, the actual rim width, and the range of tire widths that a particular rim will accommodate:

Rim No.	Actual Rim Width	Maximum Tire Cross Section
WM-0	2 ins.	2.25 to 2.50
WM-1	2¼ ins.	2.50 to 3.00
WM-2	2½ ins.	3.25 to 3.50
WM-3	3 ins.	3.50 to 4.00
WM-3.5	3½ ins.	5.00 to 6.00
WM-4.00	4 ins.	5.00 to 6.00

The tires made by all of the manufacturers are engineered to take their designed shape only when they are mounted on the correct rim width. If you're mounting much wider tires on your machine, you'd best consider replacing the rim as well if you expect to gain the full advantage of the increased tire width.

Combined wheel and tire diameter, and cross-section, although usually ideal for a given machine

under normal circumstances, occasionally involves a compromise that may not be necessary for a personalized application. The off-road boys experiment all over the place, playing with different tire diameters and widths. Generally, however, they come back to the same conclusion of the original cross-country racers, the early American pioneers, who found that the larger diameter wheels of their covered wagons put down a longer footprint which bridged the innumerable chuck holes which plagued their path. Larger diameter tires don't fall into nearly as many holes or ruts that tend to swallow a smaller hoop and deviate its course.

The fat vs. thin front tire controversy still rages. There is no cut and dried answer, for much has to do with riding style, engine power, weight of machine and type of terrain. The faster rider, capable of lofting the front wheel upon command, is less conscious of the weakness of a tall, thin front wheel and tire for he is able to lift it over the hard stuff and is more appreciative of its generally better cornering ability on fire roads. And theoretically, having less unsprung weight, the lighter front wheel and tire should prove more responsive to road irregularities. Also, in mud, the thinner tire is less apt to load up and jam. But try and tell that to the handler of a big desert sled, who wants that extra cushion of a fat 4.00 sausage to iron out his straight-ahead charge over the tulies. The 4.00 is also easier for the beginner, at least, to steer in deep, rutted sand, having less tendency to "hunt" than the 3.00. The trick with the 3.00 in soft stuff is to ride light on the bars, letting it seek its way (within limits), for it will usually go fairly straight if the operator doesn't try to man-handle it under

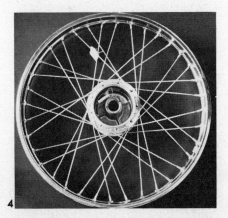

4

5

WHEELS

such circumstances (depending, too, upon the speed involved). Of course, engine displacement enters into the picture. Some of the 200cc and under machines are short on power to overcome the fat hides, in which case the tire must be proportionate to chassis weight and engine displacement.

Surprisingly, the different wheel diameters are nearly offset by the larger tire widths so that both a 3.00x21 wheel and tire and a 4.00 x18 wheel and tire have about the same overall diameter. Those first three numbers of any tire's size refer to its width and height as seen in a cutaway drawing; this is why the tire folk call those numbers the tire's "cross section." The cross section height of most tires is roughly equal to their width so that a 4.00x18 tire, for example, is about 4-ins. wide and the inflated cross section is about 4-ins. high. You can determine, then, the approximate diameter of a tire by adding twice its cross section dimension (there's a tire cross section at both the top and the bottom of the rim, remember) to its rim diameter. That 4.00x18 tire will add up as 4 plus 4 plus 18 ins. for a total of 26 ins. overall inflated diameter. A 3.00x21 tire would measure about 27 ins. in diameter (3 plus 3 plus 21 ins.). You can see, then, the two apparently different tire sizes have overall diameters that are close enough to one another to keep the machine level and evenly balanced for off-road racing.

Motorcycle rims are also available in a choice of materials including chrome-plated steel, painted high-tensile steel and aluminum at prices ranging between $18 and $30. All but the really high-performance street or cafe racers and ready-to-race moto-cross production machines are supplied from the factory with plated-steel rims. For anything but serious racing (or frequent-play racing) stock rims are fine as long as their width and diameter are suitable for the tires you want to use. The lighter weight high-tensile steel or aluminum rims will save some weight and offer more strength than the stock rims.

You do, however, have a choice of two different brands of aluminum rims: Borrani or Akront. Aluminum rims are lighter than steel because the material itself is lighter; but they're also a bit weaker if both are made to the exact configuration. Both brands of aluminum rims have an I-beam shape beneath both tire beads to give them even more strength than a steel rim. A typical WM3-18 steel rim weighs 6.1 lbs., the Akront-brand 4.4 lbs.; all without any spokes, hub or tire. The experts at the wheel shops we visited claim that they see more bent Borrani rims than Akronts. The weight savings between these two may be the result of a bit less material in the Borrani, but it may be worth it to a road racer.

There is seldom any reason to replace the hub of your wire wheel with anything other than the stock item. If you are constantly breaking hubs, the wheel can be replaced with longer spokes in a pattern with the spokes lying closer to the hub so they angle further from vertical between the rim and hub. The spokes will then cross over more of their mates than stock so that if, for example, the stock-lacing pattern was what we've described as a "cross two," you can relace the wheel in a "cross three" or "cross four" pattern. With the spokes pulling at a greater angle they actually tend to help hold the hub together rather than pulling it apart under load strains.

Many of the newer factory production moto-cross racers, and some street machines, are fitted with what are called "conical" hubs. These hubs have a brake on one side with the spokes laced into the edge of the brake drum. The side of the hub opposite the brake is as small as it can be and still leave room for the bearings and spoke holes. The hub is shaped like a cone to reach from the small flange diameter to the larger diameter of the brake drum and that's where it gets its name. There is less material in most of these hubs than in those that have a nearly constant diameter all the way from one spoke-attaching flange to the other. Some of them are even fabricated from welded-sheet steel rather than being cast aluminum. If you're considering relacing your wheel, for whatever reason, you might consider the weight-saving advantages and possible greater strength of the conical hubs. You may save a pound or two on each wheel, but the only way to tell is to contact one of the suppliers of these hubs to find out if they have a hub to fit your machine and what it weighs; then you'll have to disassemble your wheel to weigh your stock hub.

You will find it far easier to "tune" and adjust your wire wheels than to completely relace them. The various spoke's nipples around the rim can be loosened or tightened to adjust the rim so that it is pulled into concentricity with the axle. If one or both of your wheels wobbles, with no noticeable dent in the rim, you can safely assume that some of the spokes are too loose or that some ham-fisted tuner has over-tightened some of the nipples. Wire wheel truing is almost an art. Each of the spokes should be just as tight as the next; giving off a crisp ringing sound (assuming there is no glob of oil on any of them to

1. Buchanan's spoke wrench or small Crescent will fit spoke nipples best. Spokes on the 'high' side of runout are tightened no more than one full turn each time. Usually spokes opposite the wobble must be loosened the same amount. Equal tension on all spokes is the goal. When all the spokes have the same ring when tapped with a wrench, the job is right.

2. The last step is to grind or file the spoke ends flush to prevent tube damage. After they're flush with the nipple head you might cover the center 'U' groove with silver duct or masking tape. Keeps moisture out.

3. Large diameter four-shoe racing hub limits space for sharp angling of spokes. Small space between hub and rim means only a 'cross 1' pattern is possible with 36-spoke wheel. Great strength of the hub and alloy rim give the wheel sufficient rigidity for road racing. Spokes are tightened, wheel trued after each race.

dampen the sound) when tapped lightly with a wrench. To check a wheel for wobble, prop the offending end of the machine up off the floor so you can spin the wheel—the bearings and brake must be adjusted properly so the wheel will spin for a minute or so before coasting to a stop.

Block up some type of metal pointer to act as an indicator so that it is just a fraction of an inch away from the inside edge of the rim. If the wheel is running absolutely true, the distance between the indicator's point and the rim will remain constant through an entire rim rotation. If the rim wobbles, the pointer will help you to spot just where the wobble is and whether the wobble runs out toward or away from the pointer. Remember, wheel wobble can result from both lateral (side-to-side) and radial out-of-roundness. Again, the pointer will let you isolate which (it could be both) type of wobble is present. If the wheel has a lateral wobble, it can be corrected by loosening the spokes on the wobble area that are on the bulging side and tightening those that lead to the opposite side

of the hub. During adjustment, listen for the ever-constant "ping" when they're tapped with the wrench—after a little practice you can tell from the feel through the wrench handle how loose or tight the spokes are.

Always apply a drop of thread lubricant to each of the nipples a few hours before you adjust any spoke. The lubricant will loosen most seized threads and it will help to give a constant feel to each of the spoke nipples as you are adjusting them. An automotive ignition wrench set will usually include one open-end wrench that'll fit those nipples, or you can buy a special wire wheel-adjusting wrench. If you have determined that your wheel has a radial out-of-roundness, the spokes on the high side will have to be loosened and those on the diametrically opposite low side tightened to true the wheel. When working out a wheel wobble through spoke adjustment, loosen two or three of the spokes in the offending area about one turn each. The half-dozen spokes on either side of the wobble area should be loosened progressively less than that full turn

to spread the adjustment evenly. Take your time, working a maximum of a single turn of the spoke's nipples at a time. If you make a mistake in loosening or tightening the wrong spokes, they can then be quickly readjusted to their original setting. All of the work can be done with the wheel on the motorcycle just as long as you don't have to tighten one or more of the nipples any more than two full turns. If you have to tighten a nipple that much to adjust out the wobble, you may just move the threaded end of the spoke enough to rip through the rim band and into the tube. If you have adjusted any spoke nipple that much, you should remove the wheel and dismount the tire to check to see if there is a need to grind off any now-protruding spoke ends so they're once again flush with the tire-side ends of the nipples.

Don't necessarily expect the rim to be centered over the hub (as viewed from the head-on front or rear of the motorcycle). The rim on some machines is offset to clear either the brake or the chain—if in doubt the only way to be sure is to check another machine just like yours to see where the rim is positioned.

If you're one of those riders who is extremely conscious of saving weight on your machine, you may have already mentally computed that you can save as much as four or five pounds per wheel by replacing the steel rim with one of aluminum, and by replacing your full-width hub with a conical hub. It sounds like a ridiculously small amount; you could save that much by going on a weekend crash diet to save rider weight. The weight we are talking about, however, is unsprung weight and that makes it rather special. The front forks and rear shock absorbers and their springs are there to control wheel movement in an effort to keep the wheels and their tires in contact with the ground as much as possible. You cannot do much steering, stopping or accelerating if the tires are up in the air. The heavier the tire and wheel (and, of course, the brake, axle, bearings and lower half of the fork and shocks), the higher they'll bounce after each bump and the harder it is for the forks and rear shock absorbers to control them and keep them on the ground. Every bit of weight below the front

3

WHEELS

and rear springs is part of the unsprung weight which the forks and shock absorbers must control. Since a typical front tire and wheel assembly complete with brake (a Kawasaki Mach III) is about 43 lbs., a savings of 4 lbs. is nearly 10%—its beneficial effect on the machine's handling can be nearly as great as trimming 10% off the total weight of the bike and that would have to be nearly 40 lbs.! This is the reason, other than potentially greater strength, why so many road racers and moto-crossers have aluminum rims and/or lightweight hubs. Cast-alloy-wheel assemblies can save even more unsprung weight for the road racer or street rider.

There's little chance that the off-road racers will want to use cast alloy wheels. The flexing of the spokes, as the machine's weight hangs off of them, serves as a much-needed spring for the off-road racer that helps to keep the wheel from destroying itself and the rest of the machine as well. But, given a year or so who knows what the cast wheel folks will come up with for boondock riders.

It's been a long rocky road convincing the street riders that alloy wheels are, in all respects, superior

to spoked wheels and it probably would have been even tougher had it not been for the Yamaha factory. When Yamaha started marketing many of their road machines with alloy wheels it started critics thinking. If the Yamaha factory is starting to use these wheels, then they really must be the way to go. For many enthusiasts, to have a factory use a product is like giving it an official stamp of approval.

Generally speaking, if you're going to be doing some racing or traveling in fast company it would be wise to go with a cast alloy wheel using a disc brake. If weight is a concern, check them closely; some alloy wheels are actually heavier than the wheels they're replacing while others are considerably lighter. Stick with a wheel that has been proven under actual racing conditions and you're assured of getting a product that can handle your particular situation.

Most of us will never get within 100 miles of a race track so we'll probably look for different qualities in a wheel than a pure racer would—ease of installation for in-

stance. Several wheels enable the use of stock brake components which makes installation a breeze, while others require adding a disc brake unit. If you're not too handy with a wrench, or have no desire for a disc brake, it'd be wise to go with the wheel using the stock brake. However with many of the bikes coming with stock rear disc, some wheel manufacturers are making complete bolt-on kits for these bikes.

If you're into custom and show bikes, the steel wheel was made especially for you. They usually sport a highly chromed finish and are available in many different rim diameters and widths to accommodate those skinny front tires as well as those fat rear tires. These also come in a variety of styles using both the stock drum brake components and also a bolt-on disc brake kit; some front wheels are even available that use no brake at all. Some of these wheels are built more for looks than pure strength so remember what the wheel was originally intended for and use it accordingly.

1. Just the right combination of braking, acceleration and sharp shock (note bent rim at 2 o'clock) tore this hub apart. This failure can be arrested with 'cross 4' pattern that makes opposing spoke pairs pull at a tangent to the hub's circumference and at each other. This failure was caused by a combination of wrong spoke pattern and a weak hub.

2. For dirt riding there's no replacement for tire locks (security bolts, rim clamps, etc.). These beauties fit under the inner tube and when tightened pinch the tire bead against the rim. This then permits the air pressure to be very low (or even flat) without the tire spinning on the rim, tearing the valve stem.

3. Rubber cover on the back side of the tire lock protects the tube from damage or corrosion of the metal frame. Locks are sized to rim width.

4. Street riders, drag and road racers often use sheet metal screws in rim and tire bead to eliminate slippage without throwing wheel out of balance from heavy locks. Riding on a flat for long will tear tire bead.

5. Some rims come with serrations to arrest tire slippage. Serrations are most effective at tire lock or screw location. If rim is smooth a sharp chisle will make nice serrations.

1

2

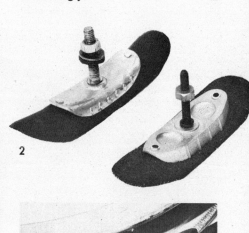
3

4

5